SEEING AND BEING

Carolyn Porter

SEEING AND BEING

THE PLIGHT OF THE PARTICIPANT OBSERVER IN EMERSON, JAMES, ADAMS, AND FAULKNER

WESLEYAN UNIVERSITY PRESS
MIDDLETOWN, CONNECTICUT

*Parts of the chapters on Emerson and Faulkner have appeared, in somewhat dif-
ferent form, in the following journals:*
"*Method and Metaphysics in Emerson's* Nature," The Virginia Quarterly Review,
Vol. 55, No. 3 (Summer, 1979), pp. 517–530.
"*The Problem of Time in* Light in August," Rice University Studies, *Vol. 61, No.
1 (Winter, 1975), pp. 107–125.*
"*Faulkner and His Reader,*" *in* Faulkner: The Unappeased Imagination: A Collection of Critical Essays, *ed., Glen O. Carey (Troy, N.Y.: Whitston Publishing Co.,
1980).*

LIBRARY OF CONGRESS CATALOGING IN PUBLICATION DATA

Porter, Carolyn, 1946-
Seeing and being.

Includes bibliographical references and index.
1. American prose literature—History and criticism.
2. Alienation in literature. 3. Point of view
(Literature) 4. Capitalism and literature. 5. Lukács,
György, 1885–1971. I. Title.
PS366.A44P67   810'.9'353   80–29234
ISBN 0–8195–5054–X

DISTRIBUTED FOR WESLEYAN UNIVERSITY PRESS BY
COLUMBIA UNIVERSITY PRESS
136 SOUTH BROADWAY, IRVINGTON, NEW YORK 10533

MANUFACTURED IN THE UNITED STATES OF AMERICA
FIRST EDITION

To my parents

CONTENTS

I be and I see my being, at the same time.
—EMERSON

PREFACE

IN THIS STUDY, I attempt, through an analysis of major works by Ralph Waldo Emerson, Henry Adams, Henry James, and William Faulkner, to identify a developing pattern in American literary history, one which emerges from, and constitutes a revelatory response to, that feature of capitalist society to which Georg Lukács gave the name *reification*. In the broadest sense, reification refers to a process in the course of which man becomes alienated from himself. This process is generated by the developing autonomy of a commodified world of objects which confronts man as a mystery "simply because," as Marx put it, "in it the social character of men's labour appears to them as an objective character stamped upon the product of that labour." The effects of this process as Lukács describes them, however, are by no means limited to the experience of the laborer, but in fact infiltrate the consciousness of everyone living in a society driven by capitalist growth.[1]

The reifying process endemic to capitalism produces a new kind of world and a new kind of man. It generates, on the one hand, a "new objectivity," a "second nature" in which man's own productive activity is obscured, so that what he has made appears to him as a given, an external and objective reality operating according to its own immutable laws. On the other hand, it generates a man who assumes a passive and "contemplative" stance in the face of that objectified and rationalized reality—a man who seems to himself to stand outside that reality because his own participation in producing it is mystified. Whether he responds to this condition by attempting to reunite self and world "in thought," that is, by means of a transcendent subjectivity, or by adopting a neutral and objective attitude in order to observe and measure the workings of a rational system of laws, he remains imprisoned within the contemplative stance. Thus, when Emerson becomes a "transparent eyeball," joyfully announcing "I am nothing; I see all," he articulates the position of both the transcendent visionary poet (to whose role he himself aspires) and the neutral scientific observer (whose role he wishes to counteract). That is, the detached observer, like the visionary seer, appears to himself to occupy a position outside the world he confronts. But as Emerson's self-contradictory formulation reveals, what is thereby repressed is man's material and active participation in the world he presumes, godlike, to watch. At the same time, the rationalized and objectified world harbors its own repressed contradiction: it presents itself as operating according to knowable laws, but in fact operates irrationally. In moments of crisis, however, the detached contemplative observer may be forced to recognize his own participation in the reality he presumes to observe; such, for example, was Heisenberg's dilemma. Further, as Heisenberg's indeterminacy principle indicates, the observer may at the same time face the limits of his rationalized world; the fabric of objectivity may be rent asunder, revealing a world in which "details . . . are subject to laws," but the "totality" is "ruled by chance." In each case, the crisis reveals, at least fleetingly, what has been reified—not man per se and not some primary nature beneath the objectified world of immediacy, but instead that "sensuous human activity" encompassing both, which constitutes, in Marx's view, history itself.[2]

The pattern I will identify originates in Emerson's heroic struggle to "be and see [his] being at the same time," a problem closely related to that embodied by Faulkner's Darl Bundren, whose dilemma is precisely that he is nothing and he sees all. In other words, the "I" who sees the world which was severed from the "I" who inhabits it in Emerson's transparent eyeball now confronts itself across a chasm of schizophrenia. In _The Education of Henry Adams_ and _The Golden Bowl,_ we may observe the widening of that chasm between seeing and being as well as the compensatory strategies designed to overcome it, but it is not really until we confront Thomas Sutpen that the full force of reification becomes apparent. For with his "pale eyes . . . at once visionary and alert," Thomas Sutpen unites in one figure both the transcendent seer and the detached, neutral observer, and so reveals the depth of the reifying process in the American history which his career both reenacts and exposes.[3]

By bringing this pattern into focus as a developing problem from Emerson through Faulkner, I wish to call into question one of the more persistent critical hypotheses about American literature, that which follows upon and emphasizes D. H. Lawrence's identification of the American desire to "get away"—away from society, from history, from institutions and bonds of every kind. According to Richard Poirier, for instance, "the classic American writers try through style temporarily to free the hero (and the reader) from systems, to free them from the pressures of time, biology, economics, and the social forces which are ultimately the undoing of American heroes and quite often of their creators." R. W. B. Lewis finds in our literature "the hero of a new adventure: an individual emancipated from history, happily bereft of ancestry, untouched and undefiled by the usual inheritances of family and race." The tendency which Lewis identifies in the hero, and Poirier in style, Richard Chase locates in the form of the American "romance-novel," which reveals an "assumed freedom from the ordinary novelistic requirements of verisimilitude, development, and continuity." More recently, Irving Howe has eulogized the "Edenic visions" of the American Renaissance, visions which "posit an end to history," even an "end to the memory of history," thereby enunciating the major theme in the postwar understanding of the Emersonian tradition—ahistoricism. By "ahistoricism," I mean, then, a set of assumptions about the American romantic tradition which are related, on the one hand, to the theory of American exceptionalism, and on the other, to an emphasis on Adamic innocence, and which, taken together, yield a reading of that tradition in which an "end to the memory of history," along with a faith in the transcendent sovereignty of the individual, are seen as definitive.[4]

My point, however, is not to dispute the findings of Lewis and Chase; given the questions they put, their answers are indisputable. I wish rather to shift the ground of the questions themselves. Rather than asking what is peculiar or exceptional about American literature's classic tradition when it is juxtaposed to its European counterparts, I wish to ask whether, given the kind of society confronting Emerson, for instance, his response to it is adequately characterized as fostering "imaginative desocialization," to use Quentin Anderson's disparaging term. In other words, if we attempt to rehistoricize Emerson—clearly the fountainhead of the American romantic tradition, and the locus classicus of American ahistoricism—by understanding him as speaking to and about a society poised on the verge of the most accelerated capitalist development in modern history, we will find his response, I think, far more complex, and a good deal less "ahistorical" than Anderson's treatment of him would lead us to suspect. Furthermore, once Emerson himself is securely resituated in a particular society undergoing radical transformation as a result of the acceleration of capitalist forces, the problems he was facing and his means of addressing them take on a distinct and distinguishable social weight. His effort to reunite man with himself, and to build up his resistance to social forces acting to undermine that union, no longer appear as part of a program for "coming out of culture," but, on the contrary, as a vital, if ultimately doomed, attempt to thwart a reifying process the effects of which Emerson—unlike most of his reforming contemporaries—felt keenly. One of my purposes in discussing Emerson, then, is to call attention to these social forces to which he was responding, so as to give the lie to any claim that his revolt was directed against Society per se, rather than against the society he saw, and saw coming in the future. Having done this, I think we can then come to understand his project in *Nature* in particular as something besides the building of an idealist metaphysical system, although it is certainly that. But it is that only as part of a strategy for dealing with the world which capitalism was unfolding everywhere in and around Emerson's Boston.[5]

My other purpose in discussing Emerson is to identify those features of reification which emerge so forcefully in his major work of the 1830s and 1840s—both those which he addressed, and those which crept into his own philosophical strategy for overcoming reification. Once the implications of that strategy are understood, it becomes possible to comprehend Adams' dilemma in *The Education of Henry Adams* and James's in *The Golden Bowl* as fundamentally related to Emerson's problems in *Nature*.

In both *The Education* and *The Golden Bowl*, we find the detached contemplative stance to which Emerson's method finally relegated him once again reconstituted, albeit with results in which the contradictions are both more evident and more disturbing. In taking the role of the visionary seer to its limits, James exposes and struggles to redeem the complicity of that seer in the world she confronts, and in taking rationalization to its limits, Adams reveals both the incoherence of the vision afforded the neutral observer and the instability of that observer's detached position. Finally, by following the pattern through to Faulkner, we may observe the effects of the deepening structure of reification after a century of capitalist development in America.

It is customary at this point to explain one's choice of writers. To do so in this case would, however, be misleading, for I did not choose these authors as exemplars of the effects of reification. On the contrary, only after several years of study did I arrive at the conclusion that Lukács' concept of reification might serve to explain a set of issues I first identified in Emerson's essays. In *Nature*, for example, I saw Emerson struggling to formulate a basis for overcoming the gap between the me and the "Not Me," and arriving at a position strikingly similar to Giambattista Vico's, viz., that man can only understand that which man has made. Emerson's strategy was to enlarge this hypothesis to encompass nature itself, so as to overcome that alienation between "Me and It" which he saw as his fundamental problem. Man could be restored to unity with his world, Emerson decided, once man realized that he had made it. Yet as a result of his strategy, worked out formally for the first time in *Nature*, alienation resurfaced in a new form—between an "I" who sees the world, and an "I" who inhabits it. If he was to avoid facing the disruptive implications of this new internal split, Emerson had to posit a dynamic, fluid reality; thus the "transparent eyeball" had to float on the "currents of Universal Being." Needing as he did an active reality to support the "bipolar unity" of "Me and It," but lacking the means of grounding that reality in a material base, Emerson in effect abstracted the historical dimension to which Vico had turned in his repudiation of Descartes. Emerson's heroic poet therefore provided a locus for the "bipolar unity" of "Me and It," but this unity had been purchased at the price of a dematerialization, since the "I" who sees and the "I" who inhabits the world could only be conceived as a unity in the abstract fluidity of the Over-Soul. The contradiction implicit in such a conclusion surfaces quite vividly with the statement "I am nothing; I see all," in which the "I" who is negated in the first clause miraculously returns in the second. It would seem that Emerson could "be and see [his] being at the same time" only by ceasing to be at all, save as a transparent eyeball.[6]

One is inclined, when faced with such contradictions in Emerson's thought, to accept the commonplace notion that Emerson is a bit windy-headed; like Whitman, he was, perhaps, rather too sanguine about self-contradiction to be taken seriously. But because I had begun to see the same contradictions emerging in other places, I was forced to pursue a different hypothesis—that the split between observer and participant (as I came to formulate it for myself) so evident in Emerson's thought was not peculiar to Emerson, but stemmed from the nature of the problem he was confronting. Roughly labeling that problem "alienation," I tried to discover why certain features of his response to it should reappear in, of all places, the work of William Faulkner. That Henry Adams should adopt the posture of a detached spectator of his own life, fetishizing a role not unrelated to Emerson's transparent eyeball, seemed understandable within the terms of a common New England tradition—one in which Adams not only saw himself, but in which he saw himself trapped. That Henry James developed, in his narrative experiments, a detached spectator as the locus and register of social experience was likewise within the bounds of reason; after all, he too, despite his cosmopolitan upbringing, was linked to Emerson through his father. But that Faulkner's narrative strategy should display conflicts and tensions which bear a distinct similarity to those emerging in Emerson defied comprehension, unless those conflicts stemmed from problems rooted in a ground larger than that circumscribed by any of the available critical theories about American literature.

It was not that Faulkner was unrelated to the American Renaissance. His work had often been compared to Hawthorne's, but the latter was after all on the opposite side of the fence from Emerson; Emerson supposedly wanted to transcend history while Hawthorne made it clear that no such transcendence was possible. Faulkner has always served as a kind of historical ballast in American literary history, developing the Hawthornian line of historical determinism in contrast to the Emersonian line of romantic freedom. How, I asked myself, can Faulkner exhibit the pronounced tendency to re-problematize Emersonian alienation in a series of narrative experiments designed to undercut the detached posture of the reader himself—for this was the conclusion at which I had arrived about Faulkner's major period from *The Sound and the Fury* to *Absalom, Absalom!*. The answer to that question—to telescope a long period of searching down (very Faulknerian) blind corridors and chasing a series of red herrings—arrived only when, quite accidentally, and in another connection entirely, I happened upon Lukács' essay "Reification and the Consciousness of the Proletariat."

This discovery was followed by my first serious reading of Marx, and led in the end to the conclusions adumbrated in this essay: that the problem of alienation as Emerson addressed it in 1836 evoked from him a critical response whose peculiar configuration was to prove so penetrating in its capacity to diagnose the reifying process of capitalist society that this configuration, within which lurked contradictions aplenty, had surfaced again and again as that society moved forward into the twentieth century; that the detached observer and the visionary poet shared the contemplative stance of reified consciousness and were both therefore vulnerable to the same disruptive contradictions; that Faulkner, far from occupying a regional Southern locale in the American literary landscape, was addressing contradictions stemming from that same American capitalist society at whose birth Emerson had served as unwitting midwife; and that, if all this were true, we could no longer either luxuriate or despair in a belief that American literature's classic tradition was defined primarily by a flight from society and the constraints of civilized life, but must at least entertain the possibility that, as a result of the relatively unimpeded development of capitalism in America, its literary history harbors a set of texts in which is inscribed, in its own terms, as deep and as penetrating a response to history and social reality as any to be found in the work of a Balzac or a George Eliot.

In the course of the inquiry just described, I found, of course, other writers whose works might have found their way into this study. Indeed, once I arrived at the conclusion that Lukács' essay provided a crucial explanation for Emerson's project, it became suspiciously easy to find other cases of the contemplative stance.

Melville, Poe, and Thoreau, in the nineteenth century, provided ample evidence of reification and its consequences, as did Fitzgerald, Hemingway, and Wallace Stevens in the twentieth. Among these, Melville was the most tempting candidate for inclusion—not least because he could serve as a referent for and a bridge to Faulkner. I have resisted the temptation to include Melville, as well as others, for several minor reasons, and one major one. First, I already had more than enough territory to cover with the four writers I felt, in the end, I had to include. Second, I thought that since a century was marked out by Emerson's *Nature* and Faulkner's *Absalom, Absalom!,* and was punctuated in the middle by the careers of James and Adams, these four writers would suffice to demonstrate the historical scope as well as the developing complexities of reification—my main purpose. While it might serve to amplify the resonance of my claims, the case of Melville would not, I ultimately decided, appreciably strengthen them. But the major reason for my choices is also the simplest to put: it was in the work of the four writers I finally decided to discuss that I had come upon the evidence for the claims I am making in the first place. In the work of Emerson, James, Adams, and Faulkner, I am convinced there is clear evidence not only of the reifying process, but of crucially revealing efforts to resist its force. That other writers have been engaged in similar projects may or may not be the case. I happen to think, for example, that Melville was and that Thoreau in fact was not, that Wallace Stevens was, and that Fitzgerald emphatically was not. That Emerson, James, Adams, and Faulkner were, I believe I can demonstrate. Although there are many detached observers in American literature, they do not necessarily face the kind of crisis we find in the works of these writers, a crisis in which the observer discovers his participation within the world he has thought to stand outside. It is this crisis which Emerson brilliantly evades, Adams and James resist, and Faulkner forces his reader to face, and it is this developing response to reification which I wish to analyze.

I should add a word about what I do *not* attempt to demonstrate. First, I do not wish to argue that all American literature ought to be seen as explicable in the terms I am using. Since I am on record in the following pages as calling into question certain monolithic dogmas, I do not wish to try to create one myself. Second, because these terms are drawn from a Marxist tradition, I wish to make it clear that I am not trying to allegorize American literary history as either a struggle against or a reflection of the forces of capitalism. As for struggle, in the writers under consideration, we can see a struggle against reification, but, as we shall see, that struggle is doomed to failure, because of reification's penetration of their own responses. The struggle against capitalism itself may also be doomed, but it is a different kind of struggle, one in which some, at least, consider victory possible. As for reflection, I have tried to thwart any such implication from arising in every way I could find, but perhaps this is the place to state clearly and emphatically that I am not arguing that the texts under consideration reflect, or constitute linguistic equivalents for, a reifying process going on in society as a whole. Rather, these texts occupy a place *within* that process itself, and their production is itself therefore "social" in the deepest sense.

Marxist criticism has a well-earned reputation for finding in literature a reductive reflection of socioeconomic conflicts, and thus for operating on the basis of an implied (when not, as in the case of Lucien Goldmann, explicit) homology between the two. Such procedures are discredited because they tend to cancel out the rich complexity not only of the text, but also of the social reality it is supposed to reflect. One of the virtues of Lukács' analysis of reification is that it enables us to understand the texts under consideration as the locus of a social production in which those features which reveal most about the society generating the need for such a production may well be features having no apparent relation to its immediate social context. This is why, save in the case of Emerson (for reasons which do not contradict the principle itself) we do not need to examine in detail what was happening in society at the time these writers were active, because we can see the reifying process acting within the texts they produced. In other words, these texts constitute and record a series of "social projects" in and of themselves, projects in whose rhetorical and narrative complexities lie sedimented the social contradictions generated by the reifying process.

Because Emerson has been dehistoricized so thoroughly, it is necessary to clarify his relation to the cultural and social transformations in which he was caught up. Emerson's case affords a rich opportunity to demonstrate how the most abstract theoretical concerns are rooted in social conditions. By employing one of Gramsci's critical tools, hegemony, as elaborated by Raymond Williams, I try to reconnect Emerson to the society he manifestly did not transcend. No writer transcends his or her historical and social context; some just succeed at understanding it more thoroughly and responding to it more fully than others. Each of the writers with whom I am concerned succeeds in these terms. In *Nature, The Education of Henry Adams, The Golden Bowl,* and *Absalom, Absalom!* are inscribed the results of what, to use Jean-Paul Sartre's phrase, each author succeeded in "making of what he [had] been made." In the cases of Adams and James, once we have the reifying process in view, the social forces which helped to "make" them are readily apparent in the concerns to which their work was devoted. In the case of Emerson and for different reasons, that of Faulkner, those forces have been partially obscured and thus need to be reviewed.[7]

As I have indicated, Emerson's transcendental metaphysics have fostered a tendency to dehistoricize him; we need therefore to reconnoiter the cultural ground on which he fought his battle with alienation. Once we identify the extent to which that process had already saturated social relations, especially in the Northeast, it then becomes possible to understand (and incidentally to appreciate) just how radical was Emerson's critical response to the social transformation he was witnessing. His disaffection with reformers, for example, turns out to represent not an antisocial persuasion, but a profound understanding of the infiltration of human consciousness by the very destructive social forces whose effects the reformers were trying to combat. Emerson's critical understanding in fact penetrated well beneath the hegemonic struggle itself, to address the roots of the problem he saw expressed there.

Faulkner presents a different problem. Clearly enough, he has not been dehistoricized. But because he is our preeminent Southern novelist, Faulkner's social and historical context has been largely defined by his Southernness. Although *Absalom, Absalom!* seems to me to explode such a view in and of itself, I have become convinced of the necessity, peculiar though it may sound, of rehistoricizing Faulkner, as an American rather than a primarily Southern novelist. By this I mean not only that the social scope of the novels Faulkner "made," as he once put it, encompasses more territory than the South, but also that the experience on which they were based—the forces which contributed to making Faulkner who he was—were likewise not peculiarly Southern. In short, Faulkner's social context is only in an immediate sense Southern. The further he penetrated that immediate Southernness, the more profound became his vision of its more inclusive American roots. He did not, as Cleanth Brooks says, "set down" the figure of Thomas Sutpen in a South to which his "innocence" made him an alien; he *found* Sutpen in that South. Accordingly, I will argue that, while Faulkner's vision is certainly marked by its comprehension of the slave economy and plantation culture by which Eugene Genovese has defined Southern distinctiveness, it situates that culture within a larger capitalist society of which it was, as Kenneth Stampp and others have argued, an integral part. What Faulkner came to see, as a result of his concern with the past (this in itself, perhaps, distinctively Southern) was what Edmund Morgan has since demonstrated—that American freedom was built upon and sustained by American slavery.[8]

Each of the four parts of this book has two chapters. Part 1, chapter 1, offers a critical discussion of ahistoricism designed to establish the theoretical bases of my claim that the imputed ahistoricism of the Emersonian tradition in American literature is called into question, once we conceive those features of our culture which have served to support certain versions of American exceptionalism as a function of the contradictions inherent in capitalism itself. These contradictions, to be sure, surface more rapidly in a society where there is no *ancien régime* to overthrow, and no monarchical state apparatus to be disassembled, but for that very reason they may generate a literary response in which social and historical forces are deeply penetrated rather than romantically evaded or denied. Chapter 2 provides a fuller elaboration of Lukács' concept of reification, establishing the key points of reference for the specific authorial projects to be examined, and a brief rehearsal of each. Part 1, then, serves as a staging device for the analyses which follow.

In part 2, chapter 3, I attempt to situate Emerson in a society undergoing radical transformation, and thus displaying that rhetorical struggle for cultural hegemony in the context of which Emerson ought to be understood. In chapter 4, I examine Emerson's project in *Nature,* where he establishes his method for combating reification and displays, within that very method, the extent to which reification has already saturated the era's most insightful diagnostician of its effects. The strategy worked out in *Nature,* as I proceed to demonstrate, is then applied in "Circles" and "Fate," where its implicit contradictions become more apparent.

In part 3, I analyze *The Golden Bowl* in chapter 5 and *The Education of Henry Adams* in chapter 6, in order to demonstrate the deepening structure of reification and to examine two radically different, though equally heroic, critical struggles against its destructive power—struggles in which the complicity of the detached observer occupying the contemplative stance of reified consciousness surfaces with potentially shattering effect.

In part 4, chapter 7, I provide external evidence supporting my claim that it should not be surprising that in *Absalom, Absalom!* Faulkner delivered a major critical treatment of the American "innocent," in his conception of Thomas Sutpen—since Faulkner's understanding of his own family's history, and ultimately of the South's history as well, could not fail to generate a view powerfully influenced by radical individualism and the self-made man. In chapter 8 I turn to the internal evidence. After tracing the developing narrative strategy, from *The Sound and the Fury* through *Absalom, Absalom!,* by means of which Faulkner attempted to undermine the reader's detachment from the text he confronts, I turn to *Light in August* and *Absalom, Absalom!,* the two novels in which the implications of that strategy become clear. By examining the distance he crossed between these two novels, I demonstrate how Faulkner arrived at a strategy for relating his narrative experiments to his thematic concern with history, a strategy which reveals in retrospect the fate of that reified consciousness which first emerged in Emerson's *Nature.*

ACKNOWLEDGMENTS

THIS BOOK ORIGINATED in a dissertation written under the direction of David L. Minter, and although it has metamorphized into a fundamentally different project, it still bears the mark of his influence and testifies to his continued support. My debt to him is the kind which one can never discharge, but which one is happy to continue owing.

I wish to thank Henry Nash Smith, who read two different earlier drafts of the book with scrupulous attention and provided support and stimulus even when (indeed, especially when) he disagreed with my argument. I owe an unaccountable debt to Michael Rogin, who read each chapter as it emerged with an unrelenting critical interest, the effect of which has been a much strengthened and clarified argument. I also wish to thank Masao Miyoshi, Richard Hutson, James Breslin, Carol Christ, Michael Harper, and Richard Slotkin, all of whom read an earlier draft of the book and all of whom made comments which helped me considerably in its revision. I am indebted to Hayden White for reading an earlier version of the first chapter and for providing encouragement when I most needed it. The contributions made by all of these friends and colleagues have helped to eliminate many weaknesses in my argument; those that remain are entirely attributable to me.

I wish also to express my gratitude to the students in my Faulkner seminars at Berkeley, in whose company I developed so many of my ideas about Faulkner's narrative techniques; with their boundless energy and their remarkable critical insights, these students were more helpful than they could possibly have known or than any teacher has a right to expect.

The University of California, Berkeley, supported my work financially with a Regents' Summer Faculty Fellowship and a Humanities Research Grant. A grant from the National Endowment for the Humanities allowed me to spend a summer at the School of Criticism and Theory at the University of California, Irvine, where an abundance of theoretical provocation aided me in my work.

Finally, I wish to thank my husband, Paul Thomas, without whose knowledge of Marx I would often have lost my way, and without whose patience and faith the undertaking could never have been completed.

PART ONE

OBSERVERS AND PARTICIPANTS

It is not a question whether a grey, everyday existence or a fantastic unreality is represented, but whether the more profound how *of an event is articulated or remains silent.*

—LUKÁCS

Chapter One

AMERICAN AHISTORICISM

Myth deprives the object of which it speaks of all History.
—ROLAND BARTHES

IN 1952 C. Vann Woodward wrote an essay, "The Irony of Southern History," in which he cautioned Americans against their illusory innocence, their belief, in Toynbee's words, that "history is
something unpleasant that happens to other people." Focusing on
the difference between Southern and American history, the difference between an experience of moral failure and military defeat,
and one of "success and victory . . . fostering . . . illusions of innocence and virtue," Woodward proceeded to draw certain paral-
lels between the antebellum South and contemporary America in
an effort to warn us of "the danger that America may be tempted
to exert all the terrible power she possesses to compel history to
conform to her own illusions." By the time the essay was reprinted
in 1968, of course, Woodward's theme of "irony" had found historical confirmation, as he noted in an "extended footnote" remarking on how "history has begun to catch up with Americans."
From a rather different perspective, Louis Hartz had issued a similar
warning in 1955. In *The Liberal Tradition in America,* having examined "the death by atrophy of the philosophic impulse" which
followed from the "colossal liberal absolutism" dominating American political thought, Hartz asked whether "a people 'born equal'
[can] ever understand peoples elsewhere that have to become so."
Hartz, in other words, was calling for a transcendence of the "ir-

rational Lockianism" which had served as the political vehicle for American innocence, in response to the dangers attendant upon the United States maintaining that innocence as a leading actor on the international stage. His warning went as unheeded as Woodward's had.[1]

One of the more striking features of these historians' arguments for the student of American literature is the difference between their attitude toward American innocence and that of the literary critics who have been exploring its literary expression ever since the 1950s. R. W. B. Lewis, whose 1955 study, *The American Adam*, has deservedly become a landmark, was by no means uncritical of the myth whose career he set out to explore, but when he turned in his "Epilogue" to the contemporary scene, he suggested that in the face of the "new hopelessness" he found in its literature, there was "an occasional vitality in American fiction" which usually showed "traces of the hopeful or Adamic tradition." Remarking how "ours is an age of containment" in which "we huddle together and shore up defenses," Lewis suggested that "the moral and artistic adventurousness" of the "Adamic tradition" "may help release us a little from our current rigidity" and serve to counter "our tired attention to the burden of history." For Lewis, insofar as the Adamic faith remained alive and well, and had not lapsed into "arrested development," it sounded a note of hope, not of danger.[2]

It would appear that while the historians were struggling to awaken us from our dreams, the literary critics were analyzing them with such brilliance that we became mesmerized all over again. Richard Chase's study of the "American romance-novel" as a "freer, more daring, more brilliant fiction" than its English counterpart, with its "solid moral inclusiveness and massive equability" followed close upon Lewis' book, and had the effect of solidifying the view that American fiction is marked by "a willingness . . . to ignore the spectacle of man in society" in favor of "a tendency to plunge into the underside of consciousness." Almost ten years later, Richard Poirier's *A World Elsewhere* was still mining the same vein, demonstrating how the ahistorical tendencies of the Adamic tradition are registered in a style designed to accommodate "the American obsession with inventing environments that permit unhampered freedom of consciousness." Huck Finn now lights out for the territory of language, and the by-now-standard contrast with English fiction supports the by-now-standard conclusion: "the strangeness of American fiction" derives not from "the environment in which a novelist finds himself," but rather from an "environment he tries to create." Poirier, to be sure, translates the argument to a more subtle level when he shifts the ground from genre to style, but the premiss remains that American fiction is strange, and that its strangeness results from the tendency of American writers not "to criticize existing environments," but "to displace them" by creating "a world elsewhere" in language. It would seem that the cultural myth which Lewis found at work in nineteenth-century America has become a critical myth with an extraordinary power to blend with modernist impulses, and to infiltrate our reading of American texts at every level. The myth of Adamic innocence has virtually assumed the status of a given, fostering our desire to examine the linguistic environment a novelist tries to create while allowing us to dismiss the environment in which he finds himself, and thereby leading us to reenact the nineteenth-century American's effort to put an "end to the memory of history." What was for Woodward and Hartz a delusion in need of correction has become for us a self-regenerating myth of American ahistoricism. Despite such revisionary efforts as Harry Henderson's to reconstitute the "historical imagination" of the American novelist, ahistoricism continues to enjoy a curious if unhealthy resilience in the critical mind as the sovereign feature of a tradition originating with Emerson, and never apparently coming to an end. Even when this sovereignty comes under fire from within a temporarily repoliticized academy, the myth remains essentially intact. If we look at two recent discussions of American ahistoricism, we can begin to see why the myth persists as well as why it ought to be called into question.[3]

Quentin Anderson's *The Imperial Self* is clearly the "cry of its occasion" and cannot be taken seriously as the responsible revision of literary history to which it apparently aspires. Yet its very status as a kind of outburst, as a reactionary assault on those elements in American culture which Anderson in 1971 held responsible for the Columbia University uprising of 1968, has the salutary effect of revealing not only his own ideological assumptions, but at least some of those informing the "new critical era" which he sees as valorizing Emerson, Whitman, and James, the "imperial selves" of his title. By decreeing "where history was, let art now be," according to Anderson, the new critics made of these writers the benign exemplars of that individualism which served in the 1950s as the bearer of the transcendental imagination. Had these critics not been taken in by aestheticism, they might have seen what Anderson sees—the surreal picture of Emerson, Whitman, and James ingesting into consciousness what ought to have been properly understood to be indigestible—society itself. These writers constitute for Anderson a kind of rogue's gallery of infantile egos, each one caught in the act of stepping "out of time" and the "constraints of civilized life." Deploying a narrowly conceived Freudian analysis, Anderson traces his victims' neurosis to the failure of their fathers. While it is James who epitomizes the displacement of history by aesthetics, it is Emerson who first initiated "a counterpoint between his strand of the American imagination and temporalized thought of every kind." What Anderson means by "temporalized thought" is that of Hegel, Marx, Nietzsche, and Freud, or as he puts it, "the mainstream of nineteenth century thought in Europe." The upshot of this argument is that what we have proudly called individualism is really "imaginative desocialization," itself the effect of that dangerous neurosis marking Emerson and Norman O. Brown alike—the imperial ego.[4]

If this line of thought is to replace New Criticism, one can only long for its return. But while his polemic on behalf of the father, the family, and society (read "constraints") is less than convincing, Anderson's charge against New Criticism is half true. Only half because the new critics were not, on the whole, conscious devotees of aestheticism as a retreat from history. As Gerald Graff has argued quite legitimately, the new critics must be seen in the light of those they were fighting, both within their own field of criticism and in the larger cultural world. On the one hand, they reacted against "hedonistic impressionism" and "genteel moralism," while on the other, they struggled to reconstitute a counterweight to scientism in the humanities. Despite the price exacted by an interpretive technique which usually had to commit secretly the fallacies it officially proscribed, the victory of the new critics within their own discipline ought not to be despised but respected. There is sufficient "hedonistic impressionism" operating today in imposing guises to make the relative chastity of the new critics rather appealing. (Unhappily, even "genteel moralism" has made a fitful return in John Gardner's *On Moral Fiction*.) From our vantage point it is clear that aestheticism displaced historical concern in the "new critical era," but from the standpoint of the new critics themselves, it was precisely history—seen as the repository of a humane tradition—that required protection. Thus to say that the new critics replaced history with art is itself an ahistorical claim, ignoring as it does the historical circumstances of the new critics themselves.[5]

These circumstances are particularly clear in the Agrarian wing of the new critical movement, and it was among these men—Cleanth Brooks, Robert Penn Warren, John Crowe Ransom, and Allen Tate—that the battle against scientism and technological domination was waged most vociferously. But while they won the battle within the discipline, they clearly lost the one beyond its boundaries. (One need only attempt to explain to an undergraduate class Ezra Pound's concern with truth in order to learn once again that poetry and truth have achieved something close to the status of a binary opposition.) Such a battle could not, of course, be won, given the weapons used. A "romantic defense of poetry as a substitute or support for religious values," in Graff's words, was from the start reactionary and futile, as is painfully clear when we look at René Wellek's defense of New Criticism. Wellek goes well beyond Graff in his staunch refusal to countenance *any* of the charges against the new critics. By attending to the particular positions of the new critics and the internal debates among them, Wellek delivers a salutary corrective to the misguided assumption that New Criticism constituted a unified movement. Yet his own defense of that movement only serves to reemphasize its limitations, especially when he argues that "New Criticism . . . believes in a philosophy of history," and then identifies that philosophy as the one commonly associated with T. S. Eliot:

There used to be once a perfectly ordered world, which is, for instance, behind Dante's poetry. This world disintegrated under the impact of science and skepticism. The "dissociation of sensibility" took place at some time in the seventeenth century. Man became increasingly divided, alienated, specialized as industrialization and secularism progressed.

The reunification of sensibility, then,

requires a rejection of technological civilization, a return to religion, or, at least, to a modern myth and, in the Southern critics, . . . a defense of the agrarian society surviving in the South.

However valiantly Wellek tries to relate this "basic scheme" to a "venerable ancestry" reaching back through F. H. Bradley to Hegel, and through Hegel and Marx to Schiller, the scheme itself remains self-evidently idealist and reactionary. For such a scheme—especially in its Southern Agrarian version—reflects the persistent "illusion," as Raymond Williams calls it, "that it is not capitalism which is injuring us, but the more isolable, more evident system of urban industrialism," so that "the transition from a rural to an industrial society is seen as a kind of fall." The failure to distinguish between industrialism and capitalism, as we shall see, plays a significant role in allowing the dominant culture of early nineteenth-century America to celebrate technological advances while excluding from its frame of reference the capitalist mode and relations of production in which they are grounded. The progressive philosophy of history of nineteenth-century romantic historians like George Bancroft indeed feeds off of just such a reduction of capitalism to industrialism, and industrialism to technology—a point which reveals the extent to which the twentieth-century Southern Agrarians were operating within the same illusion fostered by the grandfathers of their liberal foes. One could put the dilemma in structuralist terms by saying that the opposition between an agrarian past and an industrial future is a binary one; each term derives its meaning from its opposition to the other, and neither has much, if anything, to do with the actual social reality to which it presumes to refer. The only difference between the Whig progressivism of the nineteenth century and the Southern Agrarianism of the twentieth would be that the ethical valences of the opposition have been reversed; what the Whigs saw as progress, the Agrarians saw a century later as decay. But neither side has broken free of the binary opposition itself, nor can it, so long as the illusion persists that the source of our problem is scientific rationalism itself. It is noteworthy in this regard that when Emerson appealed to the philosophy of history to which Wellek refers, he did so through the mouth of the orphic poet;

Emerson seemed aware in 1836 at any rate that such a philosophy had more rhetorical than historical weight.[6]

It remains as yet unclear whether a reactionary ideology dedicated to saving traditional values is not to be preferred to the more current celebratory glee at the alleged disappearance of Man, but whatever one's position, it is undeniable that the new critics failed to provide a viable counterforce to scientism, and not least because they themselves too easily fell into a scientistic trap. John Crowe Ransom's claim that new critical interpretation was disinterested, unlike science which was practically oriented, can serve to illustrate the basic theoretical weakness of new critical strategy. Despite both Wellek's and Graff's valiant apologias, it is impossible to ignore the secret desire revealed here to seize the enemy's weapons. And whatever the intentions of its proponents, New Criticism did have the effect of severing literature and history, of exalting the aesthetic over the social. Herein lies the half-truth of Anderson's claim. But as we have seen, his cure for this weakness in the new critic's position, and in particular for the movement's virtual deification of that supreme vehicle of the Imagination, Henry James, is merely to replace freedom with necessity as the normative term in literary evaluation. Thus Anderson's position signals a kind of return of the repressed, the determinism of the left in the 1930s resurfacing today on the right. Abstract "temporalized thought" occupies a position here roughly analogous to that once held by social realism, and literature which does not recognize its obligations to the abstraction must be exorcised. Meanwhile, the exceptionalism shared by American critics and writers alike only resurfaces with its valences reversed. Anderson charges the new critics with turning "all negatives to positives," particularly "imaginative desocialization" to "individualism"; yet to turn positives to negatives as he does remains an abstract operation which leaves the basic opposition intact. The realist/romantic opposition, as always superimposed on the European/American one, continues to prevail. By manifestly ideologizing the opposition, Anderson's argument merely highlights its inadequacies.[7]

The same thing happens, moreover, when the opposition is ideologized from the left. In "New World Epics: The Middle-Class Novel in America," Myra Jehlen tries to account for the ahistoricism of nineteenth-century American literature by reference to the "ideological hegemony" of American liberalism. Like Anderson, Jehlen accepts "anti-historicism and the disengaged, abstract concept of personal identity" as a given, but for her the problem is rooted not in the failure of the fathers, but in their success. "The Founding Fathers," she says, created a political "structure which was so well suited to the basic needs of men and societies" that no alternative need ever be conceived. Not only Emerson and James, but Hawthorne and Melville as well, were unable to develop a potent social critique of American society because they were victims of the "ideological hegemony" of American liberalism. Quoting Raymond Williams, who is working with Antonio Gramsci's idea of hegemony, Jehlen argues that this ideology "is lived at such a depth" and "saturates society to such an extent" that it "constitutes the limit of common sense." Because America was for these writers *already* "a world elsewhere," because it was already constituted in effect as a utopia, "other systems than the contemporary" were "literally unthinkable." Consequently, history was in their eyes "an affliction brought on by a poor constitution."[8]

Here again, the target is American individualism, but Jehlen charges this individualism with complicity in the social and political status quo against which it ostensibly rebels, while for Anderson, American individualism represents a deluded denial of such complicity. Jehlen actually complains at one point that American writers were insufficiently individualistic by comparison with the French novelists to whom she juxtaposes them. The opposition between American and European traditions can apparently support the right and the left with equal convenience. Yet Jehlen's argument presents a far more powerful case than Anderson's, one worth pursuing a bit further in order to identify the sources of that power.

The privileged term in Jehlen's opposition is the nineteenth-century French novel. The protagonists of *Le Rouge et le Noir, Madame Bovary*, and *Le Père Goriot*, she explains, "first try to realize themselves within society, and failing," become "outcasts and subversives, with the approval of their authors." It is this "possibility of active dissent" which is missing for a Melville, an Emerson, a James, a Faulkner, for in their eyes, genuine dissent amounts to blasphemy. Thus, even Melville "cannot reconcile himself to being alienated," and thereby joins Emerson, Hawthorne, and James in supporting "the case for social constraints, for law and order, for conformity to conventional roles." Jehlen's explanation for the difference between American and French novelists is inscribed in her title, "New World Epics." She appeals to Lukács's early *Theory of the Novel*, where he distinguishes at length between novel and epic. Lukács describes "the hero of the novel" as "the product of estrangement from the outside world," and Jehlen takes up this description as appropriate to the European novel's protagonist, whose "condition reflected the personal alienation inevitably inflicted by bourgeois society." America, on the other hand, was an "integrated civilization"—another Lukácsian term—one in which people were not, as in Europe, "thrown back on themselves, on the 'autonomous life of interiority' for values and meaning in a universe become subjectively anomic." This distinction is crucial to Jehlen's argument, and she reiterates it forcefully; "in Lukács' terms, middle-class America *was* an integrated society," she insists, "like Athens and Renaissance London, and very unlike nineteenth century London and Paris." Accordingly, when Emerson promised his reader, "Speak your latent conviction and it shall be the universal sense," he was assuming an "underlying identity of interest" between the individual and society, as opposed to his European counterpart's "recognition that the individual is inevitably separate from society."[9]

This is an ambitious argument, one of whose major virtues is its effort to reconstruct American romanticism in a social context. Unfortunately, that effort leads only to a conclusion which negates the force of that context. No one would dispute the dominance of middle-class values in nineteenth-century America, but when Jehlen elevates this dominance into a "cosmology," she merely substitutes a myth of liberalism for all those other myths which have been constructed to account for, and intentionally or not, to reconstitute, American ahistoricism. Yet because Jehlen tries to couch the traditional claim in social and political terms, a fissure opens between the argument she wants to make and the tools she has assembled to make it. A social residue clings to terms like "ideological hegemony" and "alienation," and the appeal to the Marxist perspective represented by Lukács and Williams constitutes a counterforce within the essay to Jehlen's own mythologizing tendencies. The realm of social reality designated and then blocked off by Jehlen's Marxist vocabulary returns to vitiate the essay's thesis. Yet the singular value of Jehlen's approach lies precisely in the fact that we are allowed a glimpse of what the standard opposition between American and European traditions must repress if it is to operate. We can see, for instance, what has been abstracted when the abstractions used are Lukács' "integrated civilization" and "estrangement," and Raymond Williams's "hegemony."

For the pre-Marxist Lukács of *The Theory of the Novel*, the epic is the product of an "integrated civilization" called Greece, and specifically, the Greece of Homer. The Greece upon which he meditates here is to be sure a homogeneous world, one whose homogeneity is in fact so profound that "even the separation between man and world, between 'I' and 'You,' cannot disturb" it. It is, in short, an ideal world where the very need for meaning does not yet exist, meaning being immanent in all things. (Even Greek philosophy represents a decline from this blissful state, being "born only when the substance had already begun to pale.") There can be no "new world epic" in Lukács' sense of epic, because the epic is an expression of an ideal historical beginning from which the novel represents a kind of fall into the need for meaning. The novel only appears, to quote the definition Jehlen herself uses, in an age "in which the extensive totality of life is no longer directly given, in which the immanence of meaning in life has become a problem yet which still thinks in terms of totality." Lukács, of course, was later to repudiate most of this argument as utopian, but even at this early stage in his career, when he had worked his way through Hegel but not yet through Marx, Lukács' utopian conception is at least attached to a historical moment, which is one reason that it cannot be appropriated for Jehlen's purposes. For in calling America an integrated civilization "in Lukács' terms," Jehlen effectively accords it the utopian status which she defines as the disabling delusion for Melville and Emerson. In other words, by grafting Lukács' at least theoretically historical distinction between two eras—that of epic and that of novel—onto the difference between America and France in the nineteenth century, Jehlen effectively reconstitutes the ahistorical, exceptionalist perspective she wishes to discredit in American writers.[10]

The problem here is not merely that Jehlen misappropriates Lukács' terms, but that in so doing, she falls into a contradiction. One cannot have it both ways. One cannot say that America was an integrated society and at the same time indict it for falling prey to the "ideological hegemony" of the middle class, because, to put it simply, a society cannot be both bourgeois and integrated, "in Lukács' terms" or in anyone else's. Jehlen fails to see this contradiction clearly, but she tries indirectly to account for it by admitting the "paradoxical" quality of American society's integration. No sooner is middle-class America likened to Renaissance London than their difference is taken as a sign of "how ideologically particular American ideals really were." Once these are set next to "Chaucer's or Shakespeare's Englands" we find, not surprisingly, that American ideals were "characteristically middle-class." They presupposed, that is, a universe which is "essentially a natural marketplace" where "individualistic ambition" is likewise natural. Once elevated to the status of a "new world cosmology," this middle-class construction of the universe serves, in Jehlen's view, to explain "the special dilemma of American writers," for this cosmology simultaneously sanctifies and frustrates the individual's freedom, valorizing the self-made man, but denying him the "open future" necessary for the fulfillment of his ambition by placing him in "a world structured by the absolute necessities we associate with theology or myth," by trapping him, that is, in the "static absolutism" of the liberal state. But at this point, we are no longer confronting an "integrated society," but a bourgeois society, one in which the paradoxical freedom of the individual for which Jehlen is trying to account can be explained readily enough without recourse to a "new world cosmology" based on the "ideological hegemony" of liberalism. Indeed, it *has* been explained, by Marx in his essay "On the Jewish Question."[11]

Marx points out that "where the state exists in its completely developed form"—as in "the free states of North America"—the "*political character of civil society*" is abolished. "The consummation of the idealism of the state," is "the consummation of the materialism of civil society," for the "bonds which had restrained the egoistic spirit of civil society" are "removed along with the political yoke." In other words, the rights of man ensured by the U.S. Constitution are the rights of egoistic, bourgeois man, regarded as an isolated monad. Politically emancipated as a citizen, man is regarded in the "celestial" sphere of the state as free. But "a state may be a *free state* without man himself being a *free man*." Thus, when the state consummates its political emancipation, civil society is thereby shorn of the constraints previously imposed by the integration of political, religious, and social relations at work in a feudal and monarchical regime, and is dissolved into atomistic individuals. The result is a man who is at once an "*abstract citizen*" and an "*egoistic* man," whose freedom is based not upon a human relationship between man and man, but upon the separation of man from man. His status as a citizen is merely a "*political lion's skin*" for his identity as an atomized member of civil society, a member whose freedom consists in the right to pursue his self-interest, and who therefore tends to view that society as "a system which is external to the individual and as a limitation of his original independence." What makes that independence seem to him original, furthermore, is that "man as a member of civil society—*non-political* man—necessarily appears as the *natural* man." Once civil society undergoes "dissolution . . . into independent individuals," the "*egoistic* man" who is the result of that dissolution appears as "an object of direct apprehension and consequently a natural object," while "political man" becomes "abstract . . . an *allegorical, moral* person." It is this "double existence" of the politically emancipated, but not yet humanly emancipated, man which accounts for the paradox to which Jehlen points. The contradiction between the individual's imputed freedom and actual entrapment stems not from a "new world cosmology," which both liberates and limits the individual, but from the *actual* political and social conditions he inhabits as "*egoistic* man" in a bourgeois society fully supported by a secularized state. Since these conditions existed in both France and the United States in the nineteenth century, the question becomes how does American bourgeois society differ from its French counterpart?[12]

The difference lies, according to Jehlen, in "the different ways in which the middle-class achieved hegemony in Europe and America." We may agree with this claim without ever discovering in

Jehlen's argument any discussion of this historical difference. She merely asserts that "in Europe . . . the rise of the there insurgent middle class is associated with an attack on such static absolutism" as is to be found in America. But surely it makes a difference what the content of "such static absolutism" is, that is, whether it inheres in the class rule of an entrenched nobility or in the liberal ideology supporting a politically emancipated state. For Jehlen, however, one absolute is like another, "whether personal or social," and thus the middle-class insurgency of Europe registers an understanding of "personality and history . . . as continuous processes and capable therefore of only relative and mutable definition." Anderson's temporalized thought rears its ungainly countenance once more. The historical issue is left abstract, and so is the meaning of hegemony.[13]

To any reader of Raymond Williams' *Marxism and Literature*, the contradiction inherent in Jehlen's use of the term "absolute hegemony" will be readily apparent. Because Williams' concept of hegemony is important in my own argument, I shall try to indicate briefly why this is the case. For Williams, hegemony is a concept whose value consists primarily in the fact that it "includes and goes beyond" the concept of "ideology," beyond, that is, the "formal and abstract system of meanings and values which is the expression or projection of a particular class interest." Introduced by Gramsci in order to get beyond the rigid category of class rule as the direct determinant of all social and political formations, the concept of hegemony provides, in Williams' view, a useful tool for integrating cultural formations within one's vision of society understood as a total, dynamic process, and for avoiding the pitfalls of "abstract models" such as base/superstructure, ideology, and the like, which tend to reduce our vision of society to a tableau depicting the domination of one class by another. Hegemony, in short, allows us to understand the dynamic interplay between social and cultural formations in a way that the abstract "ideology" does not. Williams' discussion is characteristically intricate and far-reaching, but the main point here is that he explicitly insists upon the need to avoid turning hegemony "into an abstract totalization," a form in which "it is readily compatible with sophisticated senses of the superstructure, or even ideology" and becomes "more static, more abstract than in practice, if it is really understood, it can ever actually be."

In practice, that is, a hegemony, no matter how dominant, "is never either total or exclusive."[14]

Williams' treatment of residual cultural formations provides an example of the kind of analysis which the concept of hegemony facilitates. The residual cultural form of organized religion in England, Williams explains, exhibits on the one hand values like "absolute brotherhood" which are oppositional or alternative to the dominant culture, as well as "a larger body of incorporated meanings and values" on the other, which support that culture, such as "official morality." Within the hegemonic process, at work in the interstices of those social and political forms which loudly proclaim their ideological content, Williams is saying, a living social process is going on; and here, with the aid of delicately honed concepts such as "the residual" and "the emergent," the "oppositional" and the "alternative," we may be able to see "the relatively mixed, confused, incomplete, or inarticulate consciousness of actual men" which "is procedurally excluded as peripheral or ephemeral" when we look only at the ideological as the "decisive form" of consciousness. Unfortunately, Jehlen reduces hegemony to ideology in its most abstract form when she summarizes this discussion by saying, "the content of alternative or oppositional cultural forms is lent by either residual or emergent ideologies." It then follows that, since residual values "are associated with the Old World and thus rejected by the very process of national emergence," and since emergent opposition to the dominant hegemony is "precluded by that same peculiarly ideological origin in American which identified nationhood itself with a specific vision of both nation and state," no oppositional or alternative social formation is thinkable in America. The entire thrust of Williams' discussion—to gain cognitive access to the dynamic interplay among cultural and social formations in a society—is turned around in Jehlen's argument, blocking from view precisely those dimensions of social reality which cannot be encompassed by the category of ideology to which she reduces everything.[15]

"Ideological hegemony," like "static absolutism," "new world cosmology," and "integrated civilization," functions to mystify by remythologizing, contradictions which are simply inherent in bourgeois society, and nowhere is this mystification more striking than in Jehlen's appeal to the concept of alienation. In her initial account of European society, Jehlen clearly and accurately characterizes alienation as a condition "inevitably inflicted by bourgeois society." Yet when she comes to distinguish between European and American societies, alienation in Europe becomes a willed response to social conditions. It is "born of the recognition that the individual is inevitably separate from society." But alienation is not born of any recognition; it is, by Jehlen's own admission, inflicted on one and all by bourgeois society. Thus, she must admit that Melville was alienated and then explain his difference from Balzac by claiming that Melville could not "reconcile himself to being alienated" while Balzac drew "all his inspiration" from this condition. But if we reconstitute "alienation" in its full social meaning, it becomes clear why the social reference of the term undermines the purposes Jehlen wants it to serve. In *The Holy Family*, Marx too distinguishes between two responses to "self-alienation," to what Lukács was to call reification, but the distinction derives from somewhat different grounds than national history:

The property-owning class and the class of the proletariat represent the same human self-alienation. But the former feels at home in this self-alienation and feels itself confirmed by it; it recognizes alienation as its own instrument and in it it possesses the semblance of a human existence. The latter feels itself destroyed by this alienation and sees in it its own impotence and the reality of an inhuman existence.

Marx's distinction between the way in which the property owner and the worker experience "self-alienation" is precisely analogous to Jehlen's distinction between American and French responses to it. Emerson "affirms the underlying identity of interest" between individual and bourgeois society, while his European counterparts are "embattled with the bourgeois ethos." Yet when faced with the self-evident case of Melville's alienation, Jehlen is driven to make a claim whose implications contradict her own thesis, the claim that Balzac draws "all his inspiration" from alienation while Melville "cannot reconcile himself" to it. For what can this mean except that the American writer exhibits a proletarian consciousness, while his French opposite is profoundly bourgeois? This is hardly the point Jehlen wishes to make, but in fact close to its exact opposite. Alienation will not serve Jehlen's purposes because it leads in two directions at once in her argument. On the one hand, in its European setting, alienation designates a chosen political opposition to the status quo, while on the other hand, in its American context, its actual social residue emerges. In Europe, one recognizes alienation as "a focus for individual political judgment," while in America, one undergoes it as an inescapable social condition. This fissure reveals a possibility Jehlen struggles to recontain within the bounds of her thesis when she acknowledges that perhaps "the absolute hegemony that the middle class was able to claim in America . . . enabled a more complete ideological development than was attained in Europe."[16]

Here lies the essay's most powerful insight, for Jehlen here provides an entry into that rehistoricized comprehension of American literature which her own thesis demands that she block. Her effort to recontain the American writer's alienation within the bounds prescribed by her argument only sets in relief the centrality of reification as a social, rather than an ideological, formation. In explaining the American writer's response to alienation by reference to the "ideological hegemony" of liberalism, Jehlen obscures the very social and historical reality off which liberalism feeds. Ironically, it is Louis Hartz whose study of American liberalism exposes most vividly the hidden implications of Jehlen's argument.

If American history is, as Hartz argues, distinguished by the dominance of liberalism, perhaps we would do well to explore in our literature the complexities generated from within a liberal, capitalist society rather than looking to Europe for the different complexities our literature has supposedly either lacked (Jehlen's and Anderson's claim) or escaped (Chase's and Poirier's). Unlike Jehlen's, Hartz's discussion of America's liberal tradition accepts, as its "master assumption," "the reality of atomistic social freedom" in a capitalist America. The account of liberalism's dominance which Hartz provides acquires a good deal of its extraordinary force from his rigorous adherence to this master assumption, which echoes Marx's analysis of the egoistic bourgeois whose rights the emancipated state is designed to safeguard. Hartz audibly despairs over the ideological limitations of American political theory, much as Jehlen clearly laments the limitations of American writers whom she regards as in thrall to an "absolute hegemony." But such self-contradictory terms only obscure the consequences of the facts with which Hartz begins—that the decisive difference in America's history was made by the absence of a monarchical state or a feudal society to be overthrown. This is a familiar point, which makes it all the stranger that no critic of American literature has emulated Hartz in tracing its consequences as Hartz traced them in American politics. Why should we continue, like the historians Hartz criticizes, "repeating endlessly that America was grounded in escape from the European past," all the while failing "to interpret our history in the light of that fact"? In other words, why should we not begin with the same master assumption that Hartz did—that social reality in nineteenth- and twentieth-century America has been different from the contemporaneous social reality of England or France because in America, as Marx put it, "bourgeois relations of production" were "imported together with their representatives" and "sprouted rapidly in a soil in which the lack of historic tradition was compensated by a superabundance of humus"? If the middle class in America lacked the need to be insurgent, it confronted by the beginning of the nineteenth century a set of geographical, social, and political conditions which were to foster a relatively, even uniquely, unimpeded capitalist expansion. Political independence secured, the Constitution in place, and the Louisiana territory purchased, the only insurgency required of the American middle class was that which was necessary to "remove" the Indians, a task which, as Hartz explains, differs from the "destruction of a social order to which one belongs oneself," because the first "can actually be completed," while the second "goes on in a sense forever."[17]

The very absence of obstacles to capitalist expansion, I am suggesting, means that the atomistic social freedom of egoistic man is unleashed in nineteenth-century America with a force unparalleled in Europe. From this viewpoint, the difference between a Balzac's and a Melville's response to alienation is not a matter of Melville's inability to "reconcile himself to being alienated," as a result of his distinctively American submission to the "absolute hegemony" of liberalism, but rather a matter of his social condition as the inhabitant of a nation in which an unimpeded capitalist expansion has accelerated the process of alienation so powerfully that his very experience of alienation is likely to outstrip Balzac's. What we need to understand is that if America is different, it is not only because of what it has lacked, but also because of what that lack has fostered— a social reality constituted of the individual's atomistic freedom, a social reality breeding an extreme form of alienation.

Such a viewpoint on American literature does not, of course, rule out the importance of the struggle for hegemonic dominance. Unimpeded capitalist expansion hardly precludes the development of class conflict and the hegemonic process attending it. Thus one might well pursue the line of inquiry suggested by Jehlen's claim that the difference between American and French traditions reflects a difference in the way in which the middle class achieved dominance in the two countries. Fredric Jameson has offered a possible model in his discussion of the disparity between the novel tradition in France and England. Like Jehlen, Jameson appeals to a basic *Gemeinschaft/Gesellschaft* distinction, and also like Jehlen he takes as basic the question of how the middle class achieved its hegemony in each country. But Jameson goes on to historicize the comparison. Associating "rhetoric" with a "relatively homogeneous public or class to which the speaker addresses himself," and, in contrast, "style" with "the increasing atomization of middle class life," Jameson points out that the "rhetorical strain" lasts longer in England than in France, style displacing rhetoric in the latter "at one stroke . . . in 1857, with the publication of *Madame Bovary*." Jameson then suggests that we can account for the earlier "modernization" of the French novel by reference to the earlier supremacy in France of the bourgeois over the *ancien régime*. Not until 1830 does the French aristocracy really lose its central role, and not until 1848 does the bourgeoisie secure its dominance, only to discover its new enemy, the proletariat. After 1848, in other words, the "process of social atomization and monadization of which the modern literary language—stylistic rather than rhetorical, profoundly subjectivistic rather than collective" begins in France, while in England, where "the older feudal aristocracy is able to maintain its control of the apparatus of the state to the very middle of the First World War," effecting as it does a class compromise with the bourgeoisie, the novel remains, all the way to Ford and Conrad, a form whose "linguistic priorities . . . are those of the spoken rather than written composition.'' [18]

This summary does not of course do justice to Jameson's argument, which Jameson in any case only offers as a synecdochic model for a Marxist stylistic criticism. Yet the model suggests how we might pursue the issue of hegemony in the American literary tradition as a means of constructing a literary history bearing some relation to its European counterparts other than that of a binary opposition which merely serves to privilege one tradition over the other, depending on whether one favors the romantic or the realistic. From this perspective, Charles Feidelson's demonstration in *Symbolism and American Literature* of the precocious birth of modernism in America may ultimately prove the most valuable study produced during the postwar period.

Of course, Feidelson's study is by no means the only one which suggests that American literature exhibits features associated with modernism. Roy Harvey Pearce, for example, claims in *The Continuity of American Poetry* that the '''Americanness' of American poetry is, quite simply, its compulsive 'modernism'.'' Pearce, however, grounds this modernism in an ''antinomian, Adamic impulse'' which, as his title implies, remains continuous throughout the history of American poetry. Somehow the issue of modernism, whose complexity is currently stimulating such widespread discussion, has been reduced in Pearce's analysis to the status of a corollary to American innocence. By comparison, Feidelson's analysis is far more historically specific, focusing attention on the American Renaissance in particular. Further, his discussion of Gide raises the question of the relation of American modernism to its French counterpart in a context sufficiently specific that it might even be answered. Why should anomie, atomization, subjectivism, a concern with language—all features of modernism as Jameson defines it—appear in the literature of pre–Civil War northeastern America? The question for Marxist criticism is how this early evidence of modernism is related to the accelerated pace of capitalist expansion during the pre–Civil War years. In short, if we take into account that American society was, as both Hartz and Marx suggest, becoming a capitalist society in the opening half of the nineteenth century, and one whose social features were first manifest in the Northeast, then the emergence of modernism there in the pre–Civil War period makes a good deal of historical sense.[19]

The essay which follows, however, is not concerned with constructing a comparative framework. Such a project must obviously be the work of many hands, for one thing, and for another, it will require us to answer a host of theoretical questions about the relation between literary production and its social context. The work already done by Williams and Jameson provides, in my opinion, the most useful beginning for this task. But neither Williams nor Jameson would claim, I am sure, that the theoretical questions at issue in any contemporary effort to relate literature and history have been answered. The need at present is to reconstitute the problems themselves, and it is in that spirit that I pursue a more limited issue raised by Jehlen's discussion, the issue of reification as a major feature of American culture. Reification, like hegemony, is a concept which has lost some of its force by being too often and too casually used. In pursuing Jehlen's suggestion, then, we must avoid the attendant dangers of abstraction, and the only way of doing so, I think, is to reconstitute the full meaning of the term itself.

Chapter Two

REIFICATION AND AMERICAN LITERATURE

The detached observer is as much entangled as the active participant.
—THEODOR ADORNO

THE CLASSIC EXPLICATION of reification is Georg Lukács' essay in *History and Class Consciousness*, "Reification and the Consciousness of the Proletariat." Here Lukács applies to the realm of classical German philosophy the methods Marx used to analyze classical economics. Divided into three sections, the essay first formulates "structural analogues" between the situation of the worker and that of the bureaucrat, the technologist, indeed of all who inhabit capitalist society; second, focuses on the "antinomies of bourgeois thought," specifically, those evident in German philosophy from Kant to Hegel; and finally outlines a resolution of these contradictions which depends upon the self-consciousness of the proletariat. It is a long, densely argued, and monumentally problematical essay, whose implications have provided Marxist theorists with an abundance of issues about which to argue. But we need not, I think, fall into a bog of Hegelian terminology in order to extract from Lukács' essay a formulation for the concept of reification. For our purposes, two questions must be answered: what is reification? and what is its relation to contradiction?

Lukács begins with Marx's description of the commodity in volume 1 of *Capital*:

A commodity is therefore a mysterious thing, simply because in it the social character of men's labour appears to them as an objective character stamped upon the product of that labour . . . the products of labour become commodities, social things whose qualities are at the same time perceptible and imperceptible to the senses. . . . It is only a definite social relation between men that assumes, in their eyes, the fantastic form of a relation between things.

As a result of his world's commodity structure, then, "A man's labour becomes something objective and independent of him, something that controls him by virtue of an autonomy alien to man." Two aspects of the "phenomenon" of reification emerge at the outset of Lukács' discussion. First, in capitalist society, a new world of objects "springs into being" in which the material and substantial qualities of things as things are hidden beneath their status as commodities. Marx dramatizes this mysterious development at one point by giving the commodity its own voice: "If commodities could speak, they would say this: our use-value may interest men, but it does not belong to us as objects. What does belong to us as objects, however, is our value. Our own intercourse as commodities proves it. We relate to each other merely as exchange-values." Notice that the commodity is not addressing us, but presumably another commodity. Marx's rhetorical strategy underlines how autonomous is the realm in which commodities live and move and have their being. We become alienated observers of this bizarre theatrical performance in which objects have "intercourse" with each other without the slightest concern for, or relation to, our illusory belief that they exist for our use.[1]

Not only does man confront an alien world of commodified objects, but his own activity becomes a "commodity which, subject to the non-human objectivity of the natural laws of society, must go its own way independently of man just like any consumer article." For the factory worker, this is nothing more (and nothing less) than the experience of daily life. The worker finds himself in the position of a "mechanical part incorporated into a mechanical system," and the more mechanized the labor process, the more the worker's "lack of will is reinforced by the way in which his activity becomes less and less active and more and more *contemplative*." The worker thus confronts his own activity in the form of an alien process which he himself does not set in motion, but merely contemplates. As the commodification of society proceeds with the expansion of capital, "the fate of the worker becomes the fate of society as a whole." Thus, both aspects of reification—an alien world of commodities with a life of their own, and an alienated consciousness which can only contemplate this independent and autonomous process, moving in accord with its own "natural laws"—are repeated in bourgeois consciousness as a whole. Not only does man "become the passive observer of society; he also lapses into a contemplative attitude vis-a-vis the workings of his own objectified and reified faculties." In other words, as a result of "the reifying process" endemic to capitalism, not only does the worker contemplate his own activity in the alienated form of commodities interacting in accord with their own laws of motion, but so does the bureaucrat, the technologist, the scientist, each of whom assumes a detached contemplative stance not only toward an objective external world, but toward the objectified constructs of his own mind, which he takes to be incorporated in the external world:

Just as the capitalist system continuously produces and reproduces itself economically on higher and higher levels, the structure of reification progressively sinks more deeply, more fatefully and more definitively into the consciousness of man.

What needs to be stressed is the "artificially abstract" nature of this "new objectivity," this "second nature" man inhabits in modern capitalism. Nowhere is this artificiality more apparent than in the scientist's laboratory.

The experimenter creates an artificial, abstract milieu in order to be able to *observe*, undisturbed the untrammeled workings of the laws under examination, eliminating all irrational factors both of the subject and the object. He strives as far as possible to reduce the material substratum of his observation to the purely rational "product," to the "intelligible matter" of mathematics.

Furthermore, the intelligible matter is reduced finally to that "supreme scientific concept which is no longer the name of anything real . . . like money, e.g., the concept of an atom, or of energy." In the posture of the scientist for whom, in the words of Marx's first thesis on Ludwig Feuerbach, "reality, what we apprehend through our senses, is understood only in the form of the object of contemplation, but not as sensuous human activity," reification takes a materialist form. The idealist's opposition to this situation, however, does not overcome reification, but only reveals more pointedly what has been submerged by it—"sensuous human activity." In Raymond Williams' terms, it is "the exclusion of activity, of making, from the category of 'objective reality'," an exclusion already evident in the scientist's posture as neutral observer, which leads the idealist to invest the transcendent subject with the active dimension lost from the objectified reality he confronts. But since, according to Marx, idealism "does not know real sensuous activity as such," the active, creative subject of idealist thought is necessarily an abstraction. In short, both the neutral observer and the transcendent seer occupy the same contemplative stance, rooted in reification. The "sensuous human activity" drained out of the objectified reality observed by the scientist is only abstractly projected onto the creative, active subject of romantic idealism.[2]

One could describe reification, then, in straightforward terms such as this: man makes his world but then it takes on the appearance of an alien, autonomous, given world. Further, as the idealist response demonstrates, we cannot, simply by taking thought, reclaim this alien world as the product of human labor, any more than the worker, by taking thought, can reclaim his commodified activity. While there comes a point, and an important one for Lukács, when this analogy between the proletariat and the bourgeois breaks down, at this stage it holds true that, for both, "the reifying process" is irreversible.

As a result of the suppression of "sensuous human activity," however, the reifying process generates conditions in which a contradiction comes into view, the contradiction between "details which are subject to laws and a totality ruled by chance." For example, the "strictly rational organization of work on the basis of rational technology," which Weber found "specific to modern capitalism" requires "rational laws" if it is to function at all. The judge in a bureaucratic state, to quote Max Weber's apt phrase, is "an automatic statute-dispensing machine." Capitalist society requires, in short, that the businessman and the bureaucrat be able to calculate and predict, and thus requires a "unified system of general 'laws'."

Yet because this system disregards "the concrete aspects of the subject matter of these laws," it is and must be incoherent. One sign of this "incoherence" is the unceasing flow of conflicts which develop between the legal system and an expanding capitalist economy. But it is in periods of crisis when the system's incoherence manifests itself most dramatically, for then it becomes clear that the "'eternal, iron' laws" are mere pretenses, that the system has no real coherence at all. Lukács is not talking about a crisis which merely exposes the hypocrisy of a legal system's claim to dispense justice; he is talking about a crisis which exposes how untenable is its claim to coherence. A depression, for example, may expose the pretense of the claim of classical economics to comprehend the economic system. The point is that the reifying process yields a world which is presented to us as operating according to known or knowable laws, but which in fact operates irrationally.[3]

In its materialist form, then, reification harbors a contradiction which exposes the rationalized reality of positivism as a "second nature." But the exclusion of "sensuous human activity" which generates this contradiction resurfaces abstractly in the idealist's response to it, as we find when we examine Kant's rationalism. Kant reintroduces the hypothesis that "objects must conform to our knowledge," contrary to the empiricist claim that "all our knowledge must conform to the objects." The irony of the Kantian revolution, however, is that ultimately, whatever it may or may not conform to, our knowledge becomes objectified. Kant's rationalism differs from its predecessors primarily in that it "undertakes to confer universal significance on rational categories," whereas all earlier forms of rationalism accorded such categories only a limited scope, acknowledging a realm of the irrational presided over by God or some other mythic presence. In Kant's system, this limit is marked by the thing-in-itself, but such a limit has the effect of driving underground the irrational—both the "content" of the forms by which we know the world and the "ultimate substance" of that knowledge. The problem posed by the thing-in-itself, as Lukács' rehearsal of subsequent German philosophy through Hegel makes abundantly evident, is insoluble; it is, in effect, the perfect expression of reified consciousness, for it defines an artificial limit to knowledge which constitutes the limit of the thinkable. Henceforth, all that lies beyond the thing-in-itself, the formalized barrier of rationalist thought, closes itself off to human cognition.[4]

On the one hand, a "methodologically purified world" emerges in which the specialized sciences may become "exact" precisely *because* of the "recognition that this problem of the thing-in-itself is insoluble." Philosophy narrows its focus to a concern with the "formal presuppositions of the special sciences which it neither corrects nor interferes with." So the same contradiction arises: our knowledge of and control over "the details of social existence" allow us to subject them to our needs to some extent, while we progressively lose "intellectual control of society as a whole." On the other hand, idealist philosophy generally and romantic aesthetics in particular struggle to rescue the subject from his alienated condition as the victim of an objectified reality whose active dimension has been excluded by being pushed into the realm of the irrational behind the iron wall of the thing-in-itself. Johann Fichte describes this *"projectio per hiatum irrationalem"* definitively when he explains the problem as "the absolute projection of an object *of the origin of which no account can be given* with the result that *the space between projection and thing projected is dark and void."* The romantic effort to restore man's active participation in making the objectified world he confronts can only reconstitute his activity on a nonsensuous, idealist ground. Ferdinand Schiller, for example, makes of the play-instinct an aesthetic principle, arguing that "man only plays when he is man in the full meaning of the word, and he is fully human only when he plays." Realizing that "man as man" has been destroyed, Schiller tries to make *"man whole again in thought."* But the dogma of rationality, as we know from the results of the New Criticism, remains "unimpaired" and "by no means superseded" when the active material substratum of life is rescued through its aesthetic transformation in art. Hegel realizes that the solution to the problem must be sought in history, but as an idealist, Hegel could not locate the subject of history within history itself, and had to "go out beyond history itself, and, there to establish the empire of Reason which has discovered itself."[5]

The solution to reification for Lukács, of course, resides in proletarian consciousness. In his final section, Lukács proceeds to articulate his identity theory, in which the proletariat is the identical subject-object of history. However, we do not need to enter these troubled waters further than to say that the recognition of history's primacy as "sensuous human activity" can only occur from a vantage point within that activity. For Lukács, that vantage point can belong only to proletarian consciousness, understood not in any immediate and empirical form, but as an imputed recognition of the mediations hidden behind the reified, immediate appearance of the world. According to Lukács, such a vantage point must be ascribed exclusively to proletarian class consciousness because it experiences its own objectification differently than does the bourgeois, as instrument rather than essence, to oversimplify grossly a complex and problematical argument. For our present purposes, it suffices to note that one of the limitations to reified thought which Lukács describes at some length here is its incapacity to conceptualize change.[6]

Reified bourgeois consciousness inhabits an illusory world "where the immediately given form of the objects, the fact of their existing here and now and in this particular way appears to be primary, real, and objective, whereas their 'relations' seem to be secondary and subjective." Marx's critique of Feuerbach in *The German Ideology* provides the most straightforward, not to mention comic, refutation of the mistaken notion, itself a result of reification, that the "sensuous world" is "a thing given direct from all eternity." Feuerbach does not inhabit the given world he presumes to live in, Marx explains, because

even the objects of the simplest "sensuous certainty" are only given him through social development, industry and commercial intercourse. The cherry-tree, like almost all fruit-trees, was, as is well known, only a few centuries ago transplanted by *commerce* into our zone, and therefore only by this action of a definite society in a definite age it has become "sensuous certainty" for Feuerbach. . . . So much is this activity, this unceasing sensuous labour and creation, this production, the basis of the whole sensuous world as it now exists, that, were it interrupted only for a year, Feuerbach would not only find an enormous change in the natural world, but would very soon find that the whole world of men and his own perceptive faculty, nay his own existence, were missing.

Only when the apparently stable and given world is understood as already mediated can it be understood as the realm of change, of what Marx called "sensuous human activity." When reified consciousness tries to apprehend change, however, it simply reifies it, as Bergson does in the form of the eternal flux. As Lukács puts it, such a flux "is and does not become, . . . it is just a becoming that confronts the rigid existence of the individual objects." An analogous chasm opens before reified consciousness when it tries to apprehend a relation between the past and the present. Here the contemplative attitude is "polarized into two extremes": on the one hand, historical change is produced by "great individuals," and on the other, it is the result of "natural laws." Neither interpretation can account for the present "in all its radical novelty." Any significant change, in short, appears to be "a sudden, unexpected turn of events that comes from outside and eliminates all mediations."[7]

Reification, then, is a process in the course of which man becomes alienated from himself. But we may also speak of both a reified consciousness, marked by its contemplative stance, and of a reified world, that "second nature" which reified consciousness experiences as already given. (For reified consciousness, "objective reality has the character of a thing-in-itself.") If we turn the question around to ask what has been reified, the answer is neither man per se nor a primary nature out there beyond the objectivized world of immediacy, but rather that "sensuous human activity" encompassing both which we shall hereafter take as the referent for "history." From this point of view, then, bourgeois man does not deny history, but rather is incapable of apprehending it at all, except in reified forms. Yet at moments of crisis, the contradictions inherent in bourgeois society surface, seem to break through the reified patina of the objectified world, revealing the incoherence of the rational systems by which its actual sensuous activity has been obscured, as well as the historically mediated nature of "objectivity."[8]

We can now leave Lukács' account of reification in order to focus on two moments of crisis in which reified consciousness confronts activity beneath the hardened surface of its reified world.

One such moment occurs when Werner Heisenberg "discovers" the uncertainty principle, a concept which seems to have provided the philosophy of science with its own private version of the thing-in-itself. The uncertainty principle is designed to recognize the interference of our instruments of observation in the behavior of the phenomena being observed, and not merely in the degree of necessary error in our measurements. In his own account of indeterminacy, Heisenberg tries in effect to recontain the problems his discovery poses for scientific method, but he cannot obscure its radical content. For indeterminacy introduces, in Heisenberg's words, "the concept of probability into the definition of state of thê object of scientific knowledge in quantum mechanics," and thus "rules out . . . the satisfying of the condition that the object of the physicist's knowledge is an isolated system." If the system cannot be isolated, then the objective reality of classical physics is punctured by the emergence of the subject. For, as Heisenberg notes, "classical physics may be said to be just that idealization in which we can speak about parts of the world without any reference to ourselves." This idealization is implicit in the Cartesian split between subject and object, a split which relies heavily upon the privileged status accorded sight by natural science. Seventeenth-century science gave "sight . . . an almost exclusive privilege," as Foucault points out, "not . . . because men looked harder and more closely," but because sight is "the sense by which we perceive extent and establish proof." Other senses are either excluded or downgraded so that the natural scientist is "content with seeing—with seeing a few things systematically." But eventually, on the level of the atomic event, the scientist's observational instrument betrays the purpose for which it was designed; that is, it undermines the measurable and systematic picture of nature it is supposed to disclose. In the realm of the atomic event, at least, the observational instrument apparently participates, and with effects which cannot themselves be strictly measured. The segment of the world we had presumed to isolate for observation proves to be related to the observer. We might say, then, that if Cartesian dualism formally acknowledged the claim that we are separate from the world we examine, the uncertainty principle acknowledges the rediscovery of our inseparability from it.[9]

Such a crisis in natural science momentarily tears the fabric of a reified objectivity, not only revealing an irrational void beyond the limits of cognition but also resituating the detached observer as a participant within the carefully framed picture he confronts. This irrationality resides not in some noumenal reality whose penetration challenges us onward in our work, for indeterminacy inheres not in the "objective" world, but rather in the very act of examining it. Indeterminacy constitutes a scandal for science precisely because it reconstitutes the objective world as one including the subject. In other words, any epistemology entails an ontology, at least since Kant, and the ontology necessitated by indeterminacy defines reality as activity. As Heisenberg puts it, "quantum mechanics has brought the concept of potentiality back into physical science." As the observer faces the fact that he stands within the world he observes, he comes to recognize a moving world in which his observation constitutes an act.[10]

A similar rupture occurs at what John Berger calls "the moment of cubism." Berger analyzes the experience of a person viewing a cubist painting in terms of a contrast between the cubist's use of space and the illusionist space of Renaissance perspective. In the cubist painting, he says, "the viewing point of Renaissance perspective, fixed and outside the picture, but to which everything within the picture was drawn, has become a field of vision which is the picture itself." Consequently, when we view a cubist painting, we observe spaces defined between objects, but the relation defined between any two objects "does not, as it does in illusionist space, establish the rule for all spatial relationships between all the forms portrayed in the picture." Berger depicts the viewer's eye as moving into the picture and back to its surface repeatedly, depositing each time the newly acquired knowledge before returning to discover another relation. Thus, the cubist painting acts as "an expression of the relation between viewer and subject," and the evaluative question appropriate to it is not "is it true?" or "is it sincere?" but "does it continue?" Berger concludes that the content of a cubist painting is "the relation between the seer and the seen," and that the works of Pablo Picasso, Georges Braque, Juan Gris, and Fernand Léger from 1907 to 1914 "do not illustrate a human or social situation, they posit" one. The situation such paintings posit is one which radically redefines the epistemological relationship between perceiving subject and perceived object as interaction rather than confrontation. The detached viewer of an illusionist space in the Renaissance painting becomes the active participant in a process of vision inaugurated by the cubist painting.[11]

In both "moments," that of indeterminacy and cubism alike, relations overtake isolated objects in a field itself constituted by
events. We can examine neither the atomic event nor the cubist
painting without participating in its activity. The shock to reified
consciousness first created by these ruptures in "objectivity" has
long since been recontained, incorporated that is, within the given
world of "fact." Yet if one reads Heisenberg's account of his work,
it remains possible to appreciate the genuine agony with which he
and Niels Bohr brought themselves to accept the results of their own
experiments. We need to be able to reinhabit such moments in order
to comprehend the phenomenon of reification at all, so accustomed
have we grown to incoherence. Lukács' account, first published in
1923, is outdated in one major respect; it does not fully appreciate
the extent to which capitalist society can tolerate incoherence. *The
Education of Henry Adams*, written some fifteen years before
Lukács' essay, can serve as an example of how the threshold of
tolerance has risen. For Adams the twentieth century is to be so
incoherent as to be unimaginable; it must therefore cease to exist.[12]

If we try to reinhabit these moments of indeterminacy and cubism,
they can serve to identify a particular result of reification and its
contradictions. For in these moments, the relation between the contemplative observer and the objectified world undergoes a momen-
tary transformation. Rather than confronting a static object, the
observer finds himself participating in a process. In a Marxist perspective, the shock of such an experience results from the inability
of reified consciousness to comprehend "reality . . . as sensuous
human activity." Historical materialism, as Marx developed and
applied it to political economy, constitutes a critical and revolutionary method precisely because it takes the interaction of man and
nature through time as its subject and its ground of observation,
establishing its point of view of necessity within the process it studies, thereby voiding all escape hatches not only into detached objectivity, but also into idealized subjectivity. But in the daily life of
reified consciousness, these moments of crisis come as a shock. Not
only is the objectified surface of rationalization torn, revealing the
irrational void lying beyond the limit of the thing-in-itself, but once
admit that observation of the world constitutes a form of participation in its activity, and you experience a curious modern version

of the Fall, for you become at least theoretically implicated and complicit in events which you presume merely to watch, analyze, and interpret.[13]

Both the moral and epistemological implications of a presumed detachment on the part of an observer become clear in Henry James's *The Sacred Fount*, a work in which very little else becomes clear. The narrator of this novella devotes himself to observing his fellow guests during a weekend visit at a country home aptly called "Newmarch" in honor of the new march of society toward sham values and deceitful relations. The narrator, whose detachment is underscored by the fact that he remains nameless in a world of Lord Lutleys and Lady Froomes, observes among the couples assembled what he takes to be an alarming array of evidence suggesting vampirism; wives, husbands, and lovers seem to be sucking their partners dry of their youth or intelligence or beauty. But as the narrator's observations carry him on in the development of his theory, the reader is forced to abandon all hope of sharing his vision because here the Jamesian lucid reflector has become opaque. When the novel reaches its climactic concluding scene—the confrontation between the narrator and Mrs. Brissenden—the narrator's theory crumbles into a "pile of ruins." And the dialogue which takes place suggests not only that the narrator has allowed his theory to run away with him, but that his constant spying is itself a supreme instance of vampirism.[14]

Read as a kind of botched parable about the perils of vampirism for the artist who assumes a cold and detached posture toward his fellow creatures, pouring his passion into the effort to arrange them according to the needs of his own design, *The Sacred Fount* illustrates the well-known concern James shared with Hawthorne about the responsibilities of the artist. But when we recall that Mrs. Brissenden's explanation of people's behavior is no more reliable than the narrator's, such a reading becomes inadequate. For if *The Sacred Fount* were merely this, merely a parable, the narrator's theory would have to be exploded by a verifiable explanation, and it is not. Instead, the final dialogue presents us with a bewildering scene in which we can form no judgment at all about the observations we have been offered, because Mrs. Brissenden is no more reliable than the narrator. The scene thus calls attention not only to the inadequacies of the narrator's theory and the limitations of his subjective perspective, but also to the circumstance which dictates these problems—the narrator, while observing with such vengeance, has also been observed, a fact he is forced to realize for the first time when Mrs. Brissenden demands to know his purposes. The closing scene reveals, in short, that he has been a participant in the events he has presented himself as merely observing. The entire narrative framework of the novel is called into question by this scene because the narrator's status as observer is undermined. Once afforded a view of him as a participant in the events he has been describing, we are faced with the realization that the narrator is a character who, like everyone else at Newmarch, has put on a mask to hide his peculiar passion. His unreliability is exposed on terms which not only destroy his theory, but more importantly, implicate him in the scene he observes in a wholly undetermined and undeterminable way. The closing scene of *The Sacred Fount* constitutes a moment of crisis not only for the narrator but for the reader as well. Mrs. Brissenden tells the narrator he's mad, and we are inclined to accept that judgment, since it allows us to retreat in safety from the fissure opened here—not that between the world "as it is" and the narrator's fabricated house of cards, but that within our own faith in the world as "objectively" accessible to cognition.

The cognitive abyss exposed in *The Sacred Fount*'s concluding scene, only to be obscured by an appeal to the irrational, reflects a disjunction inherent in a reified social world, the disjunction between an immediate rationalized objectivity and an actual "sensuous human activity." The scandal surfaces, as in the case of indeterminacy, when the contemplative posture of the observer becomes so entrenched as to seem to constitute his identity. When observation is carried to this point, reified consciousness behaves as if it were a disembodied eye, only to be faced with its own presence in the world it presumes to observe. That is, the contemplative stance of the detached observer, by virtue of the extreme to which it is taken, is undermined from within, and the observer of an immediately given world is exposed as a participant in the mediated activity of which that world is constituted. It is this scandal, I wish to argue, that haunts the worlds of Emerson, Adams, James, and Faulkner.

These are different worlds, to be sure. Ralph Waldo Emerson was born at the beginning of the nineteenth century (1803) into a family long associated with New England's religious tradition; Henry Adams, born close to midcentury (1838), grew up in a different Boston, one whose political heritage was inscribed in his family's history; Henry James, Adams' contemporary (1843), escaped his father's New England to become an expatriate, but by no means escaped America as a fictional subject; William Faulkner, born at century's end (1897), was the product of a fallen South and a frontier tradition. Emerson, the secular minister, Adams, the historian, and the novelists James and Faulkner, emerge from different social and historical circumstances—a fact which makes their shared concerns the more significant. Each of them responds critically to his society, and the related terms in which these several radical critiques take shape reveal at once the deepening structure of reification in American society as it moves from the nineteenth century into the twentieth, and the exemplary efforts of four of America's most formidable critical minds to overcome and resist that reification. According to Sartre, "Man is characterized above all by his going beyond a situation, and by what he succeeds in making of what he has been made—even if he never recognizes himself in his objectification." It is this "project," as Sartre calls it, to which Emerson, Adams, James, and Faulkner are committed, and in their attempts to go beyond the situation in which they find themselves, they all exhibit the effects of that reification for which they are trying to compensate.[15]

By examining these projects, we may trace a development in which both the contemplative stance of reified consciousness and the rationalized objectivity of a reified world, while sinking deeper into the structure of social reality, are subjected to increasingly complex critical strategies. Emerson's critical reaction to rationalization yields an idealist version of the contemplative stance whose inherent contradiction resurfaces in *The Sacred Fount*. The later James tries to recontain this crisis in *The Golden Bowl*, by means of an aesthetic theory and practice designed to account for the detached seer's com-

plicity as participant. The materialist version of reified consciousness, repressed but by no means escaped in Emerson's strategy,
resurfaces in *The Education of Henry Adams*, where the contradiction inherent in the neutral observer's detached contemplation of
a rationalized objectivity is exposed. James expands the role of the
visionary seer to its critical limits, as he struggles to account for the
complicity of the detached seer in the world he confronts, while
Adams takes rationalization to its limits, revealing the more vividly
as he struggles to comprehend it, the incoherence of the vision afforded the neutral observer. In the work of James and Adams, the
contemplative stance of reified consciousness comes into view in
an increasingly critical light, revealing both the impotence of the
neutral observer's "intellectual control of society as a whole," and
the complicity of his brother and companion in reification, the visionary seer, as a participant in the world beyond which he presumes
to stand. It is this combined impotence and complicity which we not
only find fused in the figure of Thomas Sutpen, but also must find
ways of defending ourselves against as readers of *Absalom, Absalom!* Rejoining neutral observer and visionary seer as victims of the
same reified consciousness, Faulkner devises a narrative strategy
which reveals the source of the contradiction which had first surfaced for Emerson—the exclusion of "sensuous human activity"
from the objectified world. The inability of reified consciousness to
apprehend history as sensuous human activity is here revealed as
rooted in a specific historical process, one dominated by the unimpeded capitalist development which both made America, and
made it "innocent."

In the course of the progression traceable in these projects, detached seers and observers are increasingly threatened with the recognition forced upon Heisenberg—the recognition of the seer's participation in an active reality whose status as an "object of
contemplation" is undermined. Because reification operates to exclude sensuous human activity from the objective reality the observer confronts, that activity erupts in a kind of return of the repressed. It is not, however, until Faulkner's response to this crisis
that its actual sources are revealed, for Emerson's initial diagnosis

enables him finally to evade the contradictions he bequeaths to James and Adams. They, in their turn, develop strategies designed to save the detached observer, to recontain the crisis to which his contemplative stance makes him vulnerable. If we trace this developing struggle in outline, we can see why Faulkner's treatment of the detached observer yields such explosive results.[16]

Emerson's opposition to the "mechanical powers and the mechanical philosophy" of his time stems from his disaffection with a society which is turning man "into a thing, into many things," as its faith in the "goddess of Reason" leads it to contrive systems in which man is "peddled out" and reduced to an aggregate of atomized beings making up "'the mass' and 'the herd'." In his attempt to compensate for this degradation by speaking in the name of the whole man, and in the service of his salvation from alienation, Emerson attacks the most evident feature of reification in his day— rationalization, or the tendency to mechanize man in the service of profit-making enterprises requiring calculation and measurable risks. But Emerson's critical revolt ultimately reveals the penetrating force of reification, for inherent in his resistance to rationalization is the detached contemplative stance of reified consciousness.[17]

The conviction at the heart of Emerson's career is that "the reason why the world lacks unity, and lies broken and in heaps, is because man is disunited with himself." When he set out in *Nature* to forge an "original relation" between the me and the "Not Me," he did so in the faith that within the reified objectivity confronting him as alien spectator lay "imbedded" his essential selfhood. Thus the issue in *Nature* is the same issue to which Emerson referred in a journal entry of 1839—whether "the world is not a dualism, is not a bipolar unity, but is two, is Me and It." If this is the case, "then there is the alien, the unknown, and all we have believed and chanted out of our deep instinctive hope is a pretty dream." If man's self-alienation is a given, eternal, immutable condition, then Emerson's entire project proves a fool's game.[18]

So much must be grasped in order to appreciate the purpose of Emerson's procedure in *Nature*, where he establishes the opposition between the me and the "Not Me" at the outset as a given in order to transform it into an illusion. His method, as we shall see, is based on the conviction he shared with Fichte, that the reunion of subject and object required a translation of facts into events, of substance into act. On an epistemological level, Emerson succeeded in re-unifying the subject and the object within an act—an act of signifi-cation authorized by and grounded in Spirit. By the essay's end, the "Not Me"—the "involuntary," the given and opaque "objectivity" of the world—has been dissolved and transformed into an illusion. Emerson's method is designed to serve a rhetorical purpose: to pro-vide a vantage point from which the world can be seen as fluid, volatile, and obedient to man's will. As he put it in a journal entry of February 1836, "I do not dispute" the "absolute being" of "a field of corn or a rich pasture," but "point out the just way of viewing them." In his effort to arrive at this "just way of viewing" a reified objectivity, Emerson constructed a method whose genius lay in its power to penetrate the immediate and show it to be mediated.[19]

Both the power and the limitations of that method are apparent in Emerson's summary statement:

Nature from an immoveable God . . . on which as reptiles we creep, & to which we must conform our being, becomes an instrument, & serves us with all her kingdoms. Then becomes a spectacle.

Emerson saw clearly enough that "man is not what man should be," and that bourgeois society had made him so. Further, he understood that this society was the product of human agency, that it was his-torically mediated. Yet his attempt to overcome immediacy, to re-construct the "original relation" of man to his world led finally to a metaphysics of vision. Emerson was virtually unable to concep-tualize the self except in the form of an eye. Man was for him a "subject-lens," whose self-alienation is indicated by the distorted vision resulting from a kind of false correction in that lens. Even when he tried to conceive of nonalienation, to imagine the reunion of man and nature, he could only do so by turning man into a trans-parent eyeball. Thus the problem raised by Hegel's somewhat sim-ilar attempt to unify the subject and the object within a process emerges; for Emerson's Spirit, like Hegel's Absolute Reason, comes to the rescue as the missing subject of historical mediation. And Lukács' remark about the freedom of man in Hegel's history applies to Emersonian freedom as well: it is the "freedom to reflect upon laws—which themselves govern man, a freedom which in Spinoza a thrown stone would possess if it had consciousness."[20]

Yet as Newton Arvin points out, "it is a paradox that the writer who most perfectly expressed the aspirations of the American middle-class . . . also, more than almost any other . . . anticipated its passing." Arvin calls this a "vital" paradox, and so indeed it is. For Emerson's attempt to reunite man with himself led on the one hand to a faith in Spirit's benevolence in history so total as to sanctify the contemplative stance of the most ardent capitalist entrepreneur, and to a rhetorical program, on the other, designed to persuade men that the world they confronted as given was made by man and could be radically changed by him. The same paradox emerges in the sentence Myra Jehlen quotes: "Speak your latent conviction, and it shall be the universal sense." This is a flat statement of Emerson's deepest faith in the power of man to shape his destiny, and as such may indicate his "underlying identity of interest" with a society whose creed was individualism. Yet one must remember that the statement was delivered in "Self-Reliance" not as a calm philosophical doctrine, but as both a charge to the reader to change society and a firm assurance that he could do so. Emerson's own struggle to speak his latent conviction is in retrospect belied by the degree to which it became the universal sense. Finally, however, the paradox is inscribed within the method he developed for overcoming alienation. "Cannot I conceive the Universe without a contradiction?" he asked himself. The answer was no, but his effort to do so led him to expose the sources of the contradiction he could not override.[21]

Perhaps the most energetic and sustained development of Emerson's program for the visionary seer as poet is to be found in Henry James's career as a novelist. In his third-person center of consciousness, James exploited the transparent eyeball as a lucid reflector, but as we have already noted, the lucid reflector serving as a narrative lens is not transparent and cannot blithely float in the "currents of Universal Being." As *The Sacred Fount* demonstrates, the detached seer whom James invests with the role of visionary artist is also a participant in the world he confronts, and is thus potentially implicated in the events he watches, a point by no means lost on James. Sharing Emerson's conviction that the visionary seer is intensely active, James attempted to account for the seer's agency without forfeiting his status as seer. The final result of that effort is Maggie Verver, who acts on the Emersonian belief that, having made his world, man can remake it in accord with his dreams. But Maggie's career at the same time serves in one sense to de-mystify the transparent eyeball, demonstrating how the creative subject "in action," as Lukács describes the capitalist, is "transformed into a receptive organ ready to pounce," a subject, that is, whose "activity will narrow itself down to the adoption of a vantage point" from which the world is reshaped in accord with "his best interests," and who thereby assumes a "purely contemplative" attitude. Maggie, in short, is at once the visionary poet and the capitalist entrepreneur.[22]

It is this identity, implicit in Emerson's own program, which helps to account for the contradictory response which *The Golden Bowl* has always evoked. With characteristic lucidity, F. R. Leavis stated the issue when he said that while we are meant "to watch with intense sympathy Maggie's victorious struggle to break the clandestine relation between her husband and Charlotte," it remains the case that "our sympathies . . . are with Charlotte and (a little) the Prince." The contradiction to which Leavis points is unmistakably present in the novel, although it need not lead us to agree with Leavis' diagnosis that the later James had somehow "lost his full sense of life and let his moral taste slip into abeyance." I would propose a different diagnosis, that the logic of James's career as a devotee of the Imagination led him to produce a work in which the visionary seer's valorization is achieved on the basis of a narrative strategy which exposes the crack, the something "terrible at the heart of man," as the Prince calls it, which must be there, and yet be concealed, if the redemptive project is to succeed, if what Maggie calls a "distinctly bourgeois" world is to be secure. Our conflicting responses to Maggie's career, as at once miraculous and monstrous, derive from the scrupulous logic of James's procedure, which goes beyond Maggie's in exposing the commodified society whose values are adumbrated by her redemptive project.[23]

That procedure stems from James's effort to recontain the crisis erupting in *The Sacred Fount* by means of a strategy which allows him to acknowledge the seer's complicity without sacrificing his detached contemplative stance. The success of this strategy depends upon a world constituted exclusively of and by seers who are also seen. In effect, James is led to solve the problems attendant upon reified consciousness by conceiving a completely reified society. The finally exposed condition of *The Sacred Fount*'s narrator becomes essentially the condition of everyone in *The Golden Bowl*, insofar as everyone here is simultaneously both a detached seer and a complicit participant. It is only in a world made up entirely of people constituted as seers and seen that the activity of the visionary artist can proceed without her abandoning her detached contemplative stance. Maggie is a visionary seer whose innocence consists in her failure to recognize her complicity as participant in the creation of her peculiar world. In acting to redeem that world, she takes responsibility for her complicity, thereby meeting the moral dilemma implicit in the epistemological rupture which concludes *The Sacred Fount*. But far from abandoning her detached posture as seer, she exploits and solidifies it. Thus, while Maggie's career serves to acknowledge the seer's complicity, her success both presupposes and exposes a world in which man's reified status is confirmed. At the novel's end, that is, we have a world in which man has become, in Lukács' words, at once "an element in the movement of commodities" and the "impotent observer of that movement."[24]

Such is the fate of Charlotte and the Prince, whose destiny is to be initiated into a fully capitalist world as commodities. Both purchased by Adam Verver, Charlotte and Amerigo are to fulfill their roles as commodities in significantly different ways, but their fate as pieces of "human furniture" is prophetically evident at the novel's outset. Here the Prince surveys objects perhaps more "massive and lumpish" than the "*morceau de musée*" which he constitutes, but since they reside behind "plate glass," and are soon to be confined within "the iron shutter of a shop" like the one in which he is similarly to be put on display, it is not surprising that his gaze is troubled. He is confronted with his own image in the marketplace world he is about to join, not as the prospective capitalist adventurer he hopes to become, but as the commodity he has already unwittingly consented to be.[25]

What is essential to an understanding of *The Golden Bowl* is the recognition that its world is in fact commodified from the beginning, for Maggie's redemptive action presupposes a marketplace world, and she succeeds by acting in accord with its laws. Thus, while her career valorizes the visionary artist's redemptive role, it ends by solidifying a world now thoroughly reified. By standing outside the "funny form" of her marriage as spectator, while playing an improvised role in the play she is watching, Maggie fulfills Emerson's desire to "be and see my being at the same time." But her success as transcendent seer is ironic, for it leaves her bifurcated in these very terms, doomed to be split permanently into the detached seer and the observed actress she has had to become. Her world is remade, to be sure, but it is remade on the basis of the "sublime economy of art" which, as we shall see, emulates the sublime economy of Capital.[26]

Emerson's desire to "be and see my being at the same time" assumes a rather different ironic form in Henry Adams' reputed capacity to "sit on a fence and watch himself go by." Alienated early from a society whose contradictions came almost to hypnotize him, Adams turned detached contemplation into a profession; while James exploited the spectator's role in his development of the third-person center of consciousness, Adams fetishized it. Adams had little patience for Emersonian idealism, much less for the complexities it had generated in the later novels of his friend James. But Adams was far from escaping his own Emersonian heritage. Struggling to maintain a materialist position, Adams was finally to expose the contradictions attendant upon his faith in a rationalized objectivity, just as James was forced to expose a reified world in his effort to recontain the contradiction implicit in Emerson's idealized version of reified vision.[27]

Like Emerson, Adams questioned the solidity of a society driven forward by forces which made its faith in Reason and Progress the more untenable with every passing year. Adams sought to comprehend the contradiction between the advance of scientific reason and the spread of social chaos, and did so with a logical rigor conspicuously absent from Emerson's thinking. Marshaling all the available intellectual resources for calculation and prediction, Adams demonstrated their inadequacy, but never suspended his effort to comprehend history within some intelligible framework. At the outset of their careers, Emerson and Adams occupied opposite ends of the spectrum as far as reified thought's effort to apprehend history is concerned. Emerson appealed to great men, and Adams, to "natural laws." But eventually, Emerson was saying prayers to "Beautiful Necessity," and Adams was inquiring whether men might after all be able to "react, not at haphazard, but by choice on the lines of force that attract their world." Both oscillated between the two extremes of the contemplative attitude toward history, although they moved in opposite directions.[28]

Early in life, Emerson found confirmation of his belief in the social structure's mediated status when a crisis occurred. During the panic of 1837 we find him remarking, "when these full measures come, it then stands confessed—Society has played out its last stake; it is checkmated." There is a distinct glee in the following response to the "black times":

What was, ever since my memory, solid continent, now yawns apart and discloses its composition and genesis. I learn geology the morning after an earthquake. . . . I see the natural fracture of the stone. I see the tearing of the tree & learn its fibre & its rooting. The Artificial is rent from the Eternal.

At this stage, Emerson was grateful for such evidence that the world had "failed," since it confirmed his faith in the power of man to make and remake that world. Eventually, however, reified objectivity was to take on a more powerful aspect, and the "torrents of tendency" to acquire the status of a metaphysical principle. Adams' early efforts, on the other hand, to trace the sequence of history within the terms dictated by his eighteenth-century belief in progress, led him to regard men as "mere grasshoppers kicking and gesticulating on the middle of the Mississippi River." When the panic of 1893 broke out, it confirmed Adams' belief that society had failed, but the spectator here has grown nervous in his seat. Writing to John Hay, Adams exclaimed,

For a thorough chaos I have seen nothing since the war to compare with it. The world surely cannot long remain as mad as it is, without breaking into acute mania. . . . I'm mad. I'm madder than ever. . . . I am seriously speculating whether I shall have a better view of the *fin-de-siècle* circus in England, Germany, France or India, and whether I should engage seats to view the debacle in London, Paris, Berlin or Calcutta.

He went on to say, "My dear democracy is all in pieces." Such ruptures were to occupy Adams' attention for the rest of his productive life, as he tried to comprehend them within a rational scheme. Adams had begun with the conviction that "if anything universal was unreal . . . it was his own thought, and not the thing that moved it." Yet he ended by trying to measure the "sequence of force" by reference to its "attraction on thought."[29]

Henry Adams enjoyed the freedom to reflect upon laws for many years, and he reached the conclusion that the laws did not bear reflecting upon; science itself had revealed their inadequacy by exploding them one after another. When "Madame Curie threw on his desk the metaphysical bomb she called radium," the scientist, Adams remarks, had "no hole to hide in—no one could longer hope to bar out the unknowable, for the unknowable was known." Thus when Adams hypothesized that history was a sequence of force, and set about trying to order that sequence, his purpose was to discover whether man might after all play some role in directing history's course. Adopting the attitude of the scientist, he decided that if man is to control such forces, he must be able to measure them. Only then could he hope to "react . . . by choice" and not involuntarily. Adams' effort to measure force in terms of its "attraction on thought" had the advantage of reinserting man within the historical process to be apprehended, but the man reinserted remained an observer, and Adams became an observer twice removed. For now he set about observing the reactions of "great men before great monuments," and devising a "dynamic theory" of history based on the "law of reaction between force and force—between mind and nature—the law of progress."[30]

That Adams' procedure is "unscientific" in a conventional sense, no one would question. Yet in a sense, this is precisely its value. In his effort to abide by the premises of Newtonian physics—to speak about parts of the world without reference to himself—Adams was forced to violate those premises. Because the picture of history he confronted failed to cohere, he was compelled to reinsert a neutralized self into that picture, a "manikin" designed to serve the purposes of measurement. By carrying rational observation to this point, along with his other scientific paraphernalia, Adams simultaneously carries out the program of scientific progress, and shows that program's incoherence. The problem Adams always presents to us as critical readers is that of irony. We find it impossible to take seriously his analogy between the mind and a comet, except as simply that, an analogy with no cognitive foundation. Yet Adams' endeavor to treat himself as a "barometer, pedometer, radiometer" reflects at once a bitter irony and a genuinely serious enterprise. Adams *was* the *"type-bourgeois-bostonian"* for which he took himself, and he could not help trying to carry out the rational program of the eighteenth century, to whose ideal of enlightenment he remained, like Gatsby, true to the end. It was precisely because of his struggle to remain true to these ideals that he was forced again and again to confront the contradictions in that program. Adams' fatalism, in other words, is an exemplary one, for his effort to discover whether men might have some part to play in history's direction reflects a genuine desire to disprove his own suspicion that they were atoms pushed and pulled by forces of which they were wholly ignorant. His fatalism results from the intellectual honesty with which he confronted the evidence before him.[31]

Adams' was perhaps the last great mind in America capable of following current developments in geology, physics, economics, politics, literature, philosophy, and historical research on anything approaching a global scale. The picture presented to him by this assemblage of evidence forced the question which he posed and reposed from 1893 until the end of his life, the question which *The Education of Henry Adams* was designed to raise for its reader: can man control the direction of history? *The Education*'s peculiar contradictions derive from the fact that it poses for bourgeois society the question of its own survival. *The Education* is an attempt to educate, "to fit young men in universities and elsewhere, to be men of the world, equipped for any emergency." As such, *The Education* is not a wholly futilitarian document, for it records the heroic struggle of the reified bourgeois mind to formulate a coherent basis for the future of its society. Yet its didactic purpose is inscribed upon a narrative which tells the story of that society's self-destruction. In his effort to face squarely the multiple contradictions thrown up by his didactic pursuit, Adams dismantles, step by step, in his narrative, the complacent assumptions of that society, exposing the impotence of its systems of thought in the face of the energies it has itself unleashed. It is this contradiction between the desire to educate, stemming from Adams' unregenerate reformist tendencies, and the desire to tell a story whose moral could not but reveal the futility of that "heavy dissertation on modern education" for which it was intended as a vehicle, which undermines Adams' attempt to make *The Education* cohere. But the contradiction between what Adams described as his "narrative and didactive purpose and style" makes for more than a formal problem. It generates an ethical dilemma as well.[32]

Adams is given to making pronouncements throughout *The Education* about his absolute lack of responsibility, only to find himself eventually asking "where his responsibility began or ended." Here the contradiction between the individual's imputed freedom to shape—and his consequent responsibility for—his world, and his actual freedom in capitalist society merely to reflect upon "natural laws" manifests itself most dramatically. For if the Adams whose recorded life is that of a mere "bystander," the man on the fence, observing a drama for which he takes no responsibility, the Adams who writes *The Education* with a didactic purpose thereby inadvertently reveals his status as a member of the procession going by. In other words, by pursuing his didactic goal, to "encourage foresight and to economize waste of mind," Adams betrays and undermines his contemplative stance, revealing his own participation in the spectacle he repeatedly insists he is merely watching. By the end of *The Education*, he partly admits to the contradiction in assuming the role of an "umpire," whose "attitude is apt to infuriate the spectators," but whose duty is fulfilled. The narrative strategy of *The Education*, in other words, is designed primarily to deny what the act of writing it demonstrates—that Adams was a participant in the social process he presumed merely to observe.[33]

The contradictions Adams keeps confronting in *The Education* reveal the irrationality he seeks to expose and to remedy; America has rarely had a more brilliant and incisive critic. Yet the more radical Adams' critical responses become, the more evident is the reified consciousness which delivers the judgments. For instance, Adams cannot quit blaming his age's problems on the stupidity of its men, while all the time describing their impotence. More significantly, he cannot stop trying to affect history even though he insists that he is a mere observer of it. He is after all a bit like James's Fanny Assingham, always pronouncing that he is not responsible, but never able to escape completely his sense of complicity. It is this combination of complicity and impotence whose sources Faulkner exposes.

Like Emerson, Faulkner revolts against a stolid adherence to tradition; like Adams, Faulkner brings to bear the full weight of a historical imagination on his critique of modern society; like James, he works out his critical response in terms of a complex narrative strategy. But Faulkner cuts deeper, and exposes the roots of reification from which his own critical interpretation grows. Each of these writers exhibits a deep-seated ambivalence toward his society, but in Faulkner that ambivalence achieves a certain purity, a kind of stoic and open-faced acceptance of despair in comparison with which Hemingway's concept of courageous honesty, for example, looks irremediably sentimental. Faulkner's despair, I suggest, grows out of a recognition, registered in his greatest work, that the very project he himself pursues in his fiction, the drive to go beyond one's situation, is both irresistible and doomed.

I will be concerned primarily with *Absalom, Absalom!* and *Light in August*, for in these novels Faulkner developed a narrative strategy designed to undermine the reader's detachment so as to implicate him in a "stream of event" which he presumes merely to witness. The complex demands Faulkner makes on the reader, particularly in these two novels where the moral implications of detachment are so powerfully demonstrated, stem from a strategy which undermines the reader's compulsion to contain the moving flow of narrative within some ordering frame, to remain the fixed, detached spectator of a given and preformed fictional world. *Light in August* already undermines any effort on the reader's part to maintain a secure vantage point, and does so in terms which make clear why such a vantage point is illegitimate; to order the flow of time, one must presume to stand outside it, as does Gail Hightower. Thus the novel frustrates the reader's desire to frame a coherent picture by means of a narrative structure which enforces the rule that time's flow outstrips all attempts to order it.[34]

In *Absalom, Absalom!*, however, Faulkner went further. What was demonstrated in *Light in August* is now enacted. Quentin Compson comes to us as an auditor who is forced to listen to Rosa Coldfield, to his father, and to his roommate, but who struggles to resist a narrative pull which threatens to engulf him. By refusing to speak while watching static pictures of Sutpen and his family resolve out of nothing into "painted portraits hung in a vacuum," Quentin tries to maintain a detached perspective on the story of Sutpen, and so to free himself not only from the weight of the past but from his involvement in the "stream of event" itself. But he is forced eventually to participate in the telling of Sutpen's story, a process which undermines his effort to see it as an assembled totality distinct from himself. The very endeavor to secure and maintain a detached perspective on history by imposing narrative coherence on it leads inexorably to Quentin's participation in it. Furthermore, the reader's detachment is undermined in the same way, for like Quentin, he struggles to confront a story which insists upon engulfing him. The reader can no more succeed in securing a fixed point of view from which to confront the novel as a discrete totality than Quentin can find a position outside the tale of Sutpen. In *Absalom, Absalom!*, as in life itself, by the time we find out what's going on, we are already implicated in it.[35]

We have been too much concerned with the fact that Rosa, Mr. Compson, and Quentin/Shreve produce different versions of Sutpen's story to pay sufficient attention to the medium out of which we extract these versions, the medium of conversation. For *Absalom, Absalom!* does not simply conduct us through a series of perspectives, calling attention to the limitations of each; it implicates the reader in the collective act of narrative construction of which it is constituted. By making conversation the vehicle for the novel's central action, the telling of a story, and by reiterating the physical and material substratum of conversation—breathing, air—Faulkner exploits the radical potential of speech as social act. The halting yet persistent voice of Byron Bunch which drew Gail Hightower temporarily into the moving world outside his window in *Light in August* becomes in *Absalom, Absalom!* the relentless insistence not only of Shreve's voice drawing Quentin into a conversation, but of Faulkner's voice struggling to draw the reader into one as well.

Needless to say, Faulkner cannot finally succeed at making the reader a participant. To do so would entail actually bridging the gap between words and deeds, the gap to which Addie Bundren refers in *As I Lay Dying* when she laments how "words go straight up in a thin line . . . and how terribly doing goes along the earth." Yet what Faulkner can, and I shall argue, does achieve, is a resolution to the novel which contaminates what it cannot undercut—the reader's inherently contemplative position. At the novel's end, we have only two places to stand—within the picture with Quentin, or outside it with Shreve. I do not mean that we must "identify" with one or the other of these two characters, but rather that between them they exhaust all the available epistemological positions. We cannot accept Quentin's position, for in telling and hearing Sutpen's story, Quentin has in effect fallen into history. He has become a blood relation of Charles Bon's, and thus of Sutpen's. As we shall see, there are a host of reasons why Quentin's position is closed to us, not the least of which is that we cannot afford to know history as Quentin knows it at the novel's end. The point here is that it is not a question of choice; we could not adopt Quentin's position even if we wanted to, and given his fate, we certainly do not want to. Our position must be that of Shreve, who is once again fixed and outside the picture, and as such, our position is contaminated. For when Shreve turns on Quentin in the last chapter to draw a conclusion to the story, he no longer sounds like Quentin's father, but like Sutpen himself. The conclusion he draws is that "it takes two niggers to get rid of one Sutpen." This "clears the whole ledger," he thinks, except that "you've got one nigger left" whom you can't "catch" and "don't even always see," but you still "hear." While Quentin indeed continues to "hear" Jim Bond's voice, Shreve pursues a different course; he finds a "use" for this dangling fraction by issuing a prophecy—"the Jim Bonds are going to conquer the western hemisphere." Whatever accuracy may be attributed to Shreve's prediction, the significant point is that his resolution provokes the question of accuracy in the first place. For Shreve has become not only the detached observer, confronting and assembling the story of Sutpen, but a parodic case of the scientist who quantifies and predicts. He thereby mimics the Sutpen who searches for his "mistake" at the end of a life conducted as an experiment designed to prove his immortality.[36]

Behind this ending to *Absalom, Absalom!* lies a series of resolutions-by-schizophrenia in Faulkner's fiction. Quentin's conversation with Shreve actually begins in the novel's first chapter as a dialogue between "two separate Quentins," a dialogue whose two voices are, in as literal a sense as is possible, materialized later at Harvard. The quantum leap in Faulkner's narrative strategy which *Absalom, Absalom!* represents may be indicated by looking at a similar splitting-up of a single identity in the closing pages of *As I Lay Dying*. In this novel, Faulkner uses multiple perspective to present events as constituted by subjects and objects interacting in a flux presided over by no single and detached perspective. Subjects are constituted in this novel by other subjects' objectification of them. Everyone is both a subject and an object, but no one is both at once; herein lies their alienation from each other and themselves. The reader relies most heavily on Addie and Darl for his knowledge of events. In these two characters, however, the epistemological dilemma is resolved in two equally scandalous ways; Addie's death resolves her alienation, and Darl's madness resolves his. Until he splits apart, Darl serves as a transparent eyeball. Indeed, his problem is precisely that he is nothing and he sees all. It is only when he splits in two and confronts himself as "Darl" that he knows, for the first time, that he exists. The "I" who sees the world, long since alienated from the "I" who inhabits it by Emerson's transparent eyeball, now confronts itself across the chasm of self-alienation and responds with the hysterical laughter of madness.

The advance marked by *Absalom, Absalom!*'s analogous resolution derives from Faulkner's translation of the issue from visual terms into auditory ones. Dialogue replaces sight as the means by which present events are constituted. This shift enables Faulkner to translate the epistemological dilemma from the context of reified flux to that of history as "sensuous human activity." The fact reiterated throughout the novel, that Quentin and Shreve breathe and speak through the same air breathed by those whom they try to confront as static figures in a picture, makes of dialogue a physical act whose active material substratum cannot be denied. This un-

witting exploitation of Marx's remark that language is "agitated lay-
ers of air, sound" enables Faulkner to reconstitute the isolated case
of Darl's self-alienation as the social condition of man in modern
history. For what is severed at the end of *Absalom, Absalom!* is the
bond between Quentin and Shreve formed by the "happy marriage
of speaking and hearing" in chapter 8; when that bond is cut in
chapter 9, Quentin is left in the realm of sound, hearing Jim Bond's
howling, while Shreve retreats to the realm of sight.[37]

By exploiting the potential of speech as social act—a potential
already implicit in the projects of Emerson, James, and Adams—
and by undercutting the privileged status of sight, *Absalom, Absalom!* undermines both the active self of subjectivist idealism and
the neutral observer of objectivist materialism. In other words, it
is not only Sutpen's attempt to transcend history, but also Quentin's
effort to escape it, which is doomed, and for the same reason. It is
not difficult to see that Sutpen's fate gives the lie to the Emersonian
project of self-reliance. Sutpen's story exposes the consequences
of the Emersonian denial of the flesh, the family, and the social
relatedness of every individual in the human community, past, present, and future. But what dooms Sutpen's effort at transcendence
is also what undermines Quentin's effort at detachment—the fact,
as Marx put it in *The German Ideology*, that

as soon as this active life process is described history ceases to be a collection of dead facts as it is with the empiricists (themselves still abstract),
or an imagined activity of imagined subjects, as with the idealists.

History becomes, in short, "sensuous human activity."[38]

Each of these writers struggles to overcome immediacy by reconstituting an active and dynamic realm in which man can truly be at
home. Each one also fails to gain access to that reality, and yet in
their effort to reconstitute it, the scandal we saw first in James surfaces. The contemplative stance of the detached observer, by virtue
of the extreme to which it is taken, is undermined from within. The
observer becomes a participant. Of course, the scandal must then
be recontained, for reified consciousness cannot apprehend history
as active life process without, as Lukács puts it, confronting its own

suicide. As we will see in Faulkner, however, this is precisely the conclusion at which the romantic tradition in American literature arrives. At least one detached observer in *Absalom, Absalom!* falls into the picture he tries merely to observe, and the consequence of his fall is death.[39]

Lukács identified the heroic quality in classical German philosophy in just this ability "to think the deepest and most fundamental problems of the development of bourgeois society through to the very end . . . to take all the paradoxes of its position to the point where the necessity of going beyond this historical state . . . can at least be seen as a problem," and thus "in thought . . . complete the evolution of class." If, as Lukács claims, "the *developing tendencies of history constitute a higher reality than the empirical 'facts',*" then perhaps the formal, stylistic, and thematic extremities to which American literature has resorted reflect not a flight from the constraints of civilized life, but a radical understanding of the mediated nature of the given social world. In any case, one is forced to consider this possibility after examining the projects of Emerson, James, Adams, and Faulkner in the light of Lukács' formulation of reification. For here we find a repeated struggle to overcome the immediacy of a reified bourgeois society in the course of which the limits of reified thought are not only repeatedly demonstrated but ultimately confronted and exposed.[40]

PART TWO

RALPH WALDO EMERSON: MAN AS SUBJECT LENS

Let there be worse cotton and better men.

—EMERSON

PART TWO

RALPH WALDO EMERSON: MAN AS SUBJECT LENS

Let there be worse cotton and better men.
—EMERSON

Chapter Three

EMERSON'S AMERICA

*Even if we grant that the American has freed
himself from a political tyrant, he is still the
slave of an economical and moral tyrant.*

—THOREAU

EMERSON BEGAN his intellectual career by resigning from the Unitarian ministry, an act manifestly antiauthoritarian rather than antireligious in spirit. Emerson's departure from the church has, quite properly, been regarded by critics as a decisive moment. Stephen Whicher's definitive study of Emerson's private struggles leaves no doubt that he was subject to deep crises, the first of which may be dated from the death of Ellen Tucker in 1831, a year before he left the ministry. More generally, it is customary to interpret Emerson's resignation from the pulpit of the Second Church of Boston as an act of filial revolt, an assertion of independence from the authority of the fathers. To some extent, this is probably true. Emerson was the direct descendant of seven generations of New England clergymen, if we trace his genealogy beyond the family name itself back to the Reverend Peter Bulkeley who had arrived in 1634. Emerson's use of familial rhetoric, moreover, is well known. About to leave the church, he wrote, in lines anticipating the celebrated opening paragraph of *Nature*, "I have often thought that, in order to be a good minister, it were necessary to leave the ministry. The profession is antiquated. In an altered age, we worship in the dead forms of our forefathers." The "sepulchres of the fathers" had to be abandoned if Emerson's project was to go forward.

Furthermore, upon his resignation, Emerson set off for Europe in quest of new fathers to defy, and he seems to have found them readily enough. Even his favorite, Thomas Carlyle, was not exempt from the summary dismissal he entered in his journal on the eve of his return to America:

Landor, Coleridge, Carlyle, Wordsworth. Many things I owe to the sight of these men. I shall judge more justly, less timidly, of wise men forever more. . . . it is an idealized portrait which always we draw of them. Upon an intelligent man, wholly a stranger to their names, they would make in conversation no deep impression.

It would appear that when Emerson arrived in Boston in 1833, he had asserted his independence not only of the authority embodied in his father's church, but also of that enshrined in the reigning literary figures of the mother country. Emerson's reiterated rejection of the past, then, can be quite easily read as an oedipal revolt.[1]

Yet when Emerson moved to Concord the following year, he settled in the Old Manse, a house built by his grandfather, the Reverend William Emerson, on land first purchased from the Indians by Peter Bulkeley himself. Emerson's rejection of his father's church led within two years to his resettlement in his father's house. In itself, this fact may be of no great consequence, but it does serve to suggest that Emerson's revolt had a broader focus than his familial rhetoric would imply. Such is the conclusion drawn by Michael T. Gilmore, who argues that Emerson's filial revolt had less to do with a "psychological disorder" than with a "protest against existing political authority." Gilmore calls attention to how saturated American revolutionary rhetoric had been with analogies to the family; most notably, George III had played the role of a father whose tyranny brought forth and legitimized the revolt of the "Sons of Liberty." But well before Emerson was born, these "sons" were becoming the founding fathers in the rhetoric of the reigning social order, as the need to command respect for the father displaced the need to foster rebellion against him in American society. Thus it fell to Emerson's generation, according to Gilmore, "to liberate the rhetoric of the Revolution from its current function of reinforcing political loyalty." Insofar as he touches on Emerson, Gilmore is mainly concerned to assert the political dimension of the familial rhetoric he used. But Gilmore's conclusions can be supported by other kinds of evidence, once we acknowledge the "current" focus of Emerson's criticism, and the "existing" authority at which it was aimed.[2]

For example, Emerson showed little patience with the "Universal Whiggery" of New England, whose invocation of the founding fathers led him to denounce its

cants about the policy of a Washington or a Jefferson. What business have a Washington or Jefferson in this age? You must be a very dull or a very false man if you have not a better and more advanced policy to offer than they had. They lived in the greeness and timidity of the political experiment. The kitten's eyes were not yet opened. They shocked their contemporaries with their daring wisdom: have you not something which would have shocked them? If not, be silent, for others have.

It is clearly not the past itself which Emerson attacks here, but the rhetorical use being made of the past by the dominant culture of his day. In liberating the rhetoric of the Revolution, Emerson found it largely impotent to address the current political scene: "There is nothing of the true democratic element in what is called Democracy," he remarked, "it must fall, being wholly commercial." While disparaging politicians' appeals to the founding fathers, Emerson found other uses for revolutionary rhetoric:

This invasion of nature by Trade with its Money, its Credit, its Steam, its Railroad, threatens to upset the balance of man, and establish a new Universal Monarchy more tyrannical than Babylon or Rome.

It was this commercial interest which he attacked in 1841 when he wrote in his journal,

the steamboats and stages and hotels vote one way and the nation votes the other; and it seems to every meeting of readers and writers as if it were intolerable that Broad street paddies and barroom politicians, the sots and loafers & all manner of ragged & unclean and foul mouthed persons without a dollar in their pocket should control the property of this country & . . . make the lawgiver and the law. But is that any more than their share whilst you hold property selfishly? They are opposed to you: yes, but first you are opposed to them: they to be sure malevolently, menacingly, with songs and rowdies & mobs: you cunningly, plausibly, and well bred: you cheat and they strike: you sleep and eat at their expense, they vote & threaten and sometimes throw stones, at yours.

It is the well-bred readers and writers of conservative New England, and the dominant social order they represent who draw Emerson's fire. They belong to a culturally conservative class disposed to appeal to tradition in support of its interests, but as Emerson clearly knows, its interests are those of a rising middle class. They may disparage Jacksonian politicians, and lament the growing noise of the mob, but they enjoy the prosperity based on the labor of a goodly portion of that mob. It is the authority of this class—the conservative, affluent, professional class which dominated the ruling social order of Boston, defining its cultural as well as its political values—against which Emerson revolts. It was this class from which Emerson came. It presided over his life and education, perhaps even more emphatically than it might have, had his family not become so directly dependent upon its good services when Emerson's father died. It was this class from whose church he resigned. This is not to say that filial revolt played no part in Emerson's resignation from the church and departure from Boston, but rather to insist that it was only one feature of a larger struggle to liberate himself and his readers from the hold of ideas and values inscribed in the rhetoric of the dominant culture of his day.[3]

He did not find the task an easy one; that culture's power was so strong and its values so deeply interwoven in what we would today call the socialization of New England's citizens, that those who opposed the "tyranny" of trade, Emerson lamented, "appear mad or morbid and are treated as such." In "The Transcendentalist," Emerson commented that it was a "sign of our times" that "intelligent and religious persons withdraw themselves" from the "market and the caucus," roaming the land in search of something "worthy to do," lonely and without productive work. In "Man the Reformer," he noted the growing numbers of those finding the "ways of trade unfit for them," and coming "forth from it." Looking back much later on the years in which he had begun his career, Emerson remarked that "the young men were born with knives in their brains." It was to these young men that Emerson addressed his appeal; as he put it in 1839, he was to "console the brave sufferers under evils whose end they cannot see." Like Yeats, Emerson looked about him to see that "the best lack all conviction, while the worst are full of passionate intensity," and he set out to find a means of restoring their self-trust.[4]

During the opening phase of his career, until, that is, the crisis of the early 1840s, Emerson's opposition to the dominant culture offered a critical perspective whose capacity to resist incorporation was genuinely and uniquely powerful. The criticism of Margaret Fuller and Henry Thoreau may strike us as more radical, as indeed it often is; but we should not forget that both Fuller and Thoreau apprenticed themselves as radical intellectuals to Emerson. He served both as a source of oppositional authority. Nonetheless, the means Emerson developed for carrying out his self-defined vocation, as the voice which would speak for the "whole man" against the forces dividing and peddling him out, led ultimately and inevitably to his own incorporation by the dominant culture he had set out to oppose. ("Incorporation" is Raymond Williams' term; it refers to one of the means by which a dominant culture secures its own hegemony. For our purposes, incorporation may be said to include those rhetorical strategies which enable a dominant culture to neutralize oppositional or alternative values by reducing them to a trivial status or by assimilating them within the dominant hegemony.) If we are to appreciate how and why Emerson's critical resistance was incorporated, we need to resituate Emerson in the hegemonic process of his period. For Emerson's reputation as a subjective idealist, intent upon "coming out of culture," and irremediably hostile to Society, I believe, has grown out of the failure to appreciate the fact that Emerson's revolt occurred within a particular society; it was not Society in the abstract, but *this* society which he attacked.[5]

Emerson was born the same year that Jefferson bought the Louisiana territory, a coincidence not without a certain significance in understanding the society which produced Emerson and provoked his critical response. For Jefferson's step beyond the Constitution's dictated powers was to play a large part in creating the America in which Emerson found himself in the 1830s and 1840s, a nation whose commercial expansion was palpably evident in the growing cities of the Northeast. In 1807, only four years after Louisiana was added to the nation's territory, Robert Fulton succeeded in propelling a boat by the power of steam, thus opening to an expanding population the inland waterways of a country more than double its former size, and stimulating the economic developments which were to make Emerson's Boston the scene of trade-union organization by the 1830s.

In response to an extended market, American society not only grew in geographical scope during the first fifty years of the nineteenth century, but also underwent structural changes which affected the lives of farmers as well as merchants, rural housewives as well as urban craftsmen. Nowhere were the effects of economic growth more starkly visible than in New England, where 100,000 men and women were already at work in the textile mills as early as 1815. When the Erie Canal opened in 1825 it accelerated not only the growth of trade between western farmers and eastern merchants, but also the emigration of labor from New England's depressed farms to the factories of Massachusetts and the rising cities of New York and Philadelphia, where the demand for unskilled labor mounted with each ensuing year. But the shift of population from farm to factory and city in New England is only one of the more dramatic features of a deeper social transformation fostered by capitalist expansion during Emerson's life, one which affected both urban and rural life.[6]

The Boston which Emerson departed for Concord in 1834, although it was not growing as fast as New York, nonetheless remained one of the leading commercial cities of the nation and as such reflected the forces of specialization at work in the economy. Masters, journeymen, and apprentices, for example, found themselves in an altered social and financial position. For masters had either become merchant-capitalists, removed completely from the scene of actual production, and busy with the coordination of contracts with the custom, retail, and wholesale merchants who were now embodied in three persons, or else they had remained in their workshops where they no longer occupied the position of a master in charge of a group of journeymen and apprentices, but rather that of an employer, a "boss," whose interest was increasingly allied with that of the merchant-capitalist upon whose services, as the conduit of wholesale purchase and retail distribution, the employer depended. The employer's profits, moreover, were coming to depend not on the highest prices his product could command, but on the lowest wages his employees would accept. The apprentice system was disintegrating as well, as employers found assembly-line methods more efficient, and thus had less reason to train an apprentice in all the tasks involved in making a shoe or in building a house. The cheap unskilled labor of women, children, and prisoners was displacing the apprentice, while the journeyman found his skills less in demand and his tasks more specialized and monotonous. Further, the journeyman's wages were not only failing to keep up with the rising cost of living, but in the first few decades of the century, their decline stood in marked contrast to the rise in wages of common laborers from the countryside who were taking jobs as factory "operatives" in the mills of New England. In the cities, the gap between skilled and unskilled labor was narrowing, undermining the well-being and self-esteem of that class of urban artisans which had supported the Constitution's ratification because of its promise to foster the manufacturing interest. Now that this interest was undergoing fragmentation as a result of the growing specialization in the system of manufacture and distribution, the skilled urban mechanic was losing ground both in his standard of living and in his social status as a proud and independent craftsman.[7]

By the 1840s, the same forces of specialization and rationalization were provoking protests from the mill workers. No longer did the mill "girls" of Lowell, much less the "operatives" working in less idyllic mill towns such as Fall River, find the work so attractive. (It had, in fact, never been all that attractive; the women working at Lowell had always shown a marked tendency to leave after a year or two.) As a result of improved technology and the growing competitiveness of owners, productivity in the mills rose, but of course real wages did not. According to one economic historian, by the end of the 1850s, "the average worker in the largest textile mills produced twice as much as his counterpart had during the 1830's." Yet this worker's real wages had in many cases fallen, and in no case risen in anything like a proportion commensurate with his or her doubled productivity. According to the editor of the *Voice of Industry*, writing in 1846,

It is a subject of comment and general complaint among the operatives that while they tend three or four looms, where they used to tend but two, making nearly twice the number of yards of cloth, the pay is not increased to them, while the increase to the owners is very great.

By the 1840s, the benign vision of the American factory once inspired by the mills at Lowell was insupportable.[8]

The declining social and economic status of American labor in these years is further reflected in the growing inequality in the distribution of wealth. At the end of the eighteenth century, the wealthiest 10 percent of America's families owned between one-third and one-half of the nation's wealth; by 1860, the wealthiest 10 percent owned perhaps as much as 70 percent. Between 1840 and 1860, moreover, New England's per capita income rose from 32 percent to 43 percent of the national average, and yet during the same period, according to Norman Ware, the wages of New England's "factory operatives, shoemakers, clothing workers, printers, cabinet makers, hatters, iron workers"—in short, the emerging working class—did not rise, but rather fell "in relation to the cost of living."[9]

But such statistical indicators of economic stratification tell us relatively little about the social effects of an expanding capitalism, effects penetrating the lives of those who never set foot in a factory. Consider, for example, the fact that, beginning roughly in the 1830s, as Richard D. Brown notes, clocks were for the first time becoming "a necessity in American households." Thus even traditional household manufacture could now be made more productive, since accurate calculations of cost-efficiency could be brought into the home. In the wake of such calculations, farm families participated increasingly in the market economy, purchasing services like wool carding and products like candles, both of which had long been homemade.

The newly available cheaper clocks were of course themselves a product of manufacturing methods requiring a rationalized work structure. The "American System," as it came to be called in the 1830s, had been introduced in a primitive form as early as 1799 by Whitney and North in their Connecticut factory. According to Brown, while "the assembly line with interchangeable parts" was invented simultaneously in both Britain and the United States before 1810, it was first developed and put to use in New England. By the 1850s, Americans were manufacturing on the assembly line, not only clocks and guns, but their own machines. However, mass production, the factory, and the increasing use of machinery—the developments which we associate with industrialization—grew out of capitalist relations of production already evident long before the rise of the industrial city itself. Such cities were post–Civil War phenomena in America, but the structure of reification was evident early in the century, as shown by the proliferation of insurance companies and the effort to codify the laws taking place in this period. In short, this period demonstrates that capitalism penetrates social relations well before urban industrialism develops.[10]

This point is crucial in evaluating the commonplace assumptions based on the fact that America was a predominantly agricultural society in this period. We are accustomed to visualizing the farmer of the Jacksonian era as moving west to establish an independent and self-sufficient life for himself amid the bounties of nature. But as W. Elliot Brownlee points out, the migration of farmers westward did not represent a "shift of people from a market-oriented production to comparatively self-sufficient pioneer farming activities." On the contrary, western farming was market-oriented from the outset. Farms in the West were larger and more productive than those in the East and increasingly specialized to meet the demands of the market; they were more profitable too, despite the cost of transportation to eastern markets. Not only did men speculate in western land, but those who settled on it worked to increase profits by increasing productivity—an aim which led them by the 1840s and 1850s to adopt modernized tools and methods which altered the traditional purposes and quality of agrarian life considerably. Meanwhile, like the urban artisans and the factory operatives, many an eastern farmer was being injured by the effects of capitalist expansion. According to Michael Lebowitz, the fortunes of the "expectant agricultural capitalist" of the West during the Jacksonian period were rising as those of his "embattled" counterpart in the East were falling. In short, it is hardly surprising that farming was no more impervious to the forces of specialization, rationalization, and commodification than was household manufacture or urban life, once we recognize that America was not merely a predominantly agrarian society, but a *capitalist* agrarian society.[11]

In *The Country and the City*, Raymond Williams demonstrates how crucial this distinction is when we are dealing with modern literary pastoralism. Williams argues that the oft repeated invocation of a lost rural past in English literature of the eighteenth and nineteenth century has led too many critics to ignore the rural present in which those invocations were made, not to mention the class interests of those making them. Williams notes that the changing forms of rural life reveal an agrarian capitalism in force in England well in advance not only of the enclosures of the eighteenth and early nineteenth century, but also of the industrial revolution with which, in retrospect, they are so readily identified. Although America's agricultural development is obviously marked by a different set of circumstances, both historical and geographical, there can be no doubt that by the nineteenth century, agrarian capitalism was affecting the yeoman farmer just as profoundly, if not always so disastrously, as it was his English counterpart. New land was devoted to market-oriented production, not self-sufficient farming, and the forces generating an expanded market and improved techniques for increased productivity in America in the nineteenth century were essentially those which had already led in England to campaigns like that of Arthur Young for agricultural improvement necessitating large capital investments and enclosure. Because more land was available in America, the legalized theft of enclosure was not required; this does not mean that theft did not occur, but only that it took a more anarchic form. The Indians were pushed out and the speculators moved in, buying and selling western land to farmers who often aspired to a similar entrepreneurial role. When we speak of agrarian capitalism in America, then, we must emphasize the land market rather than the labor market. As Rosa Luxemburg noted, the most important of the "productive forces" for capitalist development is the land. Once capital has begun "planning for the systematic destruction and annihilation of all the non-capitalist social units which obstruct its development . . . we have passed beyond the stage of primitive accumulation." In Europe, the "non-capitalist social units" standing in the way of capital and thus requiring "systematic destruction" were those of feudalism, and their destruction not only freed the "productive forces" of the land for capitalist development, but also "freed" the peasant, whose labor became a commodity in the marketplace. In effect, capital overcame the feudal obstacles to its appropriation of the land by the same process that it created a free labor force to work the land. In America, the "non-capitalist social units" requiring destruction were the Indian tribes, and the process did not simultaneously create a class of free laborers. Indians were "removed," rather than transformed into a labor force.

Yet the process of Indian removal and the rampant speculation in the land market during the Jacksonian era both testify to the power capital was already exercising at the time. As Williams points out, even in England the "need for greater capital to survive in an increasingly competitive market" was as decisive as "explicit enclosure" in driving people from the land. It was just such forces which made New England, among other regions of the seaboard states, the scene of an internal migration from farm to city in the early nineteenth century, while stimulating westward migration at the same time. In short, it was characteristic of rural America, as it was of "rural England, before and during the Industrial Revolution, that it was exposed to increasing penetration by capitalist social relations and the dominance of the market, just because these had been powerfully evolving within its own structures."[12]

In the light of these considerations, we must recognize that the independent yeoman farmer whose idealized status has always figured so centrally in American myth-making was displaced not by the entry of the "machine" into his "garden," but by the growth of agrarian capitalism evident in the spread of cotton plantations in the old Southwest and of grain-producing farms in the old Northwest. More particularly, as Michael Lebowitz has suggested, the *declining* farmer shared with urban laborers a common plight; both were "the victims of economic change" during the Jacksonian era, and thus constituted a significant group within the Jacksonian party, one whose importance has been neglected by historians who tend to "study dominant and emerging individiuals." Because this era is seen as one dominated by the rising middle classes, the Jacksonian appeal for "a return to an old agrarian republic, to a paradise lost" has had to be accounted for somehow, and the explanation—designed largely by John W. Ward and Marvin Meyers—lies in "the Jacksonian paradox, that a movement which idealized the past cleared the way for the future." Lebowitz reexamines this paradox from a revisionist perspective grounded in the hypothesis that the "declining or embattled man"—whether urban mechanic or farmer— is the "more unique Jacksonian" than the "expectant capitalist" with whom he was allied. On this view, the appeal to an "old agrarian republic" is less paradoxical than it appears, since people injured by change normally *do* resist it, and usually do so by calling for a return to traditional ways. Such injured groups, according to Lebowitz's hypothesis, responded approvingly to the Jacksonian attack on "the most artificial aspects of the new order: banks, bank paper, and the paper aristocracy" as did the rising middle class for whom the existing banking structure represented an economic constraint wielded by the privileged few whose ranks they aspired to join. But while "rising and declining groups could unite under the same banner" on the bank issue, this does not mean that both groups acted from the same motives. The rising men of the period saw the artificial contrivances of the bank as limiting the extension of credit; those whose fortunes were in decline saw it as devaluing wages by its circulation of paper currency. For those injured by economic and social change, the bank's destruction meant a restoration of a lost dignity and autonomy, and not the opportunity to profit from the expanding economy which was actually doing the damage in the first place. Yet both could applaud the attack on the existing bank in the name of a common belief in the providential order of nature.[13]

The Jacksonian coalition of rising and declining interests was obviously powerful, if unstable. But since it was the rising men who came to dominate the market, it was their conception of the restored natural order which ultimately prevailed in the dominant culture. Because they appealed to an agrarian tradition in the service of the "expectant capitalist," however, the contradiction in their rhetoric sometimes surfaced, as, for example, in the reaction of the employers and merchant-capitalists in Boston's building trades to a strike of the journeymen carpenters in 1825. The carpenters were demanding a ten-hour day; they were told that this would constitute "a departure from the salutary and steady usages which have prevailed in this city, and all New England, from time immemorial." The salutary and steady usages in question were those of the farm laborer, and to a degree, the urban artisan, whose workday traditionally began at sunrise and ended at sunset; it was the workday, in short, which had prevailed in a traditional culture where the artisan and the farmer shared a considerable power over their own lives and productivity. The same argument was to be repeated by the millowners of New England when the operatives demanded the ten-hour day. The very term "ten-hour day" emerges from a rhetoric marked by rationalization. But the workers were using it in a battle to preserve *their* idea of a traditional culture. Like their urban predecessors in this fight, the factory workers resented the loss of leisure time, which for them meant time for family life, for the freedom and autonomy they were losing, and not for the immoral dissipation in which the owners so often accused them of wanting to indulge. Further, the operatives especially resented the unnatural transformation of a "sunrise to sunset" working day into a rationalized structure of hours which necessitated "lighting up," as they called it, during the winter when the sun did not rise on time—at least not on the owner's time. The employers were introducing rationalized work discipline, but defending their practices by an appeal to traditional agricultural customs. In their effort to restore the amenities afforded by just such traditional customs, the workers could not but speak in the language dictated by the forces already undermining those customs, a language which the merchant-capitalist neatly avoided for obvious reasons. Under less threatening conditions than those of a strike, however, the rising bourgeois used a different rhetoric, as revealed in an anecdote related by one Lucy Larcom, a worker in the Lowell mills in its earlier days. On leaving, she was asked by the paymaster, "Going where you can earn more money?" Lucy replied, "No, I am going where I can have more time." The paymaster interpreted this strange reply in what was apparently the only framework available to him. "Ah, yes," he replied, "time is money."[14]

Clearly, the appeal to the "salutary and steady usages" of the past was issued in the service of the same interests as the statement "time is money"—the interest of the dominant social order. When we turn to the more sophisticated rhetorical strategies of the dominant culture, then, we find the same interests being served by a similar appeal to the past's residual values, and the same evidence of commodification; it is, however, a good deal more subtly done.

Certainly progress was the catchword of the dominant culture's rhetoric, and the celebrants of progress had no better exhibit than the Lowell mills. The continuing fame of Lowell is largely the result of the benign glow in which it was surrounded by what Leo Marx has aptly called the "rhetoric of the technological sublime." One of the most famous examples of Lowell's celebration is Edward Everett's Independence Day address delivered at Lowell in 1830. Taking his cue from the patriotic occasion, and calling upon the visible evidence around him, Everett praised Lowell's achievements in manufacture as a "peculiar triumph of our political independence," a "complement of the revolution." Acknowledging that "some Americans" had "contemplated with uneasiness the introduction into this country of a system which had disclosed such hideous features in Europe," and admitting that in its European form, the "industrial system" had "required for its administration an amount of suffering, depravity, and brutalism which formed one of the great scandals of the age," Everett doubtless cast his eyes dramatically over the surrounding scene before proudly announcing that such "apprehensions" about the system's installation in America "have proved wholly unfounded." America's industrialization, in the view of Everett and the countless others who reiterated this argument, is to be different, because America itself is different. Its political institutions ensure freedom, and freedom in turn

animates and gives energy to its labor . . . puts the mass in action, gives it motive and intensity, makes it inventive, sends it off in new directions, subdues to its command all the powers of nature, and enlists in its service an army of machines, that do all but think and talk.

The efficiency of labor under a free government, Everett goes on to say, stands in relation to its efficiency under a despotic one, as a power loom stands to a hand loom, as a steamer stands to a barge "poled up against the current of a river." Water is much on his mind, for obvious reasons, and the "falls and rapids of our streams," whence the mills' power is drawn, come in for their share of celebration as "natural capital." But here again, it is a political condition that has brought this capital "into action." Under the "colonial system," "the beautiful diversity of the surface—nature's grand and lovely landscape gardening of vale and mountain" had been reduced to a "dull alluvial level." Now restored to active service, an abundant supply of such natural capital will, he concludes, foster manufacturing in "salubrious spots" across the land, thus enabling America, again, to avoid the "disadvantages and evils incident to manufacturing establishments moved by steam in the crowded streets and unhealthy suburbs of large cities." There is, in effect, nothing but harmony and prosperity to be expected from America's industrialization, purified as it is to be by political freedom. The textile mills of New England, by their "bold application of capital in giving employment to labor," have providentially checked the flow of emigrants westward from declining farms; the consequent division of agricultural and industrial labor means that the mill-worker "ceases to be a producer, and becomes a consumer of agricultural produce," a development whose "aggregate effect" is indisputably to be welcomed, stamped as it is with the approval of Adam Smith. Having drawn the general conclusion that industrialization "is greatly to be desired in every country," Everett returns to the subject of Lowell itself, and delivers his famous line about the "holy alliance" between labor and capital which has been established there. (Lowell's beneficent aspect enables Everett once again to discount apprehensions, for as we know, his congratulations have a certain proximate reference. In the early years of textile manufacture in New England, millowners had had some trouble attracting to the mills the daughters of the farmers who were well-acquainted with factory conditions in England. The Waltham system installed at Lowell, with its puritan discipline, quieted some of these fears, and thus helped to solve the problem of a labor shortage. Thus do economic needs give rise to holy alliances between labor and capital.) Everett goes on to congratulate his audience for having "rolled off from the sacred cause of labor the mountain reproach of ignorance, vice, and suffering under which it lay crushed." Acknowledging that "a perfect solution" to the "hard problem in social affairs" presented by the maintenance of the holy alliance remains to be reached, Everett notes that this is perfectly consistent with the "great laws of human progress" themselves, and draws to a close with a call for vigilance which significantly registers the central grievances subsequently to be voiced by the factory operatives. Labor, Everett says, is the community's

great wealth—and its most vital concern. To elevate it in the social scale, to increase its rewards, to give it cultivation and self-respect, should be the constant aim of an enlightened patriotism.

Enlightened patriotism, as it happens, did not prove to be up to the task. By the end of the decade, factory workers were protesting their degradation in the social scale, their decreasing wages, and the lack of an education for their children; self-respect, in short, had not been fostered by Lowell's holy alliance.[15]

Before addressing the opposition, let us look at Everett's strategy for preempting it. The major themes in the dominant culture's rhetorical accommodation of industrialism to American conditions are all here. Political freedom purifies the factory system and a holy alliance clothes it in moral virtue. An "army of machines," the product of America's inventive genius, is seen as virtually human; they "do all but think and talk"—that is, they do the work, while producers become consumers. Nature's lovely landscape gardening and man's creative industry work harmoniously to foster progress and prosperity. The real power of Everett's speech lies in its genius for incorporating the residual values of the agrarian republic within the dominant culture's interpretation of social change. Everett's concern is to quiet apprehensions about American industrialization, but he carries out this task within a hegemonic process in which the dominant culture celebrates the ascendancy of the expectant capitalist while at the same time neutralizing the force of any opposition emerging from the growing numbers of the injured and the disaffected. Thus his appeal to the Revolution as the cause of America's rapid economic advance, whatever the historical value of his argument, and however sincerely he may advance it, is primarily a rhetorical tool which enables Everett to assimilate the residual republican values of independence and freedom to an emergent set of values appropriate to the expanding capitalist society of Everett's day. The political heritage provides him with a powerful rhetorical instrument; he can identify the power of both steam and the water-driven power loom with the energy of a free people. Lowell itself serves his purposes even better, for its natural capital enables him to assimilate rural values as well as political ones; having naturalized industrialization, he can envision an industrialized nation free of the smoke-infested streets of industrial cities. Clearly, there is a contradiction. Steam power's use is celebrated as the product of America's genius at the same time that its ill effects are denied any American existence. Yet what is significant is not the contradiction, but Everett's evident blindness to it. We will fail to understand this kind of rhetoric if we see it as a cynical ploy for denying the obvious.

On the contrary, it is the dominant culture's power to define the obvious which Everett's speech demonstrates. The Revolution and nature's landscape are both invested with ideological values enabling Everett to incorporate the past within a reigning vision of the present. But his need to do so is explained by the presence of critical opposition in the society, an opposition he acknowledges in order to discount.

Everett's holy alliance did not last (as a rhetorical tool, that is; it had never existed as a social reality). Even before the controversies of the 1840s arose, apprehensions about the factory system proved well founded. In 1834, a representative of the New England Association of Farmers, Mechanics, and Other Working Men looked at the mills and found them a deplorable sight:

To look at the pale and dirty and spiritless beings as they pour out of the factory to their hurried meals at the sound of a bell; and although inhumanly stinted in time, to see the lazy motion of their jaded limbs, and the motionless expression of their woebegone countenances, must give a pang to the feeling heart which can never be forgotten.

This came from a sympathetic—and clearly sentimentalizing—observer. But Lucy Larcom had worked at Lowell in its earlier and more halcyon days, and she echoes similar sentiments even if she is inclined to dismiss them as resulting from her own low spirits. While working at the mill, Lucy had written poems entitled "The Early Doomed" and "The Complaint of a Nobody." In contrast to one Samuel Goodrich, a celebrant of progress who, upon seeing the interior of a cotton mill, exclaimed that here "complicated machinery seems to be gifted with intelligence," Lucy Larcom found machines rather alien: "I never cared much for machinery," she said. "I could not see into their complications or feel interested in them." Apparently Lucy rather expected to see the power looms as human, and was disappointed when they turned out not to be. By the 1840s, however, sentimentality was left to those members of the middle class who were inclined to deplore, but ill-disposed to act. The factory operatives themselves began to organize, joining the fight for the ten-hour day begun a decade earlier by the urban mechanics. In their rhetoric, we find a different construction being placed on the meaning of freedom and independence, and a different concept of labor's relations to capital than those featured in Everett's speech. The operatives faced blacklisting if the millowners learned they were participating in the organized struggle. As a spokesman for the workers put it in the *Voice of Industry* in 1846, the blacklisting regulations "conflict with our rights as rational human beings and we are regarded as living machines and all the rules are made subservient to the interest of the employers." "Every person with intelligence and independence is marked," said another writer in the same paper, "because they have been suspected of knowing their rights and daring to assert them." By 1848, the *Voice of Industry* was ready to make Everett's holy alliance a secular one: "They who work in the mills ought to own them." A few years later, a spokesman for the National Typographical Union pointed out,

It is useless for us to disguise from ourselves the fact that under the present arrangement of things, there exists a perpetual antagonism between Labor and Capital . . . one side striving to sell their labor for as much, and the other striving to buy it for as little, as they can.

The factory operatives used patriotic rhetoric to a different rhetorical purpose than Everett once had, as when the operatives of Lowell joined with those of Pittsburgh and Allegheny to declare

that the Fourth of July, 1846, shall be the day fixed upon by the operatives of America to declare their independence of the oppressive manufacturing power which has been imported from old monarchical England, and is now being ingrafted upon the business institutions of our country.

They were calling for a strike.[16]

In 1835, Emerson complained that Everett's genius was being wasted because "he is not content to be Edward Everett, but would be Daniel Webster." Emerson found Everett's speeches less powerful than Webster's, and so they were; but Everett's less sophisticated command of the rhetoric of the "technological sublime" makes his discourse today appear rather more humane than Webster's. By the time Webster was celebrating the railroads' opening in New England towns in 1847, he was well established as the era's master of this rhetoric. Since Leo Marx has analyzed Webster's strategies on these occasions so skillfully, we need only refer to his discussion to see that Webster invokes the same set of ideas evident in Everett's speech. Webster calls attention to America's rapid progress since the days of his youth when "steam, as a motive power, acting on water and land, was thought of by nobody." The railroad represents progress, but it also fosters national unity, breaking down regional barriers between producers and consumers, enabling inland citizens to enjoy fresh fish daily. It fosters social equality as well, for the people think of it as "our railroad," and so it is, Webster announces, for "free labor" and the "indomitable industry of a free people" have done all this. The railroad affords Webster an emblem for American progress, genius, and social equality—all themes evident in Everett's speech, but notably needing more explicit defense in 1830 than in 1846. At the same time, a good deal can by now be taken for granted.[17]

Like Everett, Webster must attend to criticisms, but these are no longer treated so seriously; they are mere "idle prejudices." As Leo Marx shows, such prejudices are finally reduced in Webster's strategy to an essentially aesthetic status. The locomotive's "screams," Webster generously admits, are likely to disturb the "peace and repose" of the countryside; "an awkward and ugly embankment . . . injures the look of the fields." In effect, what Everett naturalized, Webster is content to trivialize. The textile mills were incorporated by Everett's elaborate distinction between the alluvial plain of the colonial system and the advantageous curves of the landscape which, once freed, turned that flat plain into natural capital. But since the railroad directors find it necessary to "cut and slash, to level or deface a finely rounded field," Webster finds it necessary to discount the aesthetic values of "landscape beauty." In short, both use the pastoral landscape in order to undermine the oppositional values of a residual agrarian culture, but the landscape plays a different role in their rhetorical strategies. The values embodied in Everett's landscape are integrated into an industrialized America; those in Webster's are excluded from it. The difference is, moreover, not only a result of the railroad's indisputable and spreading presence, but an indication of an advance in the hegemonic process in which the opposition of the disaffected has become sufficiently vocal to require a far more subtle strategy than Everett needed in order to neutralize it.[18]

What had happened by the time Webster spoke was that the dominant culture had "seized . . . the ruling definition of the social," as Raymond Williams calls it. Since this ruling definition still persists, Williams's explanation of this process is worth quoting. A "dominant culture . . . at once produces and limits its own forms of counter culture," he says, and further, it defines the prevailing terms in which residual values such as those embodied in nature's "lovely landscape gardening" are to be incorporated in the dominant hegemony. But no matter how powerful that hegemony is, Williams emphasizes, it remains true that "*no* mode of production, and therefore no dominant social order and therefore no dominant culture ever in reality excludes or exhausts all human practice, human energy, and human intention." In view of this feature of the hegemonic process, it is particularly important to realize not only that the dominant culture defines what counts as social, but that in so doing it necessarily excludes and selects. That is, while it incorporates the "visibly alternative and oppositional class elements" in society, "there can be areas of experience it is willing to ignore or dispense with; to assign as private or to specialize as aesthetic or to generalize as natural." Webster's treatment of the landscape relies upon just such a ruling definition of the social. In other words, he can trivialize the "offended sensibility of lovers of the landscape," in Leo Marx's words, so successfully because the residual values of agrarian life have already been specialized as aesthetic by the dominant culture. Such is not yet the case with Everett's appeal to the landscape, whose aesthetic properties remain within the boundaries of the social, and in fact provide a means for assimilating emergent social changes into the residual structure of feeling associated with an agrarian republic. What is noteworthy about the changing rhetorical strategy here is its adaptation to the force of an oppositional strategy which has developed its own uses of the pastoral landscape in accord with a quite different set of purposes.[19]

The case Leo Marx himself cites of one John Orvis, writing in Brook Farm's *Harbinger* in 1847, illustrates how social critics were using the "locally residual" values of rural life, as Williams calls them, "as a form of resistance to incorporation." In Orvis' view, the "wild picturesque waterfalls" are being "deformed by the ugly presence of mills, and their voices . . . groan at the slavish wheel." The "golden equality" of an agrarian republic is giving way before "rigorous forms of caste, of capitalist and laborer." Orvis' vision of nature's "lovely landscape" is essentially that used by Everett sixteen years earlier, but given the development of labor protest in the meantime, it is not surprising that the landscape has assumed an oppositional value. Nor, in view of its capacity to sustain such oppositional force, is it surprising that Webster is ready to jest at the injuries being done to the landscape. Webster's rhetoric in fact displaces the injuries being done to people by social forces onto a landscape where people figure only as offended sensibilities. In view of this fact, it becomes clear that one cannot say, as Leo Marx does, that Orvis is "insisting upon precisely the same metaphor Webster casually dismisses," when Orvis "uses the landscape to figure a dangerous contradiction of social value and purpose." It is not, and cannot be precisely the same metaphor, since for Orvis, the landscape embodies social values of which Webster's is devoid. In a sense, the more revealing comparison would be that between Orvis and Everett, since it is Everett's rhetorical fusion of nature and industry, of labor and capital, that Orvis exposes as contradictory. Webster's position is essentially impervious to such opposition, as Marx points out; what he does not point out, however, is *why* it is impervious—the dominant culture has already trivialized the landscape as an aesthetic value, residing beyond the boundaries of what counts as social. Further, it is not difficult to see why Marx would fail to appreciate the relationship between Webster's strategy and the oppositional forces it is designed to trivialize, since Marx himself accepts essentially the same "ruling definition of the social" upon which Webster relies.[20]

Acknowledging that Orvis "is correct when he argues the patent inconsistency between industrialization and pastoral ideals," Marx opines that Webster is also "correct when he says, in effect, that it doesn't matter," for Orvis has arrived at an "intellectual, logical, and literary truth" of little weight when balanced against the "political truth" of Webster, who understands "the facts of power." Orvis, after all, represents what the dominant culture viewed as "those queer intellectuals who flaunt their disaffection with gestures of withdrawal," while Webster, clearly the era's master of the "technological sublime," represents the same organized community to which Everett belonged: "the governmental, business, and professional elites" who published their ideas in "respectable magazines" and spoke for the "nation's dominant political, industrial, and financial groups." But a political truth is inscribed in Orvis' rhetoric as well, one which Marx does not recognize because he has effectively reconfirmed the trivialization of the aesthetic on which Webster relied. This becomes especially clear when Marx accounts for the fact that "the overt negative response to industrialization is not nearly as rare, in the written record, as one might expect," by explaining that such negativity "has a special appeal for the more literate and literary" and thus "appears in print with a frequency out of all proportion to its apparent popularity with the public." Leaving aside for the moment the written record of the working-class press, it is worth reminding ourselves that the more literate and literary are part of the public too. Obviously, the disaffection of the "literary" could not be dismissed in this fashion (or rather, displaced, in its more serious forms, to the closing section of Marx's book) were it not for the fact that Marx, like Webster, has already excluded the aesthetic from the ruling definition of the social. Marx in effect measures the "relative force" of the dominant culture's responses to industrialization against that of the disaffected and, not surprisingly, concludes that the dominant culture was dominant. But such tautologies obscure the significance of the fact that it is the voice representing the literary groups "far from the centers of influence and power" that speaks of a growing rift between capitalist and laborer, while it is the voice of Webster which reviews the aesthetic injuries done the landscape by railroad directors. What Marx automatically discounts is the possibility that Orvis might well understand the "facts of power" just as clearly as Webster, but speak for those who are actually building the railroads, rather than for those who, like the railroad directors, can be forgiven their lack of aesthetic refinement.[21]

In general, we can say that the dominant culture incorporated the residual values of the agrarian republic in order to forward the cause of innovation, while the injured appealed to the past in order to resist changes which were undermining their autonomy as free men. Such resistance was easily undermined since the dominant culture could so readily incorporate the locally residual values of a rural past, either by maintaining their harmony with industrialization as Everett did, or later by trivializing the rural as an aestheticized landscape. But while the protests of disaffected Brook Farmers like Orvis could be trivialized by these tactics, those of the injured working classes required stronger methods.

Protests about the ill effects of the factory system, the declining status and waning autonomy of farmers and mechanics, the wage earner's impotence to halt the growing disparity between wages and prices—all effects of an expanding market economy which served the interests of the rising man of the period—persisted; as grievances multiplied, they posed more difficult problems for the celebrants of progress and prosperity. Or rather, these issues would have posed problems had the dominant culture not already constructed a rhetoric for defusing the criticism; this was the essential hegemonic function of the "technological sublime." Its basic strategy was first, to reduce the social formation of capitalism to a more specific and readily isolable feature of capitalist development—industrialization, and second, to reduce industrialization to technology, the product of inventive genius, and the source of labor-saving machines. The distortions in this strategy result from its denial of the distinction between the "techniques of production and the mode of production which is their specific form," as Williams describes it; the distinction is a crucial one since "the specific character of the capitalist mode of production . . . is not the use of machines or techniques of improvement, but their minority ownership." It is, of course, not really accurate to say that celebrants of progress consciously reduced capitalism to the machine; the important point, indeed, is that they saw it in these terms. The results are vividly demonstrated in Leo Marx's discussion of one Timothy Walker's rebuttal to Thomas Carlyle's *Signs of the Times*.[22]

Carlyle's essay is one of the period's most famous and powerful critiques of industrialization, and Leo Marx treats it insightfully as Carlyle's attempt to describe alienation. Leo Marx further notes Walker's failure to see that a "basic change in the structure of society" will be required for the new technology "to fulfill the egalitarian aims of the American people," as Walker expects it to do. Nonetheless, Marx clearly sees Walker winning a point, when Walker rebuts Carlyle's invidious comparison of contemporary industrial society to that of ancient Greece. Walker made the obvious rejoinder to Carlyle—that the Greeks he admired had slaves to do their work for them. Walker then drove his point home by making a comparison of his own: "Force did for them, what machinery does for us." Marx concludes that "on this point, Walker is at his best" because he strikes a blow for the "humanistic faith of the Enlightenment," by posing the issue in terms which puncture Carlyle's comparison. "Would the souls of Greek slaves or English wage-laborers be threatened by labor-saving machines?" Marx asks, elaborating upon Walker's argument. It is all a matter of one's social and economic perspective, Marx himself concludes; "unlike Carlyle," Walker "recognizes that mechanization will hardly seem a menace to those on whom society confers little dignity of soul (or status) in the first place."[23]

But no one was pressing labor-saving machines on Greek slaves, and at least some English wage-laborers had apparently thought such machines a sufficient menace to set about destroying them. The machine means different things to Carlyle and to Walker; Carlyle has objectified capitalism as industrialization, while Walker has gone a step further, objectifying industrialization as technology. For Carlyle, the machine stands for a newly industrialized world in which "mechanization" in fact entails the erosion of the "dignity of soul" while for Walker it is a labor-saving device. As Leo Marx amply demonstrates, Walker's conception of the machine as a labor-saving device had a widespread provenance; as Theodore Parker phrased it, "The head saves the hands. It invents machines, which, doing the work of many hands, will at last set free a large portion of leisure time from slavery to the elements." As Walker put it, the nation "in which the greatest number of labor-saving machines has been devised" is the nation which "will make the greatest intellectual progress." The consequence foreseen as resulting from the proliferation of such labor-saving machines is in both cases increased leisure time for intellectual pursuits. The machine as labor-saving device is a key metaphor in the rhetorical strategy of the dominant class, enabling men like Walker and Parker to project a life of leisure emerging from the growing use of machines. Walker's comparison of machines to Greek slaves rests upon precisely this belief; machinery will do our work, he is saying, and thus force will be unnecessary. It is indeed an "Automated Utopia" he envisions, as Leo Marx points out. What Carlyle sees, though, is the factory workers themselves; his vision is markedly closer to that of the people "inhumanly stinted in time."[24]

Walker's claim that machinery does for us what force did for the Greeks, reveals a good deal about the perspective from which he viewed industrialization; it is manifestly the perspective of the owner. Walker can sympathize with the Greek slave, but he cannot even see the factory worker whose alienation so concerns Carlyle. What Walker sees replacing the Greek slave is not another kind of slave, but a machine. There are no wage slaves in Walker's vision of industrial society for the simple reason that there are no human beings at all, except "us." And should one wonder who "us" is, one has only to refer to Leo Marx's description of the interests represented by Walker and the *North American Review* in which Walker's rebuttal to Carlyle appeared—the "politically conservative, theologically liberal opinion of the New England Establishment."[25]

Speaking for the same dominant social order, in 1836 Daniel Webster delivered a speech which reveals the owner's perspective dramatically. "We commonly speak of mechanic inventions as labor-saving machines," he said, "but it would be more philosophical to speak of them as labor-doing machines; because they, in fact, are laborers." This redefinition wipes away any residual presence of the human laborer himself. So long as the machine remains a labor-saving device, there is at least some vague memory of human beings and some felt need to justify the machine in terms of social values with a human potential worth saving. When it becomes a labor-doing device, the machine is no longer saving human energy for higher intellectual pursuits; it is doing the work while the owner looks on, and is thus equatable to the laborers in the factory themselves. So much is clear from Webster's vision of the factory itself:

It multiplies laborers without multiplying consumers, and the world is precisely as much benefited as if Providence had provided for our use millions of men, *like ourselves in external appearance*, who would work and labor and toil, and who yet required for their substance neither shelter, nor food, nor clothing. These automatons in the factories and the workshops are as much our fellow labourers, as if they were automata wrought by some Maelzel into the form of men, and made capable of walking, moving, and working, of felling the forest or cultivating the fields. (Emphasis added.)

Webster is projecting social harmony between "fellow-labourers," but his metaphor outstrips its purpose here, revealing the true attitudes of the owner toward his workers. Insofar as there is any fellow feeling between the speaker and the objects of his vision here, it flows between owner and machine, for in this automated utopia there are no people, only automata, or rather, the people have become automata requiring, conveniently enough, "neither shelter, nor food, nor clothing." Webster's overindulgence in the technological sublime serves to demonstrate how a rhetoric which so often humanizes the machine sometimes ends up mechanizing the human. The *Voice of Industry* was not wrong when it said that the factory operatives were seen as "living machines."[26]

The perspective shared by Webster and Walker then is that of the owner, and the prospect they imaginatively command bears a striking resemblance to the landscape surveyed by those eighteenth-century English landowners who hired Brown or Kent or Repton to create parks around their stately homes on the model of paintings by Claude and Poussin. As Raymond Williams notes, the "pleasing prospects" thus designed consisted in "a rural landscape emptied of rural labour and of labourers." Once we notice that Webster's factory and Walker's industrial utopia are similarly emptied of human laborers as a result of their rhetorical metamorphosis into machines, it becomes evident that the opposition between the rural and the urban, or the pastoral past and the technological future, or the garden and the machine, is far less significant than the separation of production and consumption exhibited in the contemplative posture of the owner-observer of both factory and park. The idealized landscape in both cases presupposes a detached observer whose aesthetic consumption is far removed from the work of production itself.[27]

If the technological sublime enables the owner-observer to wipe away the presence of the worker from his field of vision, it is not surprising that those whose labor is producing his wealth would find their humanity threatened. Understanding that they were perceived as "living machines" inside the factory, and a mob of beasts if they raised their voices in protest against its management, the wage earners in the factories understandably called attention to that humanity. It was to this end that they employed the rhetoric of the agrarian republic. Their "rights" as free Americans having been threatened, they emphasized their "intelligence and independence" as "rational human beings." The factory system in their eyes, as we have seen, was no "complement to the revolution," but a violation of its promises. Similarly, the urban mechanics appealed to republican language in their effort to resist the injuries being done to them by the forces of rising capitalism. Their adamant demand for public education, for example, was issued in language saturated with the residual values of the republic. In 1830, the *Mechanics' Free Press* called public education "the rock on which the temple of moral freedom and independence is founded; any other foundation than this, will prove inadequate to the protection of our liberties, and our republican institutions. . . . Our government is republican; our education should be equally so." Five years later, the factory operatives echoed the same demand for education; a vigilance committee of strikers in Paterson complained that "the poor and their children in manufacturing towns and districts are kept in ignorance and regarded but little superior to the beasts that perish." Thus "deprived of any privilege except working, eating, and sleeping," they noted, people were only too likely to form mobs. Whether reduced rhetorically to living machines or to beasts, the human beings degraded by proletarianization thought of themselves as citizens of a republic. The rhetoric they used reveals this all too clearly.[28]

More particularly, it suggests that they were appealing to certain residual values in republican traditions which, taken together, constituted a concept of individual independence which is virtually impossible for us to understand today, for this republican independence was not immediately tied to upward mobility. It seems rather to have consisted in the autonomous self-respect of the nonalienated laboring man, a concept which is especially powerful in the language of the urban artisans. In contrast to the emergent individualism of the rising middle class, the artisan's independence as a man constituted a residual value under siege. According to the labor historian David J. Saposs, for example,

it was not, as many believe, the lack of opportunity to become independent producers that actuated mechanics to form trade unions. On the contrary, it seems that their only motive for organizing was to protect their standard of life as skilled mechanics. Those whose chance of setting up in business for themselves was best were the first to organize into unions.

The rhetoric of upward mobility was used by the employers and merchant-capitalists far more decisively than it was by the journeymen who organized and struck for higher wages and shorter hours. In 1825, for example, the striking carpenters of Boston were told that once they became masters they would find the ten-hour day a "pernicious" evil, and they ought therefore to realize that they were demanding what was not in their own interests as rising men; they would only regret it in the end, if the employers gave in to their demands. This response did not move the strikers. The workingmen who struck, who worked to elect their legislative candidates, who demanded shorter workdays and education for their children, were more concerned with defending themselves against further losses of self-esteem and self-sufficiency than with increasing their chances for an aggrandized fortune. Further, the leisure time for which they fought was something they were losing, not something to be gained. The fight for the ten-hour day in Massachusetts, and the struggle to maintain it in other states like New York, stemmed from experiences which made a mockery of the dominant culture's praise of "labor-saving" machines; the working classes had no leisure time for the less exalted pleasures of family life, much less "intellectual" pursuits.[29]

In his effort to protect himself from proletarianization, the skilled laborer was eventually to close ranks and exclude the unskilled, a movement already evident in the 1850s. But in the opening phases of his organized efforts at defense, the skilled worker had not yet reached this stage. In the 1830s and 1840s, workingmen's associations were hardly so exclusive. Indeed, according to Ronald G. Walters, labor organizations "created . . . troubles for themselves" by admitting "people with clashing economic interests." This laxity doubtless did contribute to the "internecine warfare" within these organizations, but it also suggests that workingmen were not yet prepared to accept their own proletarianization. They were still defending a set of values based on that individual independence which had been fostered by the apprentice/journeyman/master system, and enshrined—in their eyes—in the Declaration of Independence. Thus when they set out to defend themselves as wage earners in the 1830s and 1840s, they saw themselves not only as citizens whose rights were not respected, but as individuals injured by corporations. A writer in the *Weekly Ohio Statesman* in 1838 reveals as much when trying to explain to his readers why wages do not rise proportionately to prices:

The reason is obvious. The bankers who cause the expansion, and consequent depreciation of paper (or *increase* of prices, just as you choose—the meaning is the same), are incorporated—connected—concentrated. They act simultaneously and immediately. But mechanics and laborers are simply individuals—unincorporated—unconnected—pursuing different occupations, and frequently waging opposite pursuits.

This may not go far toward explaining the disparity between wages and prices, but it does reveal a strong grasp of the individual's impotence in the face of the collective forces he saw undermining his control over his own life.[30]

This individual's independence, in short, differed from that of the expectant capitalist conventionally associated with the Jacksonian era. Whether expressed by Whig or Democrat, the dominant culture's vision of the rising man stamped this era, just as the private, acquisitive businessman who was his heir stamped the period following the Civil War. But the independence which the working people of the 1830s and 1840s struggled to preserve was fashioned on a different model. Jefferson's yeoman farmer was an idealized version of this independent man, although Jefferson emphasized self-sufficiency more than skilled productive work. The independent urban artisan embodied the same republican virtues, but his autonomy had more to do with his status as a skilled worker than with the particular kind of work he did or the setting in which he did it. He organized primarily to defend this autonomy for himself, and through education, for his children. Even some of those who joined the reformers were able to understand the root of the worker's complaint. As one William West said in 1850,

Scarcity of employment, low wages, and fourteen, sixteen hours of labor per day . . . are indeed grievances . . . but they are not fundamental. The laborer does not belong to himself, has no right to be, and exists upon sufferance. He is emphatically a wage-slave. Herein is the fundamental evil to which he is subject.

To describe the erosion of the workingman's autonomy in terms of wage slavery, however, proved a less-than-useful means of advancing his cause, for obvious reasons. At least before the Civil War, Wendell Phillips could readily formulate the differences between a Southern slave and a free laboring man. The wage earners did compare their oppression to that of slaves in the South, just as they made the same invidious comparison to wage slaves in England, but such rhetoric did not serve them well. Their appeal to agrarian republican values was more powerful, but even here the "golden equality" of a rural past and the autonomy of the working man were values easily incorporated by the dominant culture. As if this were not enough, they had to contend with the reformers as well.[31]

According to the labor historian, John Commons, the period of the 1840s constitutes "the most astonishing junction of humanitarianism, bizarre reforms and utopias, protective tariffs and futile labor organization, known to our history." Norman Ware is more precise and less charitable: "The workers' revolt had become a farce or a tragedy in the hands of the harmonizers." Harmony, indeed, was the aim of Brook Farm's L. W. Ryckman, for instance, who said in 1845, "My object is not to array one class against the other, but, by a glorious unity of interests, make all harmony and ensure universal intelligence, elevation, and happiness." The main difference between Ryckman's attitude and that displayed fifteen years earlier by Everett is that Ryckman seems to think he can himself array social classes harmoniously, while at least Everett regards his holy alliance as a group effort. Except for this larger dose of egotism, however, there is little to distinguish the reformer's attitudes from those of the dominant culture. Indeed, the reformers who concerned themselves with the social injuries of capitalist expansion went further than Everett and Webster in their pursuit of harmony; the latter only invoked it, but the reformers tried to institutionalize it. The Fourierist program, whose chief American proponent was Albert Brisbane, exemplifies the degree to which reformers were thinking in the same terms as the industrialists and their spokesmen. Fourierism had little to offer the disaffected, not only because it required one to pull up stakes and join a phalanx, but also because it reconstituted many of the same features which caused the worker's disaffection in the first place. Fourier's program was a master plan for rationalized industrial organization, specifying everything from the architecture of the phalanstery to the distribution of profits, "5/12ths to labor, 4/12ths to capital, and 3/12ths to talent." It is no wonder that Fourierism was easily confused with the older and now discredited plans of the industrialist Robert Owen embodied in the community at New Harmony. An industrialized utopia organized in phalanxes changed nothing, as one critic pointed out, except that "the working man in the phalanx would do from inclination what, in his present work, he does to keep himself from hunger. It would become, in a sense, his religion to make the capitalist rich." If one turns to George Evans' land reform program, the same rationalizing tendencies are evident. Evans set out, in effect, to rid America of national and international trade, by erecting self-sufficient townships whose internal organization he had planned with admirable thoroughness. Not only were such plans both abstract and unattractive, but they were offered in dogmatic terms. Evans in particular combined his talents for efficient organization with a stubborn belief that his reform must precede, if not void the need for, all others; "This is the first measure to be accomplished," he was in the habit of saying, "and it is as idle to attempt any great reforms without that as it is to go to work without tools."[32]

In the face of this kind of dogmatism, laboring men and women came to behave in that deplorably recalcitrant manner which elitist vanguards have always found so trying. Horace Greeley complained that "it is much easier to get 10,000 to work for the laboring man than to get one to work for himself." It is easy to see why. One such laboring man at the first meeting of the New England Association was reported as saying

that capitalists and priests had joined hands to put down, grind and oppress the laboring man—that commerce manufacturing and foreign emigration were killing them—that there was ten times more slavery in Lowell than on the Southern plantations—that Lowell manufactured the prostitutes of New York and that the first thing we must do to elevate the working man was to collect and burn the Sunday-School books which were poisoning the minds of the young.

The parting blow is doubtless a deliberately conceived outrage aimed at those like William Ellery Channing who were trying to unite the benevolent spirit of older missionary societies with reform, thereby countering the charges of infidelity through the formation of organizations such as Channing's own "Religious Union of Associationists," later called the "Church of Humanity." But when he allies "capitalists and priests," the speaker clearly reveals his sense that Christian reformers represent the same interests as the merchant-capitalists and the millowners, no matter how sincere their sympathy with the workingman. The outburst itself is aimed at the reformers assembled at this meeting, and the rage it reveals could easily have been stimulated by the spectacle of Charles Dana, L. W. Ryckman, George Ripley, Horace Greeley, Albert Brisbane, Wendell Phillips, William Lloyd Garrison, W. E. Channing, and Robert Owen—to mention only the best-known of those present—all in the same room arguing over the shape of utopia. In the end the reformers only made it easier for the dominant culture to resist opposition, of course. The reform movements drained off middle-class disaffection, and since reformers failed to understand the sources of the working class's grievances, they were never able to mount real opposition to the dominant social order.[33]

Several points can now be made about the cultural context in which Emerson worked. First, the social changes transforming society were proceeding with such force and rapidity that even Webster confessed, "What is before us no one can say, what is upon us no one can hardly realize." The millennialism so prevalent in America during this period surely represents, among other things, people's need to project a happy ending to a drama whose outcome they could not foresee. Those injured by the changes taking place blamed the rich, the banks, the factory owners, attaching responsibility to the most visible enemies; those whose interests were served by the status quo celebrated technology and improvement; those who still aspired to power and fortune did some of both. The result was a

dominant cultural vision—formed in the discourse of both Whig and
Democrat, both industrialist and reformer—of America in transition
from a rural to an industrial society, a transition given the general
name Progress, and the general result Prosperity.[34]

Second, the dominant culture's rhetoric was designed to do more
than neutralize industrialization per se; it was caught up in a complex
hegemonic process of incorporation, selection, and exclusion. There
were, for one thing, ideological values to be secured. The master
who invoked the traditional sunrise-to-sunset workday against the
employees in 1825 acted in accord with the same interests for which
Daniel Webster spoke some twenty years later when he dismissed
the values of a rural past as aesthetic. Both were using residual
values to support an interpretation of change as progress because
it was in their interest to do so. When the workers appealed to the
past, it was to a different past from Webster's or Everett's; indeed
for these two, the past was envisioned as an undeveloped countryside, as yet unblessed by the fruits of progress. For the injured farmers and mechanics, however, the past was not so much rural as it
was republican, and it was a scene marked by the abundance of what
was now being lost—the individual's self-respect and autonomy.

Third, beneath the obvious ideological struggles lay changes in
social consciousness itself to which no one was immune, changes
generated by the encompassing forces of expanding capitalism itself.
Those who celebrated industrialization as well as those who defended themselves from the social degradation it enforced apprehended social change with minds already altered by its effects. So,
in addition to recognizing the ideological values at stake, we must
also recognize this deeper level of the hegemonic process, the level
on which commodification, rationalization, and specialization are
working to define the very terms in which change is perceived. We
have seen some reflections of this process. Those who retreat to the
countryside to establish a harmonious community in touch with nature envision a rationalized form of life, projecting the factory's specialization onto the social life of the community itself. Those who
celebrate the machine end by mechanizing human beings. As the
division of labor proceeds, so does the division between production
and consumption, so that the world of production recedes into the
distance before the eyes of the dominant social order's members.

Finally, although the wage earner is the most immediate victim of social and economic change, it is the owner, and the dominant culture which speaks in his interest, whose rhetoric is the most saturated by reification. Webster is a perfect exemplar of the way in which reified consciousness emerges in the hegemonic process of incorporation. It is not simply a matter of the ideological distortion at work in Webster's speeches; it is a matter of the translation of the very categories in which men think about, the language by which they define, and the perspective through which they see, social reality, which is operating in Webster's rhetoric. This is one of the reasons a dominant culture's rhetoric is so powerful; it not only defines the presiding values of the era, but determines the language in which those values are to be inscribed. Thus, the dominant culture can produce and limit its countercultures. It produces them in the reform movements which replicate its own rationalizing tendencies. It limits the oppositional force of the worker's movements by seeming to accept the values to which he appeals, while actually neutralizing their power. Thus the disaffected man's appeal to an agrarian republic, his reliance on revolutionary rhetoric, his defense of the workingman's autonomy, his demand for the restoration of the natural order, are all acknowledged but subtly altered in the rhetoric of the dominant culture.

Resistance would thus seem impossible, but it is not. The dominant culture can never completely incorporate all human experience; there is an active residual element which persists, often in the realms which the dominant culture excludes from its "ruling definition of the social." Such is art itself, so that it is not surprising that the most radical resistance during this period comes from men like Melville, Thoreau, and Emerson. The first two exhibit such resistance; Emerson not only exhibits it, but tries to appeal to it directly in his readers so as to support their capacity to withstand incorporation. It is his strategy for supporting such resistance to which we now turn.[35]

Chapter Four

EMERSON'S REVOLT

Every sign by itself *seems dead.* What *gives it life? In use it is* alive.
Is life breathed into it there? Or is the use *its life?*

—WITTGENSTEIN

EMERSON'S DIAGNOSIS of his society's condition is succinctly sum-
marized in "The American Scholar" when he says "I believe
man has been wronged; he has wronged himself." The effects of
this wrong were clear enough to him; it was the cause of them, and
a means of correcting them, that led to his most serious and incisive
thought.[1]

He minced no words about the symptoms. "Man," he said, has
been "metamorphosed into a thing, into many things," a victim of
that division of labor which has "subdivided and peddled out" the
"whole man," with the result that "the priest becomes a form, the
attorney a statute-book; the mechanic a machine; the sailor a rope
of the ship." What was wrong, in short, was that the autonomy of
the unalienated "whole man" was eroding before the power of
"Trade," and men were becoming machines. The vision of man as
a "living machine"—implicit in Webster's rhetoric, explicit in that
of the workingman—is for Emerson an indisputable fact, symptomatic of the human degradation resulting from society's corruption.
Like the wage earners resisting proletarianization, Emerson sought
to defend the independent republican man. Someone, he decided,
had to speak for the "whole man," and this was the task he set
himself; it was a task made necessary by society's fragmented and

divided state, a task which both "Man Thinking," and "Man the
Reformer" ought to perform. The scholar's "office is to cheer, to
raise, and to guide men by showing them facts amidst appearances."
Even though it entails his "virtual hostility . . . to society, and especially to educated society," the scholar must remind men that the
appeal to "stone-blind custom" is a "lie." The reformer faces similar obstacles in pursuing similar goals: "Everybody partakes, and
everybody confesses, . . . yet none feels himself accountable. He
did not create the abuse; he cannot alter it . . . that is the vice, that
no one feels himself called upon to act for man."[2]

Like William West, Emerson saw that man no longer belonged
to himself, but more deliberately than most of the young men "born
with knives in their brains," Emerson set out to discover why this
should be the case. He found that those who appealed to custom
and tradition in support of trade, credit, steam, the railroad, were
at best dull and at worst false. He found as well that beneath simple
hypocrisy lay a deeper saturation of consciousness by the tyrannical
forces of systems, of rationalization, and of specialization. It was
to this tyranny that he addressed his attention, for he found that the
same forces which had turned the priest into a form and the mechanic
into a machine led men to worship systems and system-makers.
Thus, he could not join the Brook Farmers because, as he put it,
"I do not wish to remove from my present prison to a prison a little
larger, I wish to break all prisons." Charles Fourier's rational planning simply replicated the fragmented state of man already apparent
in society: "It takes sixteen hundred and eighty men to make one
Man, complete in all the faculties. . . . Fourier has skipped no fact
but one, namely Life." "Faith makes its own forms," Emerson
decided, and "all attempts to contrive a system are as cold as the
new worship introduced by the French to the Goddess of Reason."
Whether the systems were those inherited from the past, or those
being contrived in the present, they served to blind men to their own
wholeness, to alienate man from himself. Feeling such systems to
be both alien and oppressive, Emerson then faced the question
whether they were necessary. In effect, his own experience confirmed the conclusion that they were not, for if he could stand off
from the church and decide that religion was not a "form," but a
"Life," then there was a real and realizable difference between the

"whole man" and the "thing" to which society was reducing him. That difference signaled the emergence of the crucial discovery that if man was wronged, he had somehow wronged himself, for men had made society, and thus had also produced the "forms," as he so often called them, in which they were imprisoned. Man could thus, he reasoned, remake that society. "What is man born for," he asked, "but to be a Reformer, a Re-maker of what man has made . . . ?"[3]

But this discovery entailed another. In effect, Emerson arrived at the conclusion that the whole man was not some ideal fantasy of his own, but represented an active force within men, a force obscured by the encrusted forms of institutions and traditions; there was, in other words, a potential energy within men themselves now held in check by their internalization of social and cultural formations. Thus he postulated an active ontological principle to which this active presence corresponded, a principle he was to call Spirit. It was this belief—that an active reality persists beneath the illusions of stasis to which men cling, and by which they are entrapped—on which Emerson was to rely in his effort to pry men loose from their adherence to the rationalized structures they inhabited. Emerson's resistance to the tyranny of form resembles William James's rejection of a block universe, based as it is on the conviction that men have translated their own created structures into omnipotent gods. In one sense, Emerson's position resembles that of Karl Marx as well. Although Emerson differed radically from Marx in regarding such structures as originating in the minds of men abstracted from their material conditions, Emerson shared with Marx a primary conviction that reality is an active process. Emerson's reiterated insistence on the impermanence of any present social or intellectual pattern echoes Marx's claim that "the present society is no solid crystal, but an organism capable of change, and is constantly changing."[4]

However, among the many traits Emerson did not share with Marx was a firm belief in his own critical perspective. The energy required for Emerson to revolt against the dominant culture of his day, and to maintain his critical distance, was, to say the least, considerable. One has only to read his journals during the 1830s and 1840s to witness his struggle to maintain his own self-trust. Whatever this

struggle may tell us about Emerson himself, it ought to tell us something as well about the power of the dominant culture over even the
most critical and resilient minds among the ranks of the disaffected.
It is not a soaring transcendence, but a perpetual resistance to which
Emerson commits himself when he says,

> God offers to every mind its choice between truth and repose. Take which
> you please,—you can never have both. Between these, as a pendulum, man
> oscillates. He in whom the love of repose predominates will accept the first
> creed, the first philosophy, the first political party he meets,—most likely
> his father's. He gets rest, commodity, reputation; but he shuts the door of
> truth. He in whom the love of truth predominates will keep himself aloof
> from all the moorings, and afloat. He will abstain from dogmatism, and
> recognize all the opposite negations between which, as walls, his being is
> swung. He submits to the inconvenience of suspense and imperfect opinion,
> but he is a candidate for truth, as the other is not and respects the highest
> law of his being.

When he wrote this in 1835, Emerson was within a year of publishing
Nature, where he would enjoin man to build his own world, as if
there were nothing to resist his efforts save his blindness to the fact
that the world was his to make. But Emerson's vision of the "candidate for truth" tells us a good deal about the bondage against which
such inspirational imperatives were directed. The contradiction between the nautical image of man "aloof from all the moorings, and
afloat" and the pendulum image of him swinging between "opposite
negations" reveals an Emerson bent on freeing himself from prison
walls he is nonetheless afraid he will never escape. Emerson is
clearly struggling to confirm his revolt here; the choice "God offers"
is the choice Emerson faced, and the depth of the force against which
he struggled is indicated by the fact that the reified immediacy of
the given objective world returns even in his vision of freedom. And
so it does in *Nature* as well.[5]

Emerson set out in *Nature* to construct a vantage point from which
to see the world as mediated—the product of man's own making
within a process of incessant change. Such a vantage point would
allow him to regard the mediated appearances congealed around him
as unnecessary, and so would enable him to remain afloat in the sea

of change. But having freed himself from the prison of the immediately given by seeing it as mediated, Emerson is in effect aloof but
no longer afloat, detached as he is from the active reality he has
discovered. *Nature* is Emerson's "entering wedge," as he told Carlyle, and as such it represents not only Emerson's attempt to penetrate the congealed and encrusted forms obscuring an active reality,
so as to formulate a metaphysics on which he can stand, but also
his effort to find a source of authority within himself so as to in-
augurate his career. It is this second, more personal, motive which
we need to keep in mind in reading the essay, for it is his need to
authorize the method by which he drives home his "entering wedge"
that leads Emerson to reconstruct the walls of his own prison.[6]

Nature is an attempt to forge an "original relation" between the
soul and the world. The question Emerson poses here is the one to
which he refers again in a journal entry of 1839, the question of
whether "the world is not a dualism, is not a bipolar unity, but is
two, is Me and It." If the world is two, Emerson continues, "then
there is the alien, the unknown, and all we have believed and chanted
out of our deep instinctive hope is a pretty dream." Accordingly,
when Emerson defines nature as all that is "Not Me," he initiates
an argument through which he will negate the referentiality of his
own term. The great issue at stake in *Nature* is not the explicit
question of nature's order and meaning, but the implicit question
of the epistemological use to which it can be put, in order to overcome our sense of alienation from the world. By the climax of the
essay the "Not Me" refers only to an illusion—a vision of nature
as opaque, alien, and fixed—an eternally given order. Emerson develops in *Nature* not a theory of nature, but a method by which
"brute nature" is dissolved. The world is thus reconstituted as a
purposive order whose purpose is to evoke the imagination. That
is, Emerson constructs and enacts a method for relating man and
nature, but his method provides more than a means for achieving
that purpose. That method relates man and nature, so as to transform
both: man emerges as maker, nature as made. Nature as an alien
presence disappears as it is used until finally, "what we are, that
only can we see." But to make sense of the closing injunction to
"Build, therefore, your own world," we must understand the
method by which "Nature . . . becomes an instrument" for Emer-

son. Specifically, we must understand that what Emerson refers to as the "doctrine of Use" functions more as a tool than as a doctrine.[7]

The problem introduced at the opening of chapter 2 of *Nature*, "Commodity," is posed in terms of the "final cause of the world," that end of nature served by what Emerson describes as a "multitude of uses" falling into four classes: Commodity, Beauty, Language, and Discipline. Emerson here develops the theory that nature's end or purpose is to be used. His optimistic view of nature as working "incessantly . . . for the profit of man" results from the perspective created by the term "commodity" itself. As commodity, nature is by definition useful, and the world is automatically domesticated as man's "floor, his work-yard, his play-ground, his garden, and his bed." By focusing first on how we indisputably use nature, Emerson temporarily excludes from consideration the hostile and alien aspects of the world. Moreover, he sets in motion a circular argument: nature is useful in the following ways, and therefore nature's end is to be used. This conclusion however raises another question. By claiming that the end of nature is to be used, Emerson must face the issue of what it should be used for. Accordingly, each class of uses generates a higher class; nature's "mercenary benefit" exists for "a farther good"; beauty, itself a higher use than commodity, is nonetheless, "not ultimate," and so on.[8]

To approach nature's "final cause," Emerson appropriates a mechanism which hypostatizes this self-regenerating "doctrine of Use." "The use of the outer creation," he tells us at the beginning of chapter 4, "Language," is to give us language "for the beings and changes of the inward creation." Because words signify natural facts, language represents still another of nature's provisions for man; it offers him a sign system for articulation. Man "is placed in the center of beings, and a ray of relation passes from every other being to him. And neither can man be understood without these objects, nor these objects without man." What language does, first, is to afford man a "vehicle of thought," a vocabulary and grammar for realizing his identity as "me." But since "the whole of nature is a metaphor of the human mind," language acquires another, higher use. Since natural facts signify spiritual facts, we can use nature's sign system to transcend nature itself, arriving at those higher laws which nature signifies. Words signify natural facts, natural facts signify spiritual facts, and to the extent that language remains fastened to "natural symbols," it can be used to reflect spiritual truth. Now it is "in view of this significance of nature," Emerson says at the beginning of chapter 5, that nature can be used as a "discipline of the understanding in intellectual truths." The relationship between words and natural facts, and between natural and spiritual facts, represents a fundamental "use of the world," because it establishes a model for transcendence which can operate endlessly. "Nothing in nature is exhausted in its first use," because the signifier–signified model can always be invoked again, using the signifier to focus on the signified.[9]

Emerson is no longer enumerating nature's uses as he did in chapters 2 and 3; he has designed a tool for using nature and proceeds to apply it in chapter 5. For instance, he says the "use of Commodity, regarded by itself, is mean and squalid. But it is to the mind an education in the great doctrine of Use, namely that a thing is good only so far as it serves." Therefore, in order that we may learn this lesson we are confronted not only with all those beneficial provisions discussed in chapter 2, but also with "grinding debt" and all those apparently negative aspects of nature omitted earlier. Nature's use as a signifier has begun to outstrip all other uses. Again, when Emerson says "therefore is Space, and therefore is Time, that man may know that things are not huddled and lumped, but sundered and individual," he is exemplifying a use of nature rather than making a discursive claim about its purpose. Or rather, he is doing both, since nature's end is now seen to be its use as a sign system. (The conflation of the epistemological model of use with a metaphysically grounded *telos* creates certain problems, as we shall see.) What the first half of *Nature* establishes is not a definition of nature, but a methodology for using nature, which becomes not something to think *about*, but something to think *with*. Once this methodology is set up, the question of nature's substantiality becomes irrelevant: "whether nature enjoy a substantial existence without, or is only in the apocalypse of the mind, it is alike useful . . . to me." The "Not Me" acquires its meaning from its relationship to me, a relationship defined by the use which the me makes of the "Not Me." The world becomes whatever man's use of it makes it. The "Not Me" loses its horror when it is appropriated by this method, for it becomes not an alien and inaccessible reality, unrelated and potentially hostile to man, but that which he uses to exercise his imagination.[10]

Emerson has overcome alienation, then, by constructing an epistemological model for relating self and world by means of a process of use. However, once the implications of this argument emerge, certain problems arise.

According to Emerson, by using nature as a sign system, we humanize it so that it becomes "the double of the man." This process of use transforms the relationship between self and world into a relationship between maker and made. What Emerson's epistemological model entails is a world knowable by man—and thereby related to him—because it is made by man. As Giambattista Vico explained, though for his own anti-Cartesian purposes, if we can know only that which we make, then what we know of nature is limited to that which we make of it, whether in the form of geometrical theorems, political institutions, or Homeric epics. Nature as an epistemological category is cast out, to be replaced by culture. The ontological question of nature's existence is rendered forever moot—a consequence Emerson initially finds problematical.[11]

By translating what is initially posed as an ontological duality between self and world into an epistemologically founded relationship, Emerson's model of use forces him to beg the ontological question. Chapter 6, "Idealism," is devoted to begging it at some length. What is most significant about this chapter is not whether Emerson proves his case, but the fact that he labors to do so at all. That is, the chapter constitutes a long testimony to Emerson's own dissatisfaction with having to beg the ontological question in the first place. "Idealism" apparently brings to a temporary halt the use of nature as a sign system which has just gotten under way, for a "noble doubt" arises as to whether, after all, Discipline can be the "Final Cause" of nature, a doubt stimulated by the question "whether nature outwardly exists."[12]

Emerson first argues that, since it remains useful whether or not it has an absolute existence, nature does not need to exist as a substance; "The relation of parts and the end of the whole remaining the same, what is the difference, whether land and sea interact, the worlds revolve and intermingle without number or end . . . ?"

Whether it be "substantial" or only an "apocalypse of the mind," nature is "alike useful" to man. However, Emerson immediately points out, this claim should not lead us to conclude that the "permanence of natural laws" is in doubt. That is, Emerson acknowledges that he is an idealist, in the sense that he regards nature as a "phenomenon" rather than a "substance," but he does not, and indeed cannot, accept the inference that his belief entails the disruption of nature's laws. For he has just been arguing that these laws—the "laws of physics," the "moral law," the "law of harmonic sound," and the like can be read in nature's "text." These laws must stand, but on what ground do they stand? If nature is a dream, then it may have "no significance but what we consciously give it." Emerson seems to evade this issue for some time, devoting most of the chapter to arguing that "it is the uniform effect of culture on the human mind . . . to lead us to regard nature as phenomenon, not as substance." As we grow up, and as our sight is cultivated by the exercise of reason, nature's "outlines and surfaces become transparent, and are no longer seen; causes and spirits are seen through them." Following the route he has already carved out from the physical through the aesthetic, intellectual, moral, and religious uses of nature, Emerson adduces examples to show that "all culture tends to imbue us with idealism." As man moves from his childlike belief in nature's existence, a belief grounded in "unrenewed understanding," to the enlightened position afforded by Reason, he learns that nature is "a spectacle," "one vast picture which God paints on the instant eternity for the contemplation of the soul." [13]

Having become an "instrument" to be used, nature turns into a "spectacle," as Emerson frankly stated in his journal. The "crack," as Emerson himself called it, which opens in "Idealism," reveals a contradiction which, so far, Emerson cannot overcome. He wants to ensure the validity of the method he is enacting, the process of use which relates man and nature, but he finds that this process has led to nature's transformation into a spectacle, whose reality is in doubt. In this chapter Emerson confronts the formal barrier of the thing-in-itself, the same problem posed for Fichte by "the absolute projection of an object *of the origin of which no account can be given* with the result that *the space between projection and thing projected is dark and void.*" Nor does Emerson pretend that the problem has been solved by his arguments in chapter 6, for at its end he admits that the ontological question is still being begged:

But I own there is something ungrateful in expanding too curiously the particulars of the general proposition, that all culture tends to imbue us with idealism. I have no hostility to nature, but a child's love to it. I expand and live in the warm day like corn and melons. Let us speak her fair. I do not wish to fling stones at my beautiful mother, nor soil my gentle nest. I only wish to indicate the true position of nature in regard to man, wherein to establish man all right education tends; as the ground which to attain is the object of human life, that is, of man's connection with nature.

The unusually gnarled syntax here reflects the anguish with which Emerson finds himself "wandering in the labyrinth" of his own perceptions, as an idealist for whom nature's "absolute existence" is not only unprovable, but irrelevant. It is as if he stood back in chilled awe from his own conclusions, begging forgiveness of his "beautiful mother," reminding her of how modestly he began the intellectual enterprise which has ended in her removal. While arguing for the "advantage of the ideal theory," Emerson has, as he knows, skirted the issue it raises: how to reconcile "the total disparity between the evidence of our own being and the evidence of the world's being." That Emerson cannot reconcile this disparity is quite clear—not only to the reader, but to Emerson as well.[14]

Emerson's solution to the problem comes in chapter 7, where Spirit is introduced as both final cause and ontological ground. Whether Spirit, as Charles Feidelson has pointed out "was always available in emergencies" to Emerson, it certainly comes to his rescue here, for it solves all the problems raised in "Idealism." The first problem raised by the "ideal theory" is that the laws revealed to man when he uses nature as a sign system, if they are to be secure despite the unverifiability of sense perception, must be sanctioned by some authority lying beyond the senses. As Emerson puts the problem in his journal, "In these Uses of Nature which I explore, the common sense of Man requires that, at last, Nature be referred to the Deity, be viewed in God." In other words, the "end of Discipline" cannot itself serve as "Final Cause," because if nature is essentially a teacher, the lessons she teaches still lack both purpose and authority. Accordingly, one function of Spirit is to authorize nature's lessons, the most important being the "moral law" revealed

by Emerson's reading of nature's text in chapter 5, "Discipline."
Further, Spirit fulfills the long-deferred need in Emerson's argument
for a *telos*. The question posed in the "Introduction," "to what end
is nature?", is finally answered in chapter 7 with the claim that
Spirit, the "dread universal essence . . . is that for which all things
exist, and that by which they are." Thus, Emerson develops the
conclusion reached in his journal entry, "that a several use of Nature
is Worship," concluding that "the happiest man is he who learns
from nature the lessons of worship." Having learned this lesson,
man finds that "the noblest ministry of nature is to stand as the
apparition of God." As final cause, Spirit not only sanctions the
lesson nature teaches, but orders those lessons in accord with a
purpose: nature is "the organ through which the universal spirit
speaks to the individual, and strives to lead back the individual to
it." Having instated Spirit as final cause, Emerson can now return
to the ontological question left suspended in the previous chapter.
Only now do we learn what really troubles Emerson about idealism.
Despite the advantages of its perspective, idealism "makes nature
foreign to me," for it reinstates the ontological distinction between
me and "Not Me" which Emerson had set out to transcend. For
all his apologies to his "beautiful mother," Emerson questions the
idealist's position not because it negates nature's "absolute existence," but because it negates man's relationship to nature by pos-
iting an unknowable other, a noumenal reality existing beyond the
reach of the process of use. Since he can now rely upon Spirit as
final cause, Emerson is ready to deal with this problem, by means
of the most brilliant strategem in the essay.[15]

"When we consider Spirit," he explains, "we see that the views
already presented do not include the whole circumference of man.
We must add some related thoughts." These related thoughts turn
out to be a redefinition of the ontological issue in epistemological
terms. By defining nature "as a phenomenon, not a substance,"
idealism introduces not an unacceptable duality which again "makes
nature foreign to me, but a *useful introductory hypothesis*, serving
to apprize us of the eternal distinction between the soul and the
world." (Emphasis added.) The original distinction between me and
"Not Me," which idealism had seemed to reinstate, becomes itself
the starting point of that "right education" whose goal is to establish

"man's connection with nature." Emerson's epistemological model can now swallow the ontological duality which generated it by treating that duality as a sign whose ontological reference resides securely in the "ineffable essence" called Spirit, and whose use yields the activity to which the entire essay has been devoted—to establish man in a "true position" toward nature. So, while the question posed by idealism—how to reconcile "the total disparity between the evidence of our own being and the evidence of the world's being"—cannot be answered, it can be, and in fact has been, used. For, when Emerson redefines the distinction between me and "Not Me" as a "useful introductory hypothesis," he describes precisely the role this distinction has played in *Nature* itself. In short, Emerson resolves the dilemma raised for him by idealism by reconstituting the duality of me and "Not Me" as itself a sign whose meaning derives not from its reference to "the total disparity" between self and world, but from its use as a signifier, the use to which Emerson has put it from the outset of *Nature* itself.[16]

At this moment in the essay, Emerson's method outstrips the purpose for which it was constructed. Setting out to forge an "original relation" between man and nature, self and world, Emerson posed the defining question, "to what end is nature?" and arrived at the hypothesis that nature exists to be used as a sign system. "Language" is the crucial stage in this argument, for it is here that Emerson concludes that nature is a text to be read, an "open book" in which "every form is significant of its hidden life and final cause." In "Discipline," he offers a reading of this text, as it were, a reading which reveals the unity of that text and the moral law at its core. But having read that text, Emerson faces a crucial problem: on what grounds can he authorize the reading he has just made? As we have seen, this is one of the questions raised by the "Ideal theory," and in turn answered by Spirit, which authorizes the lessons enunciated in "Discipline." But as "Final Cause," Spirit does more—it not only guarantees the reading of nature's text offered in "Discipline," it sanctions the method Emerson uses there. In other words, Spirit authorizes the process of use itself, and not only as final cause, but also as ontological reference for "men's connection with nature," a connection which *exists in and by virtue of the process of use itself.* What is finally at stake for Emerson in his quarrel with idealism is not only the validity of the lessons enumerated in "Discipline," but more importantly the process of use enacted there.[17]

The priority of the method's authority for Emerson accords with and helps to explain his procedure in "Spirit." Here Emerson's primary need is to ensure the process of use "infinite scope," as is clear from the way in which he introduces chapter 7:

It is essential to a true theory of nature and of man, that it should contain somewhat progressive. Uses that are exhausted or that may be, and facts that end in the statement, cannot be all that is true of this brave lodging wherein man is harbored, and wherein his faculties find appropriate and endless exercise.

Spirit, by providing the process in which the relationship between self and world consists with an "infinite scope," precludes an exhaustion of uses which would bring the process to an end, sunder that relationship, and most importantly, accord to culture a spurious finality. If we recall the essay's opening, with its rejection of given cultural forms and systems, Emerson's disquietude at the prospect of a theoretical end to the process of use should not surprise us. Setting out to forge an original relation to the universe, Emerson had ended up in "Discipline" tracing the development of culture—that set of institutions, and the concept of a static natural order to which they correspond, which he originally repudiated. Thus it becomes clear why Emerson's major tactic in chapter 6 was to retrace his steps, moving from physical to spiritual uses of nature, but this time emphasizing the dynamic quality of the process of use. Throughout chapter 6, we learn again and again that nature in use is plastic, fluid, malleable: the poet "unfixes the land and the sea, makes them revolve around the axis of his primary thought, and disposes them anew"; when subjected to the philosopher's use, nature's "solid-seeming block of matter" "is dissolved by a thought."[18]

Spirit, then, by serving as ontological referent not for sign or for signified, but for the act of signification itself, renders the process of use theoretically endless, and thus incapable of yielding a final finite end. Emerson has already tried to forestall such an eventuality by asserting that nature itself is inexhaustible, but his own model hypothesizes nature's exhaustibility. "Nothing in nature is exhausted in its first use," he tells us, but as his own example reveals, the model of use, when it transforms the physical "use of commodity" into a "moral sentence," does exhaust nature as material substance. It is only "in God," that is, with the ontological reference of Spirit, that "every end is converted into a new means." Inexhaustibility can be an attribute only of an energy which generates the process of use itself, not of that which is used. Spirit, posited as eternal energy source, precludes the exhaustion of uses in which the process would otherwise end.[19]

Nature, meanwhile, becomes "a fixed point whereby we may measure our departure. As we degenerate, the contrast between us and our house is more evident." Our alienation from nature is an entirely remediable consequence of our failure to exercise our reason. "Imagination," Emerson tells us, "can be defined to be the use which Reason makes of the material world." Accordingly, "we are as much strangers in nature as we are aliens from God," because it is only to the extent that we fail to use the world as a sign system that it remains other. "Build, therefore, your own world," Emerson's Orphic poet concludes in chapter 8. As long as one is in the act of building his world, he is in touch with Spirit and is exercising his Reason. During this process, nature becomes fluid. It is only when he is not acting in accord with Reason, not using the world as sign-system, that it appears other. Then he requires the assurance that this otherness is not a necessary ontological fact, but the result of his own failure to build his world. "The ruin or blank that we see when we look at nature, is in our own eye. The axis of vision is not coincident with the axis of things, and so they appear not transparent but opaque." At this point, Emerson seems less concerned to define man as one who makes his world than to chastise him for his failure to do so. Similarly, when the Orphic poet says "What we are, that only can we see," he issues both a call to action and an indictment. The world we see, we have in fact made, we are being told, and thus if it lacks beauty and harmony, we alone are to blame. On the other hand, the poet is holding out a promise as well; once realize that you "can form your life to the pure idea in your mind," and you may transform your world. This implicit contradiction points to the limitations of Emerson's critical program, which already in *Nature* can simultaneously inspire man to remake his world and indict the individual for the ills that beset him. This contradiction, however, is rooted in that deeper contradiction which surfaced in "Idealism," and was deftly turned to rhetorical advantage in "Spirit."[20]

The problem lies in Spirit's dual function; it is both teleological principle and ontological substratum, both final cause and energy source. As we have seen, Emerson cannot proceed to solve the idealist question until he has called upon the authority of Spirit as *telos*. Having done so, he proceeds to treat Spirit as energy source. But if the moral and natural laws inscribed in nature's text are constituted by Spirit as lessons with a purpose, the process of use becomes determined by a transcendent teleological force. As *telos*, that is, Spirit endows certain readings with an eternally fixed status; as energy source, it operates to render all readings transitory. In effect, Emerson finesses this problem in "Spirit" by calling upon Spirit to authorize the specific enactment of the process of use which is *Nature* itself. In so doing, he relies upon the authority provided by Spirit, but suspends its teleological force. Both the power and the limitations of Emerson's critical strategy are signaled by this pivotal move in his strategy.

The power derives from the newfound authority which enables Emerson to employ the process of use as a rhetorical method, one which he goes on to develop and refine in later essays, where the subject at hand serves not as a topic but as a stimulant to thought, not as something real to which the essay refers, but as a sign whose meaning is to be discovered by its use as a signifier. What is thereby enacted and adumbrated once more is the process of signification itself. The process of signification, in other words, constitutes the real content of the essay; and it is this process, rather than any particular meaning it yields which is authorized by Spirit. Thus the essays can assume the form of "untaught sallies of the spirit," which resist the force of any "tyrannizing unity" by acting always on the belief expressed in "The Method of Nature": "Seekest thou in nature the cause? This refers to the next, and the next to the third, and everything refers." This method is used, moreover, to pry his audience loose from its imprisonment within an illusory vision of the world as fixed, given, and immutable.[21]

However, the new authority of Spirit upon which Emerson relied to free him from the world's objectively fixed appearance by revealing its human mediation, returns to haunt his rhetorical project, for when you break free of the world's static appearance, you are always acting in accord with a predetermined teleological plan. That is, the authority derived from Spirit exacts its price, for it results in a new form of imprisonment; man is in effect endowed with the freedom of a sentient thrown stone; he can see what throws him, but he has no power to resist being thrown. He possesses, in short, nothing more than the freedom to contemplate the walls between which his being is swung. The roots of contradiction inherent in Emerson's critical revolt are already clear in *Nature*'s most notorious passage.

When Emerson as "transparent eyeball" says "I am nothing; I see all," he gives voice to two conflicting desires. The obvious one is the desire to reunite man with himself, to restore the whole man to his unalienated condition, at home in the world. But the less obvious and more telling desire expressed in this image is to absent one's self from the world as physical being in order to view the world from the vantage point of the disembodied eye. By detaching one's self as an eye, one assumes a perspective from which it becomes clear that nothing is permanent. The transparent eyeball fuses epistemological detachment with ontological participation, projecting as image the active relation between seer and seen that *Nature* aims to support through argument. But for the climactic vision of the eyeball to achieve its effect, we must accept—or more probably fail to notice—that this airborne bubble endowed with sight results from a beheading: "Standing on the bare ground—my head bathed by the blithe air and uplifted into infinite space, all mean egotism vanishes. I become a transparent eyeball; I am nothing; I see all." Emerson first gives us his head as floating sphere, and then focuses the image as transparent eyeball. The split neatly hidden here begins to emerge in the conclusion, "I am nothing; I see all"; the rhetorical emphasis falls on the predicates, distracting us from the miraculous return in the second clause of the "I" who has just disappeared from the first. In other words, the union is unstable.[22]

Emerson wipes away all the clutter of culture which he finds obstructing his vision in order to forge an "original relation" between man and nature, a relation free of the alienation man suffers as a result of his fixed position within a reified objectivity, but constructs a theory in which alienation resurfaces as a split between the I who sees nature and the I who inhabits it. He is content to unsettle his audience by forcing them to adopt a new point of view, but he entrusts Spirit with the course to be taken by the energy thus released. His theory fosters the act of building one's own world while limiting the means with which to construct it to the imaginative potential implied by vision, and assuming the moral ends already implicit in Spirit.

Both the power and the limitations of Emerson's rhetorical method may be seen in "Circles," published in 1841. The figure of the circle is approached as a sign which means "that around every circle another can be drawn." This proposition in turn is illustrated by a series of examples which serve not to prove the maxim that "every action admits of being outdone," but to use it as a stimulant to thought. The essay moves forward according to the same principle it enunciates—by drawing larger circles around the opening proposition, thus generating meanings of broader scope, and finally referring this process to the "eternal generator" which abides.[23]

The essay is essentially an extended argument in support of the claim, already implied in *Nature*, that "permanence is a word of degrees." The world we inhabit is "at any one time directly dependent on the intellectual classification then existing in the minds of men," and this "present order of things" is always subject to a "new degree of culture," which "would instantly revolutionize the entire system of human pursuits." Emerson reiterates at length the absolute fluidity which underlies the apparent fixedness of the world. Spirit as the "eternal generator" acts as the constantly available source of energy for man's making of history. As one of the "fountain pipes on the unfathomed sea," man can tap this energy if he will. To do so is to remake the world, whose present form is entirely mediate, a mere "wave of circumstance":

Beware when the great God lets loose a thinker on this planet. Then all things are at risk. It is as when a conflagration has broken out in a great city, and no man knows what is safe, or where it will end. There is not a piece of science, but its flank may be turned tomorrow; there is not any literary reputation, but the so-called eternal names of fame, that may not be revised and condemned. The very hopes of man, the thoughts of his heart, the religion of nations, the manners and morals of mankind, are all at the mercy of a new generalization. Generalization is always a new influx of the divinity into the mind. Hence the thrill that attends it.

This passage sounds as if it had been written by an incautious Thomas Kuhn; indeed the essay as a whole envisions a world in which Kuhn's paradigms are always capable of mutation, once viewed as temporary. Emerson has little patience here for regular science, since the power issuing from Spirit is everywhere and always available to the man who would use it. But Emerson is not as windy-headed as he might appear. The essay draws its rhetorical force from the extravagance of Emerson's claims for man's potential power, and the very extravagance of those claims is calculated to pry the reader loose from his adherence to form. This design on the reader's predisposition underlies the essay's basic rhetorical pattern—taking what the reader views as fixed and viewing it as in process.[24]

The most obvious instance of this pattern is suggested by the essay's title. The circle is not only a form, but the very "first of forms," and as such, constitutes a hypothetical test case. If the circle can be shown to refer not to an eternal principle of form, but to an eternal principle of process, then all other forms will prove similarly transitory. Emerson takes a form which can stand for all forms—intellectual, social, aesthetic, religious—and proceeds to use it as a sign which signifies not static finality, but the finitude of form itself, which represents simply "the inert effort of each thought, having formed itself into a circular wave of circumstance,—as, for instance, an empire, rules of art, a local usage, a religious rite,—to heap itself on that ridge, and to solidify and hem in the life." Just as in *Nature*, the world appears to us a "solid-seeming block of matter" unless we are in the act of using it, so in "Circles" the "extent to which this generation of circles, wheel without wheel, will go, depends on the force or truth of the individual soul." Once we assume the perspective the essay sets out to establish, we stand outside "our hodiernal circle," so that what seemed final and given as the ultimate order of things is revealed as entirely mediate: "The law dissolves the fact and holds it fluid. Our culture is the predominance of an idea which draws after it this train of cities and institutions. Let us rise into another idea: they will disappear."[25]

A shift of perspective from within a circle to a point outside its circumference allows us to view it as transcendable. By a similar shift in perspective, we can view any fixed form as a wave in the ocean of process. "You admire this tower of granite," Emerson says, but it was built by man and can be destroyed by him; "an orchard, good tillage, good grounds, seem a fixture, like a goldmine, or a river, to a citizen; but to a large farmer, not much more fixed than the state of the crop." Accumulating homely examples to show the relativity of any present perspective, Emerson labors to transfer the attribute of permanence from form to process, where it properly resides. His strategy throughout is to recognize the need for form, but to treat it in terms of process: what seems a final boundary is a "circular wave of circumstance," and what feels like inertia is the "vast ebb of a vast flow." "Nothing is secure," finally, "but life, transition, the energizing spirit." He uses culture as he had previously used nature, as the fulcrum for moving beyond any fixed form. "The use of literature," for example, "is to afford us a platform whence we may command a view of our present life, a purchase by which we may move it." The fixed appearance of things being only a matter of perspective, if we use culture properly and stand back far enough, we learn that all is process, that "every ultimate fact is only the first of a new series."[26]

But there is little danger of our standing "so far back as to preclude a still higher vision," not only because Spirit sustains a world of endless process, making all visions temporary, but also because people cling to their prison bars, in effect. They have a vested interest in the culturally maintained vision of the world; to step beyond it is to lose, in a sense literally, their grip on the world. Concluding that the "only sin is limitation," "Circles" acknowledges form as a felt need which must be resisted if any hope is to be maintained. Yet the essay's rhetorical strategy reveals Emerson's own sense of how deeply that need is rooted, and how difficult is the struggle to resist its demands. In "Self-Reliance," published in the same volume as "Circles," he acknowledges the resistance of society more bluntly, but still in terms which uphold the values on which his own resistance depends:

Life only avails, not the having lived. Power ceases in the instant of repose; it resides in the moment of transition from a past to a new state, in the shooting of the gulf, in the darting to an aim. This one fact the world hates, that the soul *becomes*; for that forever degrades the past, turns riches to poverty, all reputation to a shame, confounds the saint with the rogue, shoves Jesus and Judas equally aside.

By trying to "unsettle all things," Emerson reveals both his understanding that "people wish to be settled," and his conviction that "only as far as they are unsettled is there any hope for them."[27]

In its power to oppose the authority of the dominant culture, Emerson's strategy has much to offer. Whatever appears to be given and eternally fixed, he is arguing, once seen from the proper vantage point, is revealed as the product of man's own making. Emerson tries to unsettle the minds of his audience so as to foster the active force within them. Yet in what does this unsettled condition consist? Finally, it amounts to a changing perspective, one, moreover, which changes as we retreat from the scene before us until it takes on its true form as a "vast ebb of a vast flow." The world is motion, but the eye which confronts that motion finally occupies the same vantage point as that of the owner surveying his factory or his landscaped grounds. In "Circles," the fluid plasticity of an active reality has begun itself to be reified and set against the resisting power of people who wish to be settled. By the time he wrote "Fate," Emerson was pitting a reified principle of flux against a reified principle of inertia.

"Once we thought positive power was all. Now we learn that negative power, or circumstance, is half," Emerson announces at the beginning of the essay. Fate and liberty are both facts, but contradictory ones: "this is true, and that other is true. But our geometry cannot span these extreme points and reconcile them." Yet it is just this reconciliation which the essay sets out to accomplish. Emerson's strategy is based on the method already established in *Nature*, and employed in "Circles." He explores the meaning of the term "fate" through a series of definitions, each of which works a change on it, until finally it refers not to "irresistible dictation," but to "unpenetrated causes." Fate emerges as a sign referring not to a chain of cause and effect, but as "a name for facts not yet passed under the fire of thought, for causes which are unpenetrated."[28]

The essay begins with an open admission that "we are incompetent to solve the times," and must resign ourselves to the merely "practical question of the conduct of life." Emerson insists upon an honest confrontation of our condition; we must be "perceivers of the terror of life," if our philosophy is to be sound. This claim of open-eyed practicality returns at each stage of the argument, in the form of an outspoken recognition "that the world is rough and surly." Such a posture is an essential part of the essay's rhetorical strategy, which accepts the reader's assumed opposition to any facile negations of fate. Just as he does in "Circles," Emerson appeals here to the reader's experience before shifting his perspective on that experience. In the essay's first phase, then, Emerson generously fulfills his promise to "honestly state the facts" concerning the "immovable limitations" within which we labor with apparent futility in a world whose course is already determined by an "irresistible dictation." But he then proceeds to transpose this opposition between fate and freedom into an opposition between limitation and power.[29]

The first step in this procedure is made when Emerson defines fate as "an expense of ends to means . . . organization tyrannizing over character." Fate is thus allied with form, which from "the bill of the bird" all the way up to inherited "talents imprisoning the vital power in certain directions," acts to determine the limits of freedom. Having shifted his ground subtly, Emerson rehearses again the "odious facts." Heredity and environment act in concert to keep us confined so that what "vital force" we do possess is drained by the simple effort to survive or is wasted in "digestion and sex." Nature herself appears as "necessitated activity," and so powerfully determines our course that the "force with which we resist these torrents of tendency looks . . . ridiculously inadequate."[30]

However, having translated fate into form, Emerson has laid the basis for his next definition: "whatever limits us, we call fate." As limitation, fate offers resistance to power at every stage in its evolution from "brute" to "spiritual culture." Although the "limitations refine as the soul purifies," the "ring of necessity is always perched at the top." Limitation is no longer a sin, but a condition: "it is everywhere bound or limitation." This definition marks the turning point in the essay. Having traced "fate, in matter, mind, and

morals," as the limitation imposed by nature's "tyrannical circumstance," Emerson now turns to the means by which we resist fate.
"If fate follows and limits power, power attends and antagonizes
fate." By shifting our perspective on limitation from within to a
point without, we learn that "fate has its Lord; limitation its limits."
The shift is made by recognizing "who and what is this criticism
that pries into the matter." Man's power is signaled in the very act
by which he examines the principle of limitation. Though he "betrays his relation to what is below him" by virtue of his form—
"quadruped ill-disguised, hardly escaped into biped," he betrays his
potential transcendence of form's limitations by virtue of his ability
to observe his own limitation "from above." Seen from this vantage
point, man is "a stupendous antagonism, a dragging together of the
poles of the Universe" who represents "on one side, elemental
order, sandstone and granite, rock-ledges, peat-bog, forest, sea and
shore; and on the other part, thought, the spirit which composes
and decomposes nature." Fate is, then, merely "unpenetrated
causes." Recognizing our power and the limitation which offers
constant resistance to it, we are enjoined to use our power to sustain
our own constant resistance to fate. The "solid-seeming" reified
objectivity which Emerson had dissolved in *Nature* has been returned to its reified state, and juxtaposed against man's power to
resist it, forming an eternal tension in "the eye and brain of every
man." The young man born with a knife in his brain has come to
accept it as an eternally given condition.[31]

It is easy to regard Emerson's declining optimism as a belated
ascent to maturity. But we will fail to appreciate Emerson's rhetorical power or to understand the sources of his limitations if we
do not see that they are both grounded in contradictions inherent
in his critical position from the outset of his career. In speaking for
the whole man, Emerson appealed to a residual value all too easily
incorporated in the dominant hegemony of the rising middle class.
Taking an offensive rather than a defensive position in support of
the whole man, he was to end by sanctioning the actions of those
very businessmen whose interests were served by the dominant culture. His defiance of that culture's authority was vitiated by his

reliance on a critical strategy yielding a reified vision which confronts a reified flux; complacency was meshed with revolt from the start. Nonetheless, Emerson's utopian vision of man restored to wholeness had the compensatory effects which utopian visions so often do have—that of keeping alive for some in his audience a concept of the whole man in conditions which are fragmenting him. Such a vision can have quite powerful effects as a result of its capacity to support men's refusal to accept the unacceptable; it served to support that refusal, for example, in Thoreau.

Thoreau showed no timidity about following out the full social and political consequences of detached observation as a vocation. *Walden* and *An Essay on Civil Disobedience* reveal what may follow from reattaching the "I" who sees nature to the "I" who inhabits it on the straightforward basis of radical individualism. Vision becomes a form of action for Thoreau, who, unlike Emerson, loved nature and not the idea of nature. His "sight . . . whetted by experience," Thoreau accepted the responsibility entailed by the "perception . . . of right," arguing for "action from principle . . . and the performance of right." Emerson argued that the "candidate for truth" should remain "aloof from all the moorings, and afloat," but for Thoreau, remaining "aloof" and "afloat" not only provided a point of view from which to see the world, but necessitated a limited form of action toward it as well, primarily the negative act of refusing to pay one's taxes in order "to refuse allegiance to the State, to withdraw and stand aloof from it effectually." In short, if Emerson argued the merits of a detached vision, Thoreau argued the virtues of a detached life. Thoreau presents, perhaps more than any American thinker of comparable stature, an absolute case. One may quarrel with his theories of the state, and one may dispute the moral ambiguities of his night in jail, but one cannot charge him with confusion. In contrast to Emerson, Thoreau does not contradict himself. His value lies precisely in the rigor and fluency with which he expressed a completely consistent moral vision of life. The line he pursued cannot be pursued much further; it can only be imitated or denied.[32]

Further, the split between detachment and participation figures centrally in another of Emerson's heirs. While Thoreau accepts and defines the consequences of detachment, it is Walt Whitman who reveals the contradictions implied in the task of remaining both aloof and afloat. "Song of Myself" illustrates with startling vividness how deeply Whitman's imagination has appropriated Emerson's vision of the dynamic interaction between self and world. Accepting Emerson's challenge at the end of *Nature* to "build, therefore, your own world," Whitman generates the self out of nature as the expression of Spirit. But the Whitman of "Song of Myself" confronts the issue evaded by Emerson's reliance on the visual model introduced by the transparent eyeball, the issue which arises when the self generated from within nature becomes self-conscious. Emerson, of course, did not evade this issue forever, admitting in "Experience" that "It is very unhappy, but too late to be helped, the discovery we have made that we exist." But neither did he meet it on the dangerous terms that Whitman did in "Song of Myself." In "Experience," for example, Emerson's recognition of self-consciousness as the "Fall of Man" is followed by a discussion of the cost to our vision exacted by this lamentable discovery. "Distorting lenses" that we are, we are reminded that "once we lived in what we saw." Emerson persists in treating men as ideally "subject-lenses," whose action is abstractly conceived as vision. As Emerson grew less optimistic about our power to use our own eyes, he addressed himself more openly to the forces which inhibit vision. But he left to Whitman the problem of the contradiction inherent in his own position, the problem posed when one tries to inhabit and participate in the world made visible by the vantage point Emerson established, the material world as the scene of perpetual process.[33]

In "Song of Myself," the tension between the "I" who sees the world and the "I" who inhabits it generates a series of crises in the poem's record of self-enactment. Whitman repeatedly splits apart into a self which acts, uttering itself into being, and a self which observes, standing off to admire this creature. The poem records a process of self-realization in which an identity is discovered only to split apart into an "I" who lives through the self-enacting experience and an "I" who stands back to observe the result. By locating the "currents of Universal Being" within the transactions occurring not only between the eye and its horizon, but between all the senses working together and the material world to which they respond, Whitman's poem translates Emerson's visionary flight into a rhythmical pattern marked by the repeated struggle to reintegrate the observing self with the participating self. The interaction between self and world which Emerson cast in terms of vision becomes in "Song of Myself" a process leading the self not out of the world to a vantage point above it, where participation consists in living in what we *see*, but through a potentially endless series of crises forced upon the speaker each time he tries to confront the fluid process that *is* himself.

Emerson's influence on Whitman and Thoreau, I would suggest, is significant not only as a matter of literary influence, but as a social effect of Emerson's critical revolt. If we do not make the mistake of excluding the aesthetic from the social, it is clear that Emerson's self-avowed effort to free "imprisoned thoughts" had a far-reaching impact. It was this capacity to affect his audience that later provoked the envy of Henry Adams. Adams thought Emerson naive, of course, but he inadvertently acknowledged the power of Emerson's voice when he contrasted the Boston of George Cabot Lodge to that of "Emerson and Whitman, Longfellow and Lowell," whose "antislavery outbursts" he remembered, "shook the foundations of the state." Adams, as usual, is referring nostalgically to a lost world, one in which the "gap between the poet and the citizen" was not yet "impassable." Since this gap has only widened since Adams' day, it is the more difficult—and the more essential—to appreciate the fact that Emerson's voice *was* able to cross it.[34]

While his voice carried across the gap between the poet and the citizen, however, Emerson's philosophical program could not bridge the deeper gap between a reified vision and a reified flux. By enacting the process of use, Emerson could pursue his self-appointed rounds as a "candidate for truth," but the walls he had steered so carefully between rose up in "Fate" to hem him in. Moreover, the conclusion he reached in "Fate"—that fate is unpenetrated causes— sounds remarkably like the conviction of an eighteenth-century liberal, committed to the march of Reason and Progress. If fate is simply unpenetrated causes, then it represents the same veil of superstition which the advance of science is progressively tearing away in the eyes of the Enlightenment philosophers. Emerson rejected the mechanical philosophy of his time, but his reliance on vision allied him from the outset with those worshippers of the "goddess of Reason," whose devotion he had thought to undermine. If we return to *Nature* for a moment, it becomes possible to see why Emerson's strategy could foster, on the one hand, an idealist reaction to reification, while harboring, on the other hand, a residual faith in Reason which testifies to the power of rationalization.

As we have seen, Emerson's procedure in *Nature* is designed to overcome man's alienation in a world defined by its commodity structure, by treating commodities as signifiers. In other words, Emerson tries to compensate for the objective world's mysteriously alien character by giving that world, in effect, an artificial use-value. By using the world of objects as a sign system, we can restore our relationship to it, he tells us. One has only to put his strategy in these terms to see that Emerson's solution to the problem of alienation resembles Schiller's. As Lukács puts it, Schiller on the one hand

recognizes that social life has destroyed man as man. On the other hand, he points to the principle whereby man having been socially destroyed, fragmented and divided between different partial systems is to be made whole again in thought.

Theoretically, the process of using the objectively given, the alien, commodified world, as a sign system constitutes an activity through which man is reunited with that world in a dynamic relationship adumbrated in the process of use. Practically, however—as Emerson's career itself eventually demonstrated—the subject of this activity occupies a detached position resembling that of the man who calculates and predicts on the basis of laws. As Lukács describes him, this "subject 'in action'" is

transformed into a receptive organ ready to pounce on opportunities created by the system of laws and his "activity" will narrow itself down to the adoption of a vantage point from which these laws function in his best interest. . . . The attitude of the subject then becomes purely contemplative in the philosophical sense.

Emerson's strategy allows him to "pounce" on laws in much the same way; everything is usable, grist to his mill.[35]

The peculiar consequence of Emerson's idealism is that the man who uses nature as a sign system according to Emerson's model has only one chance of sustaining his integrity, which is to *be Emerson.* Emerson used nature as a sign system in the interests of a rhetorical purpose which accorded his vocation a social value. He demonstrated to his reader that the world is not fixed but fluid, in the effort to set him afloat and to stimulate him to remake his world. As Emerson himself enacted it, the process of use relates the me to the "Not Me" through the medium of speech. But if one chooses to follow rigorously the course outlined in *Nature*, one has only two choices: to be either an Emersonian poet or a capitalist entrepreneur. The poet retreats to a vantage point from which the world appears as a set of symbols to be used for imaginative transformation, making man "whole again in thought," while the capitalist sets about using the world, remaking it according to what he doubtless is capable of seeing as the "pure idea" in his mind. In either case, the subject of the activity undergoes what Lukács describes as a "doubling of personality, the . . . splitting up of man into an element of the movement of commodities and an (objective and impotent) observer of that movement." In the eyes of both Emerson's poet and those of the capitalist who was to assume Emerson's position, this movement "necessarily appears as an activity . . . in which effects emanate from himself," though in fact, both are cut off from that movement just as definitively as the worker who contemplates the machine he operates. It is this consequence of Emersonian idealism which resurfaces in Henry James's *Golden Bowl*, where the shared contemplative stance of the visionary poet and the capitalist entrepreneur is exposed.[36]

As this identity of poet and capitalist suggests, beneath the level on which Emerson attempted to compensate for alienation by adopting the idealist position—making man "whole again in thought"— lay a fundamental alliance between transcendent vision and neutral observation. Perhaps it was because he sensed this peril that Emerson turned in the final pages of *Nature* to the detached observation of the scientist.

No longer praising the scientist's capacity to unveil nature's laws, as he had in "Discipline," Emerson is now warning against the claims of science to exhaust the field of man's knowledge. "Empirical science is apt to cloud the sight," he argues, so that the dynamic "relation between things and thoughts" fades beneath the mounting edifice of scientific knowledge. He attacks the "tyrannizing unity" of the scientific mentality, calling it the product of "half-sight." Yet the most he can claim for his compensatory system is that it must be added to this "half-sight" in order to make it whole. In other words, the "half-sight of science" must be complemented by the integrative activity of poetic vision. Juxtaposing transcendent vision against neutral observation, Emerson calls for their reunion. But in fact they are already united by the detached perspective upon which each relies; the tyrannizing unity Emerson identifies with scientific vision is made possible by the same detached vantage point from which the poet experiences a "tranquil sense of unity." In epistemological terms, Emerson has simply pushed the formal barrier constituted by the thing-in-itself back to the level of natural laws, but these he is unable to question. Instead, he deftly contrives a means of using them. Thereby he can acknowledge the realm of the irrational excluded by rationalism's assumed provenance over the knowable without having to treat it as irrational; it simply becomes the realm of "unpenetrated causes" yet to be discovered by that very empirical science whose claims he had once insistently qualified. The reified objectivity of the material world of commodities only returns as the reified objectivity of natural laws, and man is thus free to contemplate the mechanical working-out of his world's destiny. Thus, it is not surprising that the detached vantage point of the poet in *Nature* is ultimately purified and reduced in "Fate" to that of the empirical scientist, for both occupy the position of Fichte's subject, looking across a "dark and void" abyss. This gap, in other words, does not open as a result of romantic transcendence, but inheres in the very conditions which stimulate that transcendence; the "mechanical philosophy" Emerson opposes infiltrates the means he designs to resist its hegemonic dominance. Consequently, when Henry Adams comes to reject Emersonian idealism in favor of an objective materialism, he does not thereby escape the most fundamental limitations of Emerson's protest; instead, he is forced to expose them.[37]

PART THREE

TWO CRISES OF COMPLICITY

*Education insisted on finding a
moral foundation for robbery.*
—HENRY ADAMS

Chapter Five

HENRY JAMES:
VISIONARY BEING

There is no document of civilization which is not
at the same time a document of barbarism.
—WALTER BENJAMIN

ACCORDING TO Charles Feidelson, Henry James outdoes even the romantic poets in his commitment to "visionary being." What was for a Keats "the most fleeting and fragile of achievements, if achieved at all"—transcendence into the realm of the Imagination—was for James "all-too-accessible," virtually a domesticated state of self-renewing bliss. "What was *I* thus," James askes in *Notes of a Son and Brother*, "but a man of Imagination at the active pitch?" Insofar as James "triumphantly exists" as the visionary poet who often sounds in his *Notebooks* as if he stood "literally out of this world," he plays the role of the poet as defined by Emerson with an energy unexcelled by any writer in the romantic tradition. For James, the artist is preeminently the man with "eyes greatly open" who responds to the "mystic solicitation, the urgent appeal, on the part of everything to be interpreted," the man "addicted to seeing 'through'—one thing through another . . . and still other things through *that*." For James, as for Emerson, "everything refers" in the infinite field of life when presented to the eye of the "Imagination."[1]

The role of the visionary poet as James played it, however, compelled him to confront the detached seer's problematic status as participating agent, and to develop a means for resolving the conflict between seeing and doing which finally exposes the identity of the visionary poet and the capitalist entrepreneur implicit in Emerson's program. The scene of this resolution is *The Golden Bowl*, a novel which depicts a wholly reified world where man has become, in Lukács' words, at once "an element of the movement of commodities" and the "impotent observer of that movement," while sustaining all the while the illusion that this movement is an "activity . . . in which effects emanate from himself." It is by fostering that illusion that Maggie Verver gains her peculiar power over the world; it is by exposing it as illusion, and as a necessary one, that James reveals the horror implicit in that world, the crack at its core.[2]

In order to assess James's strategy, we need to approach it in the context of the problems it was devised to meet. A career as rich and various as James's cannot be reduced to any single explanatory framework; my purpose here is to point to certain threads which form *a* figure, not necessarily *the* figure, in the carpet of James's narrative production, threads which trace James's struggle to validate the artist's visionary posture, his addiction "to seeing 'through'— one thing through another," on the basis of his redemptive activity as a devotee of "the religion of doing." In the course of this struggle, James comes to accord the visionary artist an awesome power, but also to expose an equally awesome impotence, an abyss over which that power stretches its illusory bridge.

In short, by making the seer a doer, James at the same time reveals all doers to be seers, and exposes the limits of both vision and action in a world in which reification has penetrated to a level so deep as to constitute the limits of the knowable. In order to account for the seer's complicity in events he presumes to watch, James devised a means for according the seer a participating role as the redeemer of value. But his solution demanded that the world be constituted exclusively of and by seers, all of whom are complicit in the creation of a social reality which they nonetheless perceive as fixed and given. For only in a world so constituted can the kind of activity in which the visionary artist is engaged proceed without the sacrifice of the contemplative stance to which he is committed. The crisis to which reified consciousness is vulnerable is thus recontained by a strategy which accounts for the seer's complicity as participant without undermining his detached posture, but this strategy in turn reveals the identity of the visionary seer and the capitalist in a thoroughly commodified world. The valorization of the romantic imagination is purchased at the cost of exposing a reified world.

Because it reveals the relationship between James's choice of a narrative method, and the epistemological crisis to which reified consciousness is vulnerable, *The Sacred Fount* serves as the most appropriate place to pick up the thread we wish to follow in James's career. As we have seen, the narrator of *The Sacred Fount* is seduced by that "idealization" which characterizes classical physics according to Heisenberg—the assumption that "we can speak about parts of the world without any reference to ourselves." The visionary seer falls prey to the same contradiction which surfaces for the atomic physicist when the sign of his own participation in events ruptures the detached picture they had previously constituted for him. In *The Sacred Fount*, the rupture occurs when the observer is reduced to the status of the observed, a participant in the social world he has been scrutinizing. We now need to recognize that the epistemological crisis which surfaces at the end of *The Sacred Fount* is in one sense inevitable from the outset, in that it exposes the peculiar liabilities of the first-person narrator as a vehicle for the visionary seer. Once an "I" is invested with the seer's role, he is already situated within the world about which he speaks, and therefore cannot speak about it without reference to himself. This narrator's contemplative stance is actually threatened from the moment he utters the word "I," since that utterance announces his presence as subject within a world constituted for the reader only on the condition of the narrator's absence. Such an absence, James saw, could only be marked by "he."[3]

When James addressed himself to the liabilities of the first person in his preface to *The Ambassadors*, he complained that such a "romantic privilege" opens up "the darkest abyss of romance." His concern here was not with the narrator's reliability per se. That problem he had actually exploited in "The Aspern Papers," and transformed into the basis for exploring the ambiguity of evil in "The Turn of the Screw." What drew his attention was a more fundamental issue, arising—as so often for James—out of compositional questions. In *The Ambassadors*, what precludes "the terrible *fluidity* of self-revelation" inherent in the first person are "exhibitional conditions" which require a subject-lens, but at the same time forbid an actual, self-proclaimed subject of the discourse. Thus, James's exhibitional conditions compel him to use the third person, whose peculiar feature, as Roland Barthes, following Emil Benveniste, notes, is that the "he or the non-person" "never reflects the instance of discourse" and is always "situated outside of it." The liability of the "I" who speaks, and thereby "proclaims himself as the subject" of that discourse is that he forfeits the position outside the world constituted by that discourse. As subject-lens, he must remain outside the world, in the posture of the detached seer of it. But, as *The Sacred Fount* reveals, the I inevitably falls into the world which has been constituted for the reader through his eyes; the world of *The Ambassadors* is constituted in the same way—through the eyes of a subject-lens, but by using the third person, James evades this problem. If, as Benveniste says, "it is in the instance of discourse in which *I* designates the speaker that the speaker proclaims himself as the 'subject'," a discourse from which such an I is absent, such as *The Ambassadors*, may be seen as one in which the subject is denied the privilege of so proclaiming himself. Like the narrator of *The Sacred Fount*, Strether is engaged in a process of signification, caught up in the seer's task of "seeing 'through'—one thing through another, . . . and still other things through *that*," and in both novels, the world is constituted for the reader by that process of signification, enacted by the center of consciousness. The difference between the two worlds so constituted is that between one in which the subject-lens proclaims himself as subject, and one in which he does not. In short, *The Sacred Fount* demonstrated that in order to function as a subject-lens, the center of consciousness cannot be allowed to function as a genuine subject, a speaking "I." As we shall see, Maggie Verver must deny herself the "terrible *fluidity* of self-revelation" for similar reasons; she too has exhibitional conditions to meet which preclude speech.[4]

James by no means abandoned the kind of consciousness displayed in *The Sacred Fount*, believing as he did in the supreme value of "the person capable of feeling in the given case more than another of what is to be felt for it.'' But he had learned that if such a person is to record the adventures he undergoes "dramatically and objectively,'' he cannot be allowed the privileges of speech accompanying the use of an "I.'' Among its other advantages, then, the third-person center of consciousness allowed James to finesse the problem raised by *The Sacred Fount*, enabling him to invest a participating agent in the drama with the contemplative stance of the visionary seer without thereby running the risks entailed by according the seer power to speak directly to the reader. It allowed him, in short, to acknowledge the seer as a participant without sacrificing his crucial value as seer. It is precisely this virtue of the third-person center of consciousness which draws James's attention, for example, in the preface to *The Golden Bowl*. Commenting on the Prince as the center of consciousness in Book 1, James applauds the virtues of a method designed to acknowledge the observer's participation in the events he serves to register as intense perceiver without thereby allowing that participation to disrupt the perceiver's contemplative stance. As a "clean glass held up,'' the Prince "makes us see the things that may most interest us . . . and yet after all never a whit to the prejudice of his being just as consistently a foredoomed, entangled embarrassed agent in the general imbroglio, actor in the offered play.'' The clean glass held up by the intense perceiver affords us the necessary vantage point on dramatic action without which that action would merely run into confusion, constitute no coherent sequence; but by virtue of his status as one of the "bleeding participants,'' the intense perceiver remains himself on stage, or rather, remains behind the "glass" separating him from the reader. He functions at once as a lens on the world and as an actor within it.[5]

As technique, James's exploitation of the third-person center of consciousness is designed to maintain the visionary seer's contemplative stance despite the fact that this stance removes the "lucid reflector" from the world in which she or he performs a host of nonvisual acts. The technique as James developed it in his later phase enabled him to work narrative miracles. Never again would he allow one of his lucid reflectors to be shattered after the fashion of *The Sacred Fount*. But if in *The Ambassadors* he perfected the technique, he also revealed the inverse proportion between seeing and doing both reflected in and dictated by the technique.

For there is a problem with this strategy. No matter how much the bleeding participant he may be for the reader, the Prince's action consists primarily in the adventure of his vision. For James, of course, this vision can be a genuine adventure in itself. Thus he can admire Isabel Archer's "meditative vigil," a "representation of her motionlessly seeing," as in itself an "act" which "throws the action further than twenty 'incidents' might have done." But we need not dispute the narrative economy of such a vigil in order to recognize that the act in question is essentially retrospective. That is, Isabel's act of vision takes place only after she has acted in a quite different sense, by marrying Gilbert Osmond; she sees only after, and what, she has done. There is, in short, a difference between seeing and doing, no matter how far one goes toward transforming vision into act, and action into a "process of vision." That difference becomes the subject of *The Ambassadors*.[6]

Strether, James's most intense perceiver, has an adventure in seeing which reveals how bereft his life has been of all other kinds of adventure. The visionary seer's contemplative stance here reveals his passivity and impotence, limiting conditions which prove peculiarly appropriate for the application of James's method. So long as the seer is essentially impotent, he can remain more or less pristine as the "clean glass" through which his social experience is presented to the reader. Only after she has sacrificed her freedom, for instance, can Isabel Archer assume the detached stance of the seer; having imprisoned herself, she can survey her prison walls. By the same token, Strether can see, "one thing through another," but the condition of his seeing is his impotence, his inability to act on the advice he gives Little Bilham when he tells him to "live." In both cases we have the Hegelian freedom of the sentient thrown stone. Yet even so passive a figure as the aging Strether interferes in the world on which he serves as a lens, for he is one of the "ambassadors" whose mere presence in Chad's Paris operates ironically to redirect Chad's steps to America. No matter how impotent, the seer cannot, after all, maintain a stance "literally out of this world," a fact whose moral implications were to test James's technique to the breaking point in *The Golden Bowl*. Unless the seer is a thoroughly aloof and detached spectator, he is inevitably complicit in the events he serves to record. Facing up to such a fact, let us suppose (one can imagine James saying to himself), a case in which the seer is not altogether impotent. Let us imagine a case in which his inescapable complicity in the events he observes comes to the fore as a result of some given and imputed power. How then do we account for his complicity without giving up his contemplative stance? We cannot for a moment abandon that stance, of course, since without it we are simply lost in an alien and unintelligible jungle whose untended growths can only take monstrous forms. So we must acknowledge the seer's complicity in the events his vision re- flects by some means which will not shatter the glass. In fact, of course, James's approach to the problem of the seer's complicity takes a far more tortured and circuitous route, one which leads him finally to accord the visionary seer a virtually godlike power in *The Golden Bowl*. If we are to understand the peculiar features of that power, we need to see it in the context of James's long struggle with the seer's impotence, an issue which arises already with Ralph Touchett in *The Portrait of a Lady*. In this early novel, we can see in embryo the moral dimension of the problem raised by the seer's combined complicity and impotence.[7]

As the vehicle of freedom beset by the machinations of a deceptive and corrupt Europe, Isabel Archer's career reveals the perils to which romantic innocence is destined in a densely textured social world. Seeking to transcend the limitations of the conventional, Is- abel is "ground" in its "mill." Seeking to see beyond the social surfaces, she is appropriated by their most dedicated guardians. But it is her inheritance and her attitude toward it which actually propel her into Osmond's "house of darkness." Her money makes her useful to Madame Merle and imaginable as a wife to Osmond, and her wish to use her fortune for a purpose of which she can approve enhances Osmond's suit. In short, without her money, Isabel might well have gone wrong, but she could not have gone wrong in a way which would have so beautifully exemplified the case she repre- sented for James, that of an innocence which attracts the evil by which it is undone. Thus Ralph Touchett's role as the man who invests her with the financial means for realizing her freedom ac- quires its special irony. On the one hand, Ralph acts out of generosity and genuine love. On the other, in providing Isabel with a fortune, Ralph is providing himself with an occupation for the waning years of his life, the occupation of watching Isabel. Like James, Ralph wants to see what she will do if given the opportunity to live up to the limits of her imagination. He is at once the detached spectator of the dramatic unfolding of her doom, and an unwitting agent of that doom. In trying to give Isabel's imagination the means to fulfill its promise, Ralph fails to realize that his gift will itself alter the terms of that fulfillment.[8]

Ralphs' complicity in Isabel's doom, of course, is not *The Portrait*'s central moral concern. Isabel's deception at the hands of Madame Merle and Gilbert Osmond far outstrips the bounds of Ralph's contribution to her fate. Nonetheless, as the detached observer who only wishes to contribute to Isabel's freedom in order to see what she will do with it, but who finds that this very contribution fosters the annihilation of that freedom, Ralph is placed in a position which closely resembles that of James himself, as the artist "addicted to seeing."[9]

By the time James wrote *Critical Prefaces*, he had developed a program for validating this addiction, but the preface he wrote for *The Portrait of a Lady* offers a clue as to why he needed to justify the artist's visionary stance. James tells us that the peculiar difficulty which made Isabel Archer's treatment such an appealing problem was the circumstance of her being for him "vivid . . . in spite of being still at large, not confined by the conditions, not engaged in the tangle to which we look for the impress that constitutes an identity." As an image before him of a young woman "affronting her destiny," Isabel thus constitutes a case of pure potentiality for James. Placed as yet nowhere within the social world, while nonetheless "placed in the imagination," she then elicits the central question to which the novel finally develops such a chilling answer: "What will she *do*?" It is in response to this question that, "as if . . . by an impulse of their own," all the other characters arise for James. By this account, it is both as the "germ" of James's idea, and as the central character of his drama, that Isabel presents herself as pure potentiality. For James, as for Ralph Touchett, Isabel first appears as the vivid embodiment of the American girl endowed with

a strong will to freedom and an overabundance of imagination with
which to envision her future. But once nurtured in the soil of James's
imagination, she develops all round her relations which end by placing her quite definitively—as character, in the prison of Osmond's
house, and as developed fictional subject, in the "portrait of a lady"
composed by the novel itself. In other words, the course by which
the free character in the novel travels to her doom is analogous to
the path by which the vivid and yet socially unplaced figure in
James's imagination finds its way into the fixed center of a "portrait." For if James endows his vivid little figure with the "high
attributes of a Subject" by according her imaginative freedom,
Ralph Touchett endows her with the financial means to realize her
freedom, and the outcome in both cases is the same—innocence
betrayed and freedom destroyed.[10]

Like Ralph Touchett, the visionary artist is implicated in a drama
he regards himself as merely watching, implicated because he has
already participated in the course of events by endowing his heroine
with freedom. Like Ralph's, the artist's complicity reveals a capacity to exercise power which is belied by his impotence as a spectator. Ralph's habit of keeping his hands in his pockets signals at
once his impotence and the source of his power; the gesture reflects
the passivity of a man who can only watch Isabel live while he dies,
but who also can and does empty his pockets for her. James was
to emphasize the same paradox even more pointedly in Adam
Verver's case. Adam typically thrusts "his hands down in his pockets and his shoulders expressively up," simultaneously expressing
his sense of futility and reminding us of his vast financial resources.
Impotent though he may be in his inability to control the events he
sets in motion in order to observe, the artist is implicated in them
from the moment he lays hold of the "vivid" image with which he
begins. Moreover, his responsibility as agent breeds a particularly
excruciating form of pain and repentance because he has acted out
of love. As John Bayley justly remarks, James's comment on Balzac's relation to his characters applies to James as well: "It was by
loving them that he knew them, not by knowing them that he loved."
James testifies to his love for Isabel early in *The Portrait* when he
pleads with us not to regard her lightly, despite her naiveté. Like

Ralph, in other words, James acts out of love, but like Ralph, James is at times reduced to what he will later disparage as "mere gaping contrition."[11]

As elaborated in the *Prefaces* and adumbrated in *The Golden Bowl*, James's solution to the moral dilemma reflected in Ralph Touchett's problematic complicity resembles, on the face of it, nothing so much as God's solution to a similar problem. For only God is on record as having accounted for his complicity in human events without thereby sacrificing his detached contemplative stance. And although he succeeded finally at being both spectator at and agent in the same drama, it was not easy, even for him.

Out of his love for man, God gave him the freedom to choose between good and evil. It did not go unnoticed, even to God himself, that he might bear some responsibility for the ensuing nightmare of human history. So he parted with his son in an effort to pay for his mistake, to purge his guilt. He could pass this off as an act of mercy toward the human race he so loved, rather than as one of self-punishment for his original mistake, by conveniently placing the onus of punishment on Christ, who was, however, not taken in by this shrewd deception. He knew when he had been forsaken, and by whom, although he failed, understandably enough, to see just why. God, however, was well pleased with this displaced act of contrition, but just for good measure he sealed it with the Holy Ghost, thereby following self-duplication with self-triplication. Such are the complex self-deceptions and charades required when one tries to be both spectator at and agent in, the same drama. It is hardly surprising that some have suspected God's motives, finding it more plausible that he endowed man with freedom not out of love, but out of a need for entertainment.

If the artist, like God, acts out of love when he accords his creatures freedom, the artist, like God, must accept responsibility by enacting a design for their redemption. It is this task to which Maggie Verver dedicates herself when she takes up her position in Book 2 of *The Golden Bowl* as the vehicle of the Jamesian Imagination and works at an "active pitch" to redeem her marriage. Maggie acts out of love to discharge the responsibilities of the artist understood as a devotee of what James calls in the *Prefaces*, "the religion of doing." The sovereign commandment of this religion is that "connexions are employable for finer purposes than mere gaping contrition." Such contrition is the lot of Fanny Assingham, who starts up "connexions" all round her, but cannot control them once they outstrip her expectations. Fanny claims to love all the creatures she has brought together, but behaves more like the irresponsible God who creates the world out of boredom. At times, James sounds a similar note of irresponsibility. Commenting on the artist's "ideally handsome way" of producing "in any given connexion all the possible sources of entertainment" in order to "intensify his whole chance of pleasure," James parenthesizes, "it all comes back to that, to my and your 'fun'—if we but allow the term its full extension." Fanny Assingham's defense of her meddling—that "it's all, at the worst, great fun"—contributes to the slightly sinister resonance which "fun" and "funny" gradually acquire in the course of the novel, but her gaping contrition stands in contrast to Maggie's redemptive action. For if Fanny illustrates the fate of the impotent spectator whose original vivid conception makes her at least partly responsible for, though unable to control, the "funny form" of the Ververs' marriages, it is Maggie who finally assumes responsibility for Fanny's apparently gratuitous act of conception. It is Maggie, that is, who exercises what James was to call the "civic use of the imagination" and so demonstrates the redemptive purpose of the artist committed to "action with a vengeance." When she picks up the pieces of the bowl, smashed by Fanny in a desperate attempt to destroy the evidence of her own complicity as well as the symbol of its result, Maggie dramatizes the artist's role as the redeemer of value from waste, the role James describes in the *Prefaces* when he underscores the active dimension of Art. "Art deals with what we see," first and foremost, since the artist is preeminently a "figure with a pair of eyes" situated behind a window in "the house of fiction," but it must then proceed to "any amount of doing," an operation devoted to the "literal squeezing-out of value." "Life," according to James, "is capable, luckily for us, of nothing but splendid waste. Hence the opportunity for the sublime economy of art, which rescues, which saves and hoards and 'banks' . . . investing and reinvesting these fruits of toil in wondrous 'useful' works." The waste, appalling though it may be, is nonetheless fortuitous, since it affords the artist the opportunity to redeem the "hard, latent *value"* of life. Such a defense of the visionary artist resembles the theological defense of God's action by reference to the theory of the fortunate fall; in both cases, a nightmare of human waste provides an opportunity for redemption. In neither case, however, is the defense quite convincing. What both cases testify to, nonetheless, is a power which relies for its efficacy on mystification, although in *The Golden Bowl*, it is not religious but economic mystification which sustains the artist's power.[12]

God's power over his human creatures resembles Adam Verver's over those who live at his expense. Like God, Adam Verver is "perpetually treated as an infinite agent," and this "attribution of power" is the "greatest inconvenience" to someone who wishes merely to indulge his "freedom to see." Like God's, Adam's eyes have the strange effect of making you feel as if "you were never out of their range." But Adam's mystification in the eyes of others derives from the inference they automatically make, that "as he had money, he had force." It is Maggie in the end who is called upon to express that force. But if she plays Christ to Adam's God, she also plays God to Charlotte's Christ, so that once Maggie's redemptive project is complete, she appears to the Prince much as Adam himself appeared to him at the outset—as an "infinite agent" behind a "dazzling curtain of light." Like Adam's, Maggie's power results from the attribution of force she elicits once she adopts the contemplative stance of the artist as visionary seer standing outside the picture, and thereby leaves Charlotte with the question of what she sees and dazzles the Prince with the illusion that she is virtually omniscient. In short, if the "figure with a pair of eyes" posted behind a window in "the house of fiction" is the visionary artist, in *The Golden Bowl* that figure is also the capitalist, whose eyes are "a pair of ample and uncurtained windows," and the power of both figures is an attributed power, created and sustained by the mystification which their detached posture as seers generates in others.[13]

To recapitulate: on the one hand, James resolves the problem of complicity by imputing a peculiar power to the visionary seer, who exercises that power to discharge her responsibility as artist. Maggie is a seer who apparently acts, and thus adumbrates the redemptive power of art, in accord with a design which resembles God's in demanding that scapegoats be found and sacrifices be made. On the other hand, what enables James to acknowledge the seer's complicity without sacrificing his contemplative stance is a concept of action which derives from the identity of the capitalist and the artist. The implicit analogy between Ralph Touchett's money and James's imagination in effect comes to the fore to provide the material basis for the celestial power which James imputes to the visionary artist. In his effort to account for the seer's complicity as participating agent in the drama, James accords that seer extraordinary power, but when we examine the kind of power she exercises, we find that this power results from an activity which is essentially illusory.

Maggie is by no means impotent. Unlike Strether's, her "freedom to see" is not grounded in her inability to act. She carries out a redemptive program which "saves" two marriages at the sacrifice of two passionate relationships. However one judges the outcome, it testifies to Maggie's power. But the process by which that power is developed and exercised takes a curious, if revelatory, form. For Maggie does not do anything positive, once she is in possession of her germ of suspicion. On the contrary, it is because she resists the temptation to do anything that she succeeds at rearranging relationships. To do something in the situation of doubt in which she finds herself would mean speaking to Amerigo, to her father, to Charlotte, and it is by *not* speaking that she systematically forces others to rearrange themselves in accord with her wishes. There is, in effect, only one thing Maggie could finally be said to do, and that is to adopt a new vantage point outside the world she has inhabited. When she imagines herself pacing around the pagoda, she has effectively already taken this step, and all that follows—all the theatrics in which Maggie becomes engaged as both actress and director—is essentially the result of that first step outside the picture. It is as if the very perception that they are being watched by Maggie leads Charlotte and the Prince ultimately, and apparently of their own accord, to rearrange themselves apart to assume the new roles Maggie assigns them. Yet—and this is the most curious feature of the process— Maggie's detached stance as seer, once she consciously adopts it, does not lead to any final and conclusive vision of the truth, as does, say, Isabel's when she sees how she has been deceived and trapped, or as does Strether's when he sees that he has not lived. For even, indeed especially, after she has accidentally stumbled upon the golden bowl, Maggie confesses to no knowledge save that knowledge which consists in knowing that there is something she does *not* know. Not only does Maggie's activity as doer consist in not doing anything, that is, not speaking, but her activity as seer is finally reduced to *not* seeing. The power she wields, then, is generated by the illusions she fosters in the minds of others. Similarly, Adam Verver wields enormous power essentially because of his money, but this power is activated for the same reasons Maggie's is—that he is mystified in the eyes of others. Adam's power testifies to the truth of Marx's claim that "everything which you are unable to do, your money can do for you." Adam's money does everything for him, in more ways than one. At bottom, however, it invests an otherwise unimposing little person with an aura of immense power to which everyone pays homage. Like Maggie, Adam provokes others to act rather than acting himself in some unseemly show of force, and he does so essentially because he is manifest to the world as a mystery. If Amerigo and Charlotte never know what Maggie knows, not even the reader is allowed to know with any certainty what Adam knows.[14]

Despite the fact that Maggie and Adam "do" little to produce the final outcome of events in the novel, they nonetheless clearly exercise power decisively. The reason they can do so has to do with the kind of world they inhabit, a world being reconstituted by the forces of capitalism. In such a world, a perverse power accrues to those who, like Maggie and Adam, withhold—from themselves, each other, and everyone else—their knowledge that they do not know, while that power is exercised over those who, like Charlotte, are deluded by their faith in their own capacity to know. Recognizing her position as the bewildered spectator of an arrangement between the Prince and Charlotte, Maggie exploits her own bewilderment: mystified as she is, she finds that she can in turn mystify Amerigo and Charlotte, and so rearrange them. Charlotte, on the other hand, fails to recognize her own impotence, just as she fails to see the crack in the bowl. She, not Maggie, proves the true innocent, for Charlotte believes that the world is essentially knowable and that human beings possess the power to act and the freedom to choose on the basis of that knowledge. But her world is in fact not knowable. Like Eve's, Charlotte's tragic grandeur derives from her will to know, and like Eve, she is doomed to exile, evicted from the Garden to roam the arid desert of America with another Adam. She remains a victim to the illusion fostered by Maggie's denial of knowledge because she does not realize that she inhabits an unknowable world.

What makes it unknowable is also what renders delusory Charlotte's belief in that "human" relation between man and the world in which, Marx notes, "love can only be exchanged for love, trust for trust," a relation which allows the recognition of "natural and human qualities" as inherent in a "real, individual life." That is, Charlotte operates on the false assumption that hers is still an unalienated world, in which, as Marx describes it, "if you wish to influence other people you must be a person who really has a stimulating and encouraging effect upon others," or "if you wish to enjoy art you must be an artistically cultivated person." Charlotte herself is both stimulating and cultivated, but she lives in a world presided over by the values of Adam Verver, whose influence is the product of the alienated power of money, and whose aesthetic sensibility is reflected in his concern only that "a work of art of price should look like" the authentic thing for which its seller represents it. In this world, such individual virtues as Charlotte possesses are finally of no account in themselves, because "money, as the existing and active concept of value, confounds and exchanges everything." It is not merely that "he who can purchase bravery is brave, though a coward," but that "money is . . . exchanged . . . for the whole objective world of man and nature." In such a world, the value of individual human qualities is transposed and inverted into a commodity value. Charlotte cannot see the crack in the bowl, nor can she see that the world is being reconstituted before her very eyes by this transvaluation of values, so that she herself is to become at once an "element in the movement of commodities" and the impotent "spectator of that movement." It is this same commodified world, however, which affords Maggie her power.[15]

As James's description of the "sublime economy of art" indicates, the artist who acts to redeem the "hard latent value" of life is acting out the role of the capitalist who invests and reinvests. Thus, in Book 1 of *The Golden Bowl*, the Ververs are like artists who have a "good eye for a subject," perhaps, but lack the capacity for "squeezing out" its value. Their sin lies in their waste of the Prince; having bought him, they fail to make something of him. They are like the mere hoarder of money who fails to become a capitalist by refusing to reinvest his profits. Thus when Maggie acts to redeem her marriage in Book 2, she is at once the artist whose imagination operates to develop the subject she has plucked from the "spreading field" of life, squeezing out its value, and the capitalist engaged in investing and reinvesting profits. Building upon the analogy between the two processes—that of creating capital and that of making "wondrous 'useful' works"—James could validate the latter only by exposing the degree to which his world was defined by the former. Thus the romantic triumph of the visionary imagination to which Maggie's career testifies is achieved at the cost of exposing a world in which it is not merely the artist who is confined to the posture of a spectator; everyone is reduced to that position. The ironic complicity of Ralph Touchett in Isabel's fate becomes, in *The Golden Bowl*, a complicity spread among all the characters, not excepting Maggie herself. Rather than one detached spectator confronting one splendid and doomed heroine, we have an entire world of spectators, all of whom are implicated in the creation of that "funny form" in which they live.[16]

In such a world, evil inheres in the social fabric too inextricably to be simply exposed and reviled, as it can be in *The Portrait of a Lady*. Indeed, it cannot even be directly apprehended, for to see the "thing hideously behind," as Isabel does in chapter 42 of *The Portrait of a Lady*, would mean to ruin any chance of redeeming the world's "hard, latent *value*." James says that Isabel's fireside meditation demonstrates how "the mere still lucidity of her act can be as interesting as the surprise of a caravan or the identification of a pirate," but he uses the same imagery in *The Golden Bowl* to depict not what Maggie's vision reveals, but what she has successfully suppressed. For Maggie, the "straight, vindictive view . . . figured nothing nearer to experience than a wild eastern caravan." The "spell of recognition" in which Isabel finds "the last sharpness suddenly wait" allows the reader the satisfaction of watching the thing hideously behind come to the fore, shattering illusion with revealed truth. In Maggie's world, on the contrary, the direct vision of "evil seated, all at its ease, where she had only dreamed of good" cannot be allowed to surface, for such a revelation, in shattering illusions, would shatter the world itself. Thus Maggie acknowledges the thing behind only at the end of her ordeal, as something she has evaded, refused to see, noticing how "horror itself had almost failed her." Maggie's success as seer, then, depends upon her capacity not to see, not to know, while Isabel's tragic grandeur emerges only at the moment when she does see, does know. The difference between the two testifies to a difference between their worlds. In Isabel's world there is a knowable truth beneath the illusions by which she has been victimized, and her destiny is to face that truth. In Maggie's world, to know the truth is to know that one is doomed to deception at the hands of friends, not enemies, and this as a result of social conditions that cannot be fully understood. Thus Maggie's destiny is to constitute a world on the basis of the fact that truth cannot be faced if the human relations she wishes to secure are to be sustained.[17]

In portraying Maggie's pursuit of that destiny, however, James goes beyond Maggie to reveal the conditions dictating its course; he constitutes a world in which innocence does not simply attract the evil which besets it; innocence harbors that evil in itself. Everyone intends the best, everyone tries to act for the best, and no one is really insincere. Yet at the same time, everyone is complicit in the construction of a social reality at the center of which lies a flaw. It is a world which ought to be familiar to any modern reader (especially of Max Weber)—one in which something terrible has happened which no one intended, but to which everyone has contributed, taking their cues from each other, reacting rather than initiating action, and, more often than not, attributing responsibility to the arrangement in which they are "fixed." While everyone has made this world, it nevertheless *appears* to everyone as already made, fixed, completed. In short, the reifying process has reached the point where man confronts a world he has made, and therefore ought to be able to know, but cannot know because his own productive capacity has been obscured within the congealed form of commodities. If Maggie acts to redeem value by reconstituting human relations in accord with her concept of love, James exposes that redemptive process as one which presupposes a commodified society and which only succeeds when it works in accord with the economic values which must prevail in such a society. It is the Prince whose situation most immediately reflects this commodified society, and so it is with him that we shall begin to examine its lineaments.[18]

As presented to us at the outset of Book 1, Amerigo is a man wandering the London streets, watching the crowds and now and then stopping "before a window in which objects massive and lumpish, in silver and gold . . . were as tumbled together as if, in the insolence of the Empire, they had been the loot of far off victories." Too "restless . . . for any concentration," the Prince has "strayed," upon the signing of his marriage contract, into Bond Street, where "the power of the rich peoples," with whom he is about to ally himself, is exhibited in the treasures he sees behind the "plate glass" of shopwindows. At this moment, the Prince resembles the *flâneur* as described by Walter Benjamin in "Paris, Capital of the Nineteenth Century." The "gaze of the *flâneur*," Benjamin says, is "estranged"; he is "still on the threshold, of the city as of the bourgeois class. Neither has yet engulfed him; in neither is he at home. He seeks refuge in the crowd." Benjamin is actually discussing Baudelaire, and describing the opening phase in the poet's encounter with the marketplace, before he assumes the role of bohemian and "throws his lot in with the asocial," in defiance of the economic position he has been thrust into by the commodification of art. The Prince is no Baudelaire, of course, but his situation at this moment does reflect that of the artist caught up in the transition from a society in which art was supported by patrons to one in which it must seek out buyers in the marketplace. As an impoverished European aristocrat, the Prince has, in effect, found a buyer in the Ververs, who have just agreed to pay a high price for the "*morceau de musée*" which he constitutes as a result of his "antenatal history." There can be little doubt in the Prince's mind as to the fact of his being purchased, since Maggie has explicitly told him that he is "a rarity, an object of beauty, an object of price." Thus, the images of "a crunched key in the strongest lock that could be made," and "the iron shutter of a shop" which "rattled down at the turn of some crank" arise quickly enough to reflect with foreboding the Prince's resemblance as commodity to the objects caged and confined behind the plate glass. By presenting him to us at this moment, however, when the contract has been signed, but the goods, as it were, have not yet been turned over, James affords us a vision of the Prince "still on the threshold . . . of the bourgeois class" he is about to enter, still wandering the streets and observing the market's display. Here, James relies for his intense perceiver on that part of the Prince which he does not regard as having been purchased by the Ververs, what he calls his "single self," the "personal quantity" which lies behind the "public" identity they are about to appropriate. For the same reason that Charlotte rushes across the Atlantic to spend her hour with the Prince on the eve of his wedding,—that this private personal self remains, until that event, accessible—James introduces us to the Prince at one of the last possible moments in which his personal quantity can be demonstrated.[19]

Yet at the same time, James's strategy has the effect of presenting an unalienated man confronting his own alienated self in the form of alienable wealth.

The "doubling of personality" which Lukács diagnoses in the capitalist manifests itself here in revelatory fashion. The Prince is at once "an element of the movement of commodities," and the impotent observer of that movement. In his own personal dream of an *Imperium*, in his hope for a "scientific" future full of "machinery," he anticipates joining the ranks of "those people," as he will later call them—"capitalists and bankers, retired men of business, illustrious collectors"—those from whom "effects," in Lukács' words, appear to "emanate." As it turns out, however, the Prince's desire to become one of "those people" is to be frustrated, since he is treated to abundant evidence of effects, but is unable to apprehend the activity itself from which they "emanate." Mr. Verver, in particular, represents "those people," and Mr. Verver moves in mysterious ways indeed. At the outset of his adventure in the Ververs' boat, however, the Prince sees himself on the threshold of a "new history," and so his consciousness exhibits both the illusions which capital creates and the conditions underlying those illusions. As the expectant capitalist, Amerigo anticipates joining in some as yet unspecified kind of activity, but since he is himself a commodity just purchased, the personal, unalienated self is reduced to the position of an impotent observer of the movement of commodities of which he is about to become an element. And this reduced position proves, for a long while, definitive. Thus, the only new activity to be afforded Amerigo until Charlotte renews their liaison is that of wondering what action he is expected to perform. Since it is not until Charlotte provides him with an answer (which proves to be the wrong one) to this question that the Prince meets any genuine appeal to his capacity for either action or imagination, his services as a center of consciousness are not required until the closing chapters of the Book which bears his name. We are, in other words, to imagine him continuing to wonder during the intervening pages. But the posture of baffled and impotent observer to which the Prince is reduced by his marriage, is made sufficiently clear in the opening two chapters, where James defines the peculiar form which Amerigo's commodification is to take as a Verver "possession."[20]

The Prince's failure to discover what he is expected to do, now that he has allied himself with "capitalists and bankers," results not from his commodification per se, but more specifically from the particular kind of commodity which he constitutes for the Ververs. Thus Amerigo sees himself as

some old embossed coin, of a purity of gold no longer used, stamped with glorious arms, medieval, wonderful, of which the 'worth' in mere modern change, sovereigns and half-crowns, would be great enough,

but he sees as well that the coin in question will not be offered for sale again. What makes Amerigo's purchase by the Ververs strange is that it takes him out of the circulation of commodities, placing him in the position of a possession which is "to escape being reduced to his component parts" by being sold again in the marketplace. In order to appreciate Amerigo's dilemma as commodity we should begin with Marx's analysis of commodity exchange in its simplest form. According to Marx, it is because commodities are "non-use-values for their owners and use-values for their non-owners" that "they must . . . change hands." There is a curious paradox to this process of commodity exchange. On the one hand, a commodity must be realized as an exchange-value before it can be realized as a use-value, for theoretically, if the commodity had use-value for him, the seller would not bring it to the marketplace in the first place.

He sells what he cannot use in order to buy what he needs. Or, as Marx puts it, "For the owner, his commodity possesses no direct use-value. Otherwise, he would not bring it to the market." On the other hand, the commodity "must stand the test" as a use-value before it can be realized as an exchange-value, since "the labour expended" on it "only counts insofar as it is expended in a form which is useful for others." Whatever that use may be, in short, it must be there to elicit a demand for the commodity and thus find a buyer. But finally, "only the act of exchange can prove whether that labour" expended in the production of the commodity "is useful for others." In other words, commodities must possess use-values if they are to be sold, but they must be sold before their use-value is proven. It is in this vicious circle that the Prince is caught.[21]

For the Prince, that part of himself which he is selling to the Ververs is precisely a non-use-value. For the public self that attracts them as buyers is "made up of the history, the doings, the marriages, the crimes, the follies, the boundless betises of other people," a history whose most striking features for the Prince himself are its "ugliness" and an "infamous waste of money that might have come" to him. The Prince, in short, has no use for the value which his "antenatal history" has given him, and he in effect exchanges that commodity for one he thinks he can use: "If what had come to him wouldn't do, he must *make* something different. He perfectly recognized—always in his humility—that the material for the making had to be Mr. Verver's millions." If he has sold himself as an art object, he has purchased what he thinks of as a "scientific" future. Thus, from Amerigo's standpoint, Adam Verver exchanges his daughter and his millions for a *morceau de musée* to add to his collection, while the Prince exchanges his historic value and his personal freedom for the resources with which to pursue his scientific future. This would seem sufficiently straightforward and satisfactory to all parties concerned, but as the Prince ponders the bargain he has made, his thoughts waver between the advantage he has gained—the "success" he has achieved in winning Maggie and her millions—and the price he has paid for such a prize—the sale of his public self as a commodity. The first consideration reinforces his sense of humility and his desire to resist the temptation, submission to which is so well recorded in his familial history, the temptation toward any vulgar rapacity. The

second feature of his bargain breeds mystification, and the inter-
dependence of use- and exchange-values as Marx defines it helps
to explain this mystification. Since only the act of exchange can
prove whether a commodity has a use-value, and since the Ververs
do not intend, apparently, to sell what they have purchased, the
Prince cannot see what value he has for them. If the coin is not to
be "reduced to its component parts" by sale, he asks himself, "what
would this mean, . . . but that, practically, he was never to be tried
or tested? What would it mean but that, if they didn't 'change' him,
they really wouldn't know—he wouldn't know himself—how many
pounds, shillings, and pence he had to give?" What was a non-use-
value for him is apparently a use-value for the Ververs; otherwise,
he presumes, they would not have bought him. That he is "taken
seriously," the Prince sees well enough, since he knows how much
he cost on the market. In this sense, his use-value is attested to by
the high price he has already brought on the market. But "lost there
in the white mist was the seriousness in *them* that made them so
take him." In other words, he cannot comprehend in what his use-
value is to consist for those who have bought him, since they provide
him with nothing to do. His role, as Maggie has spelled it out for
him, if only in jest, is merely to be a Verver possession, whose fate
can take the form either of being "one of the little pieces" that the
Ververs unpack at hotels or of being sent off to Adam's museum
at American City, a building likened to a "tomb." In neither case
is he going to be required to do anything; on the contrary, he is
virtually required to do nothing, save be what he is. For Adam, for
whom "the question of appearances" has reduced itself to caring
only that "a work of art of price should look like" the authentic
thing its seller represents it as being, the Prince need only appear
as what he is—a Prince, and a "deep old Italian." As for Maggie,
the Prince is called upon merely to do what he cannot help doing,
which is to attract other women. Apparently, then, the Prince has
use-value for the Ververs; in fact, his use-value has been subsumed
by an exchange-value which can never be measured so long as he
is simply hoarded, suspended above the circulation of commodities.[22]

From the vantage point of Amerigo's personal self, then, the self
which anticipates a scientific future, what this suspended state

means is simply that he is given nothing to do. Rather than being initiated into the activities of "capitalists and bankers," he remains a "Roman Prince who [has] consented to be in abeyance." But in effect, the Prince's personal self has become the repository of a use-value neither called upon nor measured through resale of the commodity possessing it. The Prince cannot understand his fate because he does not realize the significantly different terms on which the Ververs have purchased him. If his scientific future fails to materialize, it is because his use-value is of no interest to the Ververs, who, as capitalists, operate on quite different economic principles than those dictating the Prince's view of his bargain with them. These principles are fairly basic ones, which Marx describes in terms of a contrast between the "simple circulation of commodities" whose features we have already touched upon, and the circulation of money as capital.[23]

The "direct form of the circulation of commodities," Marx says, consists in "selling in order to buy." What happens in this process is that commodities are transformed into money, which is then reconverted into commodities, a pattern he designates as "C–M–C." But when this pattern is reversed, money is transformed into capital, so that one buys in order to sell, a process (M–C–M) in which money is transformed into commodities only to be reconverted into money. If the "final goal" of the first process (C–M–C) is "the satisfaction of needs," or use-value, the "motivating force" of the second (M–C–M) is exchange-value. From the hypothetical standpoint of the simple trader whose transactions take the form C–M–C, money is merely a means to an end, which is the satisfaction of his or her needs. He may sell the shoes he has made, and with the money buy a bushel of corn or two yards of cloth. Or a man might sell his antenatal history in order to purchase a scientific future. Or a woman might sell her social genius in order to purchase financial security and the freedom to exercise that genius. Such people, in short, retain the capacity for desires and needs to which the marketplace is necessary, but still subsidiary. On the other hand, the capitalist, whose transactions take the form M–C–M, is engaged in what Marx calls a "passionate chase after value" which locates him wholly within the marketplace. For him, the use-value of commodities is significant not because of any needs they may fulfill for him, but because their use-value is the source of the demand for them in the marketplace, the demand on which he counts in order to complete the cycle by selling them at a profit. The capitalist purchases a commodity always with an eye to its potential exchange-value, and never to its use-value per se. The capitalist becomes therefore the "bearer" of the "movement of capital" in which "the valorization of value takes place." Both money and commodities are "mere forms" through which value passes as a "self-moving substance," which "changes its own magnitude . . . and thus valorizes itself independently." The capitalist not only looks at commodities and sees money, but further, looks at both commodities and money and sees value increasing. Thus, Adam Verver is wholly unconcerned with use-values. Even though Adam is no longer in the business of making money, no longer involved in the "transcendent calculation and imaginative gambling all for themselves," he remains committed to the same "passionate chase after value" he began at the age of twenty, and his success as collector testifies to the same "sensibility to the currents of the market" which had previously served him so well by fostering his instinct for "getting in, or getting out, first."[24]

We can now see why Amerigo's desire to discover his use-value for the Ververs is frustrated. The Prince has sold himself as the repository of European history in order to acquire the financial means to pursue a scientific future, in accord with the pattern C–M–C. What he fails to see is that by selling himself as a commodity in the market presided over by Adam Verver, he is being purchased, not to satisfy any need, but because he is "an object of price," a commodity whose potential exchange-value is enormous, in accord with the pattern M–C–M. The Prince's straightforward honesty as seller of one commodity (his public identity), and buyer of another (his scientific future), would be all very well if he were dealing with another such innocent trader in a relatively primitive marketplace where most people trade in order to meet their needs and satisfy, as well as possible, their desires. But the Prince's desires are by no means so limited as to be met in such a simple market, and luckily, neither is what he has to sell, as the Ververs demonstrate by paying such a high price for him. But theirs is a different and

more complex marketplace, where, in Marx's words, "all commodities . . . are in faith and in truth money," and where money
takes the form of commodities in order to become capital. In this
market, as James's metaphor for the Prince as coin already suggests,
the Prince is "in faith and in truth money," not money to be spent,
and not, in the end, money to be hoarded either, but money to be
made. Until Charlotte marries Adam and faces a similar—though
not identical—problem, leading to her proposal that she and Amerigo renew their old relationship, the Prince remains bewildered,
awaiting news of his use-value. But Charlotte stimulates his imagination once again, and acknowledges his use-value by her appeal
to that personal self which the Ververs have failed to acknowledge.
One might put it then that by coming together again at the end of
Book 1, Charlotte and the Prince complete the operation C–M–C.
That is, having sold themselves as glittering public personages, the
social faces of the Verver family, they have at last found a way to
spend their newly acquired resources; by renewing their love, they
satisfy their desires. Having sold a commodity for money, and the
social position it accords them, they now spend their earnings, their
freedom in particular, to reap their reward.[25]

But if Charlotte and Amerigo have thereby completed the process
begun when they sold themselves as commodities, they are now to
be faced with an unforeseeable consequence of their deed—the completion by Maggie of the process begun with her father's purchase
of the Prince. If the innocence of Charlotte and Amerigo consists
in their assumption that they live in a world where money is a means
to an end, the innocence of Maggie and Adam consists in their failure
to recognize that as capitalists they cannot simply hoard their
wealth. When they purchase the Prince, for example, they initiate
the circulation of money as capital, but then they behave like a
"capitalist gone mad" in that they stockpile their wealth, failing to
allow its self-valorization. If the Prince in Book 1 is suspended above
the stream of circulation, it is because the Ververs have purchased
him for his exchange-value, but do not exchange him. Like the other
art objects they have accumulated, whether "stored in masses
. . . in warehouses, vaults, banks, safes" all over Europe, or carried
about to make their houses "a little less ugly," the Prince is simply

hoarded. If he is to return a profit, he must reenter the circulation of money as capital, and his renewed liaison with Charlotte effectively accomplishes that reentry. In response to that development, Maggie is finally to complete the process her father initiated, thereby wiping out any vestige of a world in which money is a mere means to an end. Finally, both Amerigo and Charlotte are to fulfill their destiny as commodities in the fully capitalist economy in accord with whose operation the novel resolves its conflicts, although theirs destinies are to be different.[26]

The Prince, who initially lacks any use-value for the Ververs, acquires one because a demand is created for him, a demand which takes the form of Charlotte's renewal of their bond. In other words, if the Prince's value for Maggie has always been expressed in his attractiveness to other women, Charlotte actualizes that value into a positive demand which threatens Maggie with the loss of the Prince. Maggie must now purchase Amerigo herself, and at the price of her father—a price whose magnitude testifies to how much Charlotte's liaison with the Prince has increased his value. In retrieving the Prince, Maggie realizes a sizable profit on her father's initial investment, thanks to Charlotte, whose "unhappiness," as Maggie graciously acknowledges, was "necessary" to "build . . . up and start" her own initiation as capitalist. The process begun by Adam (M–C–M) is completed by Maggie when she pays for the Prince at the price of her father. In exchange, she herself is "paid in full" with a Prince whose exchange-value has appreciated as a result of Charlotte's demand. Unlike Amerigo, Charlotte was purchased in the first place for her use-value; she was to make the Ververs' life grander and to put Maggie's conscience at ease. Although in the end she fulfills a different purpose, Charlotte's destiny as commodity proves true to its origins since it is to be fulfilled by her use, while the Prince's, true as well to his origins as a commodity with exchange-value, is to be achieved by the value he has accrued.[27]

If the novel begins with an exchange viewed through the Prince's eyes as C–M–C, it ends with another exchange, viewed through Maggie's eyes as M–C–M. Between its opening and closing pages, the novel has reconstituted its world on the basis of a capitalist economy in which "the valorization of value" outstrips the mere satisfaction of human desires.

It is true, of course, that Maggie all along appears to be working out her design in order to satisfy her own desire for the Prince's devotion, but even Maggie's sexual desire for the Prince—so long suppressed by her need to reorchestrate their arrangement—is finally treated in monetary terms. In the novel's closing scene, as Maggie awaits the Prince, her suspense is described as that of "the creature to be paid" as to the "certification of the amount." When the Prince appears, Maggie sees him as "holding the money-bag for her to come and take it." From the outset, when the Prince sees Charlotte as a "long, loose silk purse, well-filled with gold pieces," James has depicted the sexual object of desire as itself the repository of money. Thus the Prince's proffered money-bag may signal the satisfaction of a desire, but that desire has long since acquired its primary meaning as a "passionate chase after value." Maggie, in fulfilling her desire, has effectively joined that chase. The novel, then, depicts "the creation of 'interests that [are] the extinction of other interests," in the words James uses to describe Adam's career as capitalist. Even Maggie's final reward, product though it is of her self-transformation into Lukács' "subject 'in action'" who adopts a vantage point from which the world conforms to her "best interests," arrives in terms which register "extinction" as well as "creation." Charlotte and the Prince, in fulfilling their destiny as commodities, have become "high expressions . . . of human furniture," attesting to the "rare power of purchase." Whatever "natural and human qualities" they had possessed have been submerged as a source of value because money is now the "active concept of value" which "confounds and exchanges everything." The Prince's personal, single self is nowhere in evidence in the novel's closing scene, save as the impotent observer he was in its opening chapter. The difference is that his vision has narrowed itself considerably; while he had begun by surveying the marketplace to be placed in his grasp by Adam Verver, he has been engulfed by that marketplace, whose high priestess he now worships. The world he had set out to discover, as the second Amerigo, is now reduced to Maggie herself, for he sees "only" her. And Charlotte's value has been transformed so that it now resides in her "mastery of the greater style," the style by means of which she has learned to hide her loss and her pain. It is no wonder that Maggie, the visionary seer, is last seen with her eyes "buried" in the Prince's "breast" out of "pity and dread" of his devoted gaze.[28]

Before examining Maggie's "sublime economy," it is worth stressing that the novel's resolution is accomplished on grounds which presuppose a commodified world. What makes the Prince's condition peculiar, for example, is not that he is a commodity; this, after all, he has readily consented to become in exchange for Maggie's fortune. In marrying her, he acts as both buyer and seller, selling his antenatal history in order to purchase a scientific future. What distinguishes his situation is that his business transaction, itself conceived as an act of self-initiation into the marketplace world, seems to remove him from that world, whose "machinery" he is so eager to embrace. Because of his peculiar status as an art object hoarded by the Ververs, he is artificially suspended above the stream of circulation, a condition which stands in conflict not with his status as man, but with his status as commodity, for commodities must change hands. By the end of the novel, of course, this is essentially what has taken place. The Prince's use-value has been proven in the only way possible—through another exchange. When Maggie pays for him by giving up her father, the Prince can at last assess his own worth to her—although he is able to assess little else.

Once we comprehend the Prince's situation in these terms, it should be clear why it is pointless to draw back in shock from the spectacle James presents in this novel—of men and women bought and sold in the marketplace; to do so amounts to a sentimental denial of the premise on which the novel proceeds to resolve the conflicts whose development it records—that the world is a marketplace. No one in *The Golden Bowl* is exempt from the force of commodification; everyone either bears a price tag or can be seen examining one, deciding whether or not to pay the price. In short, commodification is not something to be overcome; it defines the state of the world in which everyone lives, and when the "sublime economy of art" is demonstrated through Maggie's success in retrieving her husband's affections, it operates to redeem the Prince's "hard, latent *value*" by allowing his real status as commodity to be expressed and recognized. To realize one's value in such a world is to fulfill one's destiny either as a commodity in the marketplace or as a capitalist presiding over it. But in order for Amerigo's destiny as commodity to be fulfilled, Maggie's destiny a capitalist must be accomplished.[29]

As I have suggested, Maggie's primary action consists in stepping outside the picture to assume the contemplative stance of the detached observer. Even this act, however, is represented as an act of vision, for when Book 2 opens, Maggie is already situated outside the picture. It is her recognition of this fact which James depicts in the opening pages of the novels's second half, for it is this process of recognition which serves to register and to authenticate her detached stance.

At first, Maggie simply finds herself standing apart, scrutinizing the "funny form" of her family's life together. Maggie has, "for months and months," "carried on her existence in the space left her for circulation" outside the "outlandish pagoda" which "figured the arrangement" of the Ververs' peculiar married life, but only recently has she "ceased merely to circle," and stepped "unprecedently near." Having "ceased to take comfort in the sight" of this "ivory tower, visible and admirable doubtless, from any point of the social field," Maggie has "knocked" on "one of the rare porcelain plates," and heard "a sound sufficiently suggesting that her approach had been noted." The pagoda itself, like James's "house of fiction," is marked with "apertures and outlooks" "far aloft," but has no door. Thus, if Maggie's "raised eyes" contemplate these windows in the bizarre structure from her own "garden level," she is equally aware of the possibility that she is being watched from within. Although she has again "sought . . . a measure of relief" in "renewed circulation," she has nonetheless "done, a little, something she was not always doing" by stopping to contemplate with a critical interest the "funny form" around which she moves. Much as Adam has been described as enjoying "the great clearance" of space around the "palladian church" representing the Prince, Maggie has space to move, albeit "a space that sometimes seemed ample and sometimes narrow." But if as church, the Prince "hadn't proved angular" for Adam, the pagoda has begun to disturb Maggie. In this vision, Maggie knocks on the wall of the pagoda, as if "for admission." But if she seems to want in, the need to be admitted in itself signals the fact that she is outside the building, and it is this posture of exclusion and detachment which is both reinforced and activated by James's next elaborate figure for Maggie's situation.[30]

As Maggie sits before the fire, waiting for the Prince to dress for dinner, she examines a "projected vision" in which the "arrangement" has become a "family coach" pulled by Amerigo and Charlotte, while Maggie and her father "were seated inside together, dangling the Principino." As she watches it pass, she sees herself "suddenly jump from the coach." The picture suggests to Maggie first that "the exertion was *all* with" Charlotte and Amerigo, and second, that perhaps the peculiar form of their lives is after all a result of the fact that she has "abandoned *them*." She therefore sets out to correct both of these failings on her part by offering the Prince "the flower of participation." In other words, she wants to shoulder her part of the burden, the exertion of making the family coach move, and thereby to make up for having abandoned them. Inaugurating her plan for renewed participation, she tries to take up a position trotting alongside Charlotte and Amerigo, as it were, eagerly intent upon sharing with them both "whatever the enjoyment, the interest, the experience might be." But she soon discovers that they are intent upon "preventing her freedom of movement." They insist, as it were, that she stay in the coach with her father. "The word for it," Maggie decides, "was that they were *treating* her, that they were proceeding with her—and, for that matter, with her father—by a plan that was the exact counterpart of her own. It was not from her that they took their cue, but—and this was what in particular made her sit up—from each other." Only with this discovery does Maggie face the full significance of her detached stance, for she now recognizes that "they were arranged—all four arranged," but while Amerigo and Charlotte were arranged together, "she . . . was arranged apart."[31]

Like Amerigo at the beginning of Book 1, his "fate . . . sealed," and like Charlotte, "fixed as a pin stuck, up to its head, in a cushion," after her marriage to Adam, Maggie regards herself as placed in an arrangement "sustained by an ideal distinguishably different from her own." But the crucial difference between Maggie's apprehension of her fixed condition and Charlotte's or Amerigo's apprehension of theirs is that Maggie's is grounded in, and derives initially from, her assumption that she has participated in making the arrangement. That is, when Maggie enthusiastically inquires of each of them in succession about the Matcham house party, wishing to make up for her previous failure to share the burden of pulling the family coach, she is acting on the assumption that she has abandoned them, an assumption which reflects her belief that she has played a role in creating the "funny form" figured by the pagoda. The Prince, on the contrary, at the outset of his venture is in no position to assume that his marriage is the result of his own personal agency; purchased for a history he did not make but was made by, he relies on Fanny to discover what will be made of him as a result. By the same token, Charlotte's response to Adam's proposal is thoroughly conditioned by her insistence that she is not responsible for the outcome. She acts, that is, so that "it shouldn't be said she . . . had withdrawn from his view, so to speak, a single inch of her surface." Charlotte's interview with Adam consists, on her part, of a tissue of veiled warnings, for she insists upon according him the role of providing agent, while she assumes that of humble recipient. Further, she requires written notes of approval from Maggie and the Prince, as if to dramatize their implication in her acceptance. Both Amerigo and Charlotte, in short, read their situations as the product of other people's arrangements, nor are they altogether wrong to do so. For as Maggie herself realizes, "Charlotte had been 'had in,' as the servants always said of extra help," to meet a need, and the Prince had been purchased as "an object of price." In fact, of course, they too are finally implicated in the situation Maggie confronts, but they cannot see themselves as agents in the way she does, because they have never in fact been agents in the way she is, much less the way she is about to become at the beginning of Book 2. Their participation in creating the peculiar form she scrutinizes consists in reactions which follow from and testify to their shared assumption that their situation is wholly produced by others, a given condition in which they have somehow, mysteriously, been fixed and placed. When Maggie finds herself placed, "arranged apart," however, she is facing a set of conditions which she has, even if unwittingly, played a crucial role in creating, by virtue of marrying Amerigo and then neglecting him. Her role in producing the "funny form" is a necessary precondition for her final success at rearranging its contents; having made her world, she can, in Emersonian fashion, remake it in accord with her design. Yet in so doing, she demonstrates the consequences of reified vision, for her task of remaking serves to alienate her as seer from the world she remakes, the world in which she is seen. That is, if at the outset of Book 2, Maggie recognizes her role as participant (thereby facing the kind of crisis that erupts at the end of *The Sacred Fount*), the very act of recognition serves to place her outside the form she confronts. If she interprets her envisioned leap from the coach as a sign of her own implication in the peculiar form of her marriage, a sign that she has abandoned *them*, her efforts to join "them" generate a contradictory revelation—that she has already leapt from the coach by adopting the detached stance of the seer. Acting on the assumption that she has been a participant in the making of her world, she finds herself an alien observer of it. On the one hand, she then proceeds to act as the visionary artist, redeeming value; on the other, in so doing, she solidifies her own self-alienation as seer and seen. The crisis is recontained by a process which remakes the world in accord with the interests of one who stands, as seer, outside it, permanently severed from herself as a participant within it. That process is already under way in the elaborate conceits James constructs at the beginning of Book 2.[32]

As Maggie peruses the pagoda's surface, she is both the observer and the observed, watching from outside, but also watched from within by those looking down on her—as Charlotte and the Prince will, in fact, one day look down from the balcony at Portland Place when she returns from Regents Park with Adam and the Principino. The coach then appears in the form of a projected vision in which Maggie sees herself and interprets the behavior of the figure she sees; she now confronts herself "as if this person were somebody else," and she waits "with intensity" to see "what, in particular . . . the figure in the picture [would] do." Here again, she is in effect both Ralph Touchett and Isabel Archer, both seer and seen, but she is now watching herself as well, and so occupies both positions at once. But it is only with the failure of her effort to share the burden of exertion with Charlotte and Amerigo that the real implications of both visions stand revealed. She now recognizes that her imagined posture as both seer and seen—the posture implicit in the pagoda vision—is real, and rooted in the arrangement she has confronted, an arrangement whose form she has already begun to alter, not however by offering her "flower of participation," but rather by standing off to observe it. On the one hand, having leapt from the coach, she finds herself politely, tenderly, helped back into it. On the other hand, she remains the observer of this very operation, the detached seer who stands confronting her own picture, and stands there "very much alone." By virtue of the "light" it has "spread," her failure becomes "the perfection of . . . success," for she now recognizes her true position as that of the one "arranged apart," observing from a detached position no one yet knows she occupies. Merely by recognizing her detached stance, Maggie has already in fact leapt from the coach, even though she does not yet fully comprehend the consequences of that act—chief among which is that she has thereby abandoned her father. If the couple seated "inside together" and holding up the Principino to the windows of the coach as "an infant positively royal" is here Maggie and her father, at the end of the novel the royal couple will be Adam and Charlotte, whose "august emergence" from their "chariot" both Maggie and Amerigo will await as if anticipating the "visit of Royalty." But if Maggie has not yet faced the sacrifice of her father, she has already adopted the posture of the seer looking down on herself as seen by the others, and ready to rearrange the picture they see. By recognizing her stance outside the picture, as seer, Maggie has found that she is herself a figure seen by others. But if in that picture she is a figure seen as arranged with Adam, as seer she is in fact already utterly isolated.[33]

That isolation, moreover, proves definitive. Maggie's detached stance enables her to rearrange the picture she sees, but having rearranged it to suit her own ends, she solidifies her double posture as both seer and seen. At the novel's end, she will occupy a window far aloft, standing within the same balcony from which she "had seen Amerigo and Charlotte look down together at the hour of their return from the Regent's Park." Looking down now "from within" "the ivory tower," "to follow with her eyes her father's departure," Maggie will have taken possession of the pagoda. But, invisible to the creatures below and mystified in the Prince's eyes, the Maggie who has become a seer remains isolated, hidden behind the mask she has donned for the play she has directed, a mask which she can never remove since the play has been taken by everyone for reality. Indeed, it *is* reality, the only reality now remaining, for Maggie's design has recontained the crisis in which it was born by completing the process begun with her marriage, a process which reconstitutes her world as a wholly reified one.[34]

In order to appreciate how Maggie's design is accomplished, we need to understand the extent to which her world is already reified. Maggie is not alone in playing the double roles of observer and observed. Everyone in the novel plays this role. From the opening pages in which the Prince paces Bond Street, gazing into shopwindows, to the final scene in which Maggie watches her father's coach disappear, everyone plays the role of "a figure with a pair of eyes," and everyone is sooner or later subjected to the scrutiny of other people's eyes. Indeed, it is on the basis of everyone's double posture as seer and seen that the story told in the novel *gets* told, for events themselves are presented as visual acts. When, for example, Maggie, the Prince, and the Assinghams return from church to find Adam and Mrs. Rance in the billiard room at Fawns, the only events presented are a series of perceptual acts. Adam saw "the look in his daughter's eyes—the look with which he *saw* her take in exactly what had occurred in her absence: Mrs. Rance's pursuit of him to this remote locality." Maggie, in turn, "saw *him*" take in her look. Finally, Adam sees in Mrs. Assingham's face the evidence that "she had seen . . . what they were both seeing." Or again, when Charlotte first appears at Mrs. Assingham's, we are treated to a lengthy and erotically charged description of her through the Prince's eyes, while Charlotte deliberately does not meet his gaze; the event of her arrival is thereby translated into her offering herself to him as a vision to be consumed and his taking her as just that. Both of these "visual events" serve narrative purposes: the scene at Fawns serves the needs of the plot, leading as it does to Charlotte's invitation, and the scene at Fanny's establishes the power of the sexual attraction between the Prince and Charlotte.[35]

James's strategy here is not designed to represent the ordinary social interactions of ordinary people—however one defines the ordinary. Lest we forget, we are repeatedly being reminded just how extraordinary are the four principal characters in the drama, most often by Fanny Assingham. Yet even such transcendently extraordinary creatures lead lives behind the scenes in which they come to us as vehicles of vision, either monstrously perceptive or disastrously blind. There is, after all, a Principino in the distance, "ordered" forth from time to time, and we presume he is the consequence of some act not definitively visual. And we presume that the same unmentionable act takes place at Gloucester. Still, James has designed the novel in a way which privileges sight at every turn. What cannot be presented as seen through some character's eyes is not presented at all.[36]

Not only is the reader at the mercy of these exacting "exhibitional conditions," but so are the characters, for what people see, and the way they are seen, taken together, constitute social reality in this novel, where James testifies resoundingly to his claim that "experience is our apprehension and our measure of what happens to us as social creatures." People apprehend and then measure, watch and then interpret, acting on the cues they regard themselves as given by others. Like the poet in Wallace Stevens's "Of Modern Poetry," these people act, but they act on a stage, and in the only way the modern stage allows—as actors who lack a script and must improvise lines in response to the cues they read in the behavior of others.[37]

Thus, for example, when Charlotte arrives at Fanny's, and the Prince faces a small crisis in Fanny's absence, he waits for Charlotte to define the terms of their encounter. That it *is* a crisis for him is signaled by his immediate need to reasure himself that "he had done nothing he oughtn't." His conscience newly swept clear, he only waits "to learn how she proposed" "to arrange appearances" so that he might "help her, . . . arrange *with* her." After a few moments in which the Prince characteristically forces Charlotte to speak first, he finds that she "was arranging," and so "could be trusted to arrange." The "particular appearance she would . . . go in for,"— "that of having no account whatever to give him"—strikes the Prince as an admirable choice, and he immediately takes up the same line, helping her arrange. There is nothing particularly sinister about Amerigo's behavior here; he simply wants to be as much the gentleman as he can. In light of his understanding that the woman always gives herself away, the Prince's role as *galantuomo* is to help her

cover up this terrible fact. The task proves more difficult at their
next encounter, when Charlotte presses him for an hour of his time
in which to help her find a wedding gift for Maggie. The Prince finds
such a proposal "a little disconcerting . . . on the very eve of his
nuptials," and it requires more effort this time to respond to his cue
and fall in with Charlotte's arrangements. But fall in he does. In her
polite but resolute insistence, Charlotte compels him to agree in
order to avoid making her "beg of him." Such cruelty "would only
magnify," and he sees that he must minimize "fuss." "Apparent
scruples," he concludes, "were, obviously, fuss," and he again
finds the note to strike. "He was simply to be, with the girl, always
simple . . . that would cover everything." In both of these moments,
there is manifestly something to be covered, but for the Prince it is
not the history of his liaison with Charlotte itself which requires his
collusion in the appearances she arranges, but rather her abject pain,
her compulsory renunciation of him. As a *galantuomo*, he reacts
consistently in accord with his compassionate desire to help her
through this dark hour. Thus the deception of Maggie and her father
has already begun, and in response to the noblest of impulses. Charlotte arrives, heroically looking her loss in the face, and the Prince
falls in with her arrangement of appearances out of his desire to help
her through this crisis. The Prince's capacity for "immediate submission to the sight of what [is] clearest" makes him a party to the
deception of Maggie at the outset of his "new history."[38]

The Prince is not alone in taking his cues from others. The other
visual act we have mentioned—that of the mute communication in
the billiard room at Fawns—serves as a cue to both Maggie and
Fanny. Having seen Adam as besieged by Mrs. Rance, they both
take what they see as a cue to do something, and what they do is
to bring Charlotte to Fawns. Adam, in turn, reads Charlotte's presence—with a bit of interpretive aid from Fanny—as a cue to him,
a cue to which he readily responds. One might trace this process
all the way through to the renewal of Charlotte and Amerigo's relationship, a renewal which itself displays the same exchange of
cues.

After two years of marriage to Adam, Charlotte responds to the
cues she sees Maggie and Adam sending. As she explains to Fanny,
she has had "simply to see the truth of the matter—see that Maggie

thinks more, on the whole, of fathers than of husbands," and she proceeds to act in accord with her vision of the father and daughter as inseparable despite all her conscientious efforts to displace Maggie in her husband's affections. She cues the Prince on the basis of this vision, and he responds willingly; he exists in such a state of "abeyance" that he longs for nothing more than "the straight tip." Alone at Portland Place on that rainy afternoon, he is pondering how it is that this "was what it all came back to again with these people among whom he was married—that one found one used one's imagination mainly for wondering how they contrived so little to appeal to it." He is struck by the fact that he has not been called upon to do anything for them "worthy . . . of the personal relation," such as "plot or lie for them." Such services, after all "were consecrated to affection quite as much as to hate." Although such traditions represent, as he recognizes, "what he had once for all turned his back on" in marrying Maggie, they are after all the traditions embodied in the Prince's heritage, the antenatal history which gave him his exchange-value for the Ververs. Thus, when Charlotte gives him his cue, she calls upon him to perform precisely the services for which his heritage has trained him, and stimulates his imagination as it has not been stimulated since his marriage.[39]

It would seem that in Charlotte's eyes his public and his personal selves are no more separable than his use- and exchange-values are in Maggie's. But if for the Ververs, use-value is subsumed by exchange-value, for Charlotte, exchange-value is altogether lost in use-value; the Prince as Prince is no different for her from the Prince as the man she loves, a point which is clear from her attitude toward him as he rejoins her on the "monumental staircase" after dispatching Maggie home to her father:

she would have been half willing it should be guessed how she drew inspiration, drew support, in quantity sufficient for almost anything, from the individual value that, through all the picture, her husband's son-in-law kept for the eye, deriving it from his fine unconscious way, in the swarming social sum, of outshining, overlooking and overtopping.

Here, as is so often the case, Charlotte thinks of herself as being on exhibit. Nor is she unaware of Amerigo's exhibitional splendor. But unlike Maggie's pride, which is expressed in her desire to stand off and watch the Prince attract other women, Charlotte's pride in him is only fully expressible when she is the woman he attracts. If Charlotte has misread her cues, and in turn miscues the Prince, she does so out of an apprehension of his value as an individual in whom public and private selves are unified, and out of a quality of devotion to that individual of which no one else in the novel seems capable. It is this very unalienated vision, however, which both makes Charlotte valuable, and makes her blind to the Ververs' peculiar manners. For "the truth of the matter" as she sees it is in fact the truth; Maggie does on the whole favor fathers over husbands. What Charlotte cannot see, however, is that Maggie herself is capable of deception.[40]

In any case, Charlotte's apparent certainty about the Ververs' peculiar simplicity, once Amerigo has picked up the cue, relieves him of his own uncertainty about them. "The difficulty is, and will always be, that I don't understand them," the Prince confesses, but then accepts Charlotte's view—that Maggie and her father are "extraordinarily happy." Therefore, "it doesn't matter, really, that one doesn't understand," the Prince concludes, adding, "besides, you do—enough." So Amerigo's turning point is reached, characteristically, by a signal of his reliance on Charlotte's vision. Just as he waited for her to come upstairs upon seeing her arrive in the street, needing to "let her visit to him be all of her own choosing," so now he trusts himself to her eyes, again submitting to what is clearest. If his readiness to respond has already fostered the arrangement by which he and Charlotte have deceived Maggie, it now fosters his own self-deception. He has something to do, a service to perform, consecrated to the highest "privilege, duty . . . opportunity"—that of taking care of Maggie and her father, who are so "beatifically" happy with each other. He doesn't understand why this should be so. He doesn't even, doesn't especially, understand why Adam married Charlotte in the first place. But there they are, placed in circumstances which afford them the opportunity to live out a fabulous, a unique, destiny.[41]

The "funny form" which Maggie confronts at the beginning of Book 2, then, has arisen as a result of a process in which people are in turn seers and seen, readers and senders of cues. The point is, however, that no one save Fanny Assingham has yet occupied the stance of spectator watching the entire scene while at the same time remaining within it. By the end of Book 1, Fanny has been effectively silenced as a meddling participant in the arrangement which has developed out of her original conception. If she "was really at the bottom of it," as she admits, she is now removed to the position of impotent spectator. She can still read the cues, but she can no longer send them. Since Fanny's artistry serves as a foil to Maggie's in Book 2, it is important to understand Fanny's position.[42]

In her last dialogue with Bob in Book 1, Fanny has reached the summit of contrition. She confesses to having "fallen in love with the beautiful symmetry" of her plan out of the foolish belief that "one sees people's lives for them better than they see them for themselves." Her excuse is that "these people clearly *didn't* see for themselves." "They were," Fanny explains, "making a mess of such charming material . . . wasting it and letting it go." Charlotte in particular "was a piece of waste." In short, Fanny explains her behavior as arranger by reference to the same redemptive purpose of art which Maggie will fulfill, and James define, in the *Prefaces*. By this point, moreover, Fanny can see how the "funny form" has arisen, as a result of everyone's being so "improbably *good*," and of Maggie in particular, taking so seriously the job of making up to her father for her marriage, and then making up to the Prince for this by allowing him Charlotte "to cheer his path," and then by making up once more to her father for his resulting deprivation of Charlotte. Fanny can afford to see the vicious circle as begun by Maggie because she has now decided that Maggie will somehow save them all. But Fanny herself is now utterly helpless, as Charlotte has made abundantly clear by demonstrating her indifference to Fanny's disapproving eyes. From the moment Charlotte has decided to take advantage of her situation—a moment signaled when she publicly displays herself in relation to Amerigo at the "state" party—she immediately makes her intentions clear to Fanny, whose dismay Charlotte just as immediately dismisses as a sign of Fanny's failure of vision. Thus, when the Prince follows suit, Fanny remains an observer, but becomes an impotent one, because no one cares any longer what she sees. It is harder, of course, for the Prince to give up Fanny's eyes than for Charlotte to become indifferent to them, but once he does so, Fanny has lost her last shred of power in the world whose peculiar form she has unwittingly helped to create.[43]

Charlotte and Amerigo move "beyond" Fanny, in Charlotte's words, in two related senses. From Charlotte's point of view, they are beyond Fanny's understanding, but they are also therefore beyond the need to care how she sees them. In short, Fanny loses control over them as a seer from the moment she ceases to be for them a "pair of eyes" in whose field of vision they exist. From this moment on, they think they are unseen seers. Regarding themselves as beyond both Fanny's lapsed vision and the Ververs' simplicity, Charlotte and Amerigo behave in accord with a deluded belief that, as personal, private selves, they are unseen by anyone. As Maggie discovers, they are sending each other cues while assuming that no one else can read those they send each other. (Fanny does not need to read their cues any longer, of course, since she knows what they are doing, but her knowledge no longer matters.) Now, like Fanny, Maggie in Book 2 is a detached seer for whom the "funny form" has come into view. But unlike Fanny, Maggie is able to exercise power as seer because it matters enormously to Charlotte and the Prince how she sees them. In other words, Maggie has only to make herself felt as seer in order to terrorize them—which she knows full well when she explains to Fanny why Charlotte and Amerigo have just consented to attend another party together:

> They've been afraid not to—lest it should disturb me, aggravate me, somehow work upon me. As I insisted that they must, that we couldn't all fail . . . they had to yield to the fear that their showing as afraid to move together would count for them as the greater danger. . . . Everything that has come up for them has come up, in an extraordinary manner, without my having by a sound or a sign given myself away—so that it's all as wonderful as you may conceive . . . and that's how I make them do what I like!

Maggie's power, then, derives from her recognition that she is at once seer and seen. As with James's artist, everything here depends first on her capacity to see, but the "amount of doing" which Maggie goes in for depends as well on her being seen there watching, a "figure with a pair of eyes" in whose field of vision Charlotte and Amerigo finally move. Everyone in fact is both seer and seen, both the sender and the receiver of cues, but only Maggie recognizes this fact and exploits it to her advantage.[44]

From the moment Maggie steps outside the family coach, she remains within Charlotte's and Amerigo's field of vision only as an actress playing a role, thereby exploiting the very conditions already established in Book 1. If everyone acts on cue (in a kind of continuing play of the signifier) Maggie self-consciously acts by sending forth cues and quickly finds that "Charlotte had but wanted the hint" and the Prince "likewise only required . . . the straight tip." As an actress in the play she now watches from a distance, Maggie is always "heroically improvising" lines and thus cuing Charlotte and Amerigo in ways which first alarm them with the knowledge that they are themselves being watched, as if in a play, and then force them apart into new roles which are to put an ocean between them.[45]

Always watching from her detached position, Maggie never gives "a sound or a sign" to indicate how little she actually knows. As actress in the play she is silently directing, Maggie keeps to her role as innocent, first refusing to tell the Prince what she knows in the scene at Portland Place when he finds her in possession of the golden bowl, and then denying any knowledge at all of the plot—Maggie's plot now—when confronted by Charlotte in the drawing room at Fawns. In this last scene, Maggie again circles a building, but she is no longer denied a view inside its windows. By this time, Maggie's presence as seer has had its impact on everyone. As they sit playing bridge in the smoking room, Maggie circles the table and realizes that she is "more present to the attention of each than the next card to be played." "Watching them from her corner," she is also "holding them in her hand." When she retreats to the terrace and circles the house, she is even more forcefully aware that "her companions, watched by her through one of the windows" are figures in a "play of which she herself is the author." Pursued and brought inside again by Charlotte, Maggie delivers her lies with the mounting fervor of an actress who knows she will soon be allowed to rest. But as author, Maggie is now fully in charge of the play.[46]

If everyone is in truth both seer and seen, Maggie alone now controls what they see and how they are seen. Having seen the bridge party as Charlotte must see it, Maggie plays one final scene with Charlotte, this time pursuing the poor creature outside the house from which she has fled in terror. Charlotte has gotten the wrong volume of her novel; Maggie brings her the right one. Maggie lies once more, accepting the role Charlotte needs her to play—the role of the daughter who has worked against her mother-in-law's intimacy with her father. Insofar as Maggie remains within the field of Charlotte's vision, she remains there only to act out what she at least regards as fiction—all the while watching herself play the role she is improvising. At the novel's end, the Prince sees Maggie as an "infinite agent," about whose mysterious machinations he innocently wants to enlighten Charlotte. But Maggie cannot allow him to enlighten Charlotte, any more than Maggie can allow him to enlighten his wife by confessing to his adultery. For Maggie's power—the power which has brought him back to her as a worshipper—rests on her perceived status as a transcendent seer, a status which depends for its efficacy on their shared speechlessness. Knowing what she does at the end—that all she has contrived is a play but that the play is nonetheless real, and all that *is* real in a world constituted of actors responding to cues—Maggie is elevated to the balcony as seer, but she cannot, understandably, bear to look any longer.[47]

Maggie's self-imposed silence is crucial to the success of her redemptive design, for reasons which derive from the reified conditions which she exploits. It is, notably, Charlotte whose "way" is "systematically" to speak, as she tells Maggie in their climactic confrontation at Fawns. When Charlotte asks Maggie whether she has "any ground of complaint," she speaks from her "natural desire to know," a desire which, as she quite accurately remarks, Maggie has done "little justice." It is not that Charlotte herself is incapable of lying, of course; James makes it clear from the outset how readily Charlotte can do so when he presents her lying to the Prince about the price of the bowl. But Charlotte's lies, as this incident itself proclaims, are inevitably transparent and self-exposing. Maggie's, on the contrary, are both opaque and self-validating. Maggie exhibits no natural desire to know, but instead a profound need neither to know nor to be known. For only by "not, by a hair's breadth, deflecting into the truth," can Maggie rearrange her world. The world thus reshaped in her interests has no place for any natural desire to know, and so Charlotte is doomed to inhabit "some darkness of space that would steep her in solitude and harass her with care."

Ultimately, Charlotte adopts her own saving interpretation of the role in which she has been cast when she accuses Maggie of working against her relationship to Adam. Like Maggie, she dons a mask for her appointed role in the play, and thus becomes, in Maggie's eyes, "splendid." But unlike Maggie, Charlotte never knows how she has been manipulated. The Prince is therefore led to pronounce her "stupid," because of her failure to understand Maggie. But as his bright idea about enlightening Charlotte indicates, he doesn't understand Maggie either. But he is no more "stupid" than Charlotte, after all. It is only that neither of them can be expected to understand what Maggie sees—that the "exhibitional conditions" upon which the new world she has brought to completion depend require submission and silence.[48]

It is a similar "submission and silence" which Henry Adams declares the most appropriate response to his world, a world whose waste struck him as forcibly as it did his friend James. For Adams, however, the waste was not "splendid," but simply appalling. Eventually, of course, it was to become just as appalling to James. With the outbreak of World War I, James was brought up short by a spectacle of human waste the likes of which shocked even his Olympian imagination. As he put it in a letter written in August, 1914,

The plunge of civilization into this abyss of blood and darkness by the wanton feat of those two infamous autocrats is a thing that so gives away the whole long age during which we have supposed the world to be, with whatever abatement, gradually bettering, that to have to take it all now for what the treacherous years were all the while really making for and meaning is too tragic for any words.

Nonetheless, within a matter of days, he was testifying, in another letter, to his faith that in the face of this "funeral pall of our murdered civilization," the writer "can still . . . *make* a little civilization, the inkpot aiding, even when vast chunks of it, around us, go down into the abyss." It was this same faith that James had expressed only six months earlier in a letter responding to one from Henry Adams. Adams' letter has been lost, but we can easily take James's word that it had been a "melancholy outpouring" marked by "unmitigated blackness." James agrees with Adams' viewpoint, but only by means of a remarkable transformation:

Of *course* we are lone survivors, of course the past that was our lives is at the bottom of an abyss—if the abyss *has* any bottom; of course, too, there's no use talking unless one particularly *wants* to. But the purpose, almost, of my printed divagations [James's recently published *Notes of a Son and Brother*] was to show you that one *can*, strange to say, still want to—or at least can behave as if one did. Behold me therefore so behaving— and apparently capable of continuing to do so. . . . You see I still, in presence of life (or of what you deny to be such), have reactions—as many as possible. . . . It all takes doing—and I *do*. I believe I shall do yet again— it is still an act of life. But you perform them still yourself—and I don't know what keeps me from calling your letter a charming one! There we are, and it's a blessing that you understand—I admit indeed alone—your all-faithful

Henry James

Whether Adams' letter could be thus made out as "charming" is a moot point, but James was right at least in one respect. For all his "unmitigated blackness," Adams had performed acts of life which violated his own stated principle that "silence, next to good temper, was the mark of sense." The holocaust which so shocked James was for Adams long overdue, but Adams had performed his own acts in the name of a purpose not so different from James's. Although James's "sublime economy of art" was unavailable to Adams, he nonetheless sought, like James, to preserve his civilization, even as vast chunks of it seemed to him to be going down into the abyss, and like James's, his effort led him to expose that abyss.[49]

Chapter Six

HENRY ADAMS:
THE POSTHUMOUS SPECTATOR

But we, who cannot fly the world, must seek
To live two separate lives: one, in the world
Which we must ever seem to treat as real,
The other in ourselves, behind a veil
Not to be raised without disturbing both.
—HENRY ADAMS, *"Buddha and Brahma"*

H ENRY ADAMS SHARED Emerson's inability to rest within the con-
fines of Boston, but although "his first steps led toward Concord," he could find no stopping place there. As he pointed out,
though "he did not lack the wish to be transcendental," he "perpetually fell back into the heresy that if anything universal was unreal
. . . it was his own thought, and not the thing that moved it." Adams'
disdain for the *type-bourgeois-bostonian* was only increased by his
belief that he himself never really escaped its limitations. He was
certainly not disposed to exclude Emerson from the Boston he allied
with the "Paris of Louis-Phillippe, Guizot, and de Tocqueville, as
well as the London of Robert Peel, Macaulay and John Stuart Mill,"
all of which he saw as "varieties of the same upper-class bourgeoisie."
He granted Emerson's protest against his world, but judged it
"naif."[1]
    Nevertheless by the time Adams made this judgment, his own
protest was aimed at a similar target—a society smugly settled into
its "ruts," and his critical project took a distinctly Emersonian turn
insofar as it was aimed at defining a basis for maintaining values

other than those dictated by commerce. Emerson moved to Concord but continued preaching, intent upon impressing his audience with his belief that they resided in a world defined by motion, so that they too might free themselves from their self-imprisonment in a bourgeois society confirmed by their Unitarian ministry as the final solution to the universe. A quarter of a century later, Adams left Boston only to find the same bourgeois society displaying itself in Paris and London, where "the system had proved so successful that even Germany wanted to try it, and Italy yearned for it." And, though famous for his irony, Adams was never more dramatically ironic than when he wrote his friend Charles Milnes Gaskell that he did "not care to imitate Carlyle and Ruskin and Emerson and all the rest of our protesting philosophers by trying to make a living by abusing the society of our time." That he did not care to make a living from such abuse is partly a result of the fact that he did not need to make a living at all, at least not after his marriage. But even more deliberately than Emerson, he enacted the role of the "candidate for truth," and remaining "aloof" and "afloat" made him far more abusive of his society than Emerson had ever been.[2]

   After his wife's suicide, Adams made a fetish of remaining aloof, of refusing to capitulate to the "unthinking corporations" of his age, but the role of observer to which he thereby committed himself did not lead to any ecstatic faith in his ability to build his own world. Quite the contrary. It led to profound doubt as to whether the world of relentless and accelerating motion he observed was even real, much less invested with a humanly convenient *telos*. As he confided to Henry Cabot Lodge, "what troubles me most has been always the sense of unreality. I cannot believe that it is not all a dream." Such a view had its benefits, particularly for a man deeply concerned about his responsibility toward the world he stood off to observe. If that world seemed unreal, its claims to one's active energies were silenced; one is not responsible for one's dreams. But Adams refused to allow himself this luxury. His denial of his own responsibility for his society's behavior assumed proportions too exaggerated to be taken at face value. Adams insisted on his role as spectator while behaving very much as if the drama he watched was real after all, and the most significant evidence of this behavior is *The Education of Henry Adams*.[3]

What made the world appear like a dream for Adams was his wife's suicide, but in *The Education* this appearance of unreality surfaces as a result of the crisis which Lukács was later to depict— that in which the irrational breaks through the surface of a rationalized, objective reality, revealing the contradiction between details "which are subject to laws" and "a totality ruled by chance." The "sum and term of education," according to Adams, arrived with the vision of the world to which he was treated as a result of his sister's death. The world suddenly stood revealed as

an insanity of force. For the first time, the stage-scenery of the senses collapsed; the human mind felt itself stripped naked, vibrating in a void of shapeless energies, with resistless mass, colliding, crushing, wasting, and destroying what these same energies had created and labored from eternity to perfect. Society became fantastic, a vision of pantomime, with a mechanical motion.

It is this eruption of "anarchic and purposeless forces" which Adams struggles to measure and control within a rational pattern in *The Education*. If "society became fantastic," Adams was nonetheless willing in the end, "to admit it real in the sense of having some kind of existence outside his own mind," but he "could not admit it reasonable," and so set about defining a rational program for comprehending it.[4]

Like Emerson, the Henry Adams whose education is recorded in the first twenty chapters of *The Education* confronts the "alien," the "unknown," and with it, the possibility that "all we have believed and chanted out of our deep instinctive hope is a pretty dream." Again and again, this young man encounters ignorance in those who are supposed to know, and impotence in those who are supposed to lead. His education ends in failure and his society is exposed as both smug and obtuse, "a vision of pantomime, with mechanical motion." In the second half of the book, then, Adams devises a strategy for bridging the gap between the "dream of man" for order and the apparently "purposeless forces" driving him, all unaware, into chaos, a strategy culminating in the "dynamic theory of history." Convinced that "the sequence of men led to nothing and that the sequence of their society could lead no further, while the mere sequence of time was artificial, and the sequence of thought was chaos, he turned at last to the sequence of force." The "anarchic

. . . forces" of nature which he had once seen embodied in Mont Blanc were by now erupting around him in the form of explosives, dynamos, and the discovery of radium, and so he undertook to "arrange" a historical sequence by measuring forces.[5]

How, then, does one measure a sequence of force, especially when "no one saw the same unit of measure" even in the other discredited sequences? Adams replied that in order to "reduce all these forces to a common value, this common value could have no measure but that of their attraction on his own mind." Man's reaction to force, in short, would have to serve as the "unit of measure" in the "sequence of force." It is with this purpose in view that Adams constructed *The Education*, where he inserts himself in history as "manikin" in order to measure the motion of force. The manikin, he insists, "has the same value as any other geometrical figure of three or more dimensions, which is used for the study of relation." Forced in effect to acknowledge his presence in the picture in order to bring it into focus, Adams objectifies himself, and the figure so objectified functions, as we shall see, as an observer. Set against the historical period to which he has been a witness, this observer serves as a register of its accelerated motion and force. In short, compelled to put himself in the picture, Adams puts himself there theorectically as a detached observer. But once Adams has thus climbed on the fence to watch himself go by, the figure in the procession turns real, as it were, exposing what Adams has tried to repress—that the figure was a participant in, as well as an observer of, the events whose progress he is designed to measure. In the preface, Adams was to acknowledge this ironic development with his characteristic evasiveness when he remarked of the manikin that "it must have the air of reality . . . must be treated as though it had life. Who knows? Possibly it had!"[6]

Faced with the limits of rationalization, Adams struggled to push the Kantian barrier of the thing-in-itself back so as to encompass and recontain the crisis, a procedure which required him to secure the neutral observer's detached contemplative stance. In Heisenberg's terms, Adams was trying to maintain "that idealization in which we can speak about parts of the world without reference to ourselves." The Adams who serves as manikin is objectified and referred to in the third person in order to safeguard the integrity of the picture being presented, and the objectivity of the sequence of force being measured. But because the "isolated system" to be scrutinized has already been punctured by the presence of the subject within the picture, and this in response to the incoherence of the picture without that presence, Adams is forced in the end to acknowledge the manikin's status as a living participant.[7]

It is because of this repressed recognition of his role as participant that Adams feels a responsibility toward his reader. Like Maggie Verver, he may occupy a detached stance as spectator, but he is also an actor in the play, and as such complicit in its outcome. The very writing of *The Education* presupposes Adams' recognition of his status as a participant, and the consequent responsibility to be discharged. The more pronounced his denial of that responsibility, the more evident is his sensitivity to it. While at work on *The Education* in 1906, he wrote his brother Brooks, wearily denouncing his contemporaries: "I cannot, for the life of me, see why I am called upon to instruct them. If any damneder fools ever lived on earth than my generation of Americans, my laborious studies have not discovered them, and the proof is that they were self-satisfied beyond record." But no matter how often and how vociferously Adams disavowed his need to instruct his "fellow-insects," he nonetheless harbored that need; his eighteenth-century values remained far too entrenched for him to abandon his faith in education altogether. As he said in a letter of 1892, life "has only two responsibilities, which include all the others: one is bringing new life into existence; the other, educating it after it is brought in." In short, Adams' disclaimers about instruction, like his loquacious insistence on the value of silence, are likely to seem as disingenuous as his disapproval of abuse as a vocation.[8]

In order to understand *The Education* in these terms, we must abandon certain well-worn attitudes toward Henry Adams. By the time he wrote *The Education*, Adams saw himself as an instance of failure whose only possible value lay in stating the lesson of that failure. His critics have largely followed his lead, dividing only on the question of what the lesson itself teaches: either the perils or the potential virtues of a defection from rational objectivity. Thus, according to Ivor Winters, Adams demonstrates the mental disintegration of which the "romantic tradition" to which he belongs harbors such an abundant supply. Speaking less caustically, William Jordy agrees with Winters in faulting Adams for allowing an emotional need for certainty to override intellectual rigor. Adams' admirers, on the other hand, do not defend him against such charges; rather, they value him for the very reasons that Winters attacks him. In their view, Adams was an artist whose genius for finding symbols to express his age was suppressed by his family's political vocation. As Robert Spiller puts it, Adams was "unable to reconcile his natural inclination to literature with the family directive toward action" until late in life when he overcame his inhibitions toward art and set about discovering "an organic aesthetic form." Thus Adams' failure becomes the occasion of literary valor, and teaches the lesson that art unifies and redeems what science and reason fail to achieve. This, however, was not the lesson Adams sought to teach, nor was it, I think, the most important lesson he himself learned from writing *The Education.*[9]

Adams' continuing power as an author does not stem from his indisputable literary skills alone; it stems as well from his tendency to unsettle his readers, calling into question the very rationalist assumptions "in defense of" which Winters presumes to speak. The defense of Adams on aesthetic grounds, moreover, no matter how insightful the critical exegesis to which it has led, would seem to be a form of self-defense as well. For once Adams is identified as a romantic—as he is by both Winters and Spiller—his radical insights can be neutralized; this accomplished, it matters little whether one excuses his scientific theorizing in the name of art, or derides it as a sign of mental disintegration. In either case, the threat posed by Adams' thought is neatly deflected, and we are relieved of the burden of taking seriously what he himself took seriously—the issue of education itself.[10]

Furthermore, to treat Adams as a case of romantic confusion, as Winters does, is to ignore the very real commitment to rationalism displayed throughout Adams' career as well as in *The Education* itself. For Adams ought to be taken at his word when he calls himself "a child of the seventeenth and eighteenth centuries." Had he not been intent upon defending the provenance of Reason against threats whose seriousness even an Ivor Winters could never have imagined, Adams would not have set out so diligently to find "a scale for the whole," or a "common ground" on which to establish an "agreement of view." What seems to lie behind this view of Adams— whether one attacks or celebrates the alleged defection from rationalism—is a tendency to see him as an artistic soul chafing at the family's political bit. But this is a false vision of Adams' career, which itself both testifies to his original desire for power and exposes the distortions which can follow from simply opposing art to life.[11]

In fact, Adams sought power from the outset of his career, and did so often against the wishes of his family, which occasionally seems to have thought him more suited to a literary vocation. When we examine that career it becomes clear that we ought to take with more seriousness than we have the description Adams gives in *The Education* of his attitude when taken to visit the White House at the age of twelve:

As for the White House, all the boy's family had lived there, and, barring the eight years of Andrew Jackson's reign, had been more or less at home there ever since it was built. The boy half thought he owned it, and took for granted that he should some day live in it. He felt no sensation whatever before Presidents. A President was a matter of course in every respectable family.

Despite Adams' coy tone, this is probably a fair statement of his expectations at the age of twelve. Indeed, why shouldn't it be? His grandfather and great-grandfather had both been presidents, and as late as 1859, Adams still expected to see his father in the White House. Political power was inherent in the name Adams, and Henry took his name with solemn respect, as his early aspirations indicate. That he took up a pen in response to those aspirations rather than running for or accepting office reflects not a retreat from the family's historic commitment to political power, but an intelligent "reaction"—to use one of Adams's favorite words—to social and political developments which in effect resolved the "feud between Quincy and State Street" by elevating the capitalist values of the latter over the republican values of the former. In this "capitalist society" ruled by the "bankers," to hold political office was either to serve State Street, or to resist it at the cost of becoming a "caged rat." Adams saw that "[John] Hay needed no office in order to wield influence," and he saw as well that such political influence as could be exercised by an Adams in defense of "his eighteenth century" and "his Quincy" would have to be built on a different basis than political office, assuming it could be built at all. In the early years of his career, Adams tried to make journalism his base of influence. When that course was blocked, his adherence to his eighteenth-century ideals in the face of State Street's mounting dominance tended increasingly to nourish his snobbish disaffection and detachment. But his posture of lofty disdain grew at least partly out of the frustration of his early ambitions, ambitions whose disappointment reflect as much upon the social changes he witnessed as upon the character of Henry Adams. The political fortunes of the Adams family, insofar as it remained faithful to its principles of republican virtue, were doomed by the rise of State Street, a fact to which both *The Education* and Adams' career testify abundantly. We need to have that career in focus in order to appreciate the rhetorical purposes informing *The Education*, purposes stemming at least in part from a repeatedly deflected quest for power and influence.[12]

When Adams sailed for Europe in 1858, he had a plan. He would spend two years abroad, learning Latin, French, and German, and studying law in preparation for two years of legal studies at home. Then he would go to St. Louis and practice law, which he thought would provide "a support to fall back on if necessary," but would mainly serve as "the best grounding" for any future career. Henry defended this plan against the criticism of his older brother Charles, who seems to have appointed himself Henry's chief counselor while he was abroad and beyond the reach of the family counsel. Charles opposed Henry's plans for a career in law, urging him to write, but the literary vocation Charles proposed drew nothing but refusals from Henry, who confessed himself no wit, and expressed contempt for the role of "a writer of popular sketches in magazines; a lecturer before lyceums and College societies; a dabbler in metaphysics, poetry and art.'' But he was not averse to writing per se, and in fact prophetically proposed as his first publishable work, a piece on "Prussian schools.'' Nonetheless, he saw writing as a means to an end, an adjunct to more serious endeavors. "Adams the scholar prefers to live,'' he wrote Charles,

but Adams the scholar would rather disconsolately die and let Adams the lawyer do as he can than make one of that butterfly party which New Yorkers seem to consider their literary world. To become more, the law must be my ladder; without it, you might as well at once press me out into so many pages of *The Atlantic Monthly.*

The law, in short, offered a position from which to "work *up,*'' and Adams clearly planned to work up the ladder of power. His theory was "that an educated and reasonably able man can make his mark if he chooses.'' Should he fail to do so, as he put it, "why, then,—I fail and that's all. . . . But if I know myself, I can't fail.'' Nor at this point did he see the Adams family as declining; indeed, assuming that it retained "the requisite ability,'' he expected the "house of Adams'' to "get its lease of life renewed'' in the impending political crisis.[13]

A certain Franklinesque tone, as well as an air of fraternal competition, marks Adams' outlook here. Henry was doubtless struggling to maintain his chances alongside two older brothers, one already a politician and the other studying law for the same reasons Henry planned to do so. As Henry was later to point out to his friend Gaskell, "My father and brothers block my path fatally, for all three stand far before me in the order of promotion.'' In 1858, Henry was biding his time, refusing to give in to his brother's arguments against the law as ladder. Attractive as Europe became to him as a treasure of aesthetic experience, he stuck to his plan, returning to Washington and his parents' establishment in the center of congressional politics to pursue his course in the law. But he found in Washington too many opportunities to wait another two years before working his way up the ladder. He began writing secret letters to the Boston *Advertiser* and finally produced the "Great Secession Winter of 1860–61,'' a culmination of his observations during the chaotic events leading up to Lincoln's election. With this course of action he was "well-satisfied,'' as he wrote Charles, since his letters to the

Advertiser "had some good influence in shaping the course of opinion in Boston." For the next decade, journalism would continue to serve as his primary means for exerting influence.[14]

When in 1861 Charles Francis Adams was appointed to the Court of St. James, Henry gave up his legal studies to accompany his father as a private secretary—a job he had already been doing in Washington while helping to influence opinion in the interests of his father's party by his journalism. Although upon his arrival he wavered between his obligation to his father and his impatience to share with Charles the risks of the Civil War itself, Adams opted for England on the ground that his role there would prove more useful to the Union cause. Incidentally, of course, it might prove more useful to Henry's ambitions as well. Simply being a member of the Adams family, now settled in London, and deeply involved in the war's most delicate and important diplomatic mission, placed him on the scene of the power brokers. His anonymous correspondence with the *New York Times* gave him access to the public, whose opinion he tried once again to shape in order to pressure William Seward, the Secretary of State, into waking up to the British threat. It was this position which Adams felt most suited to occupy—close to the scenes of power, but working behind them with his pen. In Washington he had found this position both useful and exhilarating; in London it proved frustrating and guilt-producing, as he was wont to complain to Charles. His brother replied by urging him to quit the legation and strike out on his own in the British press. But Henry reminded Charles that the legation provided his sole source of information. The family's position in London placed him in a position to watch events and write letters to the American press which might influence the course of those events, however indirectly. Furthermore, he occupied a traditional family training post. For three generations Adamses had been diplomats, and Henry's father and his grandfather had both begun their political careers as secretaries to their fathers' diplomatic missions.

Further, Henry found himself in a propitious spot for a young man of twenty-three. His behavior as a journalist, moreover, showed no timidity; on the contrary, it exhibited a good deal of eagerness and no small degree of hubris, for he wrote, boldly, of an impending war with England. Like the narrator of *The Sacred Fount*, however, Henry Adams' secret status as spy was finally exposed.[15]

Anonymity was crucial to his self-appointed mission as influential journalist. His own father was unaware of the private vocation of his private secretary, and as Henry well knew, his father's delicate mission would be severely compromised if Henry's journalistic identity was revealed. Thus, when his article on the Manchester cotton industry, rerouted to the Boston *Courier*, was accidentally published with his by-line, his career as a secret journalist came to an abrupt halt. He could not afford to continue, lest his *New York Times* correspondence be similarly exposed. Although he forestalled this danger, Adams was nonetheless stung by the sarcasm with which the London press derided him for his jocular remarks about the refreshments served at a Manchester ball. He wrote Charles saying

my most efficient channels of action are now cut off . . . I feel ashamed and humiliated at leading this miserable life here, and since having been blown up by my own petard in my first effort to do good, I haven't even the hope of being any more use here than I should be in the army.

Minor though this incident may appear, it signals a recurrent pattern of forced retreat to higher ground in Adams' life. Accepting a position close to those wielding power, Adams had set out to exploit his opportunities for acquiring it. This opportunity now lost for the moment, he took a step back and looked to the future. He reassessed his talents, but not his ultimate goals. As he told Charles, he recognized that his mind was "balanced . . .in such a way that what is evil never seems unmixed with good, and what is good is always streaked with evil . . . in short, a mind which is not strongly positive and absolute," and therefore one which "cannot be steadily successful in action." Forced though he was into this honest reappraisal of his own temperament, however, he did not lose his interest in power. His ambitions were deflected from the immediate field of action, but this only stimulated him to dream larger dreams of power. He went on, for example, to propose to Charles the need of a "national school for our own generation" which might "start new influences not only in politics, but in literature, in law, in society, and throughout the whole social organism of the country." As he was pushed back from immediate participation, the scope of his imagined power widened.[16]

Deflected from the law and impressed by his experience in London with the futility of public office, Adams wrote Charles of his revised plans on the eve of his return to America:

> I never will make a speech, never run for an office, never belong to a party. I am going to plunge under the stream. . . . I do not mean to tie myself to anything, but I do mean to make it impossible for myself to follow the family go-cart.

Since the family go-cart was not proceeding with much speed in any case, this decision hardly reflects a resigned abandonment of his ambitions. On the contrary, Adams thought he could exercise more influence by becoming a congressional critic serving the interests of political reform than by repeating the failures of his brother John, who was always running for Congress and losing. Henry instead would exploit the observer's role to which he was becoming accustomed; he would be the unseen seer, the invisible observer, and—perhaps some day if all went well—the unmoved mover. When he returned to Washington in 1868, Henry took up his pen once again, and wrote the first two of what he planned as a series of articles on the annual session of Congress, these to follow upon, and make a tradition of, his "Great Secession Winter." As he was later to put it in *The Education*, it was this "permanent series of annual political reviews" which "he hoped to make, in time, a political authority," for "such a power, once established, was more effective than all the speeches in Congress or reports to the President that could be crammed into Government presses." His political perspective remained that of an Adams, but he was now directly tied not to his family's political fortunes, but to those of reform. In 1870, with Grant in office, he wrote a fellow reformer, in a gleeful mood, "It is to be regretted that the President does not know what Revenue Reform means, but I think we shall teach him as much as he will be able to learn before long."[17]

As Adams ironically anticipated, Grant proved a case for remedial instruction, and the reform movement made slight headway. Nonetheless, Adams pressed on, producing in "The Legal Tender Act" what he proudly described as "a piece of intolerably independent political abuse." Adams' theories on currency remained those of a committed eighteenth-century liberal preaching laissez-faire economic theory. His next piece, "The New York Gold Conspiracy," reflected the traditional Adams sense of moral probity, but exhibited perhaps more of the Adams capacity for abuse than his family was willing to see in print. It was a venomous exposé of Jay Gould's effort to corner the gold market, and it brought Grant under suspicion of complicity with Gould. Published both in America and in England, the article stimulated widespread discussion, and confirmed Adams' eminence as an influential political critic. Curiously, it was at this point that, as he put it in *The Education*, his family "set on him to drag him away" to Harvard. Whatever his family's motives—and it is difficult to avoid the conclusion that the piece on Gould had something to do with them—Adams relented in the end, no doubt in part because he was offered the editorship of the *North American Review* along with the teaching post; the *Review* at least gave him an authoritative platform from which he might "start new influences," as he had once proposed doing to Charles. Without this rider, it is difficult to see Adams accepting the post at all. That he sorely regretted the decision to give in to his family's wishes is evident from the evasive irony with which he describes his reasons for doing so in *The Education*: "The good people who thought it did matter had a sort of right to guide. One could not reject their advice; still less disregard their wishes." Such good people's authority is, of course, thoroughly discredited in the course of *The Education*. However one explains Adams' acceptance of the teaching post at Harvard, it is clear that he at first declined it unequivocally, and for a reason he did not fail to state clearly. He wrote Charles Eliot,

The offer you make me is not only flattering but brilliant, yet I cannot accept it. Two years ago I should have hesitated long before deciding, but, having now chosen a career, I am determined to go on in it as far as it will lead me.

The career he had chosen was the one in Washington from which he was now deflected.[18]

Once at Harvard, however, Adams made the best of his circumstances, promptly soliciting reform articles and turning the *Review* to his own purposes. He wrote Samuel Tilden asking for a piece on the "Tammany Frauds" to accompany his brother's article on the Erie Railroad, and he asked Simon Newcomb for an article on the "effect of our currency laws" on the current "emergency," which Adams thought it strange that no one had foreseen. Just as previously in England, where his forced retreat from secret journalism allowed him to read and review Charles Lyell's latest work, Adams' forced retreat from Washington now allowed him to indulge in a study of Anglo-Saxon law. As he moved back from the present scene, awaiting a better chance to direct it, but feeling a growing sense of lost opportunities, he pursued a study of history which was eventually to lead him to see the present as a tiny episode in the large scale of time, and thus to question the value of participating in it at all. Lyell had stretched the earth's age into eternity, and now his own inquiry into German law led Adams in turn to develop an interest in anthropology. Each time circumstances forced him to retreat, he became more the observer of, and less a potential participant in, the political struggle. His sole consolation was that from the vantage point of even higher ground, the participants in the struggle he watched seemed to diminish in size and importance.[19]

Accordingly, when he returned to Washington with his wife in 1877, he occupied himself with writing a biography of Albert Gallatin, while observing politics with an eye for the absurd and a sometimes complacent disdain for his former colleagues, the "children of light." Despite his growing skepticism, he still gave aid and solace where he could. No longer a journalist himself, he nonetheless stayed in touch with editors friendly to reform causes. Writing to E.L. Godkin at the *Nation*, he insisted, "To talk here is henceforward sheer waste of energy. It is to the people that the talking must be done, and it will have to be very emphatic." To Henry Cabot Lodge he remarked, "As usual the pessimists talk of the end of the world. I confess to being more interested in the practical working out of the situation." Meanwhile he worked on *The History of the United States of America*. His focus widened to the beginning of the century, and he addressed himself directly to the course of the American experiment in democracy. From this detached position, Adams came to see contemporary Washington and its corruption as part of a much longer story, whose beginning he was busily documenting, and whose end provoked increasing curiosity. The wider the scope of his vision grew, the stronger his suspicion became that even the most astute statesmen were impotent to shape historical development. Gallatin alone seemed to him a possible exception to the rule that "the element of individuality" had little to do with the direction taken by history. In 1884 Adams wrote Francis Parkman of his growing suspicion that man might soon be proven "to have as fixed and necessary a development as that of a tree; and almost as unconscious." Meanwhile, however, Adams remained in close touch with his political cohorts in the liberal wing of the Republican party. When Chester A. Arthur took office in 1881 and began enacting reforms, Adams signalled Godkin to send Carl Schurz on apace to Washington to see the president. No matter how impotent he regarded Washington's political leaders as being, he devoted a good deal of energy to bringing pressure where and when he could through his widespread connections with editors and liberal politicians. Only after December 6, 1885 did Adams assume the role of posthumous person. Here again, and for the last time, circumstances severed Adams from foundations he had built for wielding power indirectly. But this crisis proved far more decisive than any previous one.[20]

As Adams was later to tell Elizabeth Cameron, looking back on his career, the "light" had "gone out" at this point, although he was "not to blame." "As long as I could make life work," he insisted, "I stood by it and swore by it as though it was my God, as indeed it was." There is a good deal of evidence to support this testimony. Until his wife's suicide, Adams remained in touch with the world and devoted considerable energy to influencing at least that part of it centered in Washington. The Harvard professor's sphere of influence was a good deal narrower than that which Adams had once envisioned when he proposed founding a national school which would "start new influences," and the *History* was aimed at a smaller audience than "The New York Gold Conspiracy," but Adams had nonetheless fulfilled one ambition. He had returned to

Washington and taken up a position as the "stable-companion to statesmen." If he was a mere spectator, he was critically vocal one. After 1885 the spectator became silent for many years.[21]

It is impossible to overstimate Marion Adams' suicide as a force in Adams' subsequent life and thought. Oblique references to it punctuate his correspondence for the rest of his life, especially as the date of the event approached each year. Moreover, when others suffered a similar loss Adams unfailingly referred to his own, sometimes in telling ways. For example, when the John Hays lost a son in an accident in June 1901, Adams waited a month and then wrote Mrs. Hay, expressing regret that he had been too far away to be of any use. He went on to explain his deliberate delay in sending a letter of condolence:

For writing, I knew that you would be overwhelmed with letters. I knew too that almost anyone would say more than I knew how to do, for I never have learned yet that anything could be said, when silence is all that is left. I was afraid even of doing harm; for the one idea that was uppermost in my mind was that when I was suddenly struck, sixteen years ago, I never did get up again, and never to this moment recovered the energy or interest to return to active life.

Adams goes on to offer any help Mrs. Hay may wish of him, but confesses,

As a matter of medical opinion, I should say that I was not altogether the best sort of help or tonic to persons needing strength and courage. It is so long since I have got in the habit of thinking that nothing is worth the while! That sort of habit is catching, and I should not like to risk too close contact at a critical moment with a mind disposed to be affected by it.

Adams offers his aid and then derides its force, noting the infectious quality of his despair. His fear of doing harm speaks explicitly to Mrs. Hay's, to any survivor's, fragile condition, but speaks as well of Adams' complex psychological defenses. When we recall the extended period in which Marion Adams had been herself a survivor following her father's death, Adams' letter implies even more than it confesses. A "mind disposed to be affected" by nihilistic despair over the loss of her father fairly describes Marion Adams during the months preceding her suicide. Adams' fear of doing harm, one can easily infer from the circumstances, must have had a poignant history. In any case, a mixture of guilt and impotence is apparent in Adams' response to Mrs. Hay's tragedy. Clearly enough, his fear of doing harm derives from a keen sense of the guilt that may flow from even the slightest form of human action; in this letter Adams combines offers of help with such an overstated fear of the possible danger of any help he might provide that one is led to infer a rather outsized conception of his own power. At the same time he invokes such a profound sense of his own impotence—he has, after all, never gotten up again after being struck down sixteen years ago—that his fear of having any effect at all seems strangely out of place. Touched deeply by his closest friends' tragic loss, Adams inadvertently reveals the fragile balance by means of which he sustained his sanity throughout his later years.[22]

The loss of his wife by suicide brought home the issue of impotence on the most personal terms. From his own point of view, Adams had begun his career by wanting to "do good," but he had found he could do very little, and even that little might paradoxically turn into harm. By accepting the detached stance to which circumstances had led, and to which his own temperament suited him, he had minimized the immediate harm he could do in the world while aiming at a more lasting, if less immediately visible, good. But his wife's suicide forced him to recognize that, even at the distance he had put between himself and the world, he might still find himself guilty of doing harm. His letter to Mrs. Hay shows that, sixteen years after the fact, the fear "even of doing harm" was still strong in him. As a defense against this fear he pleaded impotence, his permanent incapacity to summon "the energy or interest to return to active life." The suicide of the one person in his life over whose fate he might have presumed to have some effect must prove his final impotence, unless it was to prove his final guilt. His defense against guilt, then, was the repeated profession of posthumous existence by means of which he affirmed his impotence. But the defense proved less than successful in the end, for in addition to the obvious and endless pain it inflicted on him, his wife's suicide enforced a recognition of responsibility from which he could not wholly escape.[23]

So silent was Adams on this subject that we cannot be sure of any inferences we may draw. My own opinion, however, is that rather than confirming Adams' hypotheses about man's impotence as a historical creature, his wife's death led him eventually to accept a responsibility, if not to the world as he had left it, at least to the world of his nieces and nephews. In any case, it would be a mistake simply to attribute the later Adams' notorious pessimism to his sense of personal impotence; he was far too self-conscious to project, blindly and willfully, his own impotence on society. The evidence suggests rather that his wife's suicide led first to a more entrenched detachment, but eventually to a review of his own life, a review conducted to answer the question of whether his own failure had any useful lessons to teach the future.

Whereas before he had fancied himself standing on a "stool high enough to see the crowd"—and presumably high enough to catch its attention from time to time— he now adopted the role of a self-consciously indifferent spectator:

When one cares for nothing in particular, life becomes almost entertaining. I feel as though I were at a theatre—not a first class but a New York theatre.

He played with the metaphor when it suited him, laughing sardonically about how he "always did like the theatre," though admitting that his "only ambition was to write the play." The old hubris is still there, as it had been from the start, working in Adams' mind to make even this obstinate pose of passivity an artificial defense against his long-thwarted desire for power. The pose assumes its most exaggerated form when Adams portrays himself as a posthumous person. As he put it in a letter to a friend thirteen years after Marion's death,

When one has eaten one's dinner, one is bored at having to sit at the table. Do you know that I am sixty in six weeks, and that I was only forty-seven when I finished my dinner?

He could sometimes astonish people with this pose, as when he refused an invitation to address the American Academy of Arts and Letters by saying to its president, "Do you know, Mr. Johnson, that I have been dead for fifteen years?" The pose served to support his need for privacy, and allowed him to remain in his seat, simply watching the spectacle and repeating to himself the question of whether it was tragedy or farce, while awaiting his impending demise. But Adams incoveniently lived on until 1918, and he did not by any means remain passive. The year 1893 found him in Europe, where he received news of the financial panic at home. At this point the play he had been watching in a desultory manner took on new interest.[24]

Arriving in Quincy for a hurried conference over the family finances, Adams found he was solvent and returned to Washington to watch the show. His letters now take on a new excitement. "Much aweary, but rather amused," he reports to Hay that the "quite lunatic gold-bug" has made him "a flat-footed Populist and an advocate of fiat money. This is clever of them." He found Washington in a state of chaos that he took keen delight in observing. He recognizes his own excitement in another letter to Hay: "My lunacy scares me. I am seriously speculating whether I shall have a better view of the *fin-de-siècle* circus in England, Germany, France or India, and whether I should engage seats to view the debacle in London or Paris, Berlin or Calcutta." His brother Brooks shared his developing theories about the crisis with Henry, who began to pore over State Department statistics and stock-market reports. Long convinced that he was out of phase with his time, Adams commented, "for once I feel myself in the spirit of the age." Europe did not collapse with the speed he anticipated, but the panic had the effect of bringing him to attention again. Frustrated at the "fussing and buzzing about beer and bishops" in the England of 1895, and convinced that "the causes of every political revolution nowadays are cosmic, not to be reached by legislation," Adams set about pursuing those causes. He was in a good position to watch, and under no immediate compulsion to act. He began to pose the questions that were to lead to *Mont-Saint-Michel and Chartres* and *The Education.*[25]

At the end of the decade, Adams was deep in the study of twelfth-century France, apparently an example of *fin-de-siècle* medievalism. But merely to classify Adams' medieval research under this rubric is to ignore the frame of mind in which he undertook it. His inquiry into the medieval past, like his construction of the dynamic theory of history, was stimulated by his rage at the self-satisfied generation to which he belonged. He had been watching the show long enough to grow disgusted at the absurd antics of men·in his own century,

in whose pitiful performance he found the same impotence he had
previously seen in that of Jefferson and Madison, whom he described
as "mere grasshoppers kicking and gesticulating on the middle of
the Mississippi River." When Charles published a biography of their
father, Henry was chilled at the spectacle: "the stale smell of dead
anxieties makes me sick, and that history bores my life out. That
we saved our skins in London was God's mercy, and the work of
blind forces that no one understood or measured. Looking back I
grovel in the dust, and shake with terror at the immensity of the
danger and the impotence of our efforts." Henry James's account
of their early Boston days in *William Wetmore Story and His Friends*
evoked a similar rage at "the profundity of ignorance of Story in
becoming a sculptor, or Sumner in becoming a statesman, or Emerson in becoming a philosopher." Adams turned to Chartres in re-
vulsion from the nineteenth century, but his was not a complacent
retreat into aestheticism. He was far too angry for that. As before,
the retreat was not into the distant past, but onto higher ground.
Mont-Saint-Michel and Chartres led to *The Education of Henry
Adams* and *The Rule of Phase as Applied to History*, just as the
retreat from reform politics had once led to *Gallatin* and the *History*.
Twenty years as a posthumous spectator led Adams to a final attempt to act with some effect on history.[26]

  Among the most prominent lessons Adams had learned from surveying his life and times in retrospect was that "throughout history
the waste of mind has been appalling," and the "story" told in *The
Education*, Adams explains, "is meant to show" that however accountable the individual may be for the waste of his own mind,
"society has conspired to promote" the waste of mind in general.
Such a hypothesis may of course serve to excuse the waste of one's
own mind in particular, but as Adams makes clear from the outset,
his motive is not merely personal. "Only," he insists, "as a consciously assenting member in full partnership with the society of his
age—had his education an interest to himself or to others." It is
easy to regard such a claim as a transparent cover for base conceit,
as part of a general strategy for translating personal dissappointment
into metaphysical sour grapes. But no matter how conceited and

embittered Adams had grown—and there is no question that he was an insufferable snob—we ought to take him at his word here. For why should he cast his autobiography in the form of a treatise on education if he did not genuinely wish to accomplish more than an apology for his failures and a blasting indictment of a society which had equally declined his services as a statesman?[27]

When one considers Adams' choice of genre and the narrative strategies by which he tried to transform it into an "education," a rather complex mixture of hubris and self-affacement emerges, but the project itself cannot be reduced to personal motives. To be sure, Adams wrote Henry James that *The Education* was to be "a mere shield of protection in the grave. I advise you to take your own life in the same way, in order to prevent biographers from taking it in theirs." By casting his life in the impersonal form of a third-person narrative, and by remaining silent about the twenty years during which he had been most active and suffered the most pain, Adams hoped to block the intrusions of his biographer into his private life. Further, by having one's own say, Adams implied, one could at least define the grounds on which the biographer's judgment would eventually be made. As an autobiographer Adams protected his privacy. But the choice of autobiography itself signals a certain overweening sense of self-importance; the genre entails some conceit by definition, and after all, Adams had other choices than autobiography available to him. As a "stable-companion to statesmen," throughout his life, he possessed ample material for a conventional volume of memoirs regarding the political events to which he had so often held privileged access. Had he written such a volume, he could have exposed as much of the ignorance and good deal more of the villainy of his time than he does in *The Education* itself, without placing himself at the center of the picture.[28]

Further, had he wished merely to indict his society, he could have done so far more easily by writing a novel. If he wished, that is, to stand off completely from his world and describe its corruption, the nineteenth-century novel afforded admirable models. Balzac presented the same complacent bourgeois society, emptied of moral values and corrupt to the core, which Adams derided so vociferously in his correspondence. An even more chilling critical exposure of the same society could be found in Gustave Flaubert's *Sentimental*

Education. Further, Flaubert's title relates "education" to the theme of lost illusions which marks not only Adams' book, but so much of nineteenth-century fiction. The first twenty chapters of *The Education* depict nothing so clearly as the progressive destruction of illusions in a society from which responsible authority is absent, while fools and charlatans abound. That President Grant, for example, was "the highest product of the most advanced evolution, made evolution ludicrous." Even Grant's intimate friends "could never follow a mental process in his thought" and "were not sure that he did think." By what mental process could he have arrived at the apparently serious conclusion that "Venice would be a fine city if it were drained"? By noting such contradictions between an allegedly progressive evolution and an apparent "reversion," Henry Adams has more in mind than exposing a corrupt society destined to change "his intended future into an absurdity." If "such contradictions" as emerged from his scrutiny of the era's leading models of statesmanship reflect upon the moral idiocy of the age, they also present obstacles to education; again and again, Adams finds he can "learn nothing but cross-purpose" even "among intelligent people." His lost illusions, in short, are couched in the framework of a failed education, which serves as a negative case against which to formulate a compensatory model for education, one which would "lessen the obstacles, diminish the friction, invigorate the energy, and . . . train minds to react, not at haphazard, but by choice, on the lines of force that attract their world." Unlike Flaubert, Adams had no capacity for aesthetic self-sufficiency. "Pure narrative," he said, "is an art by itself, and does not concern me more than pure science." As the two novels he had written earlier demonstrate, Adams could not write a story without pointing a moral.[29]

Rather than an autobiography, a memoir, or a novel, Adams produced an amalgam of the three in which narrative and didactic purposes are combined. He tells the story of his life—insofar as he intends it to be told at all—and he records a good deal of the history of his era from the privileged vantage point he had occupied as an Adams. But it is the relation between these two which he is most concerned with defining, and which he treats as the central subject of the book. That is, he traces his career as observer in relation to the changing world he had observed in order first to demonstrate the failure of his own education, and then to question the necessity of that failure. Thus, in addition to his private motives, there is a public motive implicit in the very task Adams set himself when he decided to mold his autobiography in the form of an education. Rather than merely telling the story of his own life in such a way as to preserve his privacy and to defend himself against the judgments of others, he chose to cast it in a form which might actually prove useful to others. By treating himself as a "manikin," he could try to accomplish both private and public goals—both hiding and using his life as a means of measurement.

In 1908, Adams explained the plan of *The Education* to Whitelaw Reid. It was, Adams said,

a story of how an average American education, in spite of the most favorable conditions ran down hill, for twenty years, into the bog labelled Failure; and how it had to be started agian, under every disadvantage, and the blindest fumblings, to crawl uphill a little way in order at least to get a little view ahead of the field it should have begun by occupying.

He was more given to humor when writing James Ford Rhodes, for whom he compared *The Education* to "a centipede moving along in twenty little sections . . . to the bottom of a hill, and then laboriously climbing in fifteen sections more . . . till it can get up on a hill." As these remarks indicate, Adams' central strategic decision was to divide *The Education* into two parts, the first consisting in chapters 1 through 20, and the second, chapters 21 through 35. This division not only enabled him to leave a gap between the years 1870 and 1890, and so to exclude the story of his marriage, but it also served his didactic purposes. Part 1 stands to Part 2 much as "The Problem" stands to "The Solutions" in "A Letter to Teachers of Ameican History." Part 1 ends in "Failure," and demonstrates the problem to be solved in Part 2. In its most abstract form, the problem posed by Part 1 is whether history is merely mechanical development along lines of least resistance, and thus impervious to human efforts to control its course; the solution proposed in Part 2 is a "dynamic theory of history" which rests on the hypothesis that history is a "sequence of force," in which man himself figures as a "certain form of energy" capable of reacting to the forces propelling him. The "dynamic theory" is proposed for a rhetorical purpose as well, for it offers a stimulus to action, a provocation designed to foster a reaction in the reader, and as such, it is designed to counter the waste of mind promoted by society, the waste whose consequences are documented in part 1. Thus the failure of Adams' education to prepare him for the world he confronts, demonstrated in Part 1, leads to the question broached in Part 2—whether this failure is necessary. In short, Adams tries to pose these questions in a narrative framework unified by the theme of failure and the effort to evaluate its causes. The Adams whose failed education is described in Part 1 reawakens like Rip Van Winkle, twenty years later, and sets out on a new education, stimulated initially by his inability to evaluate the results of the first. Adams' strategy for unifying narrative and didactic elements breaks down in the end, not for any want of genius on his part, but rather because one cannot, in fact, sit on a fence and watch one's self go by.[30]

The first half of *The Education* traces the career of a young man named Henry Adams in quest of an education—one which will suit him to some useful purpose in life, provide him with a role to play in the historical drama and the training required to play it decently. But he discovers, once he has drifted from Boston to Berlin, Rome, London, Washington, and back to Boston once more, that the play refuses to make sense. This Adams does not take part in the play but searches for a vantage point from which to watch it and a program which will provide a key to the characters and the plot. To use Adams' metaphor, this Henry Adams "never got to the point of playing the game at all; he lost himself in the study of it, watching the errors of the players." His scrutiny proves embarrassing to the players' dignity, despite the humility with which he pretends to regard their behavior. By the time this Adams' quest for education is closed out by his appointment at Harvard (an appointment which itself is treated as a sign of American society's lack of educational resources), the clay feet of every authority he has encountered are exposed. No one, the young man keeps discovering, seems to have the dimmest explanation for his actions or the slightest ground for defending the justice of those actions. Indeed, a major burden of the first half of *The Education* is to argue that those who ought to know what they are doing, since they are the ones in charge—of politics, education, literary and artistic judgment, scientific inquiry—have in fact no idea whatsoever of what they are doing. The quest for education fails for want of any solid ground for knowledge itself. Whatever knowledge Adams has acquired by the time he sets up as a teacher of history at Harvard, is neither useful nor valid. It answers neither the question "What shall I do?" nor the question "What is true?" Indeed, the education of Henry Adams as depicted in Part 1 yields no quantifiable results and is grounded in no method of learning deserving the name of education.[31]

These conclusions are brought home by his experience at Harvard, where the still uneducated Adams finds himself in 1871—amazingly enough—appointed to teach history. By this point in the narrative, Adams has repeatedly met with signs that history is moving along lines that no one can discern, and that in fact no one is bothering to identify. But this unhappy state of affairs now assumes the status of a practical problem for a young man who has learned to swim "through oceans of ignorance" without undue worry. The Henry Adams who had once chosen to be a "Darwinian for fun" is quickly brought up short by the demands of his impending task as a teacher, for despite his detached and bemused front, he is forced to admit that "even to him education was a serious thing." It may strike the contemporary reader as yet another indication of Adams' hubris when he pronounces that "a parent gives life, but as parent, gives no more. A murderer takes life, but his deed stops there. A teacher affects eternity; he can never tell where his influence stops." Given the "oceans of ignorance" through which today's students so often feel themselves struggling in vain, the claim that a teacher affects eternity has lost much of its credibility. But every teacher still faces, even if in more modest dimensions, the dilemma Adams describes himself confronting at Harvard. No matter how skeptical about the status of his discipline's current knowledge, he must teach. For someone who believes the results affect eternity, the dilemma is likely to inspire terror at his responsibility and his failure to meet it. The terror takes the form, then, of anticipated guilt when Adams imagines his students twenty years hence turning on him "as fiercely as he had turned on his old instructors" and wonders "what answer could he make?" *The Education* itself is in a sense that answer, one which to some extent mirrors the strategy he had pursued at Harvard.[32]

No matter how ignorant, he must act, and his solution is to act

frankly . . . on the rule that a teacher, who knew nothing of his subject, should not pretend to teach his scholars what he did not know, but should join them in trying to find the best way of learning it.

This course of action is the only one available, he decides, to the teacher of history, who knows that no theory of history can be proven, but that any theory adopted has its incalculable effect on the student. Specifically, since it is "in essence incoherent and immoral, history had either to be taught as such—or falsified." Wanting to do neither, Adams can only direct his students to the questions he himself must pose as teacher. Since no historical theory can be proved to rest on secure premisses, while the teaching itself must proceed, and have its effects, the only responsible course to take is to stimulate questions. But this course of action fails at Harvard, where it "reproduced at great waste of time and money results not worth reaching." At the end of chapter 20, Adams concludes, "Education . . . had done its worst. Henceforth, he went on, submissive." The allied issues of history's chaotic and mysterious course, and man's ignorance of and impotence before it, are focused in this chapter, closing out the first part of *The Education* with the implication that Adams practiced "submission and silence" for the next twenty years.[33]

Twenty years after his failure at Harvard, Adams tries to assess the results of his education. But just as the young Adams of the first twenty chapters could find no secure vantage point from which to judge the events he witnessed, the retired Adams can find no standard against which to measure his success or failure. Satisfied with his life, which he declares now complete, Adams is unsure of its success. He discusses the question with John Hay and Clarence King, his two closest friends, and the only other models of education available for his scrutiny, only to find no answer. How is success to be measured?

Lacking the world's "consideration" and any claim to its power, Adams decides that the "chief title to consideration" owned by Hay and himself "was their right to look out of their windows on great men, alive or dead in LaFayette Square." In view of the spectacle thus afforded them—of "men who had swayed the course of empire" who were now "less valued than the ephemeral congressmen behind them"—Adams and Hay are unable to say what this power is worth in the end. Perched behind his window, however, the posthumous spectator is brought finally to attention by the strange new world disporting itself before his mystified gaze. The panic of 1893 forces him to confront the specter of "some very powerful energy . . . at work, doing what nobody wanted done." The Columbian Exposition—the first of several world fairs at which Adams would play the role of exemplary observer—stimulates him to undertake a new education:

Chicago asked in 1893 for the first time the question whether the American people knew where they were driving. Adams answered, for one, that he did not know, but would try to find out.

The "object of education" changes. No longer "studying what the world had ceased for care for," Adams decides to "find out what the mass of mankind did care for, and why." The observation of men's actions recorded in Part 1 now gives way to a study of their reactions; Adams no longer pursues an education but seems to be pursued by one in the manifold forms of energy erupting around him. As observer he remains above the crowd, watching it closely for signs of progress; as a member of the procession, he is jostled and threatened by the new energies expressing themselves in bombs and dynamos. The education Adams comes to envision as required by the future is constituted from the grounds on which the education he once sought has become impossible, the grounds of history seen as the acceleration of force in which man does not act, but can only react.[34]

Having "swept his mind clear of knowledge" in good Emersonian fashion, Adams sets out "afresh" to construct a hypothesis designed to test whether man might after all be capable of reacting to force intelligently, while at the same time describing at length the massive ignorance and inertia of his society. Most important to his purposes is the self-confessed ignorance of the scientists who "murmured *Ignoramus* under their breath" while "*Ignorabimus* . . . lay on the tips of their tongues," still awaiting a larger synthesis. For "human purposes," Adams concludes, "a point must always be soon reached where a larger synthesis is suicide." If Samuel Langley told him "that the new forces were anarchical, and . . . little short of parricidal in their wicked spirit towards science," and Jules Poincaré was prepared to usher in "a mathematical paradise of endless displacement," then the unity on which science relied for its larger synthesis was—like all other forms of unity—not the "law of nature," but merely the "dream of man." Nonetheless, science represents the only dream worth pursuing. If history is to be even minimally subject to man's control, it must be rationally apprehensible, and if it is rationally apprehensible, it must move in accord with laws which are, at least theoretically, knowable. So Adams constructs a historical hypothesis along scientific lines. He decides to treat man's reactions to the forces attracting his world as a measure of its motion, and so to propose "a law of reaction between force and force—between mind and nature—the law of progress." And his object in proposing such a law "is to triangulate from the widest possible base to the furthest point . . .he can see," so as to provide historians with a "scale for the whole," and students with a common framework to use as a basis for reaction.[35]

Given the theoretical issues which arise in the second part of *The Education*, it becomes clear that the first part is more than simply a story of failure. That story is designed, first, to prepare us for the treatment of man as a "measure of motion" to be introduced in Part 2. That is, the Adams whose quest for an education in Part 1 had failed was designed to serve as a "manikin" to be "used for the study of relation." This figure is set against the forces propelling his world, as a "measure of motion," in order to show how a child born "under the shadow of Boston State House," and dealt by birth an "excellent hand," grew up to "find himself required to play" a "game . . . of which neither he nor any one else back to the beginning of time knew the rules or the risks or the stakes." From this viewpoint, Adams' case serves as an ideal measure precisely *because* his education as an Adams ought to have trained him to react "by

choice" to the forces at work in his society. If "no child, born in
the year, held better cards than he," then his failure suggests at least
the possibility that the rules of the game had changed, that the lines
of force were moving history in new directions. Adams' failed education, taken individually, may or may not display a waste of mind,
but taken as a "measure of motion" it might serve to indicate the
rate of acceleration in the forces to which he had submitted. The
Adams who plays the role of observer in Part 1 is designed to meet
the needs of the theoretical concerns of Part 2 by serving to register
both the accelerating forces moving history and man's failure to
react with intelligence and foresight to them.[36]

In retrospect, the first part of *The Education* serves another purpose as well. It reveals the incoherence of the authoritative systems—social, political, intellectual—presiding over ninetheenth-
century society. The "problem of *Pteraspis*" seems to undermine
Darwinian evolution as a ground for a theory of progress; the inability of experts to agree on the authenticity of a Raphael drawing
renders art history a "dilettante museum of scraps, with nothing but
a wall-paper to unite them in any relation of sequence"; the political
behavior of Gladstone, Russell, and Palmerston deviates from the
"old-fashioned logical drama" which "required unity and sense,"
revealing that the "actual drama is a pointless puzzle, without even
an intrigue"; English society "had no unity; one wandered about
in it like a maggot in cheese." Adams is portrayed as always baffled,
always curious, always seeking out an education in good faith, if
with declining hope. Meanwhile, "one could not stop to chase
doubts as though they were rabbits. One had no time to paint and
putty the surface of law, even though it were cracked and rotten."
In addition to functioning as a measure of the historical forces which
render his education obsolete from the start, as observer, Adams
acts as a lens exposing rupture, discontinuity, irrationality.[37]

Part 1 thus establishes both the problem and the means which will
be used to solve it in Part 2. History is shown to be proceeding like
a purposeless force, erupting in a war no one intends or really expects, developing energies whose power no one understands, and
driving toward a concentration of forces which no one can control.
The incoherence thus revealed is registered through a neutral observer, whose authenticity is supported by his alleged disinterest-

edness. First and last, he is presented as a seeker of education only. That he had other purposes and interests is acknowledged, but always subordinated to his educational quest. This juxtaposition of the observer and the mysterious movement of history is reflected in a series of tableaux which punctuate the book's movement as a whole, and serve to bring Adams' purposes into focus.

Adams repeatedly juxtaposes men and monuments, thereby providing images of the attraction of forces on the mind at different points in time, and draws the reader's attention away from an exclusive focus either on Adams' life or on the world he inhabited, and toward the relation between the two which he wants to use as a unit of measure. In the first half of *The Education*, Adams as a boy visiting Mount Vernon introduces a series of these confrontations, the most dramatic of which is set in Rome. Here Adams takes up Edward Gibbon's posture on the "steps of the Church of Santa Maria di Ara Coeli" to look out over "the ruins of the Capitol" and pose "the eternal question:—Why! Why!! Why!!!" What makes the question personal as well as eternal is that "Rome was actual; it was England; it was going to be America." Adams focuses on the same historical progression James had in *The Golden Bowl*, but struggles in vain to find a pattern within which that progression will make sense. He can neither redeem nor explain the waste. He ventures no answers to his own questions, but merely points repeatedly to his inability to do so. The chaos of Roman history "could not be fitted into an orderly, middle-class, Bostonian, systematic scheme," and placed "conundrum after conundrum in his educational path," evoking a confusion far more serious than the moral dilemmas posed by Mount Vernon. Adams therefore disclaims any pretensions toward understanding the meaning of Rome, but sets for himself a more limited task. He tries to imagine other observers on the same spot. Conceding that "perhaps Garibaldi—possibly even Cavour" are imaginable in such a picture, he nonetheless finds it impossible to conceive of Napoleon III, Palmerston, Tennyson, Longfellow, or Browning there. He concludes that even "the greatest men of the age scarcely bore the test of posing with Rome for a background."

Adams' focus, in short, shifts from the ruins themselves and the questions they pose, to the image of men confronting them. The juxtaposition of Adams against the ruins of the Capitol is repeated several times throughout the narrative, a recurrent image which serves to underline the still undetermined relation between the observer and the observed, and to shift the focus from either one to the interaction between them.[38]

The purpose of this strategy becomes explicit in the second half of *The Education* as Adams builds toward the "dynamic theory of history." In "The Dynamo and the Virgin" he describes a trip to Amiens in the company of the sculptor Augustus Saint-Gaudens. As the two men examine Amiens' western portal, Adams steps back from the initial object of study, the cathedral itself, to look at his friend in the act of observing it, realizing that "for his purposes, St. Gaudens on that spot had more interest to him than the cathedral itself." The shift of focus here, like the same shift at Rome, initiates a consideration of other observers before the same spectacle. Edward Gibbon and John Ruskin are imagined at Amiens as a means toward advancing Adams' purposes which become explicit in the effort to ascertain "the lines of force that attract" the mind at different points in history. At Amiens, as in the case of the visitors to Rock Creek Cemetery, who stare at the sculpture Adams commissioned from Saint-Gaudens for his wife's grave, Adams forces us to ponder the observer before the monument he observes in order to reinforce the claim that "one sees what one brings." And this principle, in turn, serves not to support subjectivism, but to prepare us for a definition of the observer's perspective as a "measure of motion." The "dynamic theory of history," for which these recorded reactions prepare us, constitutes a hypothetical scheme for ordering history on the basis of a model of relation between history defined as a sequence of force and the mind which reacts to such forces, a relation measured in terms of force's "attraction on thought." As such, Adams' theory is chiefly significant not as a prediction of history's probable direction—although he risks the prediction—but as a model which includes the observer within the course of history he observes. Since the picture of history is incoherent, he devises a strategy for rendering it coherent, accessible to rational apprehension. But that strategy, by recognizing the presence of the observer within the picture to be observed, lays its own insidious traps for the Adams who clings to his rationalist principles. Adams' purpose, as he repeatedly explains, is to suggest a means of measuring historical development in the hope of controlling it in the future. Adams' theory is designed to show, if only by its inadequacy, what a twentieth-century education must take into account if it is to resist society's profligate waste of mind in conditions where such waste might prove disastrous. But the presupposition of Adams' effort is that rational cognition testifies to human freedom and makes possible human control, and this presupposition is undermined by Adams' own conclusions.[39]

The two parts of *The Education* articulate two epistemological conditions entailing two antithetical views of man's relationship to history. In Part 1, Adams confronts an alien world in which he can find no order compatible with the rational requirements of his mind. Here Adams learns to swim through "oceans of ignorance," a creature afloat on an apparently purposeless drift, the victim of external forces for which his education had failed to prepare him, along with everyone else in sight. Adams' failure to acquire an education seems to be a consequence of a given and eternal condition of ignorance, and teaches that no matter how much he deludes himself into believing the contrary, man inhabits a world whose historical movement bears no relationship to his acts. Consequently, history was "in essence incoherent and immoral" and to teach it under the pretense that this was not the case was to falsify it. No intelligible sequence is evident. The Adams who moves from birth to failure in Part 1 registers with mounting emphasis the utter impotence of man to comprehend, much less control, the "anarchic and purposeless forces" to which human life and history must submit.[40]

But the Adams who takes up the narrative in chapter 21 responds to force in a fundamentally different way from the "submissive" young man whose education was wrecked on the shoals of historical obsolescence. At Chicago, Adams confronts the "question of whether the American people knew where they were driving"; in London, Hay's successful diplomacy raises the same question in another form—is there after all a "possible purpose working itself out in history?" When he decides that Hay has "saved China," Adams is forced to lament his previous failures.

Instantly the diplomacy of the nineteenth century, with all its painful scuffles and struggles, was forgotten, and the American blushed to be told of his submissions in the past. History broke in halves.

As "education ran riot at Chicago," Adams finds himself "aghast at what [he] had said and done in all these years, and still more ashamed of the childlike ignorance and babbling futility of the society that led [him] to say and do it." Hay's efforts to impose order on the map of international relations are matched by Adams' efforts to work out the scale for viewing the possible purpose suggested by the eruption of a new force. In short, Adams no longer submits to the "anarchic and purposeless forces" previously called upon to substantiate human impotence, but sets about trying to measure them, and with all the imperialistic fervor of an Alexander: "One must seek new worlds to measure." If Adams now approaches history not as essentially impervious to his mind, but potentially knowable, he does so because the author has constructed his narrative in order to demonstrate that ignorance may, in the end not be necessary. In short, there are two possible conclusions to be drawn from the experiences described in Part 1: either history moves according to the law of mass, in which case man is merely an atom "vibrating in a void" and his education is irrelevant, or history moves along lines of force discoverable by man, in which case education may be important. There is, however, a theoretical contradiction entailed in this definition of the problem. To be knowable for Adams, history must move in accord with some law, and whether that law be called mechanical or dynamic, it remains deterministic. Insofar as Adams wants to demonstrate that ignorance is in principle unnecessary—the effect of a social conspiracy to promote waste of mind—he acts on the eighteenth-century liberal faith that freedom is grounded in knowledge; but in so acting, Adams exposes the contradiction in the rationalist program itself.[41]

Adams wants to construct an alternative to the "mechanical theory . . . accepted by science" and offers a "dynamic theory" in its place. But in order to be verified scientifically, the dynamic theory must still be tested against an isolated system. That is, the neutral observer must be able, in Heisenberg's words, to "speak about parts of the world without reference to himself." Thus the Adams whose presence in the "current of his times" is acknowledged is treated theoretically as himself an objectified manikin. Compelled to insert man within the historical movement he confronts in order to render it coherent, Adams tries to maintain the neutral detachment required for scientific verifiability by objectifying that man as a geometrical figure. The result is a split between the Adams who serves as manikin and the Adams who uses him to measure the sequence of force. That is, in the second half of *The Education*, we find Adams the detached observer observing man-as-observer reacting by means of his observation to visible emblems of invisible forces. The manikin becomes inert and the Adams who uses him remains the impotent observer of the historical sequence he has arranged. Like Maggie Verver at the end of *The Golden Bowl*, in other words, the Adams-as-actor who has been deployed in the service of restoring coherence is split apart from the Adams-as-observer who stands off to confront a fixed picture, a sequence whose outcome is determined and impervious to human intervention or control.[42]

The problem here is not that Adams is being unscientific, but rather that he is too scientific. He wants to define a "scale for the whole" on which we can agree because his rationalist assumptions dictate that control requires measurement; only if history's course can be measured can its direction be calculated, and only if this calculation can be made can man be regarded as free. Yet if this calculation is possible, man is free only to contemplate his own determined fate. In short, the proposed dynamic theory differs from the opposed mechanical theory in only one respect: in the first case, our chains are visible and in the second they are not. At the end Adams says his dynamic theory "would verify or disprove itself within thirty years." If verified, it would become a law, like any other natural law. And even if "the new man" with a "new social mind" should appear, he would himself be determined—"born of contact between the new and old energies." As a theory, Adams' model works against the rhetorical purpose it is designed to foster—the stimulation of reaction. Adams admits as much when he concludes that his attitude is likely to discourage effort. He acknowledges, moreover, that if verified, his theory would prove that "dispute was idle, discussion was futile, and silence, next to good temper, was the mark of sense." Coming at the end of five hundred pages, this statement ought to give us pause.[43]

Adams is obviously not silent. I would suggest, then, that in a kind of return of the repressed, the Adams who is theoretically drained of his active dimension in order to be used as a manikin ultimately reasserts his presence as a speaker. Having once situated himself in the historical process, he cannot remain entirely outside of it. It is this fissure between the neutral observer who calculates and predicts and the speaker who wishes to provoke a reaction which accounts for Adams' self-acknowledged failure to make the narrative and didactic elements of his project cohere.

In Part 1, Adams actually succeeds in blending story and moral, narrative and didactic style and purpose. It is only in the last fifteen chapters that the balance between narrative and didactic modes breaks down. The most obvious reason for the success of the first part in this respect is that failure serves as a unifying thread on which Adams can link his experiences in sequence. It is notable that the mechanical theory here demonstrated accords so well with the narration of failure. That is, as long as Adams is demonstrating society's ignorance and the failure of rationalism to provide the total epistemological grasp it claims to offer, he has little trouble telling his story and pointing to its moral. It is only when he tries to use that program, to make it work, that the story breaks apart from the moral it is designed to teach.

Adams' failure in Part 1 is depicted by an omniscient narrator who stands aloof from the young protagonist, whose failure he can evaluate in accord with his didactic purposes. In other words, the detached observer who serves as omniscient narrator here occupies a stable vantage point above the stream of event, and depicts the character Henry Adams as the victim of a sustained dramatic irony—Adams blunders on unaware of the fact that his eighteenth-century education has been obsolete at least since he was ten years old, that is, long before it was really under way. Further, this Adams is a submissive victim to forces beyond his comprehension. The

omniscient narrator can maintain absolute control of his story because that story's lesson consists in the claim that man can only go
on, submissive and impotent before unknowable forces. The Adams
of the last fifteen chapters, however, is no longer a manikin, for he
pursues a "new education" as an old man and must increasingly
play the role of both narrator and character. The omniscient narrator
who previously occupied a stable and detached vantage point from
which to view his protagonist's failure must now protest his detachment more vociferously than ever before because he cannot
maintain it any longer. Again and again, Adams reiterates his im-
partiality, his lack of interest in the game except as spectator and
occasional critic, and his final removal from all possible arenas of
action. But the protest accompanies new talk of duty, and new questions of whether the "conservative Christian anarchist" was "the
murderer or the murdered?" The need expressed "to account for
himself to himself somehow" immediately precedes the exposition
of the dynamic theory itself. In short, the omniscient and godlike
narrator of Part 1 emerges in Part 2 as the mortal speaker whose
effort to see is limited by, and thus all the more feverishly supported
in the face of, his time-bound status as a participant in history.
Moreover, as participant, he is trying to have some effect on history's course by teaching "reaction." As speaker, that is, Adams
acts in an effort to stimulate a reaction in his audience, but as an
observer twice removed now—watching other observers react—he
presumes to maintain his narrative omniscience. He cannot be both
at the same time. Failure as a theme, it would appear, accords with
a vision of history as mechanical development along the lines of
least resistance and viewed from a godlike vantage point above the
"stream of events," but when Adams tries to maintain such a vantage point in order to resist the necessity of failure, he cannot
succeed.[44]

Thus in the second part of *The Education*, a terrific strain develops
between the effort to observe, to maintain a detached posture outside
the stream of events so as to "triangulate" from the present and the
past into the future, and the need to sustain narrative continuity
without the benefit of a stable vantage point and a coherent interpretation. In Part 2, failure may be predicted, but it can no longer
serve as the thematic foundation of the narrator's interpretation.

Furthermore, no foundation can serve, because the narrator who has previously occupied the position of the detached observer of his own past can maintain his detachment only by becoming a visionary observer of the future. And the only means of posing as such an observer is to write science fiction.[45]

The reader, in turn, must cope with a mixture of narrative and scientific speculation here that is never satisfactorily integrated. We move forward from exposition to exposition, back and forth between Hay and Adams, once King's "scientific education" shows itself a failure and King himself dies, and up and down from the kinetic theory of gases to anecdotal entries about Henry Cabot Lodge. No larger synthesis emerges from this attempt to make the rationalist program of science work. By the time the dynamic theory of history is proposed, it is altogether unclear just what responses Adams intends to provoke, since, as we have seen, it tends only to "discourage effort." No such difficulties thwart the reader's progress until chapter 21; for even if Adams' discussions of Civil War diplomacy grow tedious, they never appear pointless or random. But after chapter 21, the narrative splits away from the educational purpose it is designed to support. The narrative chronicles accelerating and anarchic forces while the dynamic theory, if verified, dictates impotent submission.

From the outset, Adams has played the role of detached observer, but his very effort to stimulate a reaction in his audience by writing *The Education* undermines the role of observer he adopts as its narrator. Insofar as his educational purpose controls the narrative, Adams cannot escape exposure as a participant in the historical process he presumes to observe from on high, for as he himself acknowledges, submission is signalled by "futilitarian silence," and he is far from silent. Adams' effort to teach reaction in *The Education*, I would suggest, constitutes a final attempt to exert influence, and as such indicates his awareness that however loudly he might protest that he is not responsible, he has accepted responsibility for the historical developments he pretends merely to watch; as speaker, he must accept responsibility. The split between Adams as speaker and Adams as observer is inherent in the very effort he undertakes in *The Education*. The attempt to relate man and history within one sequence of interacting forces leads on the one hand to a reassertion of the neutral observer's impotence, and on the other to a recognition of his complicity as a participant, exposing the contradiction to which reified consciousness is doomed.[46]

Adams tended to imagine man's effect on history as comparable to "grasshoppers kicking and gesticulating on the middle of the Mississippi River." It is thus notable that he imagined his effect on his audience in terms of the same metaphor. In a letter to Barrett Wendell, Adams noted,

> My favorite figure of the American author is that of a man who breeds a favorite dog, which he throws into the Mississippi River for the pleasure of making a splash. The river does not splash, but it drowns the dog.

He used a similar image of water when he told his brother Brooks that "the public mind is like the Gulf of Mexico. . . . You may throw into it what you please, it will show no movement." The Adams who sat on a fence and, measuring the pace of the procession on his own pulse, assured himself that he was a mere bystander, could not finally repress the fact that he himself was part of the procession; the act of speaking to his "fellow-insects" revealed as much. Accordingly, he took responsibility for the procession's direction, no matter how insistently he proclaimed his impotence. Having tried to designate "the economies necessary for the education of the New American," he felt his "duty" done. By pushing the rationalist assumptions of reified consciousness up to and beyond their limit, he exposed their contradictions, but he remained a victim to them, unable to abandon his conviction that they ought to function yet.[47]

In *The Education*, Henry Adams depicted his society as failing to meet the demands of the rational principles on which it had been founded, and in so doing exposed the contradiction between a commitment to knowable laws dictating events and the chaotic reality denied cognitive status by those laws. In his effort to construct a dynamic theory of history, Adams struggled to overcome that contradiction, but in so doing, only revealed its effects the more dramatically. Further, the *"ignorabimus"* which he detected on the lips of the scientist fed his suspicion that the task he set himself was impossible, for if nature's unity had been undercut, history's could hardly be affirmed. But despite the breakdown of the rationalist program, so dramatically demonstrated in *The Education's* opening twenty chapters, Adams resisted the logical response of *"futilitarian* silence,"* as the *The Education*'s very production indicates. No matter how carefully he confined his initial audience to his friends, Adams nonetheless wrote an Editor's Preface in 1916 and sent it to Henry Cabot Lodge together with a copy of *The Education* and a set of instructions about its publication. Insofar as the Mississippi was the stream of history, Adams reconfirmed his status as mere insect gesticulating on its surface, but insofar as he considered it an audience, he could not thwart his desire to make a splash. Even the title to *The Education*'s final chapter reflects his ambivalent attitude toward the futile picture he had drawn and the residual hope on which he had nonetheless acted: "Nunc Age," points in two directions at once: "Now Go" ends a futile effort; "Now Act" invites a reaction which will vindicate that effort's results.[48]

As early as 1894, Adams had defined the trap to which he saw bourgeois society condemned. If a "science of history were established today," he said, it could point to a "socialistic triumph" and thus place the teacher of history "in an attitude of hostility toward existing institutions." Society would, in that case, be unlikely to "tolerate the open assertion of a necessity which should affirm its approaching overthrow." Such a science, on the other hand, could point to the continuation and growth of "the present evils of the world—its huge armaments, its vast accumulations of capital, its advancing materialism," in which case "society would shut its eyes and ears" to the scientific historian's announcements. If, finally, "science should prove that society must at a given time revert to the church . . . it commits suicide." The conclusion Adams draws from this line of reasoning may serve as testimony to the logical suicide to which his posture as impotent spectator and complicit participant led him:

If the world is to continue moving toward the point it has so energetically pursued during the last fifty years, it will destroy the hopes of the vast organizations of labor. If it is to change its course and become communistic, it places us in direct hostility to the entire fabric of our social and political system. If it goes on, we must preach despair. If it goes back, it must deny and repudiate science. If it goes forward, round a circle which leads through communism, we must declare ourselves hostile to the property that pays us and the institutions we are bound in duty to support.

In *The Education*, Adams tried to find a way out of this trap, and failed. But there is considerable justice to his claim that "our failures are really not due to ourselves alone. Society has a great share in it." Adams remained trapped by contradiction to the end, but he was right to claim that he "was not to blame."[49]

PART FOUR

WILLIAM FAULKNER: INNOCENCE HISTORICIZED

A Klee painting named "Angelus Novus" shows an angel looking as though he is about to move away from something he is fixedly contemplating. His eyes are staring, his mouth is open, his wings are spread. This is how one pictures the angel of history. His face is turned toward the past. Where we perceive a chain of events, he sees one single catastrophe which keeps piling wreckage upon wreckage and hurls it in front of his feet. The angel would like to stay, awaken the dead, and make whole what has been smashed. But a storm is blowing from Paradise. . . . This storm irresistibly propels him into the future to which his back is turned, while the pile of debris before him grows skyward. This storm is what we call progress.

—WALTER BENJAMIN

Chapter Seven

FAULKNER'S AMERICA

There can be an appalling complexity to innocence,
especially if your point of departure is guilt.
—LOUIS HARTZ

MUCH LIKE HENRY ADAMS, Faulkner grew up in a world on which his family's history was visibly inscribed. The patriarchal Falkner had not been a president, but one could hardly tell it from the monument marking his grave. William Clark Falkner's tombstone—a statue of Falkner himself on a pedestal, six feet square and fourteen feet high, with FALKNER carved in large block letters on all four sides—casts a shadow quite as long over Faulkner's life as the one cast over Adams' by the Boston State House, or over Emerson's by the sepulchres of the fathers. In his first Yoknapatawpha County novel, Faulkner described his great-grandfather's monument in a telling fashion:

He stood on a stone pedestal, in his frock coat and bareheaded, one leg slightly advanced and one hand resting lightly in that gesture of haughty pride which repeated itself generation after generation with a fateful fidelity, his back to the world and his carven eyes gazing out across the valley where his railroad ran, and the blue changeless hills beyond, and beyond that, the ramparts of infinity itself.

Within ten years, Faulkner would set this figure on a horse and call him Thomas Sutpen, a man whose indomitable "innocence" rises "like a monument" above the "stream of event" he struggles to transcend. His back turned resolutely to the world, and his eyes (both "visionary and alert," both "ruthless and reposed") gazing out "along the undivulged light rays" of his projected dynasty, Thomas Sutpen embodies the final and tragic fate of the Emersonian visionary, resolving into one figure the romantic seer who seeks to transcend history and the neutral observer who presumes to stand outside it, calculating and predicting its course. Before we can appreciate Thomas Sutpen as the virtual incarnation of reification, however, we must first recognize the historical perspective from which his fate acquires such tragic resonance.[1]

Absalom, Absalom! has usually been regarded as a novel concerned with the fall of the South, and this despite the fact that, as Cleanth Brooks was the first to remark, Thomas Sutpen does not conform to the legendary type of Southern Planter. Yet even in Brooks's treatments of the novel, the implications of this insight are finally evaded. In 1963, Brooks saw Sutpen as distinctively modern; more recently, he has decided that Sutpen is after all distinctively American. But the primary point on which Brooks insists in both versions of his argument, with an apparent sigh of relief, is that Sutpen is certainly not typically Southern. Finding in Sutpen that "naive confidence in his own ability to realize his dream, that 'American' quality of . . . innocence" which marks a Jay Gatsby or a Christopher Newman, Brooks concludes that Faulkner "set down in a society generally regarded as special in nearly every sense and certainly regarded as quite 'un-American' . . . an extreme example of 'American' innocence." Possessed by his "malignant demon of abstraction," Sutpen not only embodies the calculating, rationalist temperament we associate with Weber's Protestant Ethic, but also singularly lacks the paternalistic impulses which Eugene Genovese has argued distinguish the Southern slaveowning planter. It follows, then, that Sutpen's case is "finally attributable to his own character" (one which reflects a "characteristically 'American' aberration,") rather than to "the conditions of antebellum society in the South."[2]

This argument, however, assumes a historical vision of the Old South which *Absalom, Absalom!* explodes. Sutpen is finally no less American for being Southern, and no less Southern for being American; his ghost is not to be exorcised by an appeal to his "American" features any more than it is by an appeal to the Old South's "un-American" ones. As it happens his ghost is not to be exorcised at all. But if we are to understand why, we must begin by recognizing that it would be highly uncharacteristic of Faulkner to set down any fictional character in a social environment to which he is utterly alien, and especially to do so in terms which would enable the reader to conclude that such a character's tragic case is not securely rooted in the conditions of that society. Joe Christmas, for example, is surely an alien figure, and yet he ultimately embodies the most basic conflicts within the society which produces him without ever affording him a home in which to find the peace for which he longs. Similarly, Sutpen is certainly never fully accepted by the good citizens of Jefferson, but this hardly implies that those qualities which make him an alien can themselves, in turn, be regarded as finally alien to the larger society in which he pursues his aims. Were Sutpen a genuinely alien figure of the sort Brooks envisions, Rosa Coldfield's response to him might be explained, but Quentin Compson's could not. What shocks and bewilders Rosa Coldfield is Sutpen's failure to be a gentleman, but what shocks Quentin Compson is the realization he struggles to thwart from the outset—that Sutpen's career lies at the heart of a Southern past supposedly distinguished by its adherence to the very codes which Sutpen violates so ruthlessly. Describing Quentin's dilemma in *Absalom, Absalom!* to Malcolm Cowley, Faulkner said that Quentin "grieved and regretted the passing of an order," to be sure, "but more he grieved the fact (because he hated and feared the portentous symptom) that a man like Sutpen, who to Quentin was trash, origin-less, could not only have dreamed so high but have had the force and strength to have failed so grandly." Of what is Sutpen a symptom if not of social forces at work within Southern history? And why does his story elicit such genuine horror in Quentin if Sutpen's character can so readily be classified as an aberration?[3]

One might argue that Quentin sees not the past but the future in Sutpen's career, sees a kind of cryptic prophecy of Snopesism. But this hypothesis proves weak at best. For one thing, Faulkner distinguished Snopes from Sutpen quite decisively when a student at the University of Virginia queried him on the apparent similarity in the two characters' tendency to use people in the service of a "grand design." Faulkner replied:

Well, only Sutpen had a grand design. Snopes' design was pretty base—he just wanted to get rich, he didn't care how. Sutpen wanted to get rich only incidentally. He wanted to take revenge for all the redneck people against the aristocrat who told him to go around to the back door. He wanted to show that he could establish a dynasty too—he could make himself a king and raise a line of princes.

There is a heroic dimension to Sutpen's design which is missing from Snopes's, and it is this very heroic dimension which chills Quentin Compson. For another thing, in a letter to Cowley, Faulkner located Sutpen quite definitely in the antebellum South, as one of those who "emerged, gradually, son by infrequent son," from the ranks of the common man to join that of the "barons." In short, the social forces of which Sutpen's career is symptomatic for Quentin do not lie as yet unborn in a modern future destined to displace an aristocratic Southern past; they lie embedded in that past itself.[4]

However, it does not follow that this society was "un-American." Faulkner at least did not represent it as such in *Absalom, Absalom!*, and given his family's history in northern Mississippi, it is not surprising that he would develop such a perspective. Sutpen's "case," as Brooks calls it, is of course extraordinary, but not because it constitutes an "'American' aberration" in a paternalist antebellum Southern society. For Brooks, Sutpen is special because he not only treats "his slaves" as things "adjunctive" to his design (something we "naturally expect") but he also treats "his own children" in the same way. Acknowledging that "paternalism . . . can be cruel," Brooks nonetheless insists that "Sutpen's treatment of other human beings, including his own flesh and blood, is something else." But it is not, after all, something else. Sutpen's design is nothing if not paternalistic. What makes him so extraordinary is that his design embodies and exposes the contradictions implicit in a paternalism whose roots lie deep in the soil of American history.[5]

If we are to appreciate the magnitude of Sutpen's story, then, we must trace these roots, and this task requires us first to identify the model of the upwardly mobile slaveowner on which Faulkner fashioned Sutpen. Faulkner found this model most immediately in his own great-grandfather. William Clark Falkner served, of course, as a model for other characters in Faulkner's fiction, so that we need to bring into focus those aspects of his career which Faulkner fastened upon for the first time in developing the character of Sutpen. It is because this figure, the parvenu capitalist entrepreneur of the antebellum Southwest, has been obscured by various historical interpretations of the antebellum South that we have failed to appreciate fully the explosive implications of Sutpen's career as Faulkner treats it in *Absalom, Absalom!*. In particular, the yeoman farmer and the aristocratic planter, between them, have blocked from view the self-made man who rises to a position of entrepreneurial eminence. Wilbur Cash's influential *Mind of the South* partly revived this figure, but Cash's approach was largely dominated by his concern to deflate the aristocratic pretensions of the Southern slaveholding planter, rather than to reassess that planter as a capitalist entrepreneur. As C. Vann Woodward has noted, Cash is preoccupied with the ideal of aristocracy which the Southern planter is forever failing to achieve. And as Eugene Genovese has noted, the fact that the slaveowning planter was actually no aristocrat, while doubtless true enough, still leaves unexplained his aristocratic pretensions. Genovese himself revives the aristocratic planter as a paternalist master in a slave economy. It is this view, of course, on which Brooks partly relies in his argument that Sutpen cannot be seen as a typical Southern planter because he fails to behave as a father should. If Genovese's argument can so mislead the critic who, in my estimation, has done more than any other to penetrate the enigma of Sutpen, it is worth serious attention. Genovese's primary thesis is that the Old South was not, like the rest of America, based on a capitalist economy; it was, rather, based on a slave economy and devoted to the values of a separate paternalist culture. Such a view reaffirms at once two conceptions of the antebellum South which render *Absalom, Absalom!* unintelligible—that the South was both un-American and noncapitalist in the antebellum period. Once we recognize the quite opposite view on which Faulkner's treatment of Sutpen depends, it becomes possible to see why Sutpen *does* merit the label "American" but not, as a result, the label "aberration." Further, it becomes possible to recognize Faulkner as a novelist whose scope encompasses an American and not simply a

Southern terrain, and thus to regard his appropriation of a set of problems which first arose in Emerson's *Nature* as a development which accords with their common roots in a capitalist society.[6]

The story of William Clark Falkner's career in Tippah County, Mississippi, is not marked by a plethora of verifiable facts, but its basic contours are clear. As a boy of fourteen, William left his family in Missouri, traveling on foot through Tennessee to northern Mississippi, where his uncle, John Wesley Thompson, had settled in the small town of Ripley. His uncle had been teaching school and had begun to practice law. After trying unsuccessfully to persuade his uncle to let him read law at his office in Ripley, William Clark took a job as clerk in the town jail and began studying law at night with a local Irish schoolteacher, who had just set up an office in a log cabin. If one wonders why a small town on the frontier should breed lawyers at this rate, the reason is not difficult to find. Law provided the best opportunity for acquiring land and wealth in the Southwest, as Andrew Jackson's legal career on the Tennessee frontier a generation earlier demonstrates. William Clark's opportunism manifested itself, however, even before he began to practice law. He was present when a murderer who was about to be lynched persuaded the mob to desist by promising to recount in gory detail his murder of five members of a family. William Clark apparently offered his services as amanuensis, taking down the confession and having it printed up just in time to be sold at the hanging. He not only made a tidy profit, but gained widespread notoriety as far away as Alabama. His fame was fueled once again a couple of years later when he went off to fight in the Mexican War, only to be injured on a private errand which his enemies were later to claim had an amorous rather than a military purpose. Falkner later wrote a poem about it confirming their interpretation. In 1847, he made a judicious marriage to Holland Pearce, who came from a reputable family and whose dowry included slaves. Now taken into his uncle's law office, William Clark began amassing land and setting up the Falkner Farms. His wife, having given birth to John Wesley Thompson Falkner in 1848, promptly died of consumption; William Clark took his son to his uncle's house to be raised by the childless Thompsons.

Two years later, his fortunes once again on the rise, Falkner married Lizzie Vance, reputedly the little girl whose family had succored him when he first arrived in Mississippi, poor and hungry. Her family does not appear to have been so solicitious on the occasion of his courtship of their daughter; in fact they went so far as to threaten to leave the region in order to thwart his advances. Lizzie married him anyway, apparently regretting it later. During the years just before the Civil War, William Clark expanded his landholdings and engaged in some slave-trading. By the end of the 1850s he was worth $50,000. He had also changed his politics in response to the impending crisis, moving like many Southerners from the position of a staunch Whig through a flirtation with Know-Nothingism into the Democratic party. After running against his own uncle for the state legislature in 1855 and losing decisively, he cast an electoral vote for Buchanan in 1856.[7]

Falkner's politics were always to reveal a certain ambivalence. When he was finally murdered in 1889 by Richard Jackson Thurmond, a partner in his railroad, he had just been elected to the state legislature as a Democrat. By this time the Democratic party in Mississippi had long since been in the control of the Redeemer faction headed by L. Q. C. Lamar, a faction dominated by Old Whigs and the rising men of the New South, joined by their courtship of northern capital in the name of the South's redemption from the evils of reconstruction. By 1889, the Redeemers were having trouble keeping the poverty-stricken farmers in line. The Farmers' Alliance, forerunner of the Populists of the 1890s, was fighting for the interests of the small farmers, who increasingly felt themselves ignored by the alliance of Delta planters, northern capital and black voters which the Democratic party represented. When William Clark Falkner complained during his campaign for the legislature in 1889, "Persons unfriendly to me have circulated a report that my object in running for the Legislature is to enable me to secure favorable legislation for the railroad. This is unjust, false and slanderous," and reaffirmed his concern for the farmers' plight, there was doubtless some degree of sincerity in his claims. Falkners were indeed always to exhibit a certain sympathy for the much-oppressed farmers of the hills of Tippah and Lafayette counties. John Wesley Thompson Falkner would one day bring the young Lee Russell into his law firm and actively campaign for Russell's political mentor, Senator James K. Vardaman. But still, after years of working with Russell in his law office and of supporting his rise from redneck farmer to lawyer and state politician, J. W. T. Falkner refused to receive Russell at his home. Russell, like Sutpen, was literally turned away from the front door. Similarly, no matter how genuine William Clark Falkner's testimony may have been in 1889, the suspicion about his purposes was probably not altogether ill-founded. By this time, his own success had placed him politically well beyond any easy access to the political interests of downtrodden farmers. His sympathy with those who, like himself, started out with few advantages would doubtless have proved even harder to sustain had he lived through the following decade. In any case, his entrepreneurial status in the county had by 1889 already begun to put him at cross-purposes with the interests of those who shared his humble origins.[8]

When the war came, Falkner raised his own regiment and led them with distinction at the first battle of Manassas. Voted out of his command after the first year of the war, he came home and raised another regiment of Partisan Rangers. When Jefferson Davis ordered such guerrilla groups to disband, and when Falkner's repeated pleas for another command were ignored, he apparently quit fighting altogether. He disappeared for the last two years of the war, when he was apparently running the blockade around Memphis. At least this would explain the fact that when he returned to Mississippi at the war's end, he was hardly an impoverished man; within a year after his arrival, in a typically grandiose gesture, he deeded some land to a local college. Nor does the war seem to have stemmed the flow of his ambition, for he returned to his prewar course, expanding his landholdings and returning the Falkner Farms to productivity. He was still on that course when he started building his railroad in partnership with Thurmond in the 1870s, a venture initially funded by northern capital. By the 1880s, after a series of setbacks, the railroad was operating. Meanwhile, he was receiving royalties from his novel, *The White Rose of Memphis*. Now part owner of a lumber business as well as the railroad which he kept trying to link up to others, Falkner seems to have lacked no zeal in the years following the war in his efforts to aggrandize his social and financial position. He put a final polish to his career when he set off for a grand tour of Europe with his granddaughter, writing travel pieces which were published at home and eventually collected under the title *Rapid Ramblings in Europe*. Upon his return, he had his house in Ripley rebuilt on a hybrid design concocted from his memory of the cathedrals and stately homes he had seen abroad; the result was transcendentally grotesque. On his last business trip to New York, he ordered the statue of himself, made of Carrara marble, which still stands upon his grave in Ripley.[9]

This is hardly the story of the planter-aristocrat as he has come down to us in legend, although it is, in its essentials, not atypical of many a Southern parvenu who assumed an aristocratic posture. Old Colonel Falkner had his proverbially faithful body servant, Nathan, who swatted flies and served him whiskey. But Falkner worked hard at cultivating this leisured role. He tried to make up for his lack of education by reading Shakespeare and the Greek and Latin classics in translation. He sent his younger brother to the University of Mississippi, hoping to provide his brother with the cultural resources he himself lacked. He wrote poems, novels, travelogues, as a wealthy gentleman of leisure was supposed to do, but *The White Rose of Memphis* returned him more in profits than in literary repute. Perhaps his last and most telling pretension was the stack of books at the feet of the statue he ordered for his grave.[10]

If Falkner was no planter-aristocrat, neither was he a yeoman farmer, the type whose virtues are so often emphasized by those bent upon redeeming the South from the sins of the Slaveowner. Between them, the Planter and the Yeoman have long dominated the picture of the South; in fact, Faulkner's fiction has recently been interpreted by reference to his conflicting loyalties to both types. Ambivalent he may have been in this respect, but this had little to do with his treatment of Sutpen, who resembles William Clark Falkner in his singular failure to conform to either stereotype. But like Sutpen's, William Clark Falkner's story does embody a pattern visible in the careers of many a planter and even a few yeomen, for he was at bottom a self-made man, one who rose from orphaned poverty to entrepreneurial success in the classic American way—

by hard work, driving ambition, shrewd opportunism, colossal arrogance, and a little help from his uncle. William Faulkner, who was named after his great-grandfather, described him to Robert Cantwell in 1938 as a man who "had no humor and probably no sensibility," but "wanted to make a pile of money" and "made it." "He had to be big dog," Faulkner remarked. When his railroad was completed, William Clark named some of the stations after characters in Sir Walter Scott's novels. What apparently struck Faulkner about this was not the Southern habit of inscribing the countryside with names taken from Scott's novels—a habit Faulkner satirized in *Go Down, Moses*—but the hubris his great-grandfather's naming revealed. "The people could call the towns whatever they wanted," Faulkner said, "but by God, he would name the depots." Limited though his exploits may seem, when set against those of Morgan, Mellon, or Gould, William Clark Falkner achieved no mean splendor in the minds of the residents of Tippah County. "People at Ripley talk of him," Faulkner said, "as if he were still alive, up in the hills someplace, and might come in at any time, . . . he rode through that country like a living force."[11]

Falkner's entrepreneurial designs probably stood out all the more prominently in Tippah County, for it was far removed from the rich Delta counties around Natchez where huge plantations had been established well before 1840, the year Falkner probably arrived in Mississippi. But he clearly pursued a course fundamentally modeled on those of the Delta's wealthiest planters. Among these, for example, was one Stephen Duncan, a Natchez banker who owned six cotton and two sugar plantations in the Southwest and landed property in the North, where he had invested heavily in railroads as well. One of the more famous "cotton snobs," Duncan was clearly a capitalist entrepreneur. Others had less to build on and did not get this far by the time the war started, but they were obviously pursuing the same goal. Isaac Franklin, for instance, made his money in the slave trade and then set up as a gentleman planter, who, by 1846, owned six plantations in Louisiana and one in Tennessee, but only 700 slaves as compared with Duncan's 1,041. Those of this group who weathered Reconstruction, together with a new generation of rising entrepreneurs from both North and South, formed the nucleus of the Redeemers in the post war years. Although Falkner's politics, as we have seen, were less consistently and unambiguously Whiggish than Duncan's, and the Falkner Farms never achieved the grandeur of the Delta, it remains clear that William Clark Falkner never lost sight of his ambition to rise to a seat of entrepreneurial grandeur. His activities, before, during, and after the war were all aimed at that goal, one which—allowing for its limited scale—he in fact reached.[12]

As John Cawelti has suggested, the self-made man of the early nineteenth century, whatever the self-help guides may have solemnly pronounced about the virtues of diligence, frugality, and piety, was essentially an aspiring entrepreneur. Of course, the ideal of the self-made man could serve many purposes. According to Cawelti, the social conservative "preached the gospel of self-help" in order "to keep the recipient of his advice in a position of contented inferiority without having to undertake the responsibility of supporting him." Henry Clay could defend his "American System" against charges that it would create a "privileged aristocracy of manufacturing corporations" by claiming that "in Kentucky, almost every manufactury known to me is in the hands of enterprising and self-made men," adding the obligatory reference to these men's "patient and diligent labor" as a final sanctification by the holy Protestant work ethic. So fundamental was the appeal of the self-made man that "Democrats and Whigs vied with each other in proclaiming their devotion" to his interests, Cawelti notes, constantly bringing "to the forefront of their campaigns the log cabins which supposedly existed in the background of their candidates." The ideal was, of course, enshrined forever with the ascendancy of Lincoln, who, in a statement with a certain relevance to Sutpen, reaffirmed it as president when in 1864 he told a regiment of soldiers that "any one of your children" can in principle come to "occupy this big white house, . . . as my father's child has." But whether the ideal was invoked out of a desire to calm the workingman, to pass a bill, to elect a candidate, or to inspire soldiers in time of war, its appeal lay in a widespread and deepening ambition which expressed itself in the quest for wealth and social status. The republican ideal of autonomy may have provided a residual nucleus around which the entrepreneurial model was to be built, but such autonomy gradually receded as capitalism developed, a value more defended than pursued.[13]

No region of the nation was more likely to attract those with entrepreneurial designs than the Southwest in the first half of the nineteenth century, and for a reason which can be put in a word: cotton. Faulkner, characteristically, amplified the word:

> Cotton: a king: omnipotent and omnipresent: a destiny of which (obvious now) the plough and the axe had been merely the tools; not plough and axe which had effaced the wilderness, but Cotton.

As the Indians were "removed," the Southwest became ripe for the expansion of the cotton kingdom, promising the ambitious a chance to follow in the footsteps of men like Franklin and Duncan, though of course more typically swelling the coffers of the Franklins and Duncans themselves. Like Tidewater Virginia two centuries earlier, the Southwest offered men the opportunity to rise from poverty to eminence, and to enable their sons to expand their holdings from a position of undisputed superiority, secured by the kind of money whose age made it, as F. Scott Fitzgerald was later to put it, "non-olfactory." In fact, Tidewater Virginia's tobacco boom, though it spawned similar efforts to buy up large tracts of land for future sale if not future cultivation, had been short-lived by comparison with the cotton boom set off by Eli Whitney's invention of the cotton gin in 1793. From Andrew Jackson's youthful exploits in Tennessee before the turn of the century until the Civil War, the fortune-seekers moved, wave upon wave, into the Southwest. Few succeeded, of course, but this hardly means that few tried. And William Clark Falkner may safely be counted as one of those who succeeded.[14]

William Clark Falkner does not, obviously, constitute a literal model for Thomas Sutpen. Despite the fact that they share certain details—the fourteen-year-old orphan who leaves home to seek his fortune, the marble tombstone, the command of a regiment in the war, the initially shaky social status, the architectural hubris—the two careers take different forms. Sutpen rises from illiterate poor white to overseer to plantation owner, while Falkner rose from jail clerk to lawyer to railroad owner. But in two crucial respects these careers resemble each other. First, at the heart of them both is an incorrigible ambition to rise at all costs, to be "big dog," and second, both owned slaves. It is this figure, ostensibly a fusion of the slaveowning planter and the self-made man, whose fate Faulkner set out to explore in *Absalom, Absalom!*.

This was not, of course, the first time Faulkner had used his great-grandfather's life as a fictional resource. It had served already as a source for Colonel Sartoris. But the "Old Colonel," as both Falkner and Sartoris were called, is a remembered hero in *Sartoris,* where his son, the "Young Colonel," is himself already an old man. The Old Colonel figures more prominently in *The Unvanquished*, but even there his life is depicted from the war years until his death through the perspective of the Young Colonel as a boy growing to manhood during these same years. In other words, in neither novel do we find any concentrated treatment of the Old Colonel's own youth. There is a certain logic to this omission in the Sartoris family novels, for these are hardly Faulkner's most critical treatments of the Southern past. *Sartoris'* marked indulgence in romantic nostalgia may be attributed to its early date; it was written at the time when Faulkner was first setting up as the "sole owner and proprietor" of Yoknapatawpha County. But the short stories in *The Unvanquished* were put together during roughly the same period as *Absalom, Absalom!* and their more troubled, but no less visible, romanticism stands in stark contrast to the ruthlessness both of *Absalom, Absalom!* and of its hero. To compare the two heroes is to realize that Faulkner was playing for much higher stakes in *Absalom, Absalom!*, where he moved back beyond the postwar years into those of his great-grandfather's youth, producing a novel which appreciably undermines the nostalgia emanating from the pages of *The Unvanquished*. It almost seems as if *The Unvanquished* helped him to write *Absalom, Absalom!* by siphoning off his own romantic attachment to the cavalier legends passed down in his own family, enabling him to face—or rather, to make Quentin Compson face—the more brutal history obscured by those legends. In any case, as we have seen, the "Old Colonel" named Falkner had a checkered history, one whose deeper significance remained untapped in the character of Old Colonel Sartoris, but which emerged when Faulkner sat Quentin Compson down at Harvard to confront the awesome spectacle of

Sutpen. Now—for the first time in his career—Faulkner focused his attention on the rise as well as the fall of a family.[15]

This moment marks a genuine leap in Faulkner's career, one which needs more serious attention than it has received. In his treatment of the Sartorises, Faulkner had revealed his own saturation with the legendary tales of cavalier heroism and the romance of the Lost Cause. In *The Sound and the Fury*, he had taken a decisive step further, registering in Quentin Compson's spiritual paralysis the effects of that saturation. But in these novels, Faulkner had not tried to portray the prewar South; rather, he had portrayed the legend of the Old South as in itself a phenomenon worthy of rich fictional treatment. That legend, as he himself had experienced it, was passed on through a set of tales whose resonance seemed infinite. But in *Absalom, Absalom!*, Faulkner examined in depth the very process by which such tales create the past, and in so doing he transformed that process from one which manufactures and sustains illusions into one which also and simultaneously undercuts and destroys them. The result is a novel in which the distant past of Mississippi in the 1830s is not allowed to remain distant and disembodied behind the veneer of nostalgic memory, but rather assumes the form of flesh and blood. In other words, if Quentin Compson at the novel's outset is a "barracks filled with stubborn back-looking ghosts," by the end he has had to face a flesh-and-blood embodiment of such a ghost in the person of Henry Sutpen. Indeed, the narrative strategy of *Absalom, Absalom!* is designed to force both Quentin and the reader into a recognition of the physical and material bonds which connect present to past, the living to the dead, and thereby to destroy the illusion of history as populated with "painted portraits hung in a vacuum." But this advance in Faulkner's narrative experimentation was accompanied and, one suspects, partly stimulated by, his effort to move deeper into the past, to portray the world in which William Clark Falkner had himself risen from poverty to wealth. What this effort produced was a novel in which Faulkner confronted the legend of the Old South with its actual past, the aristocrat in decline with the raw parvenu from whom his own family had descended. For the Compsons, who had served in *The Sound and the Fury* as the vehicle for Faulkner's evocation of a proud Southern family in decline, are themselves the descendants of a parvenu named Jason Lycurgus Compson.[16]

When Faulkner got around to describing Quentin's forebears for Malcolm Cowley's *Portable Faulkner*, he depicted the Jason Compson who first appeared in Jefferson in 1820 as a man who acquired the Compson Domain from Ikkemotubbe in exchange for a horse who could win a three-furlong race, though—unbeknownst to Ikkemotubbe—that was all the horse could do. Tedious though it is to explore the discrepancies in Faulkner's genealogies, it is worth noting that this appendix, reprinted in later editions of *The Sound and the Fury*, establishes the heights to which the Compson family had risen by the time of the Civil War by expanding into five generations what had been only three in *Absalom, Absalom!* In *Absalom, Absalom!*, Quentin's grandfather, General Compson, is Sutpen's contemporary; but in the appendix, Jason Lycurgus Compson, the general's own grandfather, would have been Sutpen's nearer contemporary, since Sutpen arrived in Jefferson some thirteen years after Jason Compson did. My point is that the difference between Sutpen and Compson is not a matter of parvenu origins, but of the use to which Faulkner put the two families at different stages in his career. The appendix which documents the Compson's origins, rise, and decline, is well suited to the vision of the Compsons in *The Sound and the Fury*, where they represent a once prominent Southern family whose decline has itself given rise to the legendary aura in which its past glory is enshrined. For legends whose energy is sustained by this sort of decline, many generations are required and parvenu origins are of little consequence; in America all "aristocrats" come from such origins. But in *Absalom, Absalom!* Faulkner was directly concerned with those origins and with their shattering implications for a Quentin Compson to whom Sutpen was "trash." Thus, a grandfather who had been in Jefferson to see Sutpen appear in 1833 and was still there in the 1890s to describe Sutpen's speech habits provided a necessary link between the young Quentin of 1909 and the parvenu Sutpen of the 1830s, a connection necessary if Quentin was to face the idea that "maybe it took . . . Thomas Sutpen to make all of us."[17]

But we need not rely solely on genealogical changes in order to appreciate Faulkner's aims in *Absalom, Absalom!* The ease with which the Compsons and Sartorises can transform defeat into material for heroic legends is evident in Aunt Jennie's tales of cavalier glory in *Sartoris*, and it is not altogether absent from Mr. Compson's cynical oratory in *The Sound and the Fury*. But the Southern taletellers in *Absalom, Absalom!* enjoy no such ease in their narrative efforts; on the contrary, they are constantly frustrated. It is not difficult to see why. What commands respect in *Sartoris* and *The Sound and the Fury* are the traditional Southern virtues—military heroism, loyalty to home and family, honor in defeat. Except for military heroism—a fact which drives Rosa Coldfield, in particular, further into distraction than she has already been driven—Sutpen fails signally to fit this pattern. Mr. Compson as well is mystified by Sutpen's behavior, which he cannot explain at all, given the limits of his peculiarly cynical version of Southern romanticism. Sutpen's legendary status, unlike that of Colonel Sartoris and General Compson, derives not from a postwar decline, but from a failure whose causes are mysterious because they are implicit in his rise to wealth and power. Only Quentin, with Shreve's help, is able finally to glimpse what Sutpen's career reveals—that despite all the atrocities Sutpen commits in its name, he is dedicated to vindicating the American dream itself. Conducted in the name of equality, the principle, as Faulkner once put it, that "man, if he is man, cannot be inferior to another man through artificial standards or circumstances," Sutpen's career reconstitutes the very class structure, the very artificial standards it is designed to invalidate. With Sutpen, then, Faulkner cuts through the multilayered myths of the Old South to confront the entrepreneurial designs which had actually created the Cotton Kingdom, and in so doing, reveals the explosive consequences of understanding the slaveowning planter for the capitalist entrepreneur he was.[18]

The antebellum South's self-made man driven by entrepreneurial aspirations has been obscured, largely by two opposed historical interpretations, neither of which is congruent with Faulkner's. The first and less formidable of the two is that of the prewar South as a land of yeoman farmers, a vision first projected during the Roosevelt era by Frank Owsley and the Agrarians at Vanderbilt. Using census records, Owsley and his students found a significant majority of small farmers, and argued that they constituted the backbone of a Southern democracy; this argument called into question the traditional view of a plantation aristocracy dominating the Old South from behind white porticos and fragrant magnolias. Critics soon discredited many of Owsley's statistical methods, and subsequent research has considerably muddied the waters first stirred up by Owsley's insistence upon the hegemony of Plain Folk. Yet the literary wing of the Vanderbilt movement has continued to exercise its influence, especially over our view of Southern writers, and therefore it is worth clarifying the differences between Faulkner's social vision and Owsley's.

There is no doubt, of course, about Faulkner's recognition of, and respect for, the small farmers of the South, nor about his view of the South as populated largely by them. He once pointed out at the University of Virginia that "the elegance of the colonial plantation didn't exist" in his country, which was still frontier, a place where people "lived from day to day with a bluff and crude hardiness, but with a certain simplicity." Faulkner's fiction depicts many small farmers from the hills, usually with genuine sympathy for their straitened circumstances. But Faulkner's vision of the prewar South's class structure, as he described it to Malcolm Cowley, while acknowledging "a middle class fixed upon the land," does not finally accord with Owsley's vision, essentially because for Faulkner that class harbors men with aspirations to rise. Responding to the question of why no significant literature was produced in the South in this period, Faulkner told Cowley:

There was no literate middle class to produce a literature. In a pastoral cityless land they lived remote and at economic war with both slave and slaveholder. When they emerged, gradually, son by infrequent son, like Old Sutpen, it was not to establish themselves as a middle class but to make themselves barons, too.

It would appear that Faulkner's view has much to recommend it over Owsley's. For one thing, the political behavior of the small farmers in Mississippi suggests that they had their ambitions as well as their resentments. While their support for the Confederacy was not always wholehearted, we cannot infer from this that they were all free of the desire to emulate the Cotton Snobs. How, for example, are we to interpret the debate that occurred in the Mississippi legislature in 1852 over a bill to prohibit the importation of slaves? The small farmers opposed the bill on the grounds that the rich planters would be able to get around the restriction (as they indeed had done before), and acquire more slaves, while the small farmers would not, and thus their capacity to extend and develop their property would be seriously hindered. At the time there was a labor shortage, a problem which affected the large planters much less than the small. A small planter who had succeeded in expanding his landholdings might be unable to realize a profit for lack of a labor force to cultivate his cotton. Many of these farmers were doubtless fighting a defensive battle rather than an aggressive one; as in the Northeast, rising and declining men were often fighting concentrated wealth for different motives. But clearly, given the economic as well as the social value of slaves, the debate over their importation suggests that there was built into the small farmers' bitter conflict with the Cotton Snobs of the Delta an aspiration among some at least to close the economic distance between the two. Faulkner's vision of the antebellum farmer acknowledges, as Owsley's cannot, the dynamic quality of the social structure, reflected in the aspirations of some farmers to emerge from the ranks of the yeomanry. More important, Faulkner's view encompasses what Owsley's struggles to exclude; Owsley's thesis produces its benign and comforting picture of a Southern democracy made up of common men only by excluding as exceptions those common men who happen to be black and enslaved by those other exceptions who are white slaveowners. Such exceptions do not prove any rule; on the contrary, they constitute one. Faulkner, by contrast, clearly regards the farmer's "economic war with both slave and slaveholder" as a central feature of his social position. But whether Faulkner's historical vision is superior to Owsley's— as I think it certainly is—is less important than the fact of its difference. The difference ultimately derives from the fact that Faulkner, unlike the Agrarians of the 1930s and 1940s, did not view the Old South as a world uncontaminated by the spirit of capitalism. Given the essential continuity of both his great-grandfather's career—from Whig lawyer with landed property to railroad entrepreneur—and his grandfather's—from law partner of a Lamar protégé to banker and owner of a variety of businesses to be handed on to his sons—Faulkner could hardly have failed to recognize the long-standing presence of the entrepreneurial drive in his "country."[19]

More decisive by far than Owsley's thesis in obscuring the entrepreneurial designs of the South's rising men has been their use of slave labor and the futile and twisted defenses they were constrained to make of it. Louis Hartz put their dilemma most effectively in a classic description of John Taylor's frustrated response to it:

In the time of Jefferson the agony of the South had been complex. Not only had John Taylor been embarrassed by slavery because of liberalism, but he had been embarrassed by liberalism because even then he had nourished a Disraelian streak. Now, in the age of Fitzhugh, when both of these problems would seem to have been solved, Taylor discovered that he could not be a real Disraeli even if given a chance to be one. He was a plantation capitalist, and in the Southwest, for all of its stratified social life, he was a very new, very raw, very fierce plantation capitalist. And so the sweat that had to go into making the South medieval was even greater than the sweat that had gone into making it modern.

In recent years, new sweat has gone into making the Old South a paternalistic society based on a slave economy rather than a capitalist one. While Faulkner's vision of the antebellum South has a good deal more in common with Eugene Genovese's than with Owsley's, it nonetheless conflicts decisively with Genovese's view of the South as a paternalistic society which rightly thought of itself as fundamentally distinct from, and opposed to, the North's competitive capitalist system. Once again, the point of deepest conflict lies in the issue of the parvenu, the rising man of the period whose aristocratic pretensions Genovese reads as evidence of a distinctive paternalist ideology dominating the South. His classic statement of this position comes in his attack on Wilbur Cash in *The World the Slaveholders Made*, where Genovese argues that such pretensions ought to be taken seriously as indications of the difference between the social vision inspiring Southerners and that inspiring Northerners, rather than merely as a thin veneer covering a raw Southern parvenu. "The questions," Genovese says, "come to these: Did the rising planters of the Southwest during the 1830's have before them, as an ideal future for themselves and their children, Virginia or Massachusetts? the Cavalier or the financier? Were they, in their economy and social relations, going down a bourgeois or an aristocratic road?'' Lest there be any doubt about how distinct these roads are in Genovese's mind, it is worth quoting another passage, this one from *The Political Economy of Slavery*:

At their best, Southern ideals constituted a rejection of the crass, vulgar, inhumane elements of capitalist society. The slaveholders simply could not accept the idea that the cash nexus offered a permissible basis for human relations. Even the vulgar parvenu of the Southwest embraced the plantation myth and refused to make a virtue of necessity by glorifying the competitive side of slavery as civilization's highest achievement. The slaveholders generally, and the planters in particular, did identify their own ideals with the essence of civilization, and given their sense of honor, were prepared to defend them at any cost.

It is worth remarking, of course, that ''at their best,'' Northern ideals also constituted a rejection of the evils of capitalist society; the South in the antebellum period was by no means alone in staunchly rejecting the cash nexus as a ''permissible basis for human relations.'' But presumably, Genovese would not dispute this point, since his primary aim is to underscore the extent to which the plantation myth provided a social and cultural vehicle for such ideals which was decisively different from any the North could offer, and this because for Genovese, the paternalist ideology fits a slave economy, not a capitalist one.[20]

This claim has a good deal to recommend it on logical grounds, and in traversing those grounds over the years, Genovese has shown how deeply paternalism saturated the consciousness of the Old South. Faulkner's approach to the antebellum South in *Absalom, Absalom!* relies heavily upon a similar apprehension of paternalism's hegemony, but for Faulkner, paternalism is rooted in American, not merely Southern, history and the conflicts—both theoretical and historical—into which it led the South had their origin not in an opposition between two economic systems at war with one another. but rather in a set of contradictions inherent in American capitalist development. Again, I think Faulkner's view has much to recommend it over Genovese's, but I do not wish to argue that point so much as to call attention to the difference between the two. The ideological dominance of paternalism in the South need not be disputed in order to realize that both the plantation myth and the paternalism inscribed in it were themselves the product of capitalist expansion.

Even a brief review of the plantation legend's history reveals why the rising planter of the Southwest never faced the choice Genovese implies he made in refusing to glorify "the competitive side of slavery." As William O. Taylor has shown, it was not really until the 1830s that the plantation legend as we have come to know it first developed. Previously, the South had been regarded, at least by most cultivated Northerners, as a land of barbaric "Tuckahoes." Only with *Swallow Barn*, published in 1832, did the plantation begin to assume those trappings of pastoral grace and refinement for which it has since become famous. John Pendleton Kennedy started out in *Swallow Barn* making fun of Tidewater Virginia and ended up sentimentalizing and finally eulogizing it as an image of an ideal America. Why did this happen? Kennedy himself was no planter; he was the son of a Baltimore merchant whose country home was not in the Tidewater, but in the Cumberland district of Virginia. Taylor explores this question at length, and in the process reveals just how deeply rooted was the plantation myth in a capitalist America. For one thing, the plantation ideal could serve as the repository of traditional rural values; thus *Swallow Barn* met a widespread need to "sentimentalize country life" felt by urban dwellers who had left the provinces to make their way in the cities, where lay both the opportunities for rising, and the corruptions attendant upon them.[21]

In addition to projecting a pastoral retreat from city life, the plantation legend had other compensatory attractions to offer as well. It incorporated, for example, one of the major, if not *the* major, nineteenth-century strategies for protecting human relations from the contamination of the cash nexus—the cult of domesticity promulgated most notably by Sarah Hale in *Godey's Lady's Book*. Sarah Hale set out to combat the opportunism and corruption of the marketplace by sanctifying the home and elevating the role of wife-and-mother to the position of the mainstay of social cohesion and the fountainhead of moral influence. The ideological value of the home was itself tied to an expanding capitalism, of course. As the nineteenth century unfolded, women's position was increasingly undermined; no longer called upon to produce what they could now purchase, women moved into the only role in the marketplace available to them, that of consumer. Insofar as they remained producers, they produced words, sentiment, and influence, all in an effort to stem the tide of social atomization by an appeal to the home as the bulwark of idealism. The plantation legend served as a perfect vehicle for the values of home and hearth, as Harriet Beecher Stowe understood, with well-known consequences. In *Uncle Tom's Cabin*, she appealed to the values of the home against those of the marketplace, focusing her harshest criticism not on the South, whose paternalistic ideals she shared, but on the bourgeois rapacity of slave traders and overseers, and on the hypocrisy of Northern clergymen. Stowe did not speak for the North as against the South; she spoke for the values of the family against those of the businessman, an opposition in fact far more visible in Northern society than in Southern, where the business was cotton and the businessman a planter. As Taylor remarks, the plantation myth "was not the South's image concocted to propagandize the North, nor was it the woman's or the man's; it was the nineteenth century's. Thackeray's plantation was scarcely different." Nor did the century's more acute critical observers fail to see the actual motives being at once served and obscured by the myth. Balzac's Jacques Collin (alias M. Vautrin, alias Cheat-Death) makes those motives clear in the middle of his stunning address to Eugène Rastignat in *Père Goriot*:

> You see I have a fancy. My notion is to go and live the patriarchal life on a great estate, say a hundred thousand acres, in the United States of America, in the deep South. I intend to be a planter, to have slaves, earn a few nice little millions selling my cattle, my tobacco, my timber, living like a monarch, doing as I like, leading a life unimaginable by people here where we live crouched in a burrow made of stone and plaster.

The words "patriarchal life," of course, have a special irony in a novel demonstrating just what happens to fathers in a society increasingly dominated by the cash nexus. To a man with Balzac's knowledge of and attachment to a genuine aristocracy, the plantation myth was just as vulnerable a screen for entrepreneurial designs as the rhetoric of the "technological sublime" has proved to be. Perhaps it is partly due to a long-standing confusion in the minds of Americans over the difference between capitalist and aristocrat that they have never really been able to resist altogether the plantation myth's attractions. In any case, they have hardly ever succeeded at seeing the myth in such a critical light as Balzac sheds on it.[22]

One reason for the myth's long and virulent career, one suspects, is that it is deeply bound up with American aspirations. At least it originated with these aspirations. As Taylor notes, the creation of the impetuous Southern Cavalier and the nostalgic portrayal of plantation life were themselves, in the first instance, the work of the "New Men" of the postrevolutionary era, "aspiring men" whose appeal to traditional rural and familial values was made in response to wrenching internal anxieties about the implications and consequences of their own aspirations to rise. A disaffected Northern Whig like John Kirke Paulding, for example, having made his way up in society, was increasingly disturbed by the very social dynamism which had made that rise possible, as well as by the machine-run future it presented for America. In his efforts to devise an ideal American identity, modeled after a George Washington who embodied the virtues of the natural aristocrat and the transcendent Yankee, Paulding blended the virtues of Southerner, Northerner, and Westerner, trying to preserve a noble and manly independence without sacrificing the aspirations of the self-made man. Born in the vexed minds of the aspiring men of the 1830s, the plantation legend was revived in the 1880s and 1890s, in the service of another group of rising men—this time in the South. The Redeemers having wrested control of their states from the forces of Reconstruction— and this through the collusion of men like L. Q. C. Lamar with Northern Republicans—the aspiring men of the late nineteenth century reinvented the "Old South" while pouring their energies into building the new. The paradox is dramatized by Faulkner's own grandfather, J. W. T. Falkner, who sported the classic white suit and panama hat of the Southern Colonel while accumulating land and businesses galore from his seat in his Oxford bank. In short, the restoration of the Old South was enacted in the interests of those who were most actively engaged in exploiting the New South's resources, as C. Vann Woodward has demonstrated with implacable logic. As Woodward puts it, "this archaic romanticism, this idealizing of the past, proceeded from the mouths of the most active propagandists of the New Order. And this with no apparent sense of inconsistency, certainly none of duplicity." In neither phase of its history did acceptance of the plantation legend apparently imply an opposition to entrepreneurial designs. In both its inception and its revival, in both North and South, and both before and after the war, the plantation legend served the interests of aspiring men.[23]

But it is the aspiring men of the antebellum South with whom we are chiefly concerned here, and Genovese is certainly correct in seeing them as thoroughly committed to the plantation myth and the paternalism ascribed to it. In accounting for this, however, it is not necessary to see the myth as validating a distinct slave economy in the South; it is just as plausible, if not more so, to see the myth as validating the use of slave labor by the plantation capitalist about whose "agony" Louis Hartz is so eloquent. Nor need we interpret such validation as implying a crass and cynical excuse for slavery offered by a South under ideological siege; as we have already noted, a dominant ideology does not prevail by self-conscious hypocrisy, but by gradually developing a set of beliefs and attitudes which appear virtually congruent with common sense itself. Thus, when we note that the plantation myth, for many years, offered the Southern slaveowning planter a peculiarly effective ideological resource, we need not assume that he was insincere in his appeal to that resource, any more than we need assume that Daniel Webster or Timothy Walker were insincere in their appeals to Progress. In both cases, a dominant class's interests are at stake, but when we juxtapose the Northern and Southern wings of that class, it becomes clear that, for a while, the Southerners enjoyed certain advantages in their effort to secure hegemonic dominance.

Most notably, the Northern Whig had to trivialize the pastoral retreat as a merely aesthetic value, but the Southern Whig could incorporate it as a social one. The Northerner had to compartmentalize his society into home and marketplace, walking a tightrope between the contradictory claims of familial ties and business interests. He had to see the family as benefited by labor-saving devices which would free the workingman for self-improvement and provide his family with more leisure time. He had to accommodate the family as ideal, but he could not incorporate it very easily within his social vision. But the Southern planter could and did incorporate the values of home and hearth within his social vision, by assuming the role of patriarch over an extended family in whose interests and in whose midst he was always, in principle, working. In short, the paternalist ideology of the Southern planter could and did serve—up to a certain point, both historically and theoretically—to confirm the dominant slaveowning class's right to dominate, while in the North, the dominant class had to relegate to a peripheral cultural position the pastoral and familial values on which the Southerner could rely. What destroyed this neat congruence of self-interest and idealism was not the intrusion of the cash nexus from without, but the exposure of the cash nexus within the plantation as a unit of production. When that exposure came—as it did quite explosively in *Uncle Tom's Cabin*—the Northerner's compartmentalization of home and marketplace proved itself a blessing in disguise and the more powerful strategy after all. Stowe's zealous appeal to the familial ideal exposed the basic incompatibility of the cash nexus and the family, both black and white, whose unity it destroyed. The plantation myth, in effect, proved vulnerable for the same reasons it had once been so powerful; it had provided a means for fusing within one social vision what in the end could not be fused because they were fundamentally contradictory—family and marketplace values. Since he had never really fused these values, but merely tried to make them interdependent, the Northern Whig's own vulnerability to Stowe's searing criticism of the destructive force of the cash nexus on the family went largely unnoticed.

Why, then, did the South allow itself to become vulnerable in this way? In Genovese's view, it had no choice, devoted as it was to the "aristocratic road," a road which logically and inevitably led to Fitzhugh's embrace of a feudal economy and a paternalistic culture. But again, we need not elevate George Fitzhugh to these dizzy heights of ideological supremacy in order to appreciate the South's need to exploit a fatally vulnerable ideological resource. The fusion of family and marketplace values was fostered, ironically, by the same presence which ultimately exploded it—the black slave, whose imputed status as a member of the family was in conflict with his economic function as part of a labor force. The slave, in effect, embodied in a flesh-and-blood form the transformation of man into a thing. By implicitly acknowledging the slave's human status as a child and member of a human family, the South's paternalist ideology rendered palpable and visible what the North's compartmentalized social vision served to repress—the exploitation of human labor required for the growth of capital. What added to the white slaveowning Southerner's complex "agony," furthermore, was that he *did* often believe in his paternal role, as Genovese insistently reminds us. But this state of affairs only forced him to internalize the contradiction which the African slave's legal status externalized—that between the family ideal and the cash nexus. The two had become bound together for the slaveowner in all aspects of his social life, so that he was daily extracting forced labor from people whom he thought of as his children, and who of course sometimes *were* his children. But his self-contradictory condition had itself evolved out of the earliest phases of America's capitalist expansion, for America's paternalistic ideology was generated not only by a slave economy, but also by Indian removal.

According to Michael Rogin, "market liberalism engendered longings for paternal authority, and Indian removal gave these longings their historic task," so that in the Jacksonian era, "statesmen from all sections of America asserted paternal authority over Indians." Rogin's examination of Andrew Jackson's career demonstrates with stunning clarity the role of paternalism in the capitalist expansion to which the nation committed itself in the first half of the nineteenth century. As Rogin notes, according to Rosa Luxemburg, "Capital is . . . faced with difficulties" when confronted with "social organizations that have no desire for commodity exchange or cannot, because of the entire social structure and the forms of ownership, offer for sale the productive forces in which capital is primarily interested. The most important of these productive forces is of course the land." As Rogin points out, in America the social organization which Capital had to break up was that of the Indian tribes, whose land had become the primary productive force in American capitalist development. In presiding over both the destruction of the Indian tribes and the resulting expropriation of their land, Jackson played a central role in the stage of primitive accumulation. As the record of Jackson's dealing with the Indians demonstrates, the paternalism in whose name the Indian removal was conducted was merely "the mirror image of liberalism," setting a "single power over the mass of rhetorically equal children, whose indigenous cultural and social organization it destroyed." Particularly in the Southwest, where the Indian tribes were more entrenched, having begun to develop a plantation agriculture of their own, the "sadistic underside of American expansion" surfaced. Paternalism thus served, incongruously, to portray the Indians as children and then to remove them from their homeland. In asserting paternal authority over Indians, Americans slaughtered their self-acknowledged children. Further, "slavery helped Jackson define the paternal state in whose name he removed Indians. Marrying paternalism to liberal egalitarian assumptions, he provided a structure for American expansion." Asserting paternal authority over slaves, of course, proved a task calling for the patience of a businessman as well as the violence of the Indian fighter, but nonetheless it presumed and depended upon the same ideology called forth by the need to assert paternal authority over Indians. So if the bachelor frontiersman of the West served as the bearer of what Rogin aptly terms a "mythic flight from the significance of capitalist expansion," the Southern planter constituted a mythic reassertion of the paternalism in whose name that expansion had first proceeded. The paternal authority of the state expropriated the land on which the paternal authority of the planter could then be exercised; it was a mutually self-justifying system—one set of children was exiled or killed so that another set of children could be enslaved. Such is the ideological power of paternalism, in whose name the initial productive forces of American capitalism were accumulated.[24]

In view of such a history, we may be excused for our lack of amazement at the fact that the parvenu of the Southwest "refused to make a virtue of necessity by glorifying the competitive side of slavery as civilization's highest achievement." He had long since made a virtue of necessity by embracing the plantation myth and the paternal authority inscribed therein. In identifying "their own ideals with the essence of civilization," the Southern planters had the full force of westward expansion behind them. The paternalism in the name of which they defended the slave system as an alternative to capitalism was born with the paternalism in the name of which they and their fathers had participated in the nation's capitalist expansion, an expansion to which they remained devoted in their embrace of Manifest Destiny and their support of the Mexican War. Indeed, paternalism served the nation rather well in the first half of the nineteenth century; it served to reduce Indians and Africans to the status of docile children in the minds of their murderers and exploiters; it served to compensate for urbanization in the North and to justify exploitation in the South as well. From the outset, it served one interest, that of Capital. No matter how much the Southern planter may have regarded himself as the kind father and benevolent patriarch, and indeed, no matter how far he may have exerted himself to fulfill that role, he remained enmeshed in a capitalist economy. He was no more able to withstand or to transcend the forces unleashed by that economy than was the New England reformer who designed communities in the West on the principle of the factory.[25]

This, in any case, would seem to be Faulkner's view of the matter in *Absalom, Absalom!*, where he presents us with a man who acts in the service of a dream of paternal authority which is sufficiently grandiose to merit the analogy with King David implied by the novel's title. Sutpen embodies that paternalism embraced by Andrew Jackson in the service of capitalist expansion and his fate reflects the contradictions at the core of that paternalism. As Faulkner explained, Sutpen was "a man who wanted sons and got sons who destroyed him," as a result of his failure to recognize that he was "a member . . . of the human family." Herein lies the central irony of Sutpen's dream of founding a dynasty. In the name of his patriarchal design, Sutpen ruthlessly violates the bonds of love and of blood with stunning consistency. He repudiates one wife and refuses to recognize his eldest son; he makes a bargain for a second wife whose attractions are entirely a matter of her irrefutable respectability; he turns one son into the murderer of the other, making—as Rosa Coldfield never tires of repeating—a widow of his daughter before she can become a bride; he offers Rosa a contract for copulation and Milly Jones an insult for her failure to emulate his horse in producing male offspring. Needless to say, these are not the acts of a benign paternalistic planter in a panama hat and a white suit; these are the acts of a character of mythic dimensions in whose career is inscribed the history of America itself, revealing, for one thing, the irony of a paternal authority in the name of which Indian tribes were broken up and Africans enslaved. For when Sutpen refuses to recognize his own son, he exhibits the logical, if self-contradictory, consequence of a paternalism generated in the interest of Capital, a paternalism which logically dictates that fathers exile and repudiate their sons.[26]

What we must appreciate, if we are to understand Sutpen at all, is that in his "innocence," he never understands or even considers the social content of his design. Conceived after the primitive model of the rifle analogy, the design presents itself in Sutpen's mind as a recipe, a list of ingredients consisting of "money, a house, a plantation, slaves, a family—incidentally of course, a wife"—in short, all the things possessed by the man who turned him away from the front door. By acquiring these things, of course, Sutpen intends to prove a point, which we will come to in a moment. But, first, we must recognize that Sutpen's design mirrors the Tidewater planter's achieved social eminence, thus *reflecting* the society over which the planter presides, but *never comprehending* the conflicts and contradictions inherent in that society. Therefore, Sutpen's career in pursuit of this design can serve to expose these contradictions to us for the same reason they remain utterly obscure to Sutpen himself; he has no capacity to recognize them because they are frozen within the image he sets out to emulate. Thus, his design both compels him to found a dynasty and to repudiate his own son. Since the contradiction inheres in his design, Sutpen cannot see it, and searches always for the "mistake" he has made in following the recipe rather than questioning the recipe itself. The peculiar power of such a character, in short, lies in his capacity to confront American society with its own image, exposing its implicit contradictions, and Faulkner exploits this character for all it is worth—which proves to be a great deal.[27]

The contradiction within paternalism is not the only feature of America's history which Sutpen's career exposes. In his desire to demonstrate, once and forever, the Declaration of Independence's opening assertion, he acts in the name of America's revolutionary rejection of the European past, its assertion that the "artificial standards" and "circumstances" of class will have no place in American society. Sutpen's aim is to lay waste to the class structure so that future generations will be "riven forever free from brutehood," recognized as free men, no matter what their social origins. Yet in his effort to vindicate the principle of social equality, Sutpen reconstitutes the very class structure he set out to oppose. Once again, he is the victim of his own design; in order to prove that any little boy can live in the big white house, he must acquire the house itself and all that goes with it, and in so doing, he rises above and finally refuses recognition to the man who mirrors Sutpen's own origins— Wash Jones. In denying Jones the social recognition he demands and deserves, Sutpen brings his own life to a violent end, and provokes Jones himself to suicide and the massacre of his offspring, as a result of the realization that there is no place for him in this society, that it would be "better if his kind and mine too had never drawn the breath of life on this earth" than to live without the respect owed by free men to one another. Facing the fact which Sutpen himself had once faced at the planter's front door, that he is precisely the insignificant creature for which Sutpen's slaves have always taken him, Wash Jones sees "his whole life shredded from him and shrivel away like a dried shuck thrown into the fire.[28]

Wash Jones's apocalyptic despair not only mirrors Sutpen's as a boy but also reflects the fragility of an identity dependent upon the political concepts of freedom and equality as asserted in the Declaration of Independence. For as Karl Marx remarks, this freedom "is not founded upon the relations between man and man, but rather upon the separation of man from man," and this equality amounts to the claim that "every man is equally regarded as a self-sufficient monad." In the conditions of the politically emancipated state, identity is grounded in difference. Sutpen himself constitutes the pure case of such identity. He regards everyone as a self-sufficient monad like himself, as the bearer of atomized social freedom. In realizing his freedom, egoistic man necessarily denies his relation to other men, since his liberty as a free man is founded on his separation from them. In *Absalom, Absalom!*, that separation is always revealed by its denial of the human family. Thus, joined at last by a blood relation to Sutpen as a result of Milly's newborn child, Wash Jones sees that relation denied and is forced to recognize that it means nothing at all..Faulkner thereby exposes a world in which the identity of a free man depends upon his separation from, rather than his relation to, all other free men.[29]

Wash's identity also, of course, depends upon another difference of crucial significance in American history—that between free and unfree men, between white and black. Perhaps the most harrowing of the contradictions exposed by Sutpen's life is that between American freedom and American slavery. As Edmund Morgan has pointed out, it was the labor of slaves which produced the tobacco on which "the position of the United States depended not only in 1776 but during the span of a long lifetime thereafter." "King Tobacco Diplomacy" was to be followed by King Cotton, the economic and political significance of which is well known. Sutpen's design faithfully replicates the corrupt society which first provoked it, a society at whose political birth slavery served as midwife, and whose economic prosperity in the nineteenth century heavily depended upon slave labor. Politically, this meant that white freedom was forged by the denial of black freedom, a fact whose social consequences are registered in Wash Jones's tenuous hold on his social identity as a free man. But what adds resonance to Jones's suicidal despair are the revelations harbored within Sutpen's career regarding the contradiction between white freedom and black slavery as an implicit feature of America's noblest ideal. In pursuing his design, Sutpen asserts the principles of freedom and equality; herein lies the source of his heroic stature. At the same time, however, Sutpen's career exposes the source of that design's implicit doom—its denial of the flesh-and-blood bond between the black, whose labor is exploited to support the white, and the white, whose freedom and equality is secured by that labor. That denial is no more accidental in Sutpen's career than it was accidental in America's. Faulkner exposes this contradiction in American society by confronting us with what James Baldwin once called the "savage paradox" at its heart—that which binds the white slaveowner to the African slave he exploits in a love/hate relationship secured by the bonds of flesh and blood. By denying those bonds, Sutpen exposes their power. In repudiating his black son, he alienates his white one as well, and thereby, in one fell swoop, turns brother against brother, son against father, and black against white. His assertion of freedom compels him to deny his relation to all others, black and white, who are all members of one human family. The blood-and-flesh bonds of that family reassert their power by yielding the black dynasty which Sutpen in fact founds. But this ironic outcome is already implicit in a design which derives American freedom from American slavery.[30]

By emphasizing the ways in which Faulkner exploits Sutpen's career as a register of American history and his design as a mirror of the contradictions inherent in a capitalist society, I do not mean to dismiss as unimportant those features of *Absalom, Absalom!* which focus on the South. The South, as Faulkner acknowledged to Cowley, provided his "material." But he went on to say that this material

is not very important to me. I just happen to know it, and don't have time in one life to learn another one and write at the same time. Though the one I know is probably as good as another, life is a phenomenon but not a novelty, the same frantic steeplechase toward nothing everywhere and man stinks the same stink no matter where in time.

As Shreve's responses in *Absalom, Absalom!* indicate, Faulkner knew that the South was regarded as an alien land, a fabled country whose legends were "better than Ben-Hur." But as his narrative use of Shreve also indicates, Faulkner knew how to exploit the South's image in the service of larger purposes than merely those of representing it to outsiders. It is Rosa Coldfield, after all, who seeks in Sutpen an explanation for the Lost Cause; Faulkner was pursuing bigger game. Among other narrative purposes, Faulkner set out to trace, in the rise of an American entrepreneur, the tragic fate implicit in the American dream. Although Faulkner did not have to import such an entrepreneur into the South, it may well be that his experience as a Southerner enabled him to treat this figure with more telling results than he could have done otherwise. If we compare Sutpen to that other archetypal American hero, Jay Gatsby, whose career also serves to embody the American dream, it becomes clear that Faulkner's historical vision makes a significant difference.[31]

Like Gatsby, Sutpen is the child of shiftless people, one who rises to entrepreneurial splendor through shady means. Both Gatsby and Sutpen are self-made men who refuse to recognize the failure of their designs, maintaining to the end of their lives a belief that it is never too late to try again; both are in thrall to the future and the hopes invested in it—Gatsby's hopes to win Daisy back, and Sutpen's hopes for a son; both are underbred parvenus who have come from nowhere; both believe in schedules, in calculation and planning. Finally, both are doomed to failure; not only are their dreams shattered, but they are both murdered by men who mirror their own social origins. A general holocaust marks the end of their lives, reflecting a similar emphasis on violence in the two novels. Yet in Faulkner's hands, the failure of the American dream embodied in Sutpen's rise and fall is treated as a social phenomenon rooted in history rather than as a romantic ideal betrayed by history. Sutpen's design is not born of any Platonic self-conception; it is born of a social affront, and thus originates in history rather than in spite of it. Gatsby's pure dream is corrupted only after its incarnation in a kiss, which is why at the end of the novel Nick Carraway can retrospectively imagine that dream in all its youthful promise as a disembodied ideal. Unlike Nick Carraway, Quentin Compson has no old-fashioned Midwest in which to seek safe harbor from the swelling tide of a history destined to corrupt his ideal. He cannot, like Carraway, simply disapprove of the man who, despite being an underbred parvenu, is worthy of eulogy because he still embodies America's noblest dream. Such romantic displacement is impossible for Quentin, since the corruption of Sutpen's design does not result from the incarnation of a transcendent ideal. For one thing, the design itself is corrupt from the outset, mirroring as it does a corrupt society. But more to the point, the design's failure cannot be redeemed by an appeal to it as a disembodied ideal, transcending the historical and material world. For Sutpen fails precisely *because* he presumes to transcend the material realm of history. When "the severe shape of his intact innocence" rises "like a monument" above the "limitless flat plain," Sutpen cuts himself off from history as the "stream of event," and it is this same denial of history which dooms his design to irredeemable failure. Quentin's "nevermore of peace" registers his realization that he is immersed in the same stream of event that Sutpen was, that this material and physical realm cannot be denied. Nick Carraway flees his contamination as a participant in the holocaust he has observed, but Quentin's effort to remain a detached observer, to deny his own position as one of history's "diffused and scattered creatures" all of whom are implicated as participants in the same stream of event, is frustrated from the outset. Moreover, the reader's similar need to remain detached is frustrated by a narrative strategy designed to undermine his own contemplative observer's stance.[32]

Chapter Eight

THE REIFIED READER

*But the spectacle is not identifiable with mere gazing, even
combined with hearing. It is that which escapes the activity of men,
that which escapes reconsideration and correction by their work.*
—GUY DEBORD

AS THE CRITICAL RECORD DEMONSTRATES, we respond to the maddening puzzle of *Absalom, Absalom!* most often in one of the two ways suggested by Mr. Compson's response to the equally maddening puzzle of Sutpen's life: "It's just incredible," he complains, "It just does not explain. Or perhaps that's it: they don't explain and we are not supposed to know." The effort to explain leads to detective work. "Something is missing," as Mr. Compson put it, "you bring them [the characters and their acts] together in the proportions called for" by the "chemical formula," but "nothing happens; you reread, tedious and intent, poring, making sure that you have forgotten nothing, made no miscalculation . . . and again nothing happens." In particular, the effort to verify Quentin's knowledge about Bon has led to some elaborate poring over the text, "tedious and intent," in the effort to find that something which is missing. But even when the effort to explain takes on more judicious proportions, to order and comprehend the tragic dimensions of Sutpen's story, it cannot finally account for the telling of that story except by an appeal to imagination's superiority over reality—which amounts in the end to confessing that we are not supposed to know. On this view, Quentin and Shreve deliver up a "poem of the act of the mind in the act of finding what will suffice.'' No doubt they do. No reader can fail to notice that Quentin and Shreve create both the richest and the most convincing version of the story. But it is not sufficient to assert that they succeed because they use their imaginations more energetically than Rosa or Mr. Compson. We need to ask why they are able to do so, and to call upon the transcendental imagination is merely to restate the question, not to answer it. In effect this appeal to the imagination represents the reader's romantic transcendence, while the detective's response reflects his insistence on neutral objectivity, both of which postures, as it happens, Sutpen embodies and ought to contaminate. The options available to the reader are apparently exhausted by Walter Slatoff's frank admission that we are not supposed to know, not because the imagination accounts for what reason fails to explain, but because Faulkner couldn't bring himself to work it all out. I would suggest that none of these responses is finally appropriate, because the novel's strategy is designed to block both subjective and objective escape hatches from history as the stream of event. Nor does Faulkner's novel reflect any final and irremediable incoherence in his own narrative procedures; rather, it reveals the incoherence and contradictions within the society he portrays, as well as in the society he addresses. In short, though I would agree with Cleanth Brooks's staunch insistence that the novel forms a coherent whole, I would support this claim on different grounds.[1]

In order to understand Faulkner's strategy in *Absalom, Absalom!*, we need to look first at the narrative experiments which led up to it. I wish to suggest that from *The Sound and the Fury* through *Absalom, Absalom!* Faulkner develops increasingly complex strategies for undermining the reader's detached contemplative stance. After describing the general direction of this development, I want to focus on *Light in August*, where its thematic implications become clear, before returning to *Absalom, Absalom!* itself.[2]

The Sound and the Fury is actually Faulkner's simplest experiment in terms of technical conception. In its original form, without the appendix, the novel asks the reader to inhabit four successive points of view in order to construct for himself the story of the

Compson family. The final section, moreover, offers a retroactive perspective on the events recorded which, while it may not present a single, privileged vision of the world of the novel, at least allows us to integrate all that we have seen from a single, detached point of view. *As I Lay Dying* is conceptually more complex. Instead of a gradually emerging group of characters set against a gradually emerging background, we have a field of interacting figures recurrently emerging out of a flux. Never allowed to settle for long into any character's consciousness, frustrated in our endeavor to form an image of more than passing instants, we are less confronted with the world of the novel than pulled through it along with the Bundrens. The novel imitates life not by re-creating the world in the form of a painting, but by re-creating experience as a flow of consciousness in which some images vividly remain to haunt us, but no sense of foreground and background is secure.

In *Light in August*, Faulkner combines the interior monologue with an omniscient narrator and expands the scope of his fiction from the family to the town. Here the reader's disorientation derives from the multiplicity of plot lines rather than from the multiple perspectives of the earlier novels. While *As I Lay Dying* resists our desire for the single, fixable perspective of illusionist space by forcing us through a rapidly paced substitution of one point of view for another, *Light in August* resists the same desire by refusing to allow us to follow any single action through to its completion. Each story necessitates another, until plot lines seem to spread out indefinitely. Moreover, we are set down in medias res, so that as we move forward in time, we double back further and further into the past. In *Light in August*, it becomes clear that Faulkner's manipulation of perspective is intimately involved with his interest in time. If we compare this novel with *The Sound and the Fury*, we can begin to see the relation between time and perspective.

In *The Sound and the Fury*, time is an explicit issue for Quentin Compson, who begins his last day by twisting the hands off the face of his watch. But time remains more an explicit thematic concern than an implicit means of coercing the reader. Within each section of the novel, a single perspective is developed through which we must fill in the events of the past. But once we begin to assemble the patches of time past revealed in the opening section, we are already engaged in the most complex activity the novel demands of us. Difficult though this task is, the stable and detached perspective afforded by the final section makes it possible to put the pieces of this puzzle together. Although *The Sound and the Fury* is the sort of puzzle capable of more than one solution, more than one assembled form, it is nonetheless a puzzle that can be assembled.

Light in August, on the other hand, while it makes the issue of perspective thematically explicit in the figure of Gail Hightower, the willfully detached observer seated behind his window, implicitly manipulates the reader by casting the omniscient narrator in the role of roaming listener and interpreter. That is, Faulkner refuses us a single, fixed perspective here—not by placing us in several minds successively, but by moving us from one place and time to another as the narrator focuses his attention on one character's story only to turn away to another's. The novel's first three chapters both initiate and illustrate this strategy at work. Faulkner turns from Lena, now in sight of Jefferson at the end of chapter 1, to Byron's memories of Joe Christmas' arrival in Jefferson at the beginning of chapter 2. Not until we are five pages into the chapter do we meet Brown, the man whom we would expect the author to introduce in the next episode of a book which, so far, seems to be centrally concerned with Lena Grove. So while confusion between Bunch and Burch leads Lena to expect Burch to be at the mill when she arrives, the reader, for the same reason, expects a comic plot to develop. Instead, he is introduced to a new character, Joe Christmas, whose story seems utterly irrelevant. By virtue of his name, however, Christmas cannot be a minor character, so the reader adjusts his expectations to encompass the possibility of tragedy, only to meet in chapter 3 still another character, Gail Hightower, whose relationship to Lena and Christmas must now be established somehow. From the outset, in short, the novel disrupts any expectations of a unified plot structure. This strategy is further complicated by the demand it makes on the narrator to give each character a past.

In *The Sound and the Fury*, the present consists of three days whose events are less important as episodes in plot development than as retrospective references to events in the past, references which serve primarily to establish relations between the two. The world of the present introduced in the opening section is provided with a past in the course of the novel, and the appendix Faulkner later composed for Cowley's edition of his works merely expands this history into the past and the future; in either case the past functions to deepen the meaning and elaborate the significance of these present events. Sartre was right when he argued that this novel has no future, because its present consists in events conceived not as acts with as-yet-undetermined future consequences, but as consequences already determined by as-yet-unrevealed previous events. As we read *The Sound and the Fury*, we are pulled forward not by the desire to see what happens next, but by the need to understand why this is happening now. In *Light in August*, the narrative pull encompasses both of these needs, a point which may be demonstrated by looking at the way the two novels begin.[3]

Our confusion at the opening of *The Sound and the Fury* derives from the uncertain meaning of the word "Caddy." We must first learn its literal reference in the present, and eventually its symbolic reference to the past. Once this is done, however, the scene takes on both clarity and significance. The opening pages of *Light in August*, on the other hand, locate us in a world in motion, and present us not with a present scene whose meaning is fleshed out fully once we learn its relationship to the past, but with a moving present capable of leading us virtually anywhere. Lena Grove's quest to find the father of her unborn child, precisely by virtue of its apparent hopelessness, promises to carry us on an endless journey. The novel which proceeds from this beginning makes good on this promise; its plots proliferate at an alarming rate. But while forcing us to attend to the question of what will happen next in a present always moving forward, Faulkner also meets the demand which grows more urgent as this present grows more complex, the demand to fill in the history of the characters whose actions we witness. The reader's need to explain the present events by reference to their history, therefore, coexists (by no means peacefully) with his need to keep up with them as they pull him forward into an indeterminate future.

In *Light in August*, then, Faulkner denies not merely the ultimate validity of a detached perspective as he did in *The Sound and the Fury*, but the very possibility of one. For in *Light in August*, any fixed perspective we may hope to gain is disrupted by time's unceasing flow. In other words, the reader is compelled to order time while it is moving. I want now to explain more fully how and why Faulkner forces the reader of *Light in August* to engage in this struggle.

With the significant exceptions of Lena Grove and eventually Byron Bunch, the characters in *Light in August* are victims of ordering myths, of what Frank Kermode has called degenerate fictions. The townspeople of Jefferson form a community devoted not to fostering life, but to worshipping death, an attitude demonstrated by that "Protestant music" with its "quality stern and implacable, deliberate and without passion so much as immolation, pleading, asking, for not love, not life, forbidding it to others, demanding in sonorous tones death as though death were the boon." As the roles of Joanna Burden, McEachern, and Doc Hines make clear, the Protestant church supports and enforces that commitment to the rigid distinction between black and white which imprisons and destroys Joe Christmas. The church's capacity to redeem time, to provide that "peace in which to sin and be forgiven . . . is the life of man," derives from the paradigmatic fiction of time in which a *kairos* fills all time before and after with meaning, and thus redeems history by providing man with a place in it. But this fiction has, in Kermode's terms, regressed into myth; the Christian ordering of time has ossified into an institution committed to vengeance rather than to love, devoted to death rather than to life.[4]

It is Gail Hightower, a man who has first retreated from life into the shelter of the church, and then from the church to his seat behind a window, who finally provides us with this vision of the church, and he does so in terms which help to explain why Faulkner has situated him behind that window as a willfully detached observer. In Hightower's final reverie, the church is seen as a failure not because of the "outward groping of those within it nor the inward groping of those without," but because of the "professionals who control it and who have removed the bells from its steeples." The bells which ring the hours, ordering man's days in accord with a redemptive organization of time, are gone. Developing the metaphor further, Faulkner describes all the world's steeples as "endless, without order, empty, symbolical, bleak, skypointed not with ecstasy or passion but in adjuration, threat and doom." Clearly, Faulkner's metaphor has sexual implications; the church is figured as "one of those barricades of the middle ages planted with dead and sharpened stakes," its power marshaled not in the service of procreation but of violence. By removing the bells from the steeples, the professionals have rendered the church impotent to foster life and peace, but all the more rigid and powerful in its ability to enforce its rule, to support the empty, symbolic distinctions which remain dogma.[5]

But to notice the phallic imagery here is only to begin to see the significance of this conceit, for the bells' removal is an instance not only of the novel's elaborate concern with sexuality, but also of Faulkner's use of sound as a means of referring to that realm of continuing life which Lena Grove inhabits. The most obvious case of this technique is the insect noises which recur throughout the novel, particularly in reference to Hightower and Christmas. Faulkner reminds us repeatedly that "beyond the open window" at which Hightower sits, "the sound of insects has not ceased, not faltered," and that Joe Christmas moves through a world constantly alive with the sounds of crickets. Joe, of course, is cut off from this world, as is clear from the fact that the crickets keep "a little island of silence about him." Sounds are used to emphasize Joe's alienation not only from the natural world, but also from the human community, that community which, because the church has failed to unite it in the service of love and peace, has become devoted to death and vengeance. Sitting behind the open door of his cabin, Joe hears the "myriad sounds of . . . voices, murmurs, whispers: of trees, darkness, earth; people . . . which he had been conscious of all his life without knowing it, which were his life, thinking *God perhaps and me not knowing that too.*"[6]

These recurring sounds, then, reinforce our sense of the alienation from life from which Hightower, willingly, and Joe, unwillingly, suffer. But Faulkner's technique consists not merely in the use of "sound imagery." That is, I do not mean to say that all sounds in the novel "refer" in this way to a realm of continuing life; the case of the Protestant music makes this clear, for it is associated with death, not life. Rather, Faulkner is using certain sounds to signal the continuing life from which Joe is alienated as part of a more

basic strategy which allies hearing itself with that temporal dimension which Lena Grove embodies, the continual present which sustains on-going life, but from which the church's ossified order has
alienated it. This strategy can be seen in the novel's opening pages.

As Lena Grove sits beside the road watching Armstid's wagon
approach, Faulkner describes the scene in terms of a contradiction
between what she sees and what she hears:

> The sharp and brittle crack and clatter of its weathered and ungreased wood
> and metal is slow and terrific: a series of dry sluggish reports carrying for
> a half mile across the hot still pinewiney silence of the August afternoon.
> Though the mules plod in a steady and unflagging hypnosis, the vehicle
> does not seem to progress. It seems to hang suspended in the middle dis-
> tance forever and forever, so infinitesimal is its progress.

Faulkner creates here the impression of constant change; the
wagon's sound signals its motion, while its appearance is static. He
is appealing to our predisposition to view immobility as permanence,
but complicating our responses by attributing that permanence to
motion itself. Characteristically, Lena allies herself with the wagon's
sound, so that

> in the watching of it, the eye loses it as sight and sense drowsily merge and
> blend . . . so that at last, as though out of some trivial and unimportant
> region beyond even distance, the sound of it seems to come slow and terrific
> and without meaning, as though it were a ghost travelling a half mile ahead
> of its own shape.

As we know, Lena embodies the natural, procreative realm from
which Joe is alienated and Hightower has fled. What I want to emphasize is that the way in which Faulkner establishes Lena's alliance
with the earth's motion is by suspending her sight of the wagon
("the eye loses it") as he pursues her hearing ("the sound of it seems
to come slow and terrific"). It is by locating Lena from the start in
the "realm of hearing" that he makes her embody time's ceaseless
progression.[7]

Further, if we recall that the only order Lena seems to require is
that minimal one indicated by her single metaphysical profundity,
"My, my. A body does get around," the ease with which her hearing
outstrips her seeing is hardly surprising. For Lena Grove—and this
is essentially what undermines her credibility as a character while

heightening her value as mythic force—exists in a perpetual present, a realm in which "time has not stopped" and never does, because Lena has no need to stand back and order her life in relation to time: she quite simply *is* time, understood as the "long monotonous succession of peaceful and undeviating changes from day to dark and dark to day.[8]

By bringing us into the world of the novel through Lena's peculiar consciousness, then, Faulkner presents us with a world in motion, thereby introducing us to the task we must perform as we move through the novel to come. Beginning in medias res, recapitulating Lena's past in a brief four pages, and returning to the present where Lena has remained, waiting for the wagon, Faulkner then follows her progress until she comes in sight of the yellow column of smoke whose horrific source both we and Lena are eventually to discover. But as the novel proceeds, proliferating plots and characters, we are not content with concluding, as Lena does once again on the novel's last page, that "a body does get around." Unlike Lena Grove, we are incapable of inhabiting time without trying to order it. Set down in medias res, we need to stand back and find a way of encompassing the horrifying events we must witness. In this respect, we share with Hightower a need to retreat into the role of viewer, to secure a vantage point from which to integrate events, stories, and characters into a formal unity and so confirm our detachment from them and their implications. And like Hightower, we are forced in the end to accept defeat.[9]

In contrast to Lena, whose slow and steady progress never stops, Gail Hightower is a man who, as we are repeatedly told, "has not moved." Terrified by the "hot still rich maculate smell of the earth," Hightower has long since fled from it, "to walls, to artificial light." We need not review the details of his peculiar flight from life. For present purposes, what is important is the fact that his flight from "the harsh gale of living" has finally taken the form of a withdrawal behind his window. The view framed by that window, however, is peculiar indeed. Hightower sits here not to look out on the living world itself, but to await a vision of the instant of his grandfather's death. He no longer looks at his sign, "his monument," and "he does not actually see the trees beneath and through which he watches the street," for he is waiting to see his grandfather and his troops "sweep past like a tide whose crest is jagged with the wild heads of horses," an event occurring each evening at "that instant when all light has failed out of the sky and it would be night save for that faint light which daygranaried leaf and grass blade reluctant suspire." Appealing to photosynthesis, Faulkner makes leaf and blade suspire, breathing out their stored-up light to produce "a little light on earth though night itself has come." For some light there must be, if the ghosts are to be seen. In the only full description we are given of Hightower's daily epiphany, the contrast between sight and hearing provides Faulkner with the means to indicate both the unreality of what Hightower sees, and his nonetheless adamant belief in its reality. The ghosts "rush past . . . with tumult and soundless yelling" and are gone as "the dust . . . fades away into the night which has fully come." And yet Hightower still believes they are there, because "it seems to him that he still hears them." Hightower's detached contemplative stance affords him the most encompassing vision afforded anyone in the novel, but his vantage point is irremediably contaminated by its focus on the dead rather than the living.[10]

It is only the "steady shrilling of insects and the monotonous sound of Byron's voice" which persists in relating Hightower tenuously to the living world beyond his window. It is Byron Bunch— the single major character in the novel who allows himself to break free of the regulated order by which he has protected himself from sin and responsibility—who brings to Hightower's ears the news of Lena and Joe, and who eventually ushers Joe's mother into Hightower's house and seeks his aid when Lena needs a doctor. In short, it is because of Byron's habit of visiting and talking with Hightower that he eventually finds himself again involved with the living, hearing "the treble shouts of the generations," a participant in that world of birth and death from which he has fled.[11]

If we return now to Hightower's final reverie, we will find Faulkner revealing through Hightower why any vision which promises to encompass events and redeem time is doomed to failure. As Hightower watches himself, in mounting horror, act out his life, the "wheel of thinking turns on" and he is forced to realize that he is responsible for his wife's death, that even by becoming his dead grandfather "on the instant of his death" he has not been able to remove himself from the burden of membership in the human community, since even if he *has* become his grandfather, he is still "the debaucher and murderer of his grandson's wife." Having been drawn into the events going on outside his window, Hightower is now forced to confront what his entire life has been devoted to denying—his participation in the world of the living, with all the responsibility this entails.[12]

When he first nears this realization, the wheel of thinking "begins to slow" and he "seems to watch himself among faces, always among, enclosed and surrounded by, faces." Hightower's vision now takes the form of a "halo . . . full of faces." The wheel of thinking which becomes a halo is the complex vehicle for a metaphor whose tenor includes "all the faces he has ever seen." As wheel, the vehicle moves ceaselessly; as halo it appears to be static. The wheel/halo is Faulkner's version of Keats's urn, itself by this time translated from an emblem of Lena's eternal motion into both a womb and a tomb. For a moment, it seems that the faces "are peaceful, as though they have escaped into an apotheosis," but this peaceful vision breaks down, and for a reason similar to that which made Keats's urn turn into a "Cold Pastoral": death and historical time reassert their dominion. Joe's face is not clear, and as Hightower looks at it, he sees why: "It is two faces which seem to strive . . . to free themselves one from the other," the faces of Christmas and Percy Grimm. Significantly, these faces strive "not of themselves striving or desiring it . . . *but because of the motion and desire of the wheel itself.*" (Emphasis added.) It is, then, the motion of time itself, signaled at the novel's outset by the sound of the wagon's wheels, and now by the wheel of time itself eternally moving, which both demands and resists the effort to conceive a vision which will organize time within a redemptive vision.[13]

We can now see why the "freed voices" of those singing the Protestant hymns assume "the shapes and attitudes of crucifixions, ecstatic, solemn, and profound." Like Joe Christmas, when his body is described as "a post or a tower upon which the sentient part of him mused like a hermit, contemplative and remote with ecstasy and selfcrucifixion," those within the church are imprisoned by a degenerate fiction and thereby cut off from each other and from life's motion. In other words, those trapped within this order mirror the man forced to live outside it because of their common alienation from each other and from that "peace in which to sin and be forgiven . . . is the life of man." Joe Christmas and Percy Grimm are bound to each other in their common and unwitting enactment of a devotion to death. This is what Hightower understands when, foreseeing Joe's lynching, he thinks, "they will do it gladly, gladly" because "to pity him would be to admit selfdoubt and to hope for and need pity themselves."[14]

Yet when Christmas is finally indeed crucified, whatever the citizens of Jefferson say to each other by way of ritual celebration, Faulkner apotheosizes him. He rises "soaring into their memories" to become a face "musing, quiet, steadfast, not fading," while the siren screams on, mounting toward its "unbelievable crescendo, passing out of the realm of hearing." To transcend the realm of hearing is to die; and in an unredeemed world, to die is to join the ranks of "all the living who ever lived, wailing still like lost children among the cold and terrible stars." Those whose voices assume the "shapes of crucifixions" then, adhere to a dead faith which severs them from all the living who ever lived, and these voices therefore remain "unheeded." In other words, the bells having been removed from the steeples, the church has come to represent not merely a retreat from life, but a citadel from which the human race itself, the living as well as the dead, has been exiled.[15]

Hightower's vision reflects the larger struggle of both reader and narrator, the struggle to appropriate the ceaseless flow of time into an ordered fiction within which man can find meaning. This struggle is necessitated by the relationship between the past and the continuing present in the novel. From the moment we encounter Lena sitting in the ditch to the final moment in which the furniture salesman relates his comic story to his wife, time pushes forward, seeming never to stop despite the lengthy flashbacks into the past. Faulkner's strategy in maintaining time's flow can be most readily explained in terms of Henri Bergson's concept of memory as automatically preservative. According to Bergson, the "past . . . is necessarily automatically preserved." The present is a "certain interval of duration'' like a sentence now being pronounced. Our attention spans the interval defined by the sentence, which can be elongated or shortened, "like the interval between the two points of a compass." The interval represented by one sentence can be stretched to include two by a change in punctuation. Accordingly, "an attention which could be extended indefinitely would embrace, along with the preceding sentence, all the anterior phrases of the lecture and the events which preceded the lecture, and as large a portion of what we call our past as desired." The present, therefore, is a function of the extent of our "attention to life." The distinction between the present and the past is a result of our apparent inability to sustain that attention; the present becomes past only when it no longer commands our immediate interest. If we did not have to channel our attention toward the future, if our attention to life were not repeatedly interrupted by the urgencies dictated by the practical concern of accomplishing our particular ends, our present would include our "entire past history . . . not as instantaneity, not like a cluster of simultaneous parts, but as something continually present which would also be something continually moving," something, in short, not unlike Lena Grove. Further, it is this continually moving present which Faulkner takes pains to sustain throughout the novel.[16]

For example, the paragraph leading into Joe's history, which constitutes the longest foray into the past if not the deepest penetration of it, works primarily on the principle that memory is not a system of pigeonholes, but simply a part of the flow of our consciousness, that attention to life from which we are artificially alienated. Accordingly, "memory believes before knowing remembers," because memory represents that intuitive awareness, that attention to life which never wanes but is only interrupted, so that knowing, intelligence, must remember, must search for and select those moments from the past which it deems relevant to the present. "Memory . . . believes longer than recollects, longer than knowing even wonders," and so represents a sustained subterranean flow, fundamentally unaffected by the interruptions imposed from above by the contingencies of survival. Accordingly, Faulkner modulates into the past without interrupting the flow of the present by referring the shift to a dimension which includes both past and present within the ceaseless flux of duration. He not only introduces the shift in this way, but repeats his appeal to memory as an enduring aspect of the present like a refrain throughout the following chapters, reinforcing our sense of the fundamental continuity of time.[17]

Consequently, as the present of the novel flows on into an indeterminate future, we move simultaneously farther and farther into the past until, with Hightower's final reverie, we reach a point before the Civil War. Moving farther into the past while at the same time moving ceaselessly on into the future, the novel appropriates larger and larger chunks of time into a structure which is constantly struggling to enfold them within a unified vision. The novel not only operates on this principle but calls attention to it by deliberately, as it were, biting off more than it seems able to chew. As time moves on and plots proliferate, the novel sets itself an enormous task of assimilation: as the structure expands to encompass a lengthening history within an ordered whole, that order is continually revealing itself as inadequate to the larger demands for meaning posed by the continuously moving present. Thus there is a mounting tension in the novel between time's ceaseless motion and our attempt to impose a structure large enough to give that motion a meaning, to humanize it.

Light in August, then, enacts a struggle for a unified form which will encompass the events it records, a redemptive vision which will compensate for the inadequacy of the church's degenerate fiction. But just as Hightower's tragic vision of the human community as continuous and whole fails to encompass and redeem the events he has witnessed, and this because the wheel of time keeps turning, so the tension between the flow of time and the human endeavor to impose a plot, a redemptive order, on that monotonous succession of day and night persists unrelieved. The novel as a whole seeks to redeem a diminished world by making of Joe Christmas' death a *kairos* for which Hightower's vision can supply a context and reference, but fails ultimately because that world keeps on moving.

For the same reason, the reader must fail in his endeavor to find a fixed vantage point from which to integrate events, characters, and stories into an ordered whole, separate and detached from himself. Had Faulkner ended the novel with Hightower's final vision, this would not be so forcefully true. But by telling the story of Lena and Byron on the road out of Jefferson through an entirely new character, the furniture salesman, Faulkner reinforces the implications of time's incessant progression into the future. Lena Grove's story acts as both bracket and ellipsis, to enclose and relieve the tragedy of Joe Christmas, but also to extend and amplify its intensity. By virtue of her health, her communality, and the sheer humor of her simple responses to life, she acts as comic relief to an intensely horrifying drama; but by virtue of the persistent and endless motion she comes to embody, her story extends and sustains the horror it ostensibly circumscribes. In a sense, her statement, "My, my. A body does get around," is quite seriously a profound one.[18]

What gives it a tragic profundity, in fact, is that the body which gets around under the name of Joe Christmas is a mysterious object in his own eyes. Cut off from both social and natural worlds, Joe exists in a state of sheer *chronos*. Detached from pure duration, yet "doomed with motion," he is alienated from his own body as well, a fact which becomes particularly evident at those points when he is able to watch his own physical behavior from a distance in "motionless . . . utterly contemplative" moments. Sitting in the dietitian's closet as a child, Joe seems "to be turned in upon himself, watching himself sweating, watching himself smear another worm of paste into his mouth which his stomach did not want." Again when McEachern beats him, Joe's body is described as "wood or stone; a post or a tower upon which the sentient part of him mused like a hermit, contemplative and remote with ecstasy and selfcrucifixion." Sometimes his detachment is accentuated by a difference in velocity between his mind's and his body's movement, as in the scene in Bobbie's room after everyone but Joe has left. Before the "wire ends of volition and sentience" connect, Joe lies watching the events above him unfold in a pure succession, flowing without punctuation until, as the wire ends approach each other, Faulkner begins to intersperse the events with the connective "then." As the prose moves out of italics, "thens" pile up, reflecting Joe's increasing ability to distinguish between one moment and the next. Even after volition and sentience reconnect, however, Joe's mind still moves more slowly than his body, so that "he was in the hall without having remembered passing through the door." Finally, after gulping down the whiskey, his mind moves faster than his body, which he has to "coax . . . along the hall, sliding it along one wall" as if it were a cumbersome trunk. Whether body or mind moves faster, Joe watches himself move, and continues to watch after he has "entered the street which was to run for fifteen years."[19]

Eventually, the street runs "so fast that accepting . . . takes the place of knowing and believing." It runs so fast that Joe no sooner sees a future possibility—"*Something is going to happen to me. I am going to do something*"—than it has virtually become a past fact—"Maybe I have already done it." For Joe, the present constitutes something possible, "waiting to be done" because he views the present as already past. Bergson asserts that viewing the present as a system of possibles which anticipate a future reality entails a false determinism in which the present is spuriously imprinted with the pattern of a future whose outline is unforeseeable; Joe's predicament embodies precisely that fatalism which derives from the act of structuring the present as if it were past. According to Bergson, the possible is a concept applicable only to the past wherein we try to find the causes for the present and so posit sources for that present. But when we apply this operation to the relationship between present and future, we necessarily fail because the present can only become possible from the vantage point of the future. Joe really has no present here, because he has already imposed on it the pattern which will define the future. The contrast between Joe's and Lena's modes of anticipating the future is instructive. Lena's future and past are enfolded in a perpetual present, out of which she anticipates the future and recalls the past not as distinct states, each one causing the next, but as the indistinguishable phases of a continuous flow. Thus the feeling of being on the wagon, even of having been on the wagon, does not disrupt the present, but seems to flow out of it without a break in time. Joe's present, however, is here defined by a pattern imposed on it as if it were past, so that he does not, cannot really, anticipate the future, except as the reality already possible in, and therefore determined by, the present. Joe exists in and is doomed by a pattern imposed before it is ever actualized. If for Lena the world is open-ended and creatively evolving, for Joe "his own flesh as well as all space" is a "cage."[20]

Cleanth Brooks has recently argued that "the influence of Bergson on Faulkner has been generally overestimated and . . . its importance . . . occasionally pushed to absurd lengths." Brooks's central point, I take it, is that "Faulkner did not need to be told by Bergson or anyone else that life involves motion," so that in general, "what Faulkner got from Bergson was essentially a confirmation from a respected philosopher, of something that he already knew," and could have learned from Saint Augustine or Sophocles. "Life has always been associated with motion, " Brooks tells us, and the literary artist has always faced the problem posed by life's fluidity and the static nature of words. While I agree that Bergson's influence has been occasionally overestimated, I do not think it quite accurate to treat that influence as a confirmation of timeworn truths about life and art dating back to Sophocles. Brooks's attention to the eternal seems to have obscured his perception of the particular, for I can see no other reason for his professed ability to find "little in Faulkner's narrative treatment that can be certainly attributed to Bergson's influence."[21]

For one thing, there is a notable similarity of imagery in the two writers. Bergson at one point compares the feeling of duration to the "unrolling of a spool" of thread, as one feels "himself coming little by little to the end of his span"; reversing his implications Bergson continues, "it is just as much a continual winding, like that of thread into a ball, for our past follows us, becoming larger and larger with the present it picks up on its way; and consciousness means memory." Later, he uses thread once again to figure duration, but this time as "a thread holding together the beads of a necklace." Faulkner's imagery is more successful, but aimed at a similar goal. He compares the wagon Lena awaits to "a shabby bead upon the mild red string of road," and the road, in turn, to "already measured thread being rewound onto a spool." The point here is not that Faulkner necessarily got such images from reading Bergson, however, but rather that Bergson had, in fact, "helped" him, as he later told Joan Williams. That help would appear to have made a difference particularly to the "narrative treatment" in *Light in August*, where the "unrolling of . . . duration" which Bergson describes as both "the unity of a movement which progresses" and "a multiplicity of states spreading out" is unmistakably evident in Faulkner's narrative structure. In addition to the narrative modulation into the past on the basis of a Bergsonian concept of memory, the use of Lena Grove as a vehicle for a continual present, and the adaptation of Bergson's defense of freedom into a means for depicting Christmas' fatalism, we should also note that Bergson may have suggested to Faulkner the value of hearing as a register for motion. In "The Perception of Change," Bergson remarks that "we have less difficulty in perceiving movement and change as independent realities if we appeal to the sense of hearing."[22]

Questions of influence, as some recent critical excesses reveal, are likely to obfuscate what they should illuminate, and I am not finally concerned with assessing Bergson's influence on Faulkner. But even had Faulkner not repeatedly mentioned his debt to Bergson, *Light in August* would seem to demonstrate it incontrovertibly. That debt however, is not essentially a philosophical one; in this respect Brooks is right. Faulkner used Bergson—as he confessed to using other authors—not as a source for ideas, but as a resource for narrative tools. The distinction is important if we are to recognize that Faulkner went well beyond Bergson in developing the implications of the claim that life is motion. Bergson, after all, argued for free will as an intuited truth grounded in the durational nature of reality. No such conviction is apparent in *Light in August* where the only person who might be called free in Bergson's terms is Lena Grove, and her bovine imperviousness to the tragic events among which her body moves around with such enviable impunity renders doubtful any claim that Faulkner adopted Bergson's philosophical beliefs. Indeed, *Light in August* demonstrates in several ways the limitations of Bergson's conceptual framework.

Bergson proposed to counter modern philosophical empiricism by an appeal to a truer empiricism which would overcome the deterministic implications of Kant's legacy. However, the concept of duration on which Bergson relied to accomplish this task, though providing a powerful basis for attacking the static objectivism of the scientific materialist, landed Bergson swiftly in the idealist camp, despite his disclaimers on this score. Because duration is "psychological in essence," as Bergson himself states, it can easily be reduced to a defensive weapon by romantic idealism, allying itself with the organic and natural against the static and mechanical. As Lukács indicates, the Bergsonian reaction against Kantian rationalism cannot overcome reification, for it merely reconstitutes it in the form of a reified flux set over against a contemplative observer. So much Faulkner learned from his experiment in *Light in August*, where consciousness as memory must serve as the register of life's ceaseless motion. Christmas in particular reveals the implications of Bergson's view of time as motion, for Joe constitutes one of the most alienated men in modern literature. The point is that life's motion is asserted in this novel, and in terms which make the reader's task extremely difficult, but the continual present remains abstract. A contemplative observer seated Buddha-like behind a window looks down upon an alien world of motion, signaled by the sounds of insects. The "wheel of thinking" signals one abstract motion, the insects another. The problem here is that life's motion cannot outstrip the limits of abstraction so long as it is figured in terms of nature. That Faulkner understood this problem becomes clear in *Absalom, Absalom!*, where the duration previously grounded in nature and signaled by sound, becomes a stream of events grounded in history and represented by the sound of human voices.[23]

In *Light in August*, Faulkner employs a narrative strategy which forces the reader to acknowledge the necessary disruption of any fixed perspective by the flow of time, but in *Absalom, Absalom!* he goes a decisive step further; he forces the reader to share the burden of narrative construction actively. That is, by casting the novel's central action as an exercise of the imagination in narrative construction, Faulkner implicates his reader as a participant in the telling of a story, a strategy which serves to alter the reader's relation to the novel much as a cubist painting alters the viewer's relation to illusionist space. If, as John Berger argues, the content of the cubist painting is "the relation between seer and seen," and this painting does not so much illustrate as posit a historical situation,

Absalom, Absalom! may be said to be about the relationship not only between Quentin Compson and Thomas Sutpen, but also between the reader and the novel. As such, it does not depict a series of scenes on canvas so much as it posits a historically grounded dilemma. Our tendency to conceptualize the novel as a series of versions, as if it were essentially structured like *The Sound and the Fury*, is itself a response whose validity Faulkner has deliberately undermined. His strategy relies primarily on an opposition between sight and hearing, between pictures and voices, and it is designed not only to undercut the stability of any fixed, external vantage point, but to close the gap between seer and seen, between words as printed on a page, and words as uttered in the physical medium of air. In contrast to Joseph Frank's theory, Faulkner's strategy works against not the inherent temporality of narrative, but the inherent spatiality of the book—that spatiality which endows the reader with the freedom to "re-read, tedious and intent, poring" over pages which he can turn backward as well as forward. This freedom derives from the simple fact that the reader holds an object in his hand. He can not only reread passages he has already read; he can actually put the book down, rise from his chair, and walk away, out of the talking, the telling. It is this material spatiality which Faulkner sets out to undermine, in order to make of the reader—that emblematic figure of detachment from the "real" world—a participant in the story he reads. The result is a novel in which the protagonist, or at least the only living breathing one in the novel, sits for an entire evening, and for three chapters, "quite still, facing the table, his hands on either side of the open text book . . . his face lowered a little, brooding."[24]

In conventional terms, one could say that the reader becomes a narrator, and because the major line of action in the novel consists in narration itself, the reader is threatened with becoming a character as well. But it seems more accurate to say that the novel is itself one voice in a dialogue with the reader, who, like Quentin Compson, struggles in vain to secure a detached position from which to assemble and confront a chaotic and inexplicable set of events.

It is common to regard Shreve as the surrogate for the reader, since he is the outsider, the one who shares our amazement and incredulity at the story of Sutpen. I would not dispute this claim, but would emphasize the fact that Shreve's voice is first heard on page nine of the novel, where the "two separate Quentins" address each other. If Shreve represents the reader's interests, he does so as an interlocutor in a conversation which functions to relate him intimately to Quentin. In addition to producing a story, Shreve and Quentin verbally consummate a marriage, and when Shreve issues his prophecy in the novel's final chapter, he severs a relationship at the same time. We ought, in short, to find our identification with Shreve rather uncomfortable. Further, Quentin is also a reader surrogate, and the best means of approaching Faulkner's strategy is to appreciate his dilemma. By remaining a passive hearer, Quentin tries to secure a detached perspective on the story of Sutpen, and so to free himself from the burden of history in which he is already, as a college freshman, enmeshed. But when Shreve assumes the voice of one of the "two separate Quentins," Quentin is forced to participate in the telling of Sutpen's story, a process which, for a brief hour in the novel's eighth chapter, issues in the "happy marriage of speaking and hearing," only to subside once again in the ninth, leaving Quentin within history as a stream of event, and Shreve outside, measuring and calculating its direction.[25]

Quentin's position is established in the novel's opening chapter. Before Miss Coldfield ever speaks directly, we join Quentin as he listens to her

talking in that grim haggard amazed voice until at last listening would renege and hearing-sense self-confound and the long-dead object of her impotent yet indomitable frustration would appear, as though by outraged recapitulation evoked, quiet inattentive and harmless, out of the biding and dreamy and victorious dust.

Faulkner gradually shifts Quentin's mode of apprehension from hearing to seeing ("Her voice would not cease, it would just vanish") until Quentin's mind is wholly absorbed by a vision of Sutpen: "Out of quiet thunderclap he would abrupt (man-horse-demon) upon a scene peaceful and decorous as a schoolprize water color." A picture abrupts before Quentin like a slide projected on a screen, a picture of Sutpen "immobile, bearded and hand palm-lifted," surrounded by the wild blacks and the captive architect. Then Quentin seems "to watch" as "out of the soundless Nothing," Sutpen's

Hundred is created, the "*Be Sutpen's Hundred* like the oldentime *Be Light*." In this "soundless" vision even God's words have become objects, seen and not heard. Again, a few pages later, and "as though in inverse ratio to the vanishing voice," the "ghost . . . began to assume a quality almost of solidity, permanence," an "ogre-shape which, as Miss Coldfield's voice went on, resolved out of itself before Quentin's eyes the two half-ogre children." Ellen, "the fourth one," joins the picture now, one in which the four of them are "arranged into the conventional family group of the period," and which finally becomes a "fading and ancient photograph . . . hung on the wall behind and above the voice and of whose presence the voice's owner was not even aware." By page twenty-one, Rosa herself as a child has joined the "'musing and decorous wraiths'" whom Quentin continues to visualize: "Quentin seemed to watch resolving the figure of a little girl, in the prim shirts and pantalettes . . . of the dead time."[26]

Quentin visualizes the ghosts, then, as Hightower looking through his window once gazed out upon his grandfather's Confederate raid, and in the same way Ellen Coldfield visualizes her family, once Bon has married Judith in her imagination:

> She seemed to have encompassed time. She postulated the elapsed years during which no honeymoon had taken place, out of which the (now) five faces looked with a sort of lifeless and perennial bloom like painted portraits hung in a vacuum.

Just as Rosa's conception of Charles Bon "was a picture, an image" because Rosa was "not listening" to what Ellen told her, Quentin's conception of Sutpen and his family is also a picture, because he is not listening to Rosa, but instead watching ghosts resolve before him out of the dust. Most importantly, because Quentin is engaged in ghost-watching, he too seems "to have encompassed time," as he notices that "the sun seemed hardly to have moved." The story Rosa is telling has for him the "quality of a dream," occurring "stillborn and complete in a second" even though he knows that "the very quality upon which it must depend to move the dreamer (verisimilitude) to credulity" is an "acceptance of elapsed and yet-elapsing time." Because Quentin already knows part of the Sutpen story, "the talking, the telling" of it simply strikes "the resonant strings of remembering," issuing in pictures which "encompass" events but do not explain them. And it is because they seem to deny, to stand beyond the realm of "elapsed and yet-elapsing time" that these pictures have a "quality strange, contradictory and bizarre; not quite comprehensible." In other words, Quentin detaches himself from "the telling," which goes on in time, and confronts the images beyond "the voice," the ghosts who manifest "an air of tranquil and unwitting desolation . . . as if" they "had never lived at all."[27]

The opposition established in the novel's opening chapter—between light and the vision it supports, on the one hand, and "moving air" and the talking and hearing it sustains, on the other—is grounded in one more basic, that between transcendence of, and immersion in, the stream of event. The association between vision and the effort to encompass and transcend time finds its definitive expression in Thomas Sutpen. As his first appearance indicates, Sutpen inhabits a realm defined by light. He is imagined at the inception of his design as looking "ahead along the undivulged light rays in which his descendants who might not even ever hear his (the boy's) name, waited to be born," and again "after he would become dead, still there, still watching the fine grandsons and great-grandsons springing as far as the eye could reach." Moreover, he is usually remembered as if he *had* transcended time. For example, when he first arrives in Jefferson, he seems literally to be a "man who came from nowhere": the men on the hotel gallery simply

looked up, and there the stranger was. He was already halfway across the Square when they saw him, on a big hard-ridden roan horse, man and beast looking as though they had been created out of thin air and set down in the bright summer sabbath sunshine in the middle of a tired foxtrot.

Sutpen, it seems, has a habit of "abrupting" upon any scene he comes upon; further, he is seen as a man who is himself primarily a seer, a demonic visionary who set out once and forever to transcend time by founding a dynasty, and he commands the visionary response he gets precisely because of his remorseless dedication to transcendence, his "indomitable spirit." "He was the light-blinded bat-like image of his own torment" according to Rosa Coldfield, who shares his "impotent yet indomitable frustration," and accordingly mirrors his typically rigid and upright posture. He is preeminently the man on a horse, always appearing rigidly erect. With "his pale eyes . . . at once visionary and alert," he embodies at one and the same time the transcendent seer and the calculating observer. "Even while riding," Quentin's grandfather says, Sutpen

> was still bemused in that state in which he struggled to hold clear and free above a maelstrom of unpredictable and unreasoning human beings, not his head for breath and not so much his fifty years of effort and striving to establish a posterity, but his code of logic and morality, his formula and recipe of fact and deduction whose balanced sum and product declined, refused to swim or even float.

Sutpen's legalistic "code of logic," his innocent conviction that "the ingredients of morality were like the ingredients of pie or cake," which, once "measured" and "balanced" and "mixed" could produce "nothing but pie or cake," marks him as the detached spectator of his own destiny, a figure whose reified consciousness is signaled by eyes both "ruthless and reposed." Sutpen's ruthless pursuit of immortality, like Rosa Coldfield's ruthless narrative treatment of Sutpen as Demon, derives from a quest for revenge, and expresses an "impotent and static rage."[28]

Rosa's rage results from what she describes at one point as the "final clap-to of a door between us and all that was, all that might have been—a retroactive severance of the stream of event." Thomas Sutpen's affront leaves Rosa fixed behind "a sheet of glass" from which she observes "all subsequent events transpire as though in a soundless vacuum," leaving her "immobile, impotent, helpless." That "might-have-been which is more true than truth" then becomes "the single rock we cling to above the maelstrom of unbearable reality." Thomas Sutpen too confronts the clap-to of a door, an affront which leads to a design whose purpose and effect is to "shut that door himself forever behind him on all that he had ever known." Sutpen's design is conceived in an experience of impotence, at the moment when he hears himself saying of the plantation owner, "*I not only wasn't doing any good to him by telling it or any harm to him by not telling it, there ain't any good or harm either in the living world that I can do to him.*" As Sutpen himself admits, the "boy symbol was just a figment of the amazed and desperate child" who is sent to deliver a message and finds that it *"can't even matter"* whether it was delivered or not. To defy this impotence, Sutpen conceives of a design which hypostatizes it, beyond "the living world." Like Rosa Coldfield's dream, Thomas Sutpen's innocence lifts him above the stream of events, from which the "severe shape of his intact innocence" rises as a "monument," to transcend rather than redeem the affront, to order his life in accord with a static design. But Sutpen's design fails for the same reason that God's did; to order time and thereby fill it with meaning, one must inhabit it. God could amend the error by sending his Son into the world, but Sutpen, after trying and failing to imitate God, remains to be "articulated in this world." To appreciate Sutpen's failure, as well as his peculiar immortality, we need to understand the principle which opposes transcendence in the novel.[29]

The clearest explanation of this principle is to be found in Judith Sutpen's single recorded speech. When she gives Bon's letter to Quentin's grandmother, she contrasts her purpose with her father's in bringing home those two colossal tombstones to mark the family grave. The letter differs from the tombstone because the act of passing something on "from one hand to another" represented in the letter

at least . . . would be something . . . something that might make a mark on something that *was* once for the reason that it can die someday, while the block of stone can't be *is* because it never can become *was* because it can't ever die or perish.

The act of passing on a letter from one hand to another affirms the continuity of life from one generation to the next, and stands as the physical, palpable link between past and present. The letter functions like the "churinga," which Claude Lévi-Strauss describes as an object passed on from one generation to the next in certain tribes, to furnish "the tangible proof that the ancestor and his living descendents are of one flesh." As Judith explains, it is a matter of making an "impression." You try at first to make it by weaving a pattern, but "you are born at the same time with a lot of other people," and they are all "trying to make a rug on the same loom only each one wants to weave his own pattern into the rug." You know that "it can't matter," and yet "it must matter because you keep on trying,'' but then in the end "it doesn't matter,'' since you die. So much for transcendence. Consequently, Judith responds to impotence—the failure to make an impression which led her father to build a static monument—with the simple physical act of passing something on to someone. Put schematically, Judith thereby allies herself with time as horizontal motion, while Sutpen asserts a vertical transcendence of time. Moreover, Judith's contrast with her father is emphasized by the fact that the letter itself embodies the same principle as the act of passing it on; it is a message passed on from "one mind to another" and in particular, passed from brother to sister, reconnecting the blood relation Sutpen had denied, many years after he had failed to pass on a message. Bon's letter, as well as Judith's act, manifest physically the principle of social continuity at work in all the conversations in the novel. All the speaking and hearing, dominated as it is by a single narrative voice, represents an ongoing social act which, though it cannot found a dynasty, can create a community among the living as well as between the living and the dead.[30]

In contrast to Judith's acceptance of membership in the human community, Sutpen in effect abandons that community when he leaves his family for the West Indies. Accepting her own impotence, Judith nonetheless accepts the responsibilities Sutpen has denied; when she takes in Bon's son at Sutpen's Hundred, she does not know he is in fact her nephew, in contrast to Sutpen who presumably knows that Bon is his son but turns him away just the same. But then Sutpen does not so much deny as fail even to recognize his responsibilities, for his discovery of his own impotence as a boy prohibits him from discovering that his actions can matter in "the living world," with flesh-and-blood people who breathe the same air he does. He thus remains impervious not only to any possible pain he might cause that cannot be paid for legalistically, but also to the reasons for any possible damage done to his design by other people. What makes his actions so offensive to the citizens of Jefferson is that same innocence which makes his failure so inexplicable to Sutpen himself; just as he enters the town as a "man who came from nowhere," so the acts of those who frustrate his design seem to him to come from nowhere. He fails to understand that his actions have effects which outrun his intentions, that is, because he does not recognize intentionality in others. He is a "foe" who does not even know that he is "embattled."[31]

And yet it is because he is embattled that he endures; the counterdesigns provoked by his affronts destroy his design, but ensure his eventual articulation. The central irony of Sutpen's life is that he wins immortality not by achieving his design, which ends in the mocking figure of Jim Bond, but through the counterdesign of one whom he affronts. For it is Rosa who, although she too has revenge in mind, initiates a dialogue with the youth Quentin, and so keeps Sutpen alive. Like the architect he impresses into his service, those whom Sutpen fails to acknowledge as social creatures sharing the same world and breathing the same air with him, create of "Sutpen's very defeat the victory which, in conquering, Sutpen himself would have failed to gain."[32]

It remains to note, before returning to Quentin, that the "moving air" from which Rosa's room is protected becomes Faulkner's vehicle for moving from present to past, and for referring the shift to that stream of events moving outside Rosa's blinds. Moving air serves the same purpose that the sound of insects does in *Light in August*, but functions in a more complex way. At the beginning of chapter 2, the air "still breathed" in 1909 is the "same air in which the church bells had rung on that Sunday morning in 1833," providing Faulkner with a means for modulating into the past without calling attention to the shift. The purpose is similar to that fulfilled by "memory believes before knowing remembers," but here it is achieved by reference to a material, rather than to an abstract, substratum. As Rosa remarks, "there is no such thing as memory: the brain recalls just what the muscles grope for." Air also carries the smell of wisteria and the sound of sparrows into Rosa's office, just as it carries "the wisteria, the cigar-smell, the fireflies–attenuated up from Mississippi" to a strange room in Cambridge, joining North and South, Canadian and American, in a materially grounded social bond. Most important, air carries the sound of human voices, and so acts as the medium in which all the novel's conversations exist. Air sustains life, the physical, palpable life of breathing, smelling, hearing, and even speaking—and thus joins the "sensuous human activity" which is history to the "stream of event" constituted by the voices in the novel.[33]

As we have seen, Quentin resists listening to Rosa, since, as he eventually realizes, he has "had to listen too long." The story of Sutpen is "a part of his twenty years' heritage of breathing the same air and hearing his father talk about the man Sutpen." And so, when Shreve begins retelling it in chapter 6, Quentin thinks *"He sounds just like father,"* registering once again that growing realization that he has had to listen to too much. But as he hears Shreve tell it again, he is drawn out of his detached vantage point. Recounting his father's story of Sutpen's troops bringing the marble tombstone back to Mississippi during the war, Quentin at first follows his habit of viewing: "It seemed to Quentin that he could actually see them." But when Sutpen is seen arriving home with the tombstone, Quentin's habit is undercut: "he could see it; he might even have been there. Then he thought *No. If I had been there I could not have seen it this plain.*" Once Quentin begins to speak, to share in the telling, he is in fact participating in the stream of event for the first time in the novel.[34]

When Quentin starts talking, Shreve remarks, "Don't say it's just me that sounds like your old man," forcing Quentin now to stumble forth from his fixed detachment and acknowledge a relation to Sutpen other than that of seer and seen:

Yes, we are both Father, or maybe Father and I are both Shreve, maybe it took Father and me both to make Shreve or Shreve and me both to make Father or maybe Thomas Sutpen to make all of us.

Quentin's image of pools attached to one another by a "narrow umbilical water-cord" represents his attempt to conceptualize the community he is about to enter, a community not merely joining him to Shreve, but to his father, and Charles and Henry and Sutpen too. Like that "fierce, rigid umbilical cord" which joins Rosa to Clytie at the moment they touch, the two of them "joined by that hand and arm which held" them, Quentin's image represents the community of blood, "the immortal brief recent intransient blood" shared by the two youths in their tomblike room and by those other two, whom they are soon to join, "riding the two horses through the iron darkness" of a Mississippi Christmas Eve, sixty years before.[35]

Immersed with Shreve, then, in the process of communal telling, Quentin no longer stares at static pictures, but participates in the stream of event, and in an act of love as well, that "happy marriage of speaking and hearing wherein each before the demand, the requirement, forgave condoned and forgot the faulting of the other." But this impassioned telling finally subsides, and when it does, Quentin must face what he saw behind that door, and so fulfill the dust cloud's prophecy: that he will "find no destination but . . . a plateau and a panorama of harmless and inscrutable night and there will be nothing . . . to do but return." All that Quentin testifies to learning from Henry Sutpen is that he has come home to die. Having waited until the last chapter for this confrontation, the reader is met with nothing more than a conversation which mirrors itself:

And you are—?
Henry Sutpen.
And you have been here—?
Four years.
And you came home—?
To die. Yes.
To die?
Yes, to die.
And you have been here—?
Four years.
And you are—?
Henry Sutpen.

What the reader confronts in this passage is an issue to which we will turn shortly. What Quentin confronts here is death, the maddening rebuttal to all designs for transcendence and immortality, and this, of course, is the message of the dust cloud as well. Born into time, man struggles to deny his mortality by transcending the stream of event, but the dust is victorious, as the two rooms in which the novel's opening and closing conversations take place indicate.[36]

From Rosa's room to this one at Harvard, from September to December, Quentin has had to listen to the voices of others, each one "trying . . . to weave his own pattern into the rug," using language itself to try to transcend and encompass time, and each one failing. Thus Quentin and Shreve's dialogue is "a good deal like Sutpen's morality and Miss Coldfield's demonizing," in that each represents the effort of the "prisoner soul" which "coils ever up-ward sunward" to rise above the earth where time and death await them. Yet, on the other hand, Shreve and Quentin, in their joint act of creation, have accomplished what no one else in the novel could have, and this because they do it together, in an act of love, not vengeance. They use language, too, although not primarily to impose a design, but rather as

that meager and fragile thread . . . by which the little surface corners and edges of men's secret and solitary lives may be joined for an instant now and then before sinking back into darkness where the sprit cried for the first time and was not heard and will cry for the last time and will not be heard then either.

Yet for a brief hour, Quentin and Shreve do hear and respond. Their act of telling, in other words, differs from those of Rosa Coldfield and Mr. Compson not merely because they imagine more creatively, and so "encompass" more than either, but because of what makes this more ambitious vision possible—their joint participation in the telling, that "happy marriage of speaking and hearing" which not only allows each to forgive the other's faultings, but even enables each to take the other "up in stride without comma or colon or paragraph," voicing that relentless Faulknerian sentence which rep-resents the stream of event in *Absalom, Absalom!*[37]

But their immersion in this stream is brief and passing. It cul-minates in the closing pages of chapter 8, appropriately enough in a conversation, one between Henry Sutpen and Charles Bon, each played by Quentin and Shreve jointly, since "both of them were Henry Sutpen and both of them were Bon." This dialogue fore-shadows the one between Quentin and Shreve at the novel's end, for each dramatizes a confrontation. Bon invites Henry to shoot him; Henry replies, "You are my brother," and Bon responds with the novel's ur-sentence: "No I'm not. I'm the nigger that's going to sleep with your sister. Unless you stop me Henry." Henry, "panting and panting," jerks the pistol from Bon's hand and points it at him, but all that explodes are words: "You shall not!" At the end of the next and final chapter, Shreve, like Bon, throws down his own peculiar gauntlet, asking Quentin, "Why do you hate the

South?'' and Quentin, ''panting in the cold air, the iron New England dark,'' replies ''at once, immediately; 'I don't hate it'.'' Furthermore, Shreve has just articulated the results of Henry's impotence as the brother avenger who fails to stop his black brother from sleeping with his white sister: ''the Jim Bonds are going to conquer the western hemisphere,'' he announces, proceeding to echo Bon once more when he says, ''in a few thousand years, I who regard you will also have sprung from the loins of African kings.'' John Irwin has provided a full and convincing treatment of the psychological bases of Quentin's identification with both Bon and Henry. What concerns us here is the split which occurs in both of these dialogues—in the first between brothers, and in the second between two boys who have been joined by a ''marriage of speaking and hearing.'' When Shreve issues his prophecy, he is, like Bon, effectively challenging Quentin with a cold deduction of the consequences to follow from his impotence. While Shreve uses Bond to clear the ''ledger,'' Quentin can still ''hear'' Bond wailing, unredeemed and unredeemable like Quentin himself as he whispers, ''Nevermore of peace.'' At the novel's end, Quentin's two selves have split apart irrevocably; Quentin has fallen into the ''fluid cradle of events (time)'' where death lies waiting, while Shreve steps neatly forth to make his predictions. Furthermore, Shreve's summing-up parodies the attempt on the part of the reader to stand off and assemble a final interpretation, to detach himself from the talking, the telling.[38]

From the beginning, Faulkner has been immersing us in the stream of event which his sustained voice embodies. His strategy in this respect consists in telling us things before we can understand him, possessing us of information before we have learned where it fits in the story, while at the same time pulling us forward by withholding the crucial information about Bon's past, as well as the crucial scene in which we expect to have this information verified. By the end of chapter 1, for example, we actually know about the major events of Sutpen's life after his arrival in Jefferson, although we cannot make sense of them. As a result, when these events are related again and again in the ensuing chapters, we know them ''already,'' so that what is said almost seems to strike, as it does for Quentin, ''the

resonant strings of remembering.'' Further, as we read on, it is as
if we, like Quentin, had been brought into a room and experienced
a shock at the sight of Sutpen abrupting before us, as if we "knew"
but did not yet "believe" what we had seen. And because we, like
Rosa, were not there to see these events, we visualize them for
ourselves, much as we visualize the static picture of Rosa and Quentin in that vividly presented opening scene.[39]

By the time we reach the end of chapter 5, the events Rosa has
conjured up before us have, thanks to Quentin's father, been placed
in some sequence, but they remain for us, as for him, like Quentin's
pictures, "contradictory and bizarre," because we still lack the information which will account for them, the facts about Charles Bon's
past. "Something is missing," as Mr. Compson puts it, that something which our "chemical formula" has failed to include, so that
when we bring the characters together "in the proportions called
for . . . nothing happens." This kind of scrutinizing of the events
one has witnessed and the account one has made of them is precisely
the kind of activity in which we find Sutpen himself engaged in the
second half of the novel, as he sits

there in Grandfather's office trying to explain with that patient amazed
recapitulation, not to Grandfather and not to himself . . . but trying to explain to circumstance, to fate itself, the logical steps by which he had arrived
at a result absolutely and forever incredible, repeating the clear and simple
synopsis of his history . . . as if he were trying to explain it to an intractible
and unpredictable child.

Like Rosa Coldfield, Sutpen sits in an office addressing himself not
to his interlocutor, but to "fate itself." Further, the story as Sutpen
tells it provides an excellent example of that "idealization," as
Heisenberg calls it, "in which we can speak about parts of the world
without any reference to ourselves." For Sutpen depicts himself as
acting wholly out of his obligations to the design in his mind—that
"pure idea" which Emerson had once invited his reader to make
the world conform to—and the result is a carefully controlled series
of denials: "I did not undertake—I did not even demand . . . I accepted them . . . I could have reminded them . . . but I did not;
. . . I merely explained . . . I made no attempt . . . I declined and
resigned all right and claim that I might repair whatever injustice
I might be considered to have done by so providing for the two

persons whom I might be considered to have deprived of anything I might later possess.'' It is hardly surprising that General Compson cannot go on listening to this recital after Sutpen refers to his ''conscience,'' for there is no conscience in evidence here, no capacity for recognizing responsibility or guilt, but instead the demonstration of an innocent belief that immunity can be bought from the bonds of flesh and blood.[40]

Unlike Shreve and Quentin during the climactic chapter 8, where Shreve exhibits a manifest need to meet Quentin's repeated complaint, ''that's still not love,'' participating in a joint struggle to come up with an account of Bon and Judith, Thomas Sutpen addresses no one but himself. And he virtually treats his failed design as if it were itself a book, over which he pores, ''tedious and intent,'' trying to locate the missing fact he had forgotten, the ''mistake'' he had made, so as to explain ''a result absolutely and forever incredible.'' Shreve's summing-up is contaminated by the same resolute insistence on clearing the whole ''ledger'' and so is Mr. Compson's effort to combine ''the words, the symbols, the shapes'' standing out against ''that turgid background of a horrible and bloody mischancing of human affairs'' by means of a ''chemical formula.'' For Mr. Compson resorts essentially to a romantic interpretation of the puzzle he cannot fit together in any other way: Sutpen and his family lived in a now ''dead time,'' he says,

people too as we are, and victims too as we are, but victims of a different circumstance, simpler, and therefore, integer for integer, larger, more heroic and the figures therefore more heroic too, not dwarfed and involved but distinct, uncomplex who had the gift of loving once or dying once . . .

Just as Sutpen occupies a detached posture toward his own life as a historical creature, Mr. Compson distances what he cannot explain; that is, he heroicizes his ancestors, thereby severing his blood-and-flesh relationship to them, as fellow members of a historical community. Thus severed from his own life, the figures can be manipulated as he wills, and it is not surprising that Mr. Compson conceives of Charles Bon—the sophisticate with whom he most readily identifies—as a ''mere spectator'' with ''the detached attentiveness of a scientist watching the muscles in an anesthetized frog.'' Bon, he imagines ''took the innocent and negative plate of

Henry's provincial soul and intellect and exposed it by slow degrees to this esoteric milieu, building gradually toward the picture which he desired it to retain, accept." Mr. Compson transcendentalizes the "simpler" and "more heroic" figures in a spatialized picture of history as a kind of infinite regress of spectators: "I can see him corrupting Henry," Mr. Compson tells Quentin, describing Bon watching Henry "with that cold and catlike inscrutable calculation, watching the picture resolve and become fixed." Whether the figures in the picture are integers or symbols, in short, the viewer of the picture presumes to stand outside it, and therefore occupies Sutpen's morally impotent posture as the contemplative observer of his own life. Faulkner's condemnation of this posture as embodied in the reader gains force from the way in which he meets—or rather, refuses to meet—our expectations in the novel's final chapter.[41]

As we enter the novel's second movement in chapter 6, we are still waiting, like Bon once was, for the "answer, aware of the jigsaw puzzle integers . . . jumbled and unrecognizable yet on the point of falling into a pattern," the answer which will "reveal . . . at once, like a flash of light," the meaning of the story. As we gradually discover the relation between Bon and Sutpen, and the reason for Sutpen's repudiation of Bon, the events of Sutpen's story begin to compose a coherent picture. But while investing Quentin with the knowledge of Bon's past, Faulkner withholds from us its source, the conversation between Henry and Quentin on that night in September at Sutpen's Hundred. Thus we still don't know "quite all of it," because there is still one thing missing, the verification of Quentin's knowledge about Bon. Accordingly, we await that scene which will allow us to believe what we already know by the time Quentin and Shreve have assembled the story for us, the scene, that is, which will provide proof of Quentin's claim that he learned this crucial fact on that night when he accompanied Rosa to Sutpen's Hundred.[42]

When the confrontation between Quentin and Henry is finally depicted, however, no flash of light comes. Further, this scene not only fails to meet our expectations for verification, but repudiates the very motives for such expectations. The mirror conversation in chapter 9 serves, as it were, to confront us with our own image. It is not only that Faulkner deliberately denies us verification for Quentin's knowledge about Bon; he flaunts that denial, like a rebuke, in our faces. Given this rebuke, the debate about whether we can in fact explain, or whether we are after all not supposed to know, only demonstrates how reified our own consciousness is, for that debate merely traps us between two forms of detached contemplation. It is not that we are not supposed to know, but that we cannot know whether Quentin's statements about Bon are true, and this not because the novel is a paean to the Romantic Imagination, but rather because it is an elegy to it. In other words, if we seek an answer to the question left hanging since the end of chapter 5, the question of what Quentin found out at Sutpen's Hundred, in order to verify the information he seems to have acquired there, we mimic Sutpen in the way Shreve does at the novel's end. We seek to fulfill that need for a final explanation which will account for events by means of a "chemical formula" and this in order to sit back, satisfied with a completed picture from which we can walk away. If, on the other hand, we fall back on imagination to save us, we may avoid playing the detective, but we do not thereby avoid occupying his detached posture, as the case of Mr. Compson abundantly demonstrates. In effect, it is not only Shreve who acts as the reader's surrogate in the novel; it is everyone who speaks, not excluding Sutpen himself. Like Judith, we are responsible, no matter how little we know. Quentin is right when he suspects that "it took . . . Thomas Sutpen to make all of us," because Sutpen's story closes out and gives the lie to the dream of innocence itself, not merely as a literary theme, but as a historical reality. For the boy who was turned away from that "smooth white house" has become, even in Sutpen's eyes, a "boy-symbol," a heroicized figure, now reduced to a ghost who haunts voices "where a more fortunate one would have had a house." Further, those voices speak in the "coffin-smelling gloom" of a "tomb-like room" where men and women cry out in the dark to one another, panting for breath. No novel is more suffused with the virtual smell of death than this one. We may be joined together by that "meager and fragile thread" of speech and hearing which the novel rewinds on its spool, but when Quentin Compson cries out "I don't hate it," the thread has reached its end.[43]

This ending leaves us as readers in an impossible position, for our endeavor to assemble events into an ordered and completed whole has drawn us into the role of participants in the same activity which constitutes the novel's major line of action—narrative construction. Accordingly, when we find our expectations of an ending thwarted by the scene at Sutpen's Hundred, it is for the same reason that, as the dust cloud warns him, Quentin *"will find no destination but will merely abrupt gently onto a plateau and a panorama of harmless and inscrutable night."* For as participants in the same kind of activity which constitutes the stream of event for the participants in the novel's central line of action, we are threatened with becoming, like Quentin, trapped within the very picture we have presumed to compose.[44]

Of course, we insist upon composing that picture, upon resisting that threat. Needless to say, the preceding discussion is itself as much a form of resistance as any other reading of the novel. We cannot avoid resisting the implications of Quentin's position at the novel's end, for the simple reason that the implications are suicidal. What makes our resistance possible, moreover, is also what makes Faulkner's task itself impossible. Printed words cannot become the deeds he struggles to make them here, so that the reader can still treat the book as a spatial object. He can reread or walk away from it, just as if it were a painting on his living room wall. But insofar as Faulkner's strategy succeeds, the reader remains contaminated by his knowledge that, in thus resisting the novel's threat, he is imitating its demonic hero.

THEORETICAL POSTSCRIPT

THE WRITER AS PARTICIPANT:
MODERNISM AND CRITICAL RESISTANCE

Nevertheless there were always writers who in their life-work, despite all the resistance of the day . . . aided the development of mankind and the triumph of humanist principles in a society so contradictory in its nature that it on the one hand gave birth to the ideal of the complete human personality and on the other hand destroyed it in practice.

—LUKÁCS

THE PRIMARY AIM OF THE preceding essay has been to identify the social projects inscribed in the literary works of four major American writers. This claim has essentially two points of reference. This first is that still dominant strain of American ahistoricism discussed at the outset, whose legitimacy the argument is designed to challenge; the second is Marxist critical theory itself, some of whose tools I have tried to use and, in the process, to test. Chief among those tools, of course, has been the Lukácsian opposition between observer and participant attendant upon the developing phenomenon of reification under capitalism. My appropriation of this tool needs itself, however, to be justified, given the fact that Lukács' own critical application of the opposition to literary texts, the novel in particular, not only differs from but, in its evaluative conclusions, conflicts with my own.

Further, there is a more formidable set of issues left implicit in the preceding pages, issues which demand at least that we make them explicit. I have argued that once we understand "social" in the appropriate terms, the projects of Emerson, James, Adams, and Faulkner reveal themselves as episodes in a struggle whose literary form in no way precludes—and indeed derives ultimately from—its essentially social nature. The strategies each devises to combat, undermine, or transcend the contradictions attendant upon reification may be analyzed as narrative, rhetorical, or philosophical, but ultimately these strategies operate in and through language; it is only by conceiving language itself as not merely permeated with ideological values, but constituted out of the social interaction in which those values are born, live, and die, that we can begin to understand a literary text as part of a social process. In short, the terms on which I have treated texts as "social projects" have a broader reference than to American literary history. They have reference, theoretically, to the fundamental methodological dilemma of any Marxist criticism—the relation of text to reality.

This issue is complex—far too complex both in its historical and in its theoretical ramifications to be dealt with fully here. What I would like, nonetheless, at least to specify are the theoretical bases for my own method. The reader familiar with Marxist critical theory will have recognized by now the central sources on which I have relied. In addition to Raymond Williams' theory of cultural materialism, the linguistic theory of V. N. Vološinov—upon which Williams himself calls in his chapter on language—has helped me to formulate for myself a view of literature as itself a "social entity" which "participates in the social process." While the theoretical principles emerging from the work of Vološinov and his colleagues, Mikhail Bakhtin and Pavlev Medvedev, are more than worthy of defense and elaboration, my aim here is not so much to defend or elaborate as simply to identify these principles; their usefulness must be judged on the basis of their elaboration in the argument I have already made.[1]

The struggle against reification which I have identified as marked by observers confronted with their own participation in the world they contemplate comes into view primarily through the lens of Lukács' *History and Class Consciousness*, a work he was later to repudiate as contaminated with idealism. The circumstances surrounding this famous recantation and, indeed, the political context of Lukács' intellectual development in general are not without relevance to the questions I wish to address here. But the central question—How can we use the analytic tools which Lukács forged in *History and Class Consciousness* to rescue a modernist literary practice from the charge of ahistoricism when Lukács himself was later to use those same tools to condemn that practice?—requires us primarily to understand the difference between the observer/participant opposition as it is defined in the 1923 work and the application of that opposition which Lukács works out in his literary criticism of the 1930s and 1940s. Lukács' political fate would necessarily play a definitive role in any full account of the differences between the earlier and later versions of this opposition in his work, but I am less concerned to account for that difference than to identify it and, in so doing, to rescue a set of tools for other uses than those to which Lukács himself limited them in his own literary criticism. To these ends, I want briefly to outline Lukács' use of the observer/participant opposition in *Studies in European Realism*, where he is concerned to draw a contrast between the pre-1848 realist novel of Balzac and post-1848 modernism, whether of Flaubert or of Zola. Once his adaptation of the opposition is in view, we can see that the limits of Lukács' application of his own Marxian distinction are (1) unnecessary and (2) rooted not in his most radical Marxian assumptions, but rather in those of bourgeois aesthetics.[2]

Lukács' attack on modernism is inseparable from his valorization of realism. What the latter possesses, the former lacks, both in historical preconditions and in literary virtues.

Realism flourishes in the period between 1789 and 1848, a period in which, in France, the bourgeoisie serves as the bearer of capitalism's revolutionary phase, struggling to wrest power from the forces of aristocracy, church, and monarchy. Having secured its dominating position in the beautiful revolution of February, the bourgeoisie turns upon its new enemy, the proletariat, in the ugly revolution of the June days, fighting a battle which marks "a turning point in history on an international scale," since here "the bourgeoisie for the first time fights for the naked continuance of its economic and political rule." "All spheres of bourgeois ideology" are affected by "this change." Specifically, in the realm of the novel, the conditions enabling Balzac to see and to represent the revolutionary social changes wrought by the rise of capitalism and of the bourgeoisie inevitably begin to disappear after 1848. As Lukács puts it, "1848 destroyed the subjective conditions which made a great realism possible."[3]

What were these conditions? According to Lukács, "the great realists of old, from Swift and Defoe to Goethe, Balzac and Stendhal" were none of them "writers only." As men they enjoyed "intricate and combative" relationships with their society, and could do so because that society offered "historically significant social and ideological trends" to which they could "dedicate" themselves. In short, they were participants in history, and this condition—grounded in their historical situation as members of societies in which capitalism remained unfinished, and the class destined to rule it remained engaged in a heroic struggle for political emancipation—enabled them to produce a realist narrative from the standpoint of participants.[4]

The post-1848 bourgeois novelists, on the contrary, became spectators, alienated from a society which afforded them "nothing they could support whole-heartedly." These altered "subjective conditions" generated an altered and debased "new realism." Thus, in Zola, a "mechanical average" replaces the dialectical unity of individual experience and social significance in literary "types" to be found in Balzac. Mere "description and analysis" replace "epic plots" in which "individual and social . . . the physical and the psychical . . . private interest and public affairs" are intertwined. Zola provides "pictures" which serve as "a gigantic backdrop in front of which tiny, haphazard people move to and fro" rather than an integrated and penetrating vision of individuals as social creatures at a historical moment. The "great realists" presented "social institutions as human relationships and social objects as the vehicles of such relationships," but in the works of their followers, no such thematic coherence is in sight. Instead, we find "isolated characters of purely private interest" standing in front of "dead scenery described with admirable skill," characters whose human relationships, lacking "social motives," are so shallow that the author either "stresses the shallowness of life with angry or sentimental irony or else substitutes dead, rigid, lyrically inflated symbols for the missing human and social relationships." (One is reminded of Scott Fitzgerald's remark that, having failed to represent the relationship between Gatsby and Daisy, he covered the gap with "blankets of excellent prose.'') In essence, then, once bourgeois hegemony is secure, the writer becomes a spectator, alienated from a world in which he plays no part, a world he is inclined to "repudiate with hatred and loathing," if, like Flaubert, he has integrity. With bourgeois apologists, Lukács is not really concerned. The great artist's work suffers accordingly.[5]

The immediate question is, and has always been: How can Lukács attack the modern novelist for portraying his own historical moment just as accurately as Balzac portrayed his? If the world changed after 1848, and if the novelist's mission is, as Lukács claims, to meet "the demand formulated by Hamlet: 'to hold the mirror up to nature',," and if, furthermore, social conditions determine literary practice, how can a Flaubert be faulted for the literary effects of a historically enforced spectator's posture? If the heroic phase of capitalism made Balzac, in Fredric Jameson's words, "contemporary with a social transformation which permitted him to see objects not as completed material substances but as they issued from human work" and "to apprehend social change as a network of individual stories," then the "mechanical and 'finished' character of the capitalist world" could only make Flaubert the victim and recorder of a society in which objects were reified and human relationships were cut adrift from "social motives."[6]

Lukács is by no means unaware of this problem, but his solution only reconstitutes the problem in another guise, for his solution betrays his own mimetic principles. The modern bourgeois novelist, Lukács says, must struggle to "overcome, in the sphere of art, that coldness and harshness in bourgeois existence, and in the relationships of men with each other and with nature, which opposes such a rigid resistance to poetic presentation." How? By "seeking out the surviving live elements of these relationships in reality itself." But where do these "live elements" lie? In the novelist's "own rich and real experience." But what "rich and real experience" can the novelist have if he is relegated by his historical moment to the condition of an alienated spectator of a "finished" capitalist world. Well, it seems after all that he is *not* so relegated: "for the mechanical and 'finished' character of the capitalist world . . . is, it is true, an existing and growing evolutionary tendency in capitalism, but it must never be forgotten that it is still only a tendency, that

society is objectively never 'finished', fulfilled, dead, petrified reality." At this point, Lukács sounds remarkably like Raymond Williams: no social formation is ever complete, no hegemony absolute.[7]

How, then, do we reconcile this voice, calling for the novelist
"to swim against the current . . . of capitalism" by reconstructing
realism, with that other one which claims that "the evolution of
bourgeois society after 1848 destroyed the subjective conditions
which made a great realism possible"? On the one hand, Lukács
describes the post-1848 writer as inevitably alienated from his society, relegated to the posture of the detached spectator; on the other
hand, he asks this same writer to resist "bourgeois existence" by
"culling from his own rich and real experience" the "still living
tendencies" beneath the petrified surface of capitalist reality. How
resist if one is determined?[8]

To account for this contradiction in Lukács' argument is a formidable task, and one we cannot hope to accomplish here. But it
is surely not enough to call this, as Jameson does, an "ambiguity"
in Lukács' judgment, and then to apologize for it by noting that the
"same ambiguity is visible in Marxist revolutionary theory as well."
It is no ambiguity, but a contradiction, to argue that the writer's
social condition as spectator, and thus his literary practice, is determined by the "evolution of bourgeois society after 1848," and
then to demand that he "overcome" the "subjective conditions"
of the alienated spectator by some kind of personal fiat. Nor does
it help to "set aside that part of Lukács' work which constitutes a
set of recommendations to the artist." As we shall see, those recommendations are crucial to an understanding of Lukács' position.
In his effort to sever a faulty "judgment" from a sound "diagnosis,"
which accurately identifies an "absolute difference" between realism and a modernism "characterized precisely by its ahistorical,
metaphysical" perspective, Jameson effectively rescues Lukács as
a perceptive literary historian but not as a Marxist literary critic with
formidable theoretical powers.[9]

Lukács' argument cracks not along a fault line between diagnosis
and judgment, but rather along one which cuts through both, one
between a mimetic principle harboring a naive realism which posits
a real to be reflected in art and a genuinely historical materialism
in which the real is always in dialectical process, always undergoing

a self-transformation—one in which the artist, like everyone else in capitalist society, is himself implicated. In other words, the contradiction into which Lukács is led here develops out of a conflict between two warring epistemologies: one which underwrites the principle of mimesis and believes in an art which reflects a historical reality from which the "honest artist" himself is detached, and one which conceives the artist as a participant in social activity. To follow out the first line is to make of the "honest artist," always and everywhere, a person who, as Lukács says of Balzac, is able to transcend his own prejudices and to "inexorably depict the true essence of reality." To follow out the second is to conceive the artist in fundamentally different terms—as someone whose life is imbedded in its historical moment, but for whom that moment always and everywhere affords the possibility of resistance. In the first view, Balzac's epistemological position is itself, ironically, that of the spectator; in the second, Balzac becomes a participant, but on terms which should logically extend to include Flaubert and Zola.[10]

These two positions, the one presupposing the artist as alienated spectator and the other presupposing that all members of capitalist society, artists included, remain participants, no matter how much the victims of alienation, generate two opposed views of art which clash again and again in *Studies in European Realism*. The first places the artist always and everywhere outside the picture, as it were. At the same time, he is asked to imitate reality, to represent social reality in a form which will serve as a "poetic mirror." In the face of the examples provided by the new realists, however, this mimetic/spectator model breaks down. The emphasis subtly shifts from "mirror" to "poetic." Once the artist is confronted with the "prose" of capitalist society, merely to reflect that prose is to be Zola, whose work succeeds, according to Lukács, only insofar as it goes beyond its mechanically conceived mimetic principles. Similarly, Flaubert's work succeeds insofar as his rage at the prose of capitalist society emerges from between the lines of his perfectly composed sentences. In accounting for what does work in Flaubert and Zola, Lukács must appeal to the capacity of these new realists to go beyond the limits of their own strict literary codes, a capacity which in turn presupposes that they are not wholly alienated spectators, any more than capitalist society is itself ever wholly finished.

It is their residual status as participants, in short, which both makes them accountable for their narrative acts and partially redeems the failure of those acts. It is, further, a status they share with Balzac. In order to see this, however, we need to distinguish between what Lukács genuinely admires in Balzac's work and the terms on which he tries to account for Balzac's achievement.[11]

What Lukács admires about Balzac is that he accomplished precisely what Lukács calls upon the modern bourgeois novelist to accomplish; he constructed a realist narrative which "opposes . . . the destruction of the completeness of the human personality," a narrative which, far from merely reflecting social reality (the false strategy for which Zola is criticized), calls forth its "latent" possibilities by means of an "extreme presentation of . . . extremes." When Lukács turns to the situation of the modern bourgeois novelist, he calls for this same resistance and this same appeal to the "latent" and the "extreme":

The example of *Robinson Crusoe* shows that the struggle against the prose of capitalist reality can be successful only if the author invents situations which are not in themselves impossible within the framework of this reality (although they may never really occur) and then, given this invented situation, allows his characters to develop freely all the essential factors of their social existence.

It could be argued, and in a sense has been in the preceding pages, that the work of so marked a modernist as Henry James essentially accords with such a formulation. James, of course, was hardly a political opponent of capitalism, but his continuing experiment in narrative is as clear a case of "the struggle against the prose of capitalist reality" as we are likely to find this side of Flaubert, a novelist whom James, incidentally, admired a good deal less than he did Balzac. On this view, James tried and failed to write the Balzacian novel, and so had to "invent situations" which, like that of Isabel Archer, "may never really occur" but which do allow "his characters to develop freely all the essential factors of their social existence."[12]

I am suggesting, then, that Lukács admires Balzac's realism primarily because it is a critical realism, in which the "struggle against the prose of capitalist society" can be seen. It is when he tries to account for Balzac's preeminence as a realist by reference to a mimetic principle which removes the artist from history and makes him, ontologically, a detached spectator that Lukács falls into contradiction. "What makes Balzac a great man," Lukács tells us, "is the inexorable veracity with which he depicted reality even if that reality ran counter to his own opinions, hopes and wishes." Tolstoy is praised in similar terms for his ability to transcend his own ideological limits: "Being a writer of genius, he faithfully recorded certain essential traits of reality and thus, without his knowledge, and contrary to his conscious intentions, he became the poetic mirror of certain aspects of the revolutionary development in Russia." Such statements reveal Lukács falling into a form of bourgeois idealism. Because Balzac is an "honest artist," because Tolstoy is a "writer of genius," they are able to see the truth even when that truth contradicts their own beliefs. As is so often the case, a mechanical materialism accompanies a romantic notion of genius, underwriting the realist novelist and the scientist in the same terms. Here, "genius" is invoked to overcome the inability of the mimetic/spectator model to account even for Balzac and Tolstoy. The picture presented here of Balzac impassively overriding his own prejudices in a coolly detached observation of social reality conflicts fundamentally with the view of him as thinking "through to the end the necessities of social reality, beyond their normal limits, beyond even their feasibility." In the first instance, Balzac is conceived as a spectator; in the second, he is conceived as a participant, and one whose struggle is recognized in the same terms as that of the heroic German philosophers discussed in *History and Class Consciousness*.[13]

If the mimetic/spectator model contradicts the participant/resistance model in Balzac, that contradiction proves even more obvious when we turn to Lukács' treatment of Flaubert. Flaubert, no less than Balzac, is the "honest artist," a "writer of genius" whom Lukács deeply admires as such. Like Tolstoy, Flaubert "faithfully recorded certain essential traits of reality." How then can this alleged failure as a realist be explained? Lukács appeals to the "anti-artistic nature of capitalist society," portraying Flaubert as a great artist forced into an alienated stance from which he cannot emulate Balzac in penetrating "the superficial phenomena of everyday life in a capitalist society." At this point, it seems, no matter how "honest" the artist, and no matter how much of a genius, he cannot overcome his "subjective conditions" and relate individual experience to "social motives" in a dynamic, critical realism. Yet this is precisely what Lukács asks him to do, on the grounds that the "anti-artistic nature of capitalist society . . . does not, of course, form an unsurmountable obstacle in the path of true art and aesthetics." The fact is, however, that if the artist is defined in these hypostatized terms, capitalist society's "anti-artistic nature" does form an "unsurmountable obstacle." The artist's posture here becomes that of the detached spectator in his guise as romantic hero. But, as we have seen, such was not, in fact, Balzac's posture. Balzac, remaining in touch with the real as a social participant, forged a realist narrative in which he opposed "the destruction of the completeness of the human personality." What enabled Balzac's critical resistance to take the specific realist form it did was a combination of subjective and objective conditions: he was not merely a writer, but a social actor, and in the society he inhabited, the "destruction of the completeness of the human personality" was not yet complete. But what gives force to the label "genius" is Balzac's resistance to that destruction. The conditions necessary for Balzacian realism may indeed disappear with the expansion of capital. But what does not disappear, even for Lukács, is the capacity of the bourgeois novelist to resist the reifying process. That resistance, however, may no longer be possible within the limits of realism.[14]

The question depends upon how these limits are defined. If you explain the "fantastic element" in Balzac as Lukács does when he says it "derives from the fact that he thinks through to the end the necessities of social reality, beyond their normal limits, beyond even their feasibility," realism is thereby defined in terms which logically extend to include Kafka. But insofar as Balzac's literary practice is defined within a strictly mimetic limit, that practice is foreclosed by conditions, both subjective and objective, which undercut the force of mimesis (as in Zola), but do not undercut critical resistance to the reifying process itself. It is in tying resistance to representational narrative models that Lukács falls into self-contradiction. Such resistance can and does generate, as I have tried to show, a variety of literary strategies in which the very effort to resist reification exposes the contradictions attendant upon it. Lukács praises Balzac for exposing contradictions in bourgeois society, but fails, himself, ultimately to "think through to the end the necessities of [a] social reality" which can sometimes compel the modern novelist to depart from mimesis precisely *because* he is struggling against reification.[15]

We can now draw several conclusions about Lukács' argument in *Studies in European Realism*. Lukács reifies his own categories. The contemplative stance of the detached observer functions not as part of an epistemological dilemma which deepens and ruptures forth as capitalism expands, but rather merely as the personal "subjective condition" of the modern artist. In arguing that Balzac and Tolstoy inhabited a society in which they could still be participants, Lukács effectively stops "sensuous human activity" in June 1848. In *History and Class Consciousness*, sensuous human activity is always and everywhere operative; reification works to repress it, to obscure it from view, but that repression in turn has consequences in that it breeds crises which erupt to reveal what has been repressed, if only temporarily. It is to this view that Lukács appeals when he insists that "society is objectively never 'finished'." But by superimposing the participant/observer opposition on the shift in the artist's "subjective conditions" before and after 1848, Lukács posits a society that *is* finished. He gains thereby a set of categories which can serve, to be sure, to illuminate the literary effects of social change, but only at the cost of losing the more powerful categories of which these are an emasculated, not to mention a reified, version.[16]

Once you say that Balzac's status as a participant and Zola's as an observer are historically fixed, you are forced to conclude that the literary practice of both is determined in a sense which makes criticism of the latter unjust. If, on the other hand, you say that under capitalism, everyone is subject to reification and thus to some extent a victim of the contemplative stance, then the difference between Zola and Balzac can be described in terms which, while acknowledging the social preconditions of their literary practice, can still allow for their capacity to "struggle against the prose of capitalist reality." On this view, Balzac himself is already to some extent a victim of the reifying process at work in capitalist society, one who struggles against such forces by forging a realist narrative designed to expose their destructive power. It is because of particular social conditions, because the rise of the bourgeoisie to political power and cultural hegemony is still in process, that Balzac—in his Royalist alliance and his preference for the English model afforded by the Glorious Revolution—has a place to stand within society, but beyond the limits of the bourgeois class itself, a place which enables him to construct his preeminent realism. But it is because of a basic theoretical principle, because society is never finished, petrified, and complete, that Balzac is able—by means of that realism—to resist the reifying process. It is as a participant in this more basic sense that Balzac can forge a narrative strategy which in fact violates mimetic principles, relying on the "latent," the "extreme," and the "fantastic," and which is deployed in the service of opposing the destruction of the human personality. Balzacian realism may depend, as Lukács argues, upon the social conditions before 1848 in France, but Balzacian realism is itself a narrative strategy constructed in the service of resistance to those social conditions—a resistance whose possibility is acknowledged in the more fundamental Marxist principles of *History and Class Consciousness*.[17]

On this view, then, the social conditions in France prior to 1848 would indeed be understood as essential to the production of the Balzacian novel, but that novel would not, in turn, become the model which all critical resistance to capitalist society necessarily follows. On the contrary, it might be argued that the social conditions making Balzac's realism possible are the exception rather than the rule when we set them next to the development of bourgeois hegemony in England, Germany, or the United States. For where else in the West does this development follow a pattern with the dramatic coherence (the narrative unity, one might say) to be found in nineteenth-century France? Because the class struggle in France takes an atypically clear-cut form, France can serve Lukács, as it did Marx, as an excellent model for understanding that struggle, but as model it can also serve to obscure distinctions which have important effects on literary production, distinctions not only between the social conditions informing English as opposed to French realism (of which Lukács is by no means unaware), but also between the conditions generating realism itself as opposed to modernism (of which Lukács loses sight, one suspects, precisely because of his tendency to take the Balzacian period as a rule rather than an exception). In short, it would be worth considering whether Balzac's particular social conditions, and in consequence his particular form of literary production, are not exceptional, perhaps even unique.[18]

For our purposes, however, the central point to be made is that the principles derived from *History and Class Consciousness* generate a participant/resistance model which conflicts with the mimetic/spectator model. Specifically, these principles dictate a view of the artist, even under late capitalism, which undercuts the bourgeois idealist view of him as genius because they deny both sides of the mimetic/spectator model underlying such a view. As the "honest artist" who sees beyond the limits of his personal attitudes, Balzac becomes a case of the detached spectator as romantic overreacher. But as we have seen, this view of the artist breaks down. As long as Lukács clings to the view of the artist as "poetic mirror," he is forced to treat him as a detached spectator; but the case of Zola proves this to be a dead-end street. On the other hand, in appealing to the modern novelist to overcome the "anti-artistic nature of capitalist society," which "does not . . . form an unsurmountable obstacle in the path of true art and aesthetics," Lukács sanctions the view of the artist as uniquely capable of transcendence. But if a commitment to "true art and aesthetics" could not enable a Flaubert to overcome such an "obstacle," no one else need apply for the job.[19]

While the spectator must become a genius to fulfill the unfulfillable demands of "true art and aesthetics," the mimetic standard falls victim to self-contradiction as well. Lukács treats the failures of Zola and Flaubert as marks of a debased realism, a false because reductive version of mimesis. But the conception of the artist as still a participant, which underwrites Lukács' explanation for their limited success, calls into question the principle of mimesis itself. Indeed, what he finds fault with in both is essentially a slavish commitment to mimetic description. In Zola, this takes a straightforward positivist form; for Flaubert, the boredom of exact description is compensated by the romantic flights of *Saint Antoine*. In both cases, the critical force of Balzac's realist strategy is lacking. But once we understand it as a strategy, a narrative construction in which the "fantastic" is marshaled in the service of critical resistance, Balzac's realism has little to do with a mimetic principle. Balzac's realism succeeds not by holding up a mirror to nature, but by exaggerating the possibilities "latent" in his society so as to expose its contradictions. Once Balzac's realism is understood as a narrative construction rather than a poetic mirror, the mimetic standard is discredited. This does not mean, of course, that that construction springs from Balzac's head full blown and stands in no relation to his society or to his historical moment. (Lukács shows clearly enough how deeply related the construction is to the historical moment.) It means rather that this relationship is not one which can be properly conceived in terms of reflection. For reflection theory lies at the end of that dead-end street signposted by Zola's work, just as art for art's sake lies at the end of the dead-end street discovered by Flaubert. For the Lukács who is trapped by the mimetic/spectator model, these two streets are really one—a kind of bounded, double dead-end street on which the modern bourgeois novelist travels back and forth in mounting frustration. But for the Lukács who, contradicting himself, appeals to that novelist to swim against the current of capitalist society, there must necessarily be an exit from the twin dead ends of prosaic reflection and poetic genius, of reductive mimesis and aesthetic compensation. That exit comes into view at the moments when Lukács appeals to the novelist to overcome and resist capitalist society's dehumanizing force, only to be closed off again when that society is described not as fundamentally alienating, but as more particularly "anti-artistic."[20]

While Lukács does not finally embrace the bourgeois tactic of heroizing the alienated artist and mystifying his productions under the sign of the Imagination, he does travel a good distance down the road which leads in this direction when he accepts the distinction between the aesthetic and the social. In its more conventional bourgeois form, this road leads to the hypostasis of the artist as a compensatory figure, a man who, alienated from the social status quo, overcomes its prosaic boredom by making Art. Baudelaire and Flaubert are his fathers, and his impotence as social actor is compensated by his glorification as aesthete. The bourgeois version of this view differs from the Lukácsian in only one respect, but this proves a significant difference. Whereas the bourgeois view allows for a certain equilibrium between artist and society, Lukács refuses to accept this resolution. That is, in bourgeois aesthetics, not only does a Flaubert become the exemplar of the artist as alienated; he is also valorized on this basis. The severance of Art from the social becomes a given, for reasons we have already reviewed in our discussion of Emerson's America. The artist's critical perspective is neutralized because his works are understood to emerge from (and are treated as remaining within) an aesthetic realm beyond the limits of the social. For Lukács, however, while the artist becomes alienated in modern society, that alienation is neither valorized nor even always understood as given. While he does not accept the resolution of bourgeois aesthetics, however, he often seems to accept the precondition for it—the severance of the aesthetic from the social. I say "seems" because the very label "anti-artistic," while it presupposes the split between aesthetic and social, at the same time calls that split into question. That is, when Lukács labels capitalist society "anti-artistic," he still maintains a vision of what it would mean if that society were not anti-artistic. Consequently, despite the extent to which Lukács falls into the trap of bourgeois aesthetics, his argument also brings into focus what the latter obscures—that the artist's alienation is socially produced and that his literary response to that condition is also a social response. To carry through on these principles, however, requires us to overcome the split between the aesthetic and the social itself, and that task in turn requires an understanding of language as itself social.

Raymond Williams' recent work is partly devoted to charting a route to a theoretical position in which the distinction between aesthetic and social collapses, and among the most valuable guides he has found in that effort is the linguistic theory of V. N. Vološinov. For Williams, Vološinov's "decisive contribution was to find a way beyond the powerful but partial theories of expression and objective system," beyond, that is, the idealist subjectivism of Wilhelm von Humboldt's school and what Vološinov calls the "abstract objectivism" of Ferdinand de Saussure's school. Vološinov accepted from Saussure the primary importance of the sign for any understanding of language but rejected the Saussurean privileging of *la langue* over *la parole*. At the same time, he accepted from von Humboldt the view of language as "activity, an unceasing process," but rejected the subjectivist idealism accompanying it. For Vološinov,

Theoretical Postscript

the "actual reality of language-speech" is neither the "abstract system of linguistic forms" (privileged by the Saussureans) nor the "isolated monologic utterance" (privileged by the Humboldtian school) but rather "the social event of verbal interaction implemented in an utterance or utterances." The sign, on this view, is the locus of a meaning produced not only out of its relations with other signs, but also out of its role as the material of verbal interaction, its role, that is, in "dialogic" utterance.[21]

Vološinov's emphasis on "dialogic" as opposed to "monologic" utterance follows from his claim that both subjectivist and objectivist views of language, by taking the monologic utterance as their point of departure, drain language of its actual social dimension, although in opposing ways. Saussure's claim that "language stands in opposition to utterance in the same way as does that which is social to that which is individual" presupposes the same false opposition between individual and social upon which subjectivism grounds its view that "the psyche is individual while ideology is social." By separating *la langue* from *la parole*, Saussure reduces the individual speech act, the monologic utterance, to the status of the individual instance in biological science; that is, it becomes merely a particular example whose features are understood in relation to an overriding formal system. Subjectivism, on the other hand, valorizes the monologic utterance because it believes in an individual consciousness which is "the architect of the ideological superstructure" rather than "a tenant lodging in the social edifice of all ideological signs." But "the content of the individual psyche is by its very nature just as social as is ideology," Vološinov argues, because "the domain of ideology coincides with the domain of signs," and "consciousness becomes consciousness only once it has been filled with ideological (semiotic) content." On this view, the opposition between individual and social is radically undermined, since the "individual, as the possessor of the contents of his own consciousness . . . is a purely socioideological phenomenon." Once that opposition is broken down, moreover, the monologic utterance loses its supporting Cartesian framework. Whether monologic utterance is reduced as *la parole* or exalted as poetic creation, it preserves its false status as individual as opposed to social. It is only by regarding all utterance as dialogic, then, that this social dimension of language can be recognized.[22]

What allowed Vološinov to avoid the formalist determinism to which Saussure's theory has subsequently led, most notably in France, was not only his rejection of the *langue/parole* dichotomy, but also his reconstruction of *langage* (or "language-speech") as verbal interaction. In Vološinov's theory the "domain of signs" is just as constitutive of consciousness as it is in some branches of structuralism, but because that domain is conceived as including rather than excluding the sign's "social life," because, that is, the process of signification is active and dynamic, sustained as it is by social interaction, the constitutive function of the sign for human consciousness does not foreclose the active dimension of that consciousness. In contrast to the residual idealism of the structuralist program, Vološinov proposes a materialist theory which seeks to understand the "genuine dialectical refraction of existence in the sign" by approaching the "form of the sign" as itself always already "conditioned by the social organization of the participants involved" in the verbal interaction from which the sign emerges. In other words, the sign, itself an ideological phenomenon, can never be understood accurately in separation from its use, because it is in its use that it becomes a sign. What distinguishes this approach from Emerson's in some ways comparable one, and from subjectivist idealism in general, is that the process of signification is never monologic: "Signs emerge . . . only in the process of interaction between one individual consciousness and another."[23]

This view of the sign, then, not only enables Vološinov to overcome the most notorious failing of post-Saussurean linguistics and structuralism generally, its inability to account for historical change, but does so by restoring to language its active, social dimension. Rejecting both the romantic view of language as "an ever-flowing stream of speech acts in which nothing remains fixed and identical to itself" and the abstract objectivist view of language as "the stationary rainbow arched over that stream," Vološinov is led into significantly different metaphors in his effort to describe the living, active reality of the sign. Insisting upon the need to restore to language its social dimension, for instance, Vološinov remarks: "In order to observe the process of combustion, a substance must be placed into the air. In order to observe the phenomenon of language, both the producer and the receiver of sound and the sound itself must be placed into the social atmosphere." Or again, countering the reductive semantics following from an abstract focus on the "system of language," Vološinov argues that "meaning is the *effect of interaction between speaker and listener produced via the material of a particular sound complex*. It is like an electric spark that occurs only when two different terminals are hooked together." Thus, those who approach a word's meaning as derived exclusively from its place in an abstract system of language "want, in effect, to turn on a light bulb after having switched off the current." But, in fact, "only the current of verbal intercourse endows a word with the light of meaning."[24]

The virtue of such metaphors lies in their capacity to focus attention on the sign as neither abstract nor spontaneous but rather as socially produced and socially active. Vološinov enables us to approach language as both constituted by and constitutive of human consciousness. That is, if signs "emerge" only in the process of verbal interaction between "socially organized persons," such persons, in turn, emerge only as a result of the same process. There is no question here of how to relate individual consciousness to the ideological signs in which it embodies an abstractly conceived thought, for consciousness itself is constituted in and by those signs. But at the same time, consciousness can be seen to constitute signs; in fact, it *must* do so because it is always necessarily engaged in a dialogue with other consciousnesses, and it is from that dialogue that signs themselves emerge. In effect, once language is understood as dialogic utterance, linguistic creativity is theoretically necessary.[25]

The radical implications of Vološinov's theory for our understanding of literary production as a social rather than an aesthetic phenomenon are evident in the critical reaction of Vološinov and his colleagues, Bakhtin and Medvedev, to Russian Formalism. For our purposes, what is significant about the work of this group is its view of literature as itself a product of "ideological activity," a "social entity" whose changing forms cannot be explained within the terms of "literariness" upon which the Formalist program operates. In their efforts to formulate a "sociological poetics," Vološinov, Bakhtin, and Medvedev sought to construct a theory of literary production in which a work of literature could be understood as a "social entity" which "participates in the social process." Their project, while benefiting from the Formalist analysis of defamiliarization, called into question the Saussurean view of language upon which the Formalists relied.[26]

The Formalists' theory of literariness as defamiliarization opens a way toward understanding literary changes at the same time that it forecloses any possibility of comprehending the concrete historical dimension of these changes. In the Formalist theory, literary changes are always themselves conceived abstractly in that they represent changes in function within a closed system understood, as in Saussure's closed system of *la langue*, synchronically, That is, in making defamiliarization the dominant feature of the literary as opposed to the nonliterary, Russian Formalism makes visible changes in the literary system for which it cannot account within the boundaries of that system, since those boundaries are prescribed by a binary opposition between literary and nonliterary which, while circumscribed by the limits of the synchronic, is itself subject to historical changes. For example, what counts as literary at any particular moment in history may become nonliterary, and vice versa, not merely as a result of changes in literary taste but because, as in T. S. Eliot's concept of tradition, the text's function changes as new forms arise to reorganize the whole system of relations between texts. Thus, the quality of literariness is itself subject to historical changes whose operation it presupposes without being able to incorporate.[27]

The obstacles presented by literariness as a relational concept can be seen even more clearly when we turn to its specific applications. For example, by working from the binary opposition between the literary and the nonliterary, the Formalists demonstrated how formal devices drawn from subliterary genres (such as the detective story) could be used to "make strange" the conventions of the realist novel, thereby revealing that these *were* conventions, that is, formal devices, themselves. But while they could thus discredit any claim of realism (or indeed, of any literary construction) to mirror the real directly, they had no theoretical means for comprehending the social and historical bases for that realist construction.

The effect of this program is comparable in one sense to the effect of the Kantian thing-in-itself. In both cases, the "real" remains acknowledged (as the *noumenal* for Kant, and as the ideological content of nonliterary discourse for the Formalists), but is relegated to an inaccessible realm conceived as irrational. For Saussure, it will be remembered, the realm of speech designated by *la parole* is separated off from that of *la langue* and subordinated to it precisely because the realm of speech "resists classification under any of the categories of human facts because there is no knowing how to elicit its unity." For the Formalist, this Saussurean version of the thing-in-itself means that literature operates on a given which, whether it resides in ordinary discourse or in the formal devices of prior forms of literary discourse, remains that which is worked on, but never can be known in itself as what it is—ideological activity. That this given is regarded as ideological rather than as some kind of raw, unprocessed material does not keep it from being conceived as given, and therefore from rendering the real inaccessible to cognition.[28]

A virtue of the Formalist theory, however, is that it allows us to see what subsequent structuralist programs often obscure. If the distinguishing feature of literary discourse is that it works on ordinary discourse, making strange what the latter represents as real, literature becomes, in Tony Bennett's words, "a mode of discourse which constantly maintains 'No, the world is not like that' in relation to dominant forms of discourse which maintain that it is." There is no doubt, of course, that a literary work can operate to this effect, even with this effect as its intention; Brecht's alienation effect does work to reveal how ideologically saturated is our concept of the real. But it is one thing to identify or exploit literary discourse's capacity to say "No, the world is not like that" and quite another to conclude from this discovery that the world referred to in such a statement *is* not, at all. When defamiliarization is elevated from an analytic category to a substantive description, from a capacity of discourse per se to the distinguishing feature of *literary* discourse, literature becomes a mode of discourse in which the question of what *is* real is not only begged, but ultimately discredited altogether, as in the more recent poststructuralist movement. An enabling device for this movement can be seen clearly in the Formalist theory of defamiliarization, for the theory presupposes a given in ordinary discourse upon which literary discourse operates and without which it could not operate, a given which stands in for what it blocks off—a real which has been repressed from the moment literature is separated off from the ideological activity of which it is a part. Thus, despite the theory's capacity to reveal how thoroughly the real is mediated in all literature, no matter how realist it presumes to be, the theory breaks down in effect precisely at the horizon it opens into view, the horizon marked by the given ideological content imbedded in ordinary discourse. In severing the system of literature from the changing social forces whose effects they tried to comprehend from within the synchronic domain of *la langue*, the Formalists brought those forces into view as a problem.[29]

It is to this problem that Medvedev speaks when he argues that a work of literature "enters into the milieu of ideological activity" as one of its "phenomena." It not only "reflects . . . other . . . ideological formations" but constitutes such a formation itself: "in reflecting . . . other signs, literature itself creates new forms, new signs of ideological communication, and these signs—works of literature—become a functioning part of the surrounding social reality." Here literature is still accorded "a special place" in the "ideological milieu," but what makes literature special is not its capacity to work on and make strange some given, preformed ideological formation, but rather its peculiar double focus within an active social process; it both reflects ideological formations and constitutes one itself. On this view, the defamiliarizing function of literature is by no means denied, but neither is it seen as the generic feature of literariness. Indeed, on this view, literariness, like Literature as an aesthetic category, fades from sight. Further, since literature is itself conceived as a form of ideological activity, it cannot be regarded (as it is by Althusserians, for instance) as a category apart from ideology. In the absence of this hierarchical relation between the literary (or aesthetic) and the ideological, and between the ideological and the real, literature can no longer be separated out definitively from the social process, whether as a reflector of it or as an autonomous construction beyond its limits. Literature can no longer be defined as the Formalists, according to Tony Bennett, define it, as a "play of form upon form" in which "one set of devices" is used to "chisel the ground from beneath another" so as to "wrestle

. . . reality away from the terms of seeing they propose." Rather, because the real has not already been bled out of the system, Medvedev can comprehend the work of literature as part of the real itself, inasmuch as the coextensive domain of the sign and ideology, in and by which human consciousness is constituted, is a very crucial part of the real designated as history. While a work of literature can, to be sure, operate to defamiliarize what ordinary discourse represents as given reality, this capacity is a property not of literary as opposed to nonliterary discourse but rather of all discourse, understood as the stream of verbal communication in which all ideological activity takes place. Thus the statement implicit in literary discourse as defined by Formalism—"No, the world is not like that"—becomes audible as part of a dialogue carried on between texts understood as the utterances of interlocutors in a conversation which never ceases, a conversation which is itself the medium of all ideological activity and therefore itself part of the social process.[30]

The work of Bakhtin, Vološinov, and Medvedev more than merits the long overdue attention it has begun to receive, for it proposes an analytic framework in which the distinction between aesthetic and social collapses, affording us a means of understanding the text as itself a social entity. Its relationship to social reality becomes, then, a question not of the relationship between two different orders of existence, whether conceived as literary versus nonliterary or as text versus reality, but rather of the interaction between different forms of ideological activity. If language is understood as operating according to Vološinov's dialogic model, in short, literary production must be regarded as social to the core.

More specifically, Vološinov's model provides a way of conceptualizing the modern literary artist as engaged in the kind of social project I have tried to describe, one in which his ontological status as participant must not only be presupposed, but also be expressible. By regarding that artist as a speaker, we have a means of articulating his status as participant. By understanding a literary text as a "moment in the continuous process of verbal communication," we come to see it as an utterance in which the writer "responds to something, objects to something, affirms something, anticipates possible responses and objections, seeks support, and so on.'' For whether the addressee is real or presupposed, whether the utterance is printed or not, the situation in which utterance takes place remains that of dialogue. Further, by conceiving the modern writer as a speaker, we can begin to break free of the illusions attendant upon the image of him as alienated spectator, returning him to the stream of verbal communication in which "*word is a two-sided act . . .* determined equally by *whose* word it is and *for whom* it is meant." This means more than simply reminding ourselves of the local context in which a work was written; it means that we must understand, as I have tried to do in the case of Emerson, the extent to which that context is itself constituted by the verbal interaction which serves as the medium of ideological activity. Finally, built into this model is the recognition that no writer can be so disentangled from the social forces at work on him as to "show" them from the outside, whether from a godlike perspective or from that of the camera eye. Insofar as reification has infiltrated our critical understanding of the writer, the speaker model can serve as a means of resisting it by reminding us that the writer is always already in history.[31]

In using it to this purpose, moreover, we take our cue from the American writers I have discussed. It does not seem to me a coincidence that Faulkner's narrative strategy in *Absalom, Absalom!* depends upon its use of dialogue as a means of exposing reification; nor that Henry Adams focused so much of his frustration on the silence which he heard greeting his words; nor that Henry James constructed in Maggie Verver a heroine whose refusal to utter the truth is at once the basis of her triumph and of the triumph of commodification; nor that Emerson's literary practice is preeminently aimed at a lecture audience. In other words, the recurring presence of the speaking voice in these cases suggests a hypothesis which I shall leave for the reader's consideration: that the critical resistance to the reifying process of capitalism which Lukács fails to find in modernist literature can be found there once we identify the participant as a speaker. While the modernist program notoriously suppresses that speaker's voice, insofar as it privileges showing over telling and operates under the sign of Stephen Daedalus' artist, the arch-observer who looks down like an indifferent god paring his fingernails, that suppression is by no means definitively successful, as the career of Faulkner demonstrates most powerfully. In its grandiose resonance, Faulkner's voice may at times sound like God's, but in *Absalom, Absalom!* he uses it not to escape from the nightmare of history, but to demonstrate that no escape is possible.

NOTES

Preface

1. Karl Marx, *Capital*, trans. Ben Fowkes (New York: Vintage, 1976), 1:164, quoted in Georg Lukács, *History and Class Consciousness*, trans. Rodney Livingstone (Cambridge: MIT Press, 1971), p. 86.

2. Lukács, *History*, pp. 86–87, 97, 139, 102; Ralph Waldo Emerson, *Nature*, in *The Collected Works of Ralph Waldo Emerson*, ed. Alfred R. Ferguson, William H. Gilman, Robert E. Spiller, and Carl F. Strauch (Cambridge: Harvard University Press, 1971), 1:10 (hereafter cited as *Collected Works*). See Werner Heisenberg, *Physics and Philosophy* (New York: Harper and Row, 1962); Karl Marx and Friedrich Engels, *The German Ideology*, trans. Salo Ryanaskaya (London: Laurence and Wishart, 1965), p. 645.

3. Ralph Waldo Emerson, *The Journals and Miscellaneous Notebooks of Ralph Waldo Emerson*, ed. William A. Gilman, Alfred R. Ferguson et al. (Cambridge: Harvard University Press, 1960–), 5:278 (hereafter cited as *Journals*); William Faulkner, *Absalom, Absalom!* (New York: Vintage, 1936), p. 33.

4. D. H. Lawrence, *Studies in Classic American Literature* (New York: Thomas Selzer, 1923), p. 5; Richard Poirier, *A World Elsewhere* (New York: Oxford University Press, 1966), p. 5; R. W. B. Lewis, *The American Adam* (Chicago: Chicago University Press, 1955), p. 5; Richard Chase, *The American Novel and Its Tradition* (Garden City, N.Y.: Doubleday, 1957), p. ix; Irving Howe, "The American Voice—It Begins on a Note of Wonder," *New York Times Book Review*, 4 July 1976, p. 2. Howe writes in an appropriately nostalgic tone, on the occasion of the bicentennial, and is not himself among the major spokesmen for this theme. But the theme itself lives on, proving itself capable of apparently endless adaptation. Tony Tanner's *The City of Words* (New York: Harper and Row, 1971), for example, relocates the escape from society in contemporary American fiction.

5. Quentin Anderson, *The Imperial Self* (New York: Knopf, 1971), pp. 4, 201.

6. Emerson, *Collected Works*, 1:8, 10; Emerson, *Journals*, 7:200; 4:278.

I am indebted to James Breslin for first pointing out this syntactical contradiction in Emerson's statement.

7. Jean-Paul Sartre, *Search for a Method*, trans. Hazel E. Barnes (New
York: Vintage, 1968), p. 91.

8. Cleanth Brooks, *William Faulkner: Toward Yoknapatawpha and Beyond* (New Haven: Yale University Press, 1978), pp. 299–300; Edmund
Morgan, *American Slavery American Freedom* (New York: Norton, 1975).

PART 1   OBSERVERS AND PARTICIPANTS

Chapter 1   *American Ahistoricism*

1. C. Vann Woodward, "The Irony of Southern History," in *Southern
Renascence,* ed. Louis D. Rubin, Jr., and Robert D. Jacobs (Baltimore:
Johns Hopkins University Press, 1953), reprinted in *The Burden of Southern
History* (Baton Rouge: Louisiana State University Press, 1968), pp. 189,
191, 213, 214; Louis Hartz, *The Liberal Tradition in America* (New York:
Harcourt Brace, 1955), pp. 285, 309, 308.

2. Lewis, *American Adam*, pp. 196, 197.

3. Chase, *American Novel*, pp. vii, ix; Poirier, *A World Elsewhere*, pp.
8, 9, 6; Howe, "The American Voice," p. 2.

While the emphasis on the ahistorical achieved a certain dominance in
the 1950s, certainly the authoritative beginning of the movement was F. O.
Matthiessen's *American Renaissance* (New York: Oxford University Press,
1941). Given the theologizing of the aesthetic that was to follow, it is salutary
to reread Matthiessen's opening remarks on the "devotion to the possibilities of democracy" which binds the American Renaissance writers together
(p. ix). It is precisely this residual social orientation in Matthiessen's work
which made it for Charles Feidelson an impure mixture: "Even in this
magnificent work," Feidelson wrote, "the sociological and political bent
of studies in American literature makes itself felt indirectly." See Charles
Feidelson, *Symbolism and American Literature* (Chicago: Chicago University Press, 1953), p. 3. We owe much to these critics, and I wish to make
it clear at the outset that my implied critique of their perspective is not
intended as a direct critique of their work itself, taken as a whole. We
cannot do without the analyses of American literature they produced. The
tendency to dismiss the insights of a previous era is a danger which Marxist
critics ought especially to resist, not only because they are especially vulnerable to it, but also because Marx himself pointed out that "mankind
always sets itself only such tasks as it can solve: since . . . it will always
be found that the task itself arises only when the material conditions for
its solution already exist or are at least in the process of formation." See
T. B. Bottomore and Maximilien Rubel, eds., *Karl Marx: Selected Writings
in Sociology and Social Philosophy,* trans. T. B. Bottomore (New York:

McGraw-Hill, 1964), p. 52. The tasks performed by Matthiessen and Feidelson, to mention the inception and the apogee of the movement, may not be our tasks any longer, but our tasks would be at once different and far more difficult to perform without *American Renaissance* and *Symbolism and American Literature*. While one would need to defend the claim by appealing to a theory of cultural materialism such as that advanced by Raymond Williams, it seems to me that the work of Matthiessen and Feidelson might well be regarded as among the more significant "material conditions" necessary for the solution of today's critical tasks. At any rate, their work has certainly played such a role in this essay. See Raymond Williams, *Marxism and Literature* (New York: Oxford University Press, 1977).

Harry Henderson's *Versions of the Past* (New York: Oxford University Press, 1974) marks a great step forward toward the rehistoricization of American literature. As Alan Trachtenberg put it in his foreword to Henderson's book, "it recognizes historical thinking in American fiction where it had not been seen before." There is, however, an inherent limitation in Henderson's appropriation of "Lukács' generic approach to the historical novel" (p. 12). As Henderson notes, "Lukács had the certainty of a unified aesthetic" based on a "Marxist interpretation of history," one which Henderson rejects out of a desire to avoid the pitfalls of a too "philosophic" approach (p. 12). Whatever the shortcomings of that aesthetic, particularly when confronted with fiction falling outside the boundaries of the realistic novel, Lukács's literary criticism depends for its considerable power upon a Marxist philosophy of history. Lacking such a philosophy, Henderson locates the "common traits of history and the novel" in those attitudes toward history which he identifies as "progressive" and "holistic" (pp. 12–15). The result is a mixed blessing. While his analyses of historical novels by reference to these two attitudes clearly demonstrate a "historical imagination" at work in American fiction, the "progressive" and "holistic" finally become so intertwined as to undermine their usefulness as hermeneutic tools. In other words, when uprooted from its Marxist foundation, and resituated on the ground of two contending attitudes toward history, Lukács's "generic approach" leads to the recognition of conflicts and contradictions within that imagination which remain unresolvable for the critic and the novelist alike. Whether one diagnoses this problem from a Marxist perspective or not, it remains true that the two types of historical understanding Henderson uses prove inadequate, because his method comes too close to the "philosophic" approach he wished to avoid.

For a characteristically insightful meditation on the issues Henderson raises, see Kenneth Burke, *Attitudes Toward History* (Boston: Beacon Press, 1961). For a useful approach to the romantic historical perspective of the nineteenth century as it bears on Hawthorne's novelistic practice, see Michael D. Bell, *Hawthorne and the Historical Romance* (Princeton: Princeton University Press, 1971).

4. Anderson, *The Imperial Self*, pp. 63, 236, 17, 16.

5. Gerald Graff, "What Was New Criticism? Literary Interpretation and Scientific Objectivity," *Salmagundi* 27 (Summer–Fall 1974):72–93.

6. René Wellek, "The New Criticism: Pro and Contra," *Critical Inquiry* 4 (1978):611–24, esp. p. 616; Raymond Williams, *The Country and the City* (New York: Oxford University Press, 1973), p. 96.

7. Anderson, *The Imperial Self*, pp. 17, 4.

8. Myra Jehlen, "New World Epics: The Middle-Class Novel in America," *Salmagundi* 36 (Winter 1977):49–68.

9. Georg Lukács, *The Theory of the Novel*, trans. Anna Bostock (Cambridge: MIT Press, 1971), p. 66, quoted in Jehlen, "New World Epics," p. 52.

10. Lukács, *Theory*, pp. 32, 34, 56.

11. Jehlen, "New World Epics," pp. 53–54.

12. T. B. Bottomore, ed. and trans., *Karl Marx: Early Writings* (New York: McGraw-Hill, 1963), pp. 3–40.

13. Jehlen, "New World Epics," pp. 51, 52, 63.

14. Williams, *Marxism and Literature*, pp. 108–9, 112–13.

15. Ibid., p. 122; Jehlen, "New World Epics," p. 51. I belabor the issue of hegemony because, while this term too must inevitably fall into abstraction (as in some historians' discourse it has done already), it is a great pity to see its end unduly hastened. Any conceptual tool which enables us to penetrate the wall we have constructed between literature and the social process of which it is a part is to be highly valued. The tendency which Jehlen's use of the term demonstrates forcefully is one which Williams identifies repeatedly as a danger to which orthodox Marxism often falls prey. Speaking of Plekhanov's description of base and superstructure, for example, Williams remarks, "the analytic categories, as so often in idealist thought, have, almost unnoticed, become substantive descriptions, which then take habitual priority over the whole social process to which, as analytic categories, they are attempting to speak." See Williams, *Marxism and Literature*, pp. 80–81. Sartre attacked the same idealist tendency in Marxism when he charged "contemporary Marxism" with "neglecting the particular content of a cultural system and reducing it immediately to the universality of a class ideology." See Sartre, *Search for a Method*, p. 115.

16. Jehlen's comment is worth quoting in full: "Perhaps it is to its American avatars that one should look for the real fulfillment of individualism—and therefore to such as Melville—for the most telling critiques, exposing at once the enormous creative potential and the appalling destructiveness it renders possible. So if Melville is less tolerant of romantic rebellion than his European counterparts he is also probably better aware than they of just what it can entail." Despite its shortcomings, Jehlen's argument remains extraordinarily provocative, largely as a result of the intellectual honesty and analytic consistency to which this passage testifies.

Wrong though I think her main thesis is, her argument would hardly be worth refuting if it did not represent the thought of a very powerful critical intelligence, one from which I have learned a good deal. See Jehlen, "New World Epics," pp. 52, 55, 63, 59; Karl Marx and Friedrich Engels, *The Holy Family* in *Marx–Engels Collected Works* (New York: International Publishers, 1976), p. 36, quoted in Lukács, *History*, p. 149. Bruce Franklin argues that Melville was in fact a "proletarian artist." While this claim does not seem to me entirely accurate, Franklin does demonstrate the extent to which Melville's experience of the "worker's world" informed his understanding of bourgeois society. Particularly interesting is Franklin's discussion of "The Tartarus of Maids" and "The Paradise of Bachelors." See Bruce Franklin, "Herman Melville: Artist of the Worker's World," in *Weapons of Criticism: Marxism in America and the Literary Tradition*, ed. Norman Rudich (Palo Alto: Ramparts Press, 1976), pp. 287–309.

17. Hartz, *Liberal Tradition*, pp. 62, 4, 65; Karl Marx, "On America and the Civil War," in *The Karl Marx Library*, ed. Saul K. Padover (New York: McGraw-Hill, 1972), 2:18.

18. Fredric Jameson, "Criticism in History," in Rudich, *Weapons of Criticism*, pp. 31–50.

19. In Feidelson's view, of course, the "symbolistic method" of the American Renaissance writers does not emerge in the context of expanding capitalism, nor in any other clearly defined social context. Rather it is an intellectual phenomenon and part of "one continuous movement from the Puritan era through the new learning of Locke to the new philosophy of Emerson," and at the same time "part of the symbolist tradition that culminates in modern literature." Although it is indisputable that Feidelson's analysis of this tradition is singularly lacking in any demonstrated concern with the material, historical conditions in which the "movement" in question unfolded, and must therefore repeatedly beg the question of why these writers "anticipated modern symbolism" (for example, "because they lived in the midst of the same intellectual forces" which generated "modern symbolism," or "because the crux of modern thought was oddly accentuated by the provincial culture they inhabited"), he nevertheless demonstrates the "symbolistic program" at work in the American Renaissance. Thus, the questions Feidelson leaves unanswered become precisely the questions his argument raises, questions about the relation between the "modern intellectual conditions" of which "the intellectual situation of nineteenth century America was a kind of epitome" and the social conditions which made this the case. Nor does Feidelson's appeal to the Puritan intellectual heritage forestall such an inquiry, for if the Puritan mind's bequest "to American writing" is "a conflict between the symbolic mode of perception . . . and a world of sheer abstractions certified as 'real'," and that conflict develops out of a "Puritan rationalism" whose consequences parallel the "divided consciousness which Whitehead sees" emerging at

the time in England "under the impact of physical science," then the "modern intellectual conditions" to which Feidelson sees the "symbolistic method" responding are related to social conditions closely resembling those whose impact on modern German philosophy Lukács analyzes as a function of reification. By simultaneously using symbolism as "a way of getting at modern and American literature," and using "modern literature and American literature" as "ways of getting at that strain" of symbolism to be found "in the literary history of the last two centuries," Feidelson produced an extended analysis of a postromantic (though still idealist) response to "a world grown abstract and material," a reified world in which the "vindication of imaginative thought" attempted in the "symbolistic program" leads to a form of "intellectual suicide." Feidelson, then, not only liberated Emerson, Melville, Hawthorne, Poe, and Whitman from their status as "minor disciples of European masters" in a romantic tradition by recognizing their "title to literary independence" in the "symbolistic method," but in so doing he rewrote a major chapter in American literary history by redefining the American Renaissance as a period in which "Emerson and his colleagues," "in an attempt to find a point of departure outside the premises of dualism," "grasped a basic issue of modern thought, in which idealism and romanticism were only an episode." While Feidelson's explanation for this early genesis of modernism in America is finally inadequate, it is not, as Quentin Anderson claims, because the book is "a rather scary exhibition of the costs of denying history," but rather because it is an awesome tribute to the formidable questions which must be answered before we can even begin to understand literary history. See Anderson, *The Imperial Self*, p. 260; Feidelson, *Symbolism*, pp. 4, 105, 75, 43, 76, 90, 5; also see Roy Harvey Pearce, *The Continuity of American Poetry* (Princeton: Princeton University Press, 1961), p. 5.

Chapter 2   Reification and American Literature

1. Karl Marx, *Capital*, 1:164, quoted in Lukács, *History*, p. 86; Lukács, *History*, p. 87; Marx, *Capital*, 1:176-77.

2. Lukács, *History*. pp. 87, 89, 91–92, 100, 93, 132, 131; Marx and Engels, *German Ideology*, p. 645; Williams, *Marxism and Literature*, p. 32.

3. Lukács, *History*, pp. 102, 96, 100.

4. Ibid., pp. 111, 116.

5. Ibid., pp. 120, 121, 119, 139, 147.

6. For a basic history of identity theory as an issue in subsequent Marxist debate, see Martin Jay's history of the Frankfurt School, *The Dialectical Imagination* (Boston: Little, Brown, 1973).

7. Lukács, *History*, pp. 154, 158; Marx and Engels, *German Ideology*, pp. 57–58, 645.

8. Lukács, *History*, p. 150; Marx and Engels, *German Ideology*, p. 645.

9. Heisenberg, *Physics and Philosophy*, pp. 24, 55; Michel Foucault, *The Order of Things* (New York: Vintage, 1970), pp. 133–34.

10. Heisenberg, *Physics and Philosophy*, p. 4.

11. John Berger, "The Moment of Cubism," in *The Look of Things*, ed. Nikos Stangos (New York: Viking Press, 1971), pp. 150–59.

12. During the autumn of 1926, when he was in Copenhagen working on the problems of quantum theory with Erwin Schrödinger and Niels Bohr, Heisenberg recalls, there were "discussions with Bohr which went through many hours till very late at night and ended almost in despair; and when at the end of the discussion I went alone for a walk in the neighboring park I repeated to myself again and again the question: Can nature possibly be as absurd as it seemed to us in these atomic experiments?" See Heisenberg, *Physics and Philosophy*, p. 42.

13. Marx and Engels, *German Ideology*, p. 645.

14. Henry James, *The Sacred Fount*, ed. Leon Edel (New York: Grove Press, 1953), p. 312.

15. Sartre, *Search for a Method*, p. 91.

16. Lukács, *History*, p. 121.

17. Emerson, *Journals*, 7:271; Emerson, *Collected Works*, 1:53, 65, 92. Passages not yet published in this new edition of Emerson's works, of which only one volume has appeared, will be cited in the standard edition, *The Complete Works of Ralph Waldo Emerson*, ed. Edward Waldo Emerson, 12 vols. (Boston: Houghton Mifflin, 1904; hereafter cited as *Complete Works*).

18. *Nature* in Emerson, *Collected Works*, 1:43, 7–8.

19. "The kingdom of the involuntary, of the not me." Emerson, *Journals*, 5:333, 123–24.

20. Emerson, *Journals*, 5:125, 333; Lukács, *History*, p. 146.

21. Newton Arvin, *American Pantheon* ed., Daniel Aaron and Sylvan Schendler (New York: Delacorte Press, 1966), p. 13; Emerson, *Complete Works*, 2:45; Emerson, *Journals*, 5:337.

22. Lukács, *History*, p. 130.

23. F. R. Leavis, *The Great Tradition* (New York: New York University Press, 1967), pp. 160–61; Henry James, *The Golden Bowl* (New York: Penguin, 1966), p. 537.

24. Lukács, *History*, p. 166.

25. James, *The Golden Bowl*, pp. 541, 29, 35, 39.

26. Ibid., p. 316; Emerson, *Journals*, 4:278; Henry James, *The Art of the Novel: Critical Prefaces*, ed. R. P. Blackmur (New York: Scribner's, 1934), p. 120.

27. The remark about Adams's fence-sitting was made by Ed Howe. See Ernest Samuels, *Henry Adams: The Middle Years* (Cambridge: Harvard University Press, 1958), p. 96.

28. Emerson, *Complete Works*, 6:31; Henry Adams, *The Education of*

Henry Adams, ed. Ernest Samuels (Boston: Houghton Mifflin, 1973), p. 314.

29. Emerson, *Journals*, 5:333; "To Samuel Jones Tilden," 24 January 1883, "To John Hay," 21 September 1893, in *Henry Adams and His Friends*, ed. Harold Dean Cater (Boston: Houghton Mifflin, 1947), pp. 126, 289–90; Adams, *The Education*, pp. 63, 382–83.

30. Adams, *The Education*, pp. 452, 493.

31. Ibid., p. 456; "To Henry James," 18 November 1903, in *Letters of Henry Adams*, ed. Worthington Chauncey Ford (Boston: Houghton Mifflin, 1938), 2:414.

32. Adams, *The Education*, p. xxx; "To Whitelaw Reid," 13 September 1908, "To Barrett Wendell," 12 March 1909, in Cater, *Henry Adams*, pp. 623, 645.

33. Adams, *The Education*, pp. 458, 346, 501.

34. Faulkner, *Absalom, Absalom!*, p. 158.

35. Ibid., p. 75.

36. William Faulkner, *As I Lay Dying* (New York: Vintage, 1932), p. 165; Faulkner, *Absalom, Absalom!*, p. 378.

37. Marx and Engels, *German Ideology*, pp. 645, 37; Faulkner, *Absalom, Absalom!*, p. 316.

38. Marx and Engels, *German Ideology*, pp. 41–42, 38.

39. See Lukács, *History*, p. 181.

40. Ibid., pp. 121, 181.

PART 2   RALPH WALDO EMERSON: MAN AS SUBJECT LENS
Chapter 3   Emerson's America

1. Emerson, *Journals*, 4:27, 285; Emerson, *Collected Works*, 1:7. See Stephen Whicher, *Freedom and Fate: An Inner Life of Ralph Waldo Emerson* (New York: Barnes, 1961). Still the most useful discussion of Emerson's decision to repudiate the family vocation is Henry Nash Smith's "Emerson's Problem of Vocation," in *Emerson: A Collection of Critical Essays*, ed. Milton R. Konvitz and Stephen Whicher (Englewood Cliffs, N.J.: Prentice-Hall, 1962), pp. 60–71. The problems attendant upon the role of the intellectual without connections to the church in early nineteenth-century Boston, difficult enough in themselves, form one side of this dilemma, and an important one. For a discussion of this problem in relation to the transcendentalists as a group, see Lawrence Buell, *Literary Transcendentalism* (Ithaca: Cornell University Press, 1973), pp. 39–54. Ann Douglas' *The Feminization of American Culture* (New York: Knopf, 1977) provides a provocative treatment of the ministry's responses and adaptations to its loss of social and political power in a rising consumer society. Another side of Emerson's vocational problem, however, remains to be explored definitively. A psychological study might do much to reveal an Emerson over-

shadowed by his academically more successful brothers and pressured by self-doubt about his own intellectual powers. More attention to Emerson's self-doubt, in any case, is in order, as Joel Porte's fine essay, "Emerson in 1838: Essaying to Be" suggests. See *Studies in Biography, Harvard English Studies* 8, ed. Daniel Aaron (Cambridge: Harvard University Press, 1978), pp. 183–99.

2. Michael T. Gilmore, "Eulogy as Symbolic Biography: The Iconography of Revolutionary Leadership, 1776–1826," in Aaron, *Studies in Biography*, p. 155.

3. Emerson, *Journals*, 8:58; 4:95, 268, 114–15.

4. Emerson, *Journals*, 7:268; Emerson, *Collected Works*, 1:207, 148; Emerson, *Complete Works*, 10:311; Emerson, *Journals*, 7:271.

5. Emerson, *Collected Works*, 1:53. See Williams, *Marxism and Literature*, pp. 108–27.

6. This discussion relies mainly on Douglass C. North, *The Economic Growth of the United States, 1790–1860* (Englewood Cliffs, N.J.: Prentice-Hall, 1961); W. Elliot Brownlee, *Dynamics of Ascent: A History of the American Economy* (New York: Knopf, 1974); John R. Commons et al., *History of Labor in the United States*, 1 (New York: Macmillan, 1918); Norman Ware, *The Industrial Worker: 1840–1860* (1924; reprint ed., New York: Quadrangle, 1964); Richard D. Brown, *Modernization: The Transformation of American Life, 1600–1865* (New York: Hill and Wang, 1976); Michael Paul Rogin, *Fathers and Children: Andrew Jackson and the Subjugation of the American Indian* (New York: Vintage, 1976).

7. See Commons, *History of Labor*, 1:100–107; Ware, *Industrial Worker*, pp. 26–70.

8. Brownlee, *Dynamics of Ascent*, p. 108; Ware, *Industrial Worker*, p. 121.

9. Brownlee, *Dynamics of Ascent*, pp. 94, 103; Ware, *Industrial Worker*, p. xii.

10. Brown means by the "assembly line," as do I, not a moving belt, but simply the division of labor required for mass production even before that production becomes automated. See Brown, *Modernization*, pp. 134–35, 104–5, 112. On the codification of laws, see Perry Miller, *The Life of the Mind in America* (New York: Harcourt Brace, 1965), pp. 239–65.

11. Brownlee, *Dynamics of Ascent*, p. 117; Michael Lebowitz, "The Jacksonians: Paradox Lost?" in *Towards a New Past: Dissenting Essays in American History*, ed. Barton J. Bernstein (New York: Vintage, 1968), pp. 65–89.

12. Williams, *The Country and the City*, pp. 97–98; Rosa Luxemburg, *The Accumulation of Capital* (New York: Monthly Review Press, 1972), quoted in Rogin, *Fathers and Children*, pp. 166–67.

13. Leo Marx, *The Machine in the Garden* (New York: Oxford University Press, 1964); Lebowitz, "The Jacksonians," pp. 70, 80–82.

14. Commons, *History of Labor*, 1:158–60; Ware, *Industrial Worker*, p. 134; Larcom is quoted in Herbert Gutman, "Work, Culture, and Society in Industrializing America, 1815–1819," *American Historical Review* 78 (1973):552.

15. Leo Marx, *Machine in the Garden*, p. 195; Edward Everett, "Fourth of July at Lowell," in Everett, *Orations and Speeches on Various Occasions* (Boston: Little, Brown, 1850), 2:47–68, esp. pp. 33–37.

16. Commons, *History of Labor*, 1:320; Gutman, "Work, Culture, and Society," pp. 551–552; Goodrich, quoted in Perry Miller, *Life of the Mind*, p. 300; Ware, *Industrial Worker*, pp. 109–10, 142.

17. Emerson, *Journals*, 5:33; Daniel Webster, "Opening of the Northern Railroad," in *The Writings and Speeches of Daniel Webster* (Boston: Little, Brown, 1903), 4:105–17, quoted in Leo Marx, *Machine in the Garden*, pp. 209–10.

18. See Leo Marx, *Machine in the Garden*, pp. 211–12.

19. Williams, *Marxism and Literature*, pp. 114, 124; Leo Marx, *Machine in the Garden*, p. 212.

20. Williams, *Marxism and Literature*, p. 125; John Orvis, "Trip to Vermont," *Harbinger* 5 (July, 1847):50–52, quoted in Leo Marx, *Machine in the Garden*, p. 216; Leo Marx, *Machine in the Garden*, p. 217.

21. Leo Marx, *Machine in the Garden*, pp. 217, 219.

22. Williams, *The Country and the City*, p. 294.

23. Timothy Walker, "Defense of Mechanical Philosophy," *North American Review* 33 (July 1831):122–36, quoted and discussed in Leo Marx, *Machine in the Garden*, pp. 180–90; Leo Marx, *Machine in the Garden*, p. 189.

24. Thomas Carlyle, "Signs of the Times," *Edinburgh Review* (1829), quoted in Leo Marx, *Machine in the Garden*, p. 176. Theodore Parker, "Thoughts on Labor," *The Dial* 1 (April 1841):497–519, quoted in Leo Marx, *Machine in the Garden*, p. 201; Leo Marx, *Machine in the Garden*, p. 185; Commons, *History of Labor*, 1:320.

25. Leo Marx, *Machine in the Garden*, p. 181. Despite the fact that Marx specifies the ideological limits of the dominant class whose rhetoric concerns him, he does not himself escape those limits, but indeed reconstitutes them. The very project undertaken in *The Machine in the Garden* necessarily objectifies the machine as a cultural symbol for progress, and reduces capitalism to industrialism. This reduction becomes quite clear when Marx describes the industrial revolution as a metaphorical "expression of the affinity between technology and the great political revolution of modern times." Marx regards the "two new forces, political and technological," as constituting a "double 'revolution'," which he sees posing a threat to "the old order everywhere" from the beginning of the nineteenth century to the present. This revolution expresses the "unprecedented claim of the propertyless, working masses for a fair share of the necessities . . . of life,"

Chapter 4   Emerson's Revolt

1. Emerson, *Collected Works*, 1:65.
2. Ibid., pp. 53, 62, 148.
3. Emerson, *Journals*, 8:58, 209; 7:408; 4:27; Emerson, *Collected Works*, 1:92, 156.
4. Karl Marx, *Capital*, 1:93.
5. Emerson, *Complete Works*, 2:341–42; first draft in Emerson, *Journals*, 5:112.
6. "To Thomas Carlyle," in *The Correspondence of Emerson and Carlyle*, ed. Joseph Slater (New York: Columbia University Press, 1964), p. 149.
7. Emerson, *Journals*, 7:200; Emerson, *Collected Works*, 1:28, 45, 26.
8. Emerson, *Collected Works*, 1:11–12, 17.
9. Ibid., pp. 28, 18, 17, 21, 19, 23, 26.
10. Ibid., pp. 26, 24, 29.
11. Ibid., p. 25. Also see Giambattista Vico, *The New Science*, trans. Thomas Goddard Bergin and Max Harold Fisch (Ithaca: Cornell University Press, 1948), p. 331.
12. Emerson, *Collected Works*, 1:29.
13. Ibid., pp. 29, 25, 27, 30, 35, 36.
14. Emerson, *Journals*, 5:125; Johann Fichte, quoted in Lukács, *History*, p. 119; Emerson, *Collected Works*, 1:35–36, 37.
15. Feidelson, *Symbolism*, p. 128; Emerson, *Journals*, 5:149; Emerson, *Collected Works*, 1:38, 37.
16. Emerson, *Collected Works*, 1:37–38. This translation of the problem into a self-reflective mode is what was to make of Emerson's works, according to Charles Feidelson, "a continuous monologue in which the genesis of symbolism is enacted over and over." See *Symbolism*, p. 123.
17. Emerson, *Collected Works*, 1:23.
18. Ibid., pp. 36–37, 31, 34
19. Ibid., p. 25.
20. Ibid., pp. 39, 31, 45, 43.
21. Ibid., p. 125.
22. Ibid., p. 10.
23. Emerson, *Complete Works*, 2:301, 318.
24. Ibid., pp. 303, 310, 304, 308–9.
25. Ibid., pp. 301, 304, 311–12.
26. Ibid., pp. 302–3, 304, 307, 319–20, 312.
27. Ibid., pp. 308, 69, 320.
28. Ibid., 6:15, 4, 3, 32, 31.
29. Ibid., pp. 3, 5, 6.
30. Ibid., pp. 8, 9, 19, 11.
31. Ibid., pp. 20, 21–22, 14, 26, 23.
32. Henry Thoreau, *"Walden" and Other Writings of Henry David Tho-*

a claim which becomes "reasonable for the first time" as a result of
and technology. Significantly, Marx dismisses the "silly scholarly
versy" over the accuracy of "revolution" as a description of techr
breakthrough on the ground that "the whole issue becomes irrelev:
we recognize that we are dealing with a metaphor." We may agree
controversy in question is irrelevant without finding Marx's appro
of "industrial revolution" as a metaphor for the proletarianizatio
"propertyless, working masses" quite satisfactory. What joins the
olutions—political and technological—in Marx's mind is finally no
from what enables Walker to see the machine as affording "plenty
that technology makes it "reasonable" to think social equality
Marx's "double 'revolution'" is simply a liberal myth, fusing as
revolution of rising expectations with an advancing technology. T
is here supported on the one hand by the reduction of capitalism
trialism, and industrialism to the labor-saving machine, and on tl
by the assimilation of events such as those occurring in 1848, 1
1917 in Europe and Russia to a vision of revolution as nothing n
an attack on "the old order everywhere." Yet obviously, as with th
farmers and urban mechanics of the Jacksonian era, the "unprec
claims of the "working masses" were at least initially directed ag
rise of a new order dominated by those who were profiting fro
panding capitalism. Nothing becomes irrelevant because it is a n
on the contrary, it is often precisely the metaphor itself which rev
is relevant. See Leo Marx, *Machine in the Garden*, p. 187.

26. Daniel Webster, "Lecture Before the Society for the Di
Useful Knowledge," in *Writings and Speeches*, 13:63–78; Ware,
Worker, p. 109.

27. Williams, *The Country and the City*, p. 125. The whole c
12, "Pleasing Prospects," is well worth reading in relation to
observers and the landscapes they both made and saw.

28. Ware, *Industrial Worker*, p. 110; Commons, *History*
1:227–28, 183.

29. David J. Saposs, "Colonial and Federal Beginnings," in C
History of Labor, 1:105; Commons, *History of Labor*, 1:158 ff.

30. Ronald G. Walters, *American Reformers, 1815–1860* (New
and Wang, 1978), p. 189; *Weekly Ohio Statesman*, 1838, quoted in
"The Jacksonians," p. 77.

31. William West, *New York Tribune*, 18 June 1850, quoted
Industrial Worker, p. 171.

32. Commons, *History of Labor*, 1:12; Ware, *Industrial Worke*
210, 172, 169, 183; see also Walters, *American Reformers*, pp. (

33. Ware, *Industrial Worker*, pp. 209, 210.

34. Webster, *Writings and Speeches*, 4:43, quoted in Leo Mar:
in the Garden, p. 214.

35. Williams, *Marxism and Literature*, p. 125.

rèau, ed. Brooks Atkinson (New York: Modern Library, 1937), pp. 6, 643, 654.

33. Emerson, *Complete Works*, 3:75–76.

34. Henry Adams, "The Life of George Cabot Lodge," in *The Shock of Recognition*, ed. Edmund Wilson (New York: Modern Library, 1955), p. 755.

35. Lukács, *History*, pp. 139, 130.

36. Ibid., pp. 139, 166, 130.

37. Emerson, *Collected Works*, 1:39–40, 41.

PART 3   TWO CRISES OF COMPLICITY
Chapter 5   Henry James: Visionary Being

1. Charles Feidelson, "James and the 'Man of Imagination'," in *Literary Theory and Structure*, ed. Frank Brady, John Palmer, and Martin Price (New Haven: Yale University Press, 1973), pp. 345–46, 337; Henry James, *The Art of the Novel: Critical Prefaces*, ed. R. P. Blackmur (New York: Scribner's, 1934), pp. 59, 153–54.

2. Lukács, *History*, pp. 166, 130.

3. Heisenberg, *Physics and Philosophy*, p. 55.

4. James, *Critical Prefaces*, pp. 320, 321, 153–54; Roland Barthes, "To Write: An Intransitive Verb?," in *The Structuralist Controversy*, ed. Richard Macksey and Eugenio Donato (Baltimore: Johns Hopkins University Press, 1972), p. 139; Emil Benveniste, *Problems in General Linguistics*, trans. Mary Elizabeth Meek (Coral Gables, Fla.: University of Miami Press, 1971), p. 226.

5. James, *Critical Prefaces*, pp. 67, 328–29.

6. Ibid., p. 57.

7. Ibid., pp. 329, 154; Feidelson, "James and the 'Man of Imagination'," p. 346.

8. James, *Critical Prefaces*, p. 53. As Ralph puts it to his dying father, "I hope I shall live long enough to see what she does with herself." Mr. Touchett remarks perceptively, "You speak as if it were for your mere amusement," and Ralph agrees, "So it is, a good deal." See James, *The Portrait of a Lady* (New York: Norton, 1975), pp. 160–61, 360.

9. James, *Critical Prefaces*, p. 153.

10. Ibid., pp. 47, 48, 53, 119.

11. James, *The Golden Bowl*, pp. 180, 348; James, *Critical Prefaces*, p. 47; John Bayley, *The Character of Love* (New York: Collier Books, 1963), p. 185.

12. James, *Critical Prefaces*, pp. 347, 348, 345, 48, 223, 312, 46, 120; James, *The Golden Bowl*, pp. 87, 316.

13. James, *The Golden Bowl*, pp. 115, 128, 142; James, *Critical Prefaces*, p. 46.

14. James, *The Golden Bowl*, p. 128; James, *Critical Prefaces*, p. 119; Bottomore, *Karl Marx: Early Writings*, p. 171.

15. Bottomore, *Karl Marx: Early Writings*, pp. 193–94; Lukács, *History*, p. 166.

16. James, *Critical Prefaces*, pp. 119–20, 312; James, *The Golden Bowl*, p. 316.

17. James, *The Golden Bowl*, p. 459; James, *Critical Prefaces*, pp. 120, 57.

18. James, *The Golden Bowl*, p. 199.

19. Ibid., pp. 29, 39, 35, 38, 33; Walter Benjamin, *Reflections*, ed. Peter Demetz, trans. Edmund Jephcott (New York: Harcourt Brace, 1978), pp. 156–57.

20. Lukács, *History*, p. 166; James, *The Golden Bowl*, pp. 38, 223–24, 43.

21. James, *The Golden Bowl*, p. 43; Karl Marx, *Capital*, 1:179. The theoretical nature of Marx's discussion here must be stressed. Marx is concerned at this point to break down what happens in the marketplace to its essentials, and so his discussion necessarily simplifies the marketplace, whose existence is always nonetheless presupposed. Because he is addressing the "simple circulation of commodities," in and of itself, that is, Marx speaks of buying and selling in their simplest dimension, and can therefore refer to the seller of a commodity as if he were simply selling an object for which he has no use. But in selling what he cannot use, the seller is already in fact acting in accord with the market's "economic relations" of which he is the bearer. The point is that commodities are never merely objects.

22. James, *The Golden Bowl*, pp. 33, 38, 30, 43, 35, 36, 37, 126. Maggie "never admired him so much, or so found him heart-breakingly handsome, clever, irresistible . . . as when she saw other women reduced to the same passive pulp that had begun, once for all, to constitute *her* substance." See p. 138.

23. Ibid., pp. 223–24, 265; Karl Marx, *Capital*, 1:249.

24. James, *The Golden Bowl*, pp. 38, 124, 125; Karl Marx, *Capital*, 1:247–48, 250, 253–54, 255.

25. James, *The Golden Bowl*, pp. 35, 33; Karl Marx, *Capital*, 1:256.

26. James, *The Golden Bowl*, p. 36; Karl Marx, *Capital*, 1:254.

27. James, *The Golden Bowl*, pp. 532, 547.

28. Ibid., pp. 546–47, 59, 124, 541; Lukács, *History*, p. 130; Bottomore, *Karl Marx: Early Writings*, p. 193.

29. James, *Critical Prefaces*, p. 120.

30. Ibid., p. 46; James, *The Golden Bowl*, pp. 316, 301–2, 118.

31. James, *The Golden Bowl*, pp. 315–17, 328, 330.

32. Ibid., pp. 30, 199, 330, 315, 316, 177, 35, 330.

33. Ibid., pp. 301, 315–16, 317, 330, 327, 537.

34. Ibid., pp. 537, 301, 303, 546.

35. Ibid., pp. 130–131, 57–59; James, *Critical Prefaces*, p. 46.

36. James, *The Golden Bowl*, p. 542.

37. James, *Critical Prefaces*, pp. 64–65; Wallace Stevens, "Of Modern Poetry," in *The Collected Poems of Wallace Stevens* (New York: Knopf, 1964), pp. 239–40.

38. James, *The Golden Bowl*, pp. 61–62, 91–92.

39. Ibid., pp. 199, 265, 325, 238, 38.

40. Ibid., pp. 191, 193.

41. Ibid., pp. 234–35, 225.

42. Ibid., pp. 316, 283.

43. Ibid., pp. 289, 293.

44. Ibid., pp. 235, 236, 378; James, *Critical Prefaces*, p. 46.

45. James, *The Golden Bowl*, pp. 324, 325, 322.

46. Ibid., pp. 378, 456, 458.

47. Ibid., p. 115.

48. Ibid., pp. 467–69, 547, 533.

49. Adams, *The Education*, pp. 500, 501; "To Howard Sturgis," 4 August 1914, "To Mrs. Alfred Sutro," 8 August 1914, "To Henry Adams," 21 March 1914, in *The Letters of Henry James*, ed. Percy Lubbeck (New York: Scribner's, 1920), 2:384, 388, 360–61; James, *Critical Prefaces*, p. 120.

Chapter 6   Henry Adams: The Posthumous Spectator

1. Adams, *The Education*, pp. 63, 33, 35. "To Henry James," 18 November 1903, in Ford, *Letters of Henry Adams*, 2:414; Emerson, *Complete Works*, 2:341–42.

2. "My views on education are radically revolutionary, but no one cares. So I have always found my American audience. No one ever cares. Nothing diverts the American mind from its ruts." "To Whitelaw Reid," 9 September 1908, in Cater, *Henry Adams*, p. 621; Adams, *The Education*, p. 33; "To Charles Milnes Gaskell," 28 April 1894, in Ford, *Letters of Henry Adams*, 2:46.

3. Emerson, *Journals*, 3:259; "To Henry Cabot Lodge," 5 September 1909, in Cater, *Henry Adams*, p. 663.

4. Lukács, *History*, p. 102; Adams, *The Education*, pp. 288, 289, 317.

5. Emerson, *Journals*, 7:200; Adams, *The Education*, pp. 288, 451, 474, 382.

6. Adams, *The Education*, pp. 383, xxx.

7. Heisenberg, *Physics and Philosophy*, pp. 55, 24.

8. "To Brooks Adams," 12 April 1906, in Cater, *Henry Adams*, p. 583; "To Brooks Adams," 17 February 1909, ibid., p. 639; "To Charles Franklin Thwing," 1 July 1892, ibid., p. 269.

9. Ivor Winters, *In Defense of Reason* (Chicago: Swallow Press, 1947), p. 401; Robert Spiller, in *Literary History of the United States*, ed. Robert E. Spiller, Willard Thorp, Thomas A. Johnson, Henry Seidel Canby, rev.

ed. in 1 vol. (New York: Macmillan, 1957), pp. 1087, 1097; William Jordy, *Henry Adams: Scientific Historian* (New Haven: Yale University Press, 1952).

10. The best critical readers of Adams as artist are Levenson and Blackmur. See J. C. Levenson, *The Mind and Art of Henry Adams* (Stanford, Calif.: Stanford University Press, 1957); R. P. Blackmur, "The Harmony of True Liberalism," *Sewanee Review* 60 (Winter 1952), pp. 1–27; idem, "Henry Adams: Three Late Moments," *Kenyon Review* 2 (Winter 1940), pp. 7–29.

11. Adams, *The Education*, pp. 4, 434, 46.

12. Ibid., pp. 46, 194, 24, 343–44, 365; "To John William Burgess," 13 June 1908, in Cater, *Henry Adams*, p. 609; "If the Governor weathers this storm he has a good chance of living in the White House some day." From "To Charles Francis Adams, Jr.," 23 November 1859, in Ford, *Letters of Henry Adams*, 1:53.

13. "To Charles Francis Adams, Jr.," 3 November 1858, in Ford, *Letters of Henry Adams*, 1:4; "To Charles Francis Adams, Jr.," 18 January 1959, ibid., pp. 12–13; "To Charles Francis Adams, Jr.," 9 February 1859, ibid., pp. 18, 20; "To Charles Francis Adams, Jr.," 23 November 1859, in Ford, *Letters of Henry Adams*, 1:53.

14. "To Charles Milnes Gaskell," 24 May 1875, in Cater, *Henry Adams*, p. 67; "To Charles Francis Adams, Jr.," 13 February 1861, in Ford, *Letters of Henry Adams*, 1:88.

15. See Ernest Samuels, *Young Henry Adams* (Cambridge: Harvard University Press, 1948), pp. 112–20.

16. Samuels, *Young Henry Adams*, p. 120; "Henry Adams to Charles Francis Adams," 21 November 1862, *A Cycle of Adams Letters*, ed. Worthington Chauncey Ford (Boston: Houghton Mifflin, 1920), 1:195–96.

17. "To Charles Francis Adams," 16 November 1867, in Ford, *Letters of Henry Adams*, I:136; Adams, *The Education*, pp. 258–59; "To Jacob Dilson Cox," 8 December 1870, in Cater, *Henry Adams*, p. 52.

18. See Samuels, *Young Henry Adams*, pp. 192–99; Adams, *The Education*, p. 293; "To Charles W. Eliot," 3 July 1870, in Cater, *Henry Adams*, p. 45.

19. "To Samuel Jones Tilden," 9 November 1871, in Cater, *Henry Adams*, p.55; "To Simon Newcomb," November 1873, ibid., p. 57.

20. "But doubtless our capitalists will protect themselves. They are warned and are wiser than these children of light." From "To Henry Cabot Lodge," 6 January 1878, in Ford, *Letters of Henry Adams*, 1:304, "To Edwin Lawrence Godkin," 13 December 1881, in Cater, *Henry Adams*, p. 118; "To Henry Cabot Lodge," 6 January 1878, in Ford, *Letters of Henry Adams*, 1:305; Henry Adams, *The History of the United States of America*, 9 vols. (London: G. P. Putnam's Sons, 1891–1892); "To Samuel Jones Tilden," 24 January 1883, in Cater, *Henry Adams*, p. 126; "To Francis

Parkman," 21 December 1884, ibid., p. 133; "To Edwin Godkin," 28 November 1881, ibid., p. 117.

21. "To Elizabeth Cameron," 2 January 1891, in Ford, *Letters of Henry Adams*, 1:458; Adams, *The Education*, p. 317.

22. "To Clara Louise Stone Hay," 25 July 1901, in Cater, *Henry Adams*, p. 516.

23. Samuels, *Young Henry Adams*, p. 120.

24. Samuels, *Henry Adams: The Middle Years*, pp. 19, 285, 297; "To Rebecca Gilman Rae," 21 December 1897, in Cater, *Henry Adams*, p. 426.

25. "To John Hay," 8 September 1893, in Cater, *Henry Adams*, p. 287; "To John Hay," 21 September 1893, idem, p. 290; Ernest Samuels, *Henry Adams: The Major Phase* (Cambridge: Harvard University Press, 1964), p. 129; "To John Hay," 4 August 1895, in Cater, *Henry Adams*, p. 343.

26. "To Samuel Jones Tilden," 24 January 1883, in Cater, *Henry Adams*, p. 126; "To Brooks Adams," 4 March 1900, ibid., p. 487; "To Henry James," 18 November 1903, in Ford, *Letters of Henry Adams*, 2:414.

27. Adams, *The Education*, pp. 314, 4.

28. "To Henry James," 6 May 1908, in Ford, *Letters of Henry Adams*, 2:495; Adams, *The Education*, p. 317.

29. Adams, *The Education*, pp. 266, 262, 100, 314; "To Barrett Wendell, 12 March 1909, in Cater, *Henry Adams*, p. 645.

30. "To Whitelaw Reid," 9 September 1908, in Cater, *Henry Adams*, p. 621; "To James Ford Rhodes," 16 March 1908, in Adams, *The Education*, p. 512; Henry Adams, "A Letter to Teachers of American History," in *The Degradation of the Democratic Dogma*, ed. Brooks Adams (New York: Peter Smith, 1949), pp. 125–263; Adams, *The Education*, pp. 382, xxx.

31. Adams, *The Education*, p. 4.

32. Ibid., pp. 300, 232, 306.

33. Ibid., pp. 302, 304, 313.

34. Ibid., pp. 316, 327, 326, 338, 343, 353.

35. Ibid., pp. 376, 401, 402, 381, 455, 451, 493, 595, 434.

36. Ibid., pp. xxx, 3, 4.

37. Ibid., pp. 230, 220, 156–57, 197, 233.

38. Ibid., pp. 90–92; See also pp. 367, 477, 497.

39. Ibid., pp. 386, 314, 387, xxx, 383.

40. Ibid., pp. 301, 289.

41. Ibid., pp. 343, 363, 392, 342, 378.

42. Ibid., pp. 501, 382, xxx; Heisenberg, *Physics and Philosophy*, pp. 55, 24.

43. Adams, *The Education*, pp. 501, 500.

44. Ibid., pp. 313, 337, 501, 472, 497, 423.

45. Ibid., p. 395. Actually, science fiction would have served Adams' needs in Part 2 remarkably well. He might, for example, have projected another manikin into the world of 1938, that centennial year in which he

timidly imagined returning with Hay "for a holiday," (p. 505). H. G. Wells was well known by the time Adams wrote *The Education*, but Adams seems to have come upon Wells several years later, when he read, not *The Time Machine* or *When the Sleeper Wakes*, but *Tono-Bungay*. See "To Brooks Adams," 30 January 1910, in Ford, *Letters of Henry Adams*, 2:532.

46. Adams, *The Education*, p. 359.

47. "To Samuel Jones Tilden," 15 May 1883, in Cater, *Henry Adams*, p. 126; "To Barrett Wendell," 12 March 1909, ibid., pp. 644–45; "To Brooks Adams," 19 March 1909, ibid., p. 648; "To Brooks Adams," 17 February 1909, ibid., p. 639; Adams, *The Education*, p. 501.

48. Adams, *The Education*, pp. 401, 359; see Ernest Samuels' account of the Editor's Preface in Adams, *The Education*, p. 541.

49. Henry Adams, "The Tendency of History," in *A Henry Adams Reader*, ed. Elizabeth Stevenson (Garden City, N.Y.: Doubleday, 1959), pp. 350–59; "To Barrett Wendell," 12 March 1909, in Cater, *Henry Adams*, p. 645; "To Elizabeth Cameron," 2 January 1891, in Ford, *Letters of Henry Adams*, 1:458.

PART 4   WILLIAM FAULKNER: INNOCENCE HISTORICIZED

Chapter 7   Faulkner's America

1. William Faulkner, *Sartoris* (New York: Random House, 1956), p. 375.

2. Cleanth Brooks, *William Faulkner: Toward Yoknapatawpha*, pp. 298–300.

3. Faulkner, *Absalom, Absalom!*, p. 14; "To Malcolm Cowley," November 1944, in *Selected Letters of William Faulkner*, ed. Joseph Blotner (New York: Random House, 1977), p. 185. In fairness to Brooks, I should note that he is not really claiming that Sutpen's fate is completely separable from the conditions of antebellum Southern society. But he does seem insistent on the point that these "of themselves" do not prove sufficient determinants of the "tragedy" inscribed in Sutpen's story. In effect, Brooks sees in Sutpen's American aberration a kind of tragic flaw, one which meets the requirement of "authentic tragedy"—that the hero's downfall be tied to a feature of his own character. My point is that this character's flaw cannot be so easily used, as Brooks tries to use it, to distinguish him from antebellum Southern society.

4. Frederick L. Gwynn and Joseph L. Blotner, eds. *Faulkner in the University*, (New York: Vintage, 1965), pp. 97–98; "To Malcolm Cowley," January 1946, in Blotner, *Selected Letters*, p. 216.

5. Brooks, *William Faulkner: Toward Yoknapatawpha*, p. 300.

6. See Wilbur Cash, *The Mind of the South* (New York: Vintage, 1941); Eugene D. Genovese, *The Political Economy of Slavery* (New York: Vintage, 1961); Eugene D. Genovese, *The World the Slaveholders Made* (New

York: Vintage, 1971); Eugene D. Genovese, *In Red and Black* (New York: Vintage, 1972).

7. Joseph Blotner, *Faulkner: A Biography* (New York: Random House, 1974), 1:8–50.

8. Ibid. pp. 45, 174.

9. A picture of William Clark Falkner's monument appears in Blotner, *Faulkner: A Biography*, 1:49.

10. According to Blotner, by the time Falkner wrote *The White Rose of Memphis*, "he was a much better read and educated man" than he had been thirty years before. The novel demonstrates that "he knew the Iliad through Pope, apparently, and also Pope's major essays in verse." There were other allusions "to Dickens, Milton, Swift, . . . Defoe . . . Shakespeare . . . Byron . . . Twain, Cervantes, and Scott." See Blotner, *Faulkner: A Biography*, 1:38, and "Notes," 1:23.

11. See Myra Jehlen, *Class and Character in Faulkner's South* (New York: Columbia University Press, 1976); Robert Cantwell, "The Faulkners: Recollections of a Gifted Family," in *Three Decades of Faulkner Criticism*, ed. Frederick J. Hoffman and Olga Vickery, pp. 55–56.

12. See Paul W. Gates, *The Farmer's Age: Agriculture, 1815–1860* (New York: Holt, Rinehart, 1960), p. 148.

13. John Cawelti, *Apostles of the Self-Made Man* (Chicago: Chicago University Press, 1965), pp. 40, 43; Abraham Lincoln, "Speech before the 166th Ohio Regiment," 22 August 1864, in Abraham Lincoln, *Collected Works*, ed. Roy P. Basler (New Brunswick, N.J.: Rutgers University Press, 1953–1955), 7:512.

14. William Faulkner, *Requiem for a Nun* (London: Penguin, 1960), pp. 190–91; F. Scott Fitzgerald, *The Great Gatsby* (New York: Scribner's, 1925), p. 69.

15. The map of Yoknapatawpha County with "William Faulkner: Sole Owner and Proprietor" inscribed appears at the beginning of *The Portable Faulkner*, ed. Malcolm Cowley (1946; rev. ed., New York: Viking Press, 1967), and, in a more detailed form, at the end of the Vintage edition of *Absalom, Absalom!*; on the relationship between *Absalom, Absalom!* and *The Unvanquished*, see Estella Schoenberg, *Old Tales and Talking: Quentin Compson in Faulkner's Absalom, Absalom! and Related Works* (Jackson, Miss.: University Press of Mississippi, 1977).

16. Faulkner, *Absalom, Absalom!*, pp. 12, 75.

17. See Cowley, *The Portable Faulkner*, p. 706; Faulkner, *Absalom, Absalom!*, p. 262.

18. Gwynn and Blotner, *Faulkner in the University*, p. 35.

19. Ibid., p. 131; "To Malcolm Cowley," January 1946, in Blotner, *Selected Letters*, p. 216; Gates, *The Farmer's Age*, p. 151; Frank L. Owsley, *Plain Folk of the Old South* (Baton Rouge: Louisiana State University Press, 1950). For a critical review of the historical literature on Southern agriculture, see James C. Bonner, "Plantation and Farm: The Agricultural

South," in *Writing Southern History*, ed. Arthur S. Link and Rembert W. Patrick (Baton Rouge: Louisiana State University Press, 1965), pp. 147–74. An Owsleyan analysis dealing with Mississippi is Charles S. Sydnor's *Slavery in Mississippi* (Baton Rouge: Louisiana State University Press, 1933).

20. Hartz, *Liberal Tradition*, p. 149; Genovese, *The World the Slaveholders Made*, p. 139; Genovese, *The Political Economy of Slavery*, p. 30.

21. William O. Taylor, *Cavalier and Yankee* (Garden City, N.Y.: Doubleday, 1963), pp. 156–72, 165.

22. Taylor, *Cavalier and Yankee*, pp. 92–99, 287–94, 143; Honoré de Balzac, *Old Goriot*, trans. Marian Ayton Crawford (London: Penguin, 1951), p. 131.

23. Taylor, *Cavalier and Yankee*, pp. 179–81, 46, 204–39; C. Vann Woodward, *Origins of the New South, 1877–1913* (Baton Rouge: Louisiana State University Press, 1971), p. 157.

24. Rogin, *Fathers and Children*, pp. 166–69.

25. Genovese, *The Political Economy of Slavery*, p. 30.

26. Faulkner, *Absalom, Absalom!*, pp. 73, 80.

27. Ibid., pp. 238, 263.

28. Gwynn and Blotner, *Faulkner in the University*, p. 35; Faulkner, *Absalom, Absalom!*, pp. 290–91.

29. Bottomore, *Karl Marx: Early Writings*, pp. 24–25.

30. James Baldwin, "Many Thousands Gone," in Baldwin, *Notes of a Native Son* (Boston: Beacon Press, 1955), p. 42; Morgan, *American Slavery American Freedom*; Gwynn and Blotner, *Faulkner in the University*, p. 81.

31. "To Malcolm Cowley," November 1944, in Blotner *Selected Letters*, p. 185; Faulkner, *Absalom, Absalom!*, p.217.

32. Fitzgerald, *Gatsby*, pp. 99, 163; Faulkner, *Absalom, Absalom!*, pp. 238, 158, 373, 89.

Chapter 8   The Reified Reader

1. Faulkner, *Absalom, Absalom!*, pp. 100, 101. The major line of detective work—like so much of Faulkner criticism—begins with Cleanth Brooks. See his "What We Know about Thomas Sutpen and His Children," in *William Faulkner: The Yoknapatawpha Country* (New Haven: Yale University Press, 1963), pp. 429–33. Gerald Langford's introduction to Faulkner's revision of *Absalom, Absalom!* (Austin: University of Texas Press, 1971) raises new problems with Brooks's findings, and Brooks responds to these issues in "The Narrative Structure of *Absalom, Absalom!*" in *William Faulkner: Toward Yoknapatawpha and Beyond*, pp. 301–28. Cleanth Brooks's work on Faulkner remains, in my estimation, the most consistently sensitive and intelligent critical response to Faulkner's career as a whole. At several points, as the reader will note, my own reading accords with that of Brooks. However, in part no doubt because he insists upon defending *Absalom*'s coherence, he persists in disputing the evidence

of its factual gaps and inconsistencies—a process which has led him to become the master detective of Faulkner criticism. Critical appeals to the imagination are numerous, but perhaps the most lucid and in many ways insightful reading of *Absalom, Absalom!* from this perspective is Albert J. Guerard's "*Absalom, Absalom!*: The Novel as Impressionist Art," in his *The Triumph of the Novel: Dickens, Dostoevsky, Faulkner* (New York: Oxford University Press, 1976), pp. 302–39. See Walter J. Slatoff, *Quest for Failure* (Ithaca: Cornell University Press, 1960).

2. I do not include *Sanctuary* (1931) and *Pylon* (1935) in this discussion because I think in these novels Faulkner was more intent upon gaining control of his language than on experimenting with narrative structure. They are, therefore, essentially peripheral to the strategy for relating past and present by means of techniques which thwart the reader's effort to remain detached from the flow of time sustained in the novel. Moreover, the history of *Sanctuary*'s composition, and the fact that Faulkner turned to writing *Pylon* because he was stuck in the middle of *Absalom, Absalom!*, I would argue, support the view that these novels were less ambitious efforts for Faulkner himself. For a different approach to Faulkner's narrative experiments, see Joseph Reed, *Faulkner's Narrative* (New Haven: Yale University Press, 1973).

3. As Sartre puts it, "In *The Sound and the Fury*, everything has already happened." See Jean-Paul Sartre, "On *The Sound and the Fury*: Time in the Work of William Faulkner," in *Faulkner: A Collection of Critical Essays*, ed. Robert Penn Warren (Englewood Cliffs, N.J.: Prentice-Hall, 1966), pp. 87–93.

4. William Faulkner, *Light in August* (1932; reprint ed., New York: Random House, 1968), p. 347. The following discussion of *Light in August* is heavily indebted to Frank Kermode's discussion of fictions as representing "imaginative investments in coherent patterns which, by the provision of an end, make possible a satisfying consonance with the origins and with the middle." See Frank Kermode, *The Sense of an Ending* (New York: Oxford University Press, 1967), p. 17. I am aware that by identifying spatiality and vision with the effort to constitute these "patterns," I am violating Kermode's strictures against precisely such an identification, but I do so because I think Faulkner did so. For a discussion of this issue, see Joseph Frank's "Spatial Form: An Answer to Critics," *Critical Inquiry* 4 (Winter 1977):242–52. See also Faulkner's statement to Malcolm Cowley on the subject of "trying to say it all in one sentence . . . to put it all, if possible, on one pinhead," in Blotner, *Selected Letters*, p. 185.

5. Faulkner, *Light in August*, p. 461.

6. Ibid., pp. 370, 149, 216, 98.

7. Ibid., pp. 5–6, 440.

8. Ibid., pp. 26, 5.

9. Ibid., pp. 26, 480.

10. Ibid., pp. 80, 300, 301, 453, 55, 52, 466–67.

11. Ibid., pp. 83, 385.

12. Ibid., pp. 464, 465.

13. Ibid., pp. 462, 465–66.

14. Ibid., pp. 347, 150, 461, 348.

15. Ibid., pp. 440, 466, 465.

16. Henri Bergson, *A Study in Metaphysics: The Creative Mind*, trans. Mabelle L. Andison (1946; reprint ed., Totowa, N.J.: Littlefield Adams, 1965), pp. 137, 151–52.

17. Faulkner, *Light in August*, p. 111.

18. Ibid., p. 480.

19. Ibid., pp. 213, 114, 150, 207–10.

20. Ibid., pp. 167, 97, 104, 151.

21. Brooks, *William Faulkner: Toward Yoknapatawpha*, pp. 255, 264–65, 256.

22. Bergson, *Metaphysics*, pp. 164–65, 185, 147; Faulkner, *Light in August*, p. 6; see Blotner, *Faulkner: A Biography*, 2:1302.

23. Bergson, *Metaphysics*, p. 184.

24. Berger, "The Moment of Cubism," p. 159; Faulkner, *Absalom, Absalom!*, pp. 217–18.

25. Faulkner, *Absalom, Absalom!*, pp. 9, 316, 158.

26. Ibid., pp. 7–8, 9, 13, 14, 21.

27. Ibid., pp. 75, 74–75, 22, 11, 213, 22, 14.

28. Ibid., pp. 261, 271, 20, 31–32, 254, 171, 7, 33, 275, 263.

29. Ibid., pp. 158, 151, 143, 149–50, 261, 238, 171.

30. Ibid., pp. 127–28; see Claude Lévi-Strauss, *The Savage Mind* (Chicago: University of Chicago Press, 1966), p. 241. The letter Quentin has received from his father, telling of Rosa Coldfield's death, embodies the same kind of bond between generations; it serves as well to reinforce, on a material basis, the connection between the recent past in Mississippi and the present scene in Massachusetts.

31. Faulkner, *Absalom, Absalom!*, pp. 20, 63.

32. Ibid., p. 39. For an incisive discussion of this irony, see David L. Minter, *The Interpreted Design as a Structural Principle in American Prose* (New Haven: Yale University Press, 1969).

33. Faulkner, *Absalom, Absalom!*, pp. 31, 143, 207, 158.

34. Ibid., pp. 193, 181, 190.

35. Ibid., pp. 261–62, 140, 295, 294. The Mississippi River itself, of course, serves as yet another "umbilical" by which Quentin and Shreve are "joined, connected . . . in a sort of geographical transubstantiation." See p. 258.

36. Ibid., pp. 316, 175, 373, 8.

37. Ibid., pp. 127, 280, 143, 251, 316.

38. Ibid., pp. 351, 357–58, 373, 378, 66; See John Irwin, *Doubling and*

Incest/Repetition and Revenge (Baltimore: Johns Hopkins University Press, 1975).

39. Faulkner, *Absalom, Absalom!*, pp. 212–13, 335, 30
40. Ibid., pp. 14, 101, 263–64; see Heisenberg, *Physics and Philosophy*, p. 24 ff.
41. Ibid., pp. 328, 101, 263, 378, 89, 93, 110.
42. Ibid., pp. 313, 266.
43. Ibid., pp. 313, 101, 262, 233, 261, 8, 336, 251, 378.
44. Ibid., p. 175.

THEORETICAL POSTSCRIPT

The Writer As Participant: Modernism and Critical Resistance

1. See Williams, *Marxism and Literature*, pp. 21–44; V. N. Vološinov, *Marxism and the Philosophy of Language*, trans. Ladislav Matejka and I. R. Titunik (New York: Seminar Press, 1973), p. 180. See also Mikhail Bakhtin, *Rabelais and His World* (Cambridge: MIT Press, 1968), and Bakhtin, *Problems of Dostoevsky's Poetics* (Michigan: Ardis/Ann Arbor, 1973).

2. Georg Lukács, *Studies in European Realism* (New York: Grosset and Dunlap, 1964). On Lukács' political "self-criticism," see Morris Watnick, "Relativism and Class Consciousness: Georg Lukács," in *Revisionism*, ed. Leo Labedz (New York: Praeger, 1969), pp. 142–65. For an unusually cogent treatment of Lukács' critical attacks on modernism, see Eugene Lunn, "Marxism and Art in the Era of Stalin and Hitler: The Brecht-Lukács Debate," *New German Critique* 3 (Fall 1974):12–44.

3. Georg Lukács, *The Historical Novel*, trans. Hannah and Stanley Mitchell (Boston: Beacon Press, 1963), p. 171; Lukács, *European Realism*, p. 140.

4. Lukács, *European Realism*, p. 140.

5. Ibid., pp. 141, 91, 145, 92–93, 143; "To Edmund Wilson," Spring 1925, in *The Letters of F. Scott Fitzgerald*, ed. Andrew Turnbull (New York: Scribner's, 1963), pp. 341–42.

6. Lukács, *European Realism*, pp. 13, 156, 143; Fredric Jameson, *Marxism and Form* (Princeton: Princeton University Press, 1971), pp. 203–4.

7. Lukács, *European Realism*, pp. 155–56.

8. Ibid., pp. 155–56, 140.

9. Jameson, *Marxism and Form*, pp. 198, 200; Lukács, *European Realism*, pp. 140, 155.

10. Lukács, *European Realism*, pp. 99, 13.

11. Ibid., p. 137.

12. Ibid., pp. 6, 157.

13. Ibid., pp. 22, 137, 91, 60.

14. Ibid., pp. 91, 137, 112, 143, 6.

326 *Notes for pages 289-301*

15. Ibid., p. 60.
16. Ibid., pp. 156, 140.
17. Ibid., pp. 157, 6, 60. For a provocative analysis of Lukács' treatment of art's shifting political role after 1848, see Christine Schoefer, "The Power of Creation—Lukács and Clark on Politics and Art in France after 1848," *Berkeley Journal of Sociology*, 1980, pp. 159–83.
18. It is also by making French realism the rule that Myra Jehlen is led to make American ahistoricism the exception.
19. Lukács, *European Realism*, pp. 91, 137, 112.
20. Ibid., pp. 112, 60, 6. Flaubert said of *La Tentation de Saint Antoine* that the "subject . . . left me completely free as to lyricism, emotions, excesses of all kinds." It is noteworthy that this remark is made in the same letter in which Flaubert's often quoted remark about wanting to write "a book about nothing" is made. "To Louise Colet," 16 January 1852, in *The Letters of Gustave Flaubert, 1830–1857* ed. Francis Steegmuller (Cambridge: Harvard University Press, 1980). p. 154.
21. Williams, *Marxism and Literature*, p. 35; Vološinov, *Marxism*, pp. 48, 94, 38.
22. Vološinov, *Marxism*, pp. 60, 34, 13, 10, 11.
23. Ibid., pp. 59, 10, 21, 11.
24. Ibid., pp. 52, 46, 102–3.
25. Ibid., pp. 11, 21.
26. P. N. Medvedev, *The Formal Method in Literary Scholarship: A Critical Introduction to Sociological Poetics,"* quoted in Vološinov, *Marxism*, p. 180.
27. My discussion of Russian Formalism is heavily influenced by, and essentially agrees with, Tony Bennett's recently published *Formalism and Marxism* (London: Methuen, 1979). See also Fredric Jameson, *The Prison-House of Language: A Critical Account of Structuralism and Russian Formalism* (Princeton: Princeton University Press, 1972), and L. Matejka and K. Pomorska, eds., *Readings in Russian Poetics* (Cambridge: MIT Press, 1971).
28. Quoted in Vološinov, *Marxism*, p. 60.
29. Bennett, *Formalism and Marxism*, p. 55.
30. Quoted in Vološinov, *Marxism*, p. 180; Bennett, *Formalism*, p. 55.
31. Vološinov, *Marxism*, pp. 95, 86.

INDEX

ABOUT THE AUTHOR

A participant, not simply an observer herself, Carolyn Porter, after graduating from Rice University in 1967, taught elementary school for the Peace Corps in a village in Sierra Leone before returning to Rice for her Ph.D. Since 1972 she has been on the faculty of the University of California at Berkeley, where she is now associate professor of English. Her husband, Paul Thomas, teaches political science at Berkeley and is the author of *Karl Marx and the Anarchists*.